BEYOND CONVERSION AND SYNCRETISM

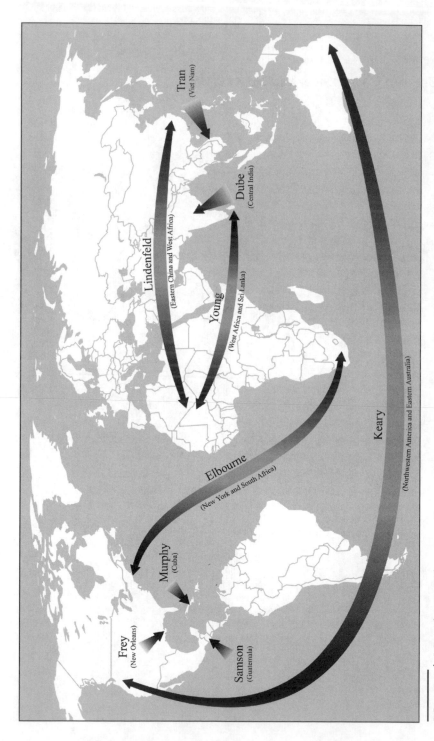

Map 0.0 | *Map showing the connections and comparisons discussed in this volume. Drawn by Mary Lee Eggart.*

BEYOND CONVERSION AND SYNCRETISM

**Indigenous Encounters with
Missionary Christianity, 1800–2000**

Edited by

David Lindenfeld and Miles Richardson

Berghahn Books
New York • Oxford

Published in 2012 by

Berghahn Books

www.berghahnbooks.com

©2012 David Lindenfeld and Miles Richardson

Library of Congress Cataloging-in-Publication Data

Beyond conversion and syncretism : indigenous encounters with missionary
    Christianity, 1800–2000 / edited by David Lindenfeld and Miles Richardson.
        p. cm.
    Proceedings of a workshop held in 2008 at Georgetown University.
    Includes bibliographical references and index.
    ISBN 978-0-85745-217-7 (hardback : alk. paper) — ISBN 978-0-85745-218-4
    (e-book)
        1. Missions—History—19th century—Congresses. 2. Conversion—
Christianity—History—19th century—Congresses. 3. Missions—History—
20th century—Congresses. 4. Conversion—Christianity—History—20th
century—Congresses. 5. Christianity and other religions—Congresses.
I. Lindenfeld, David F. II. Richardson, Miles, 1932–

    BV2120.B49 2012
    266.009′034—dc22

                                                                2011014731

British Library Cataloguing in Publication Data
A catalogue record for this book is available from the British Library

Printed in the United States on acid-free paper.

ISBN 978-0-85745-217-7 (hardback)
ISBN 978-0-85745-218-4 (ebook)

⚘ CONTENTS

🪷 ILLUSTRATIONS

Maps

Illustrations

🪷 ACKNOWLEDGMENTS

Studies of religious behaviors and beliefs are often, in one way or another, studies of hope—a commodity which has been in surprisingly good supply in the recent past in Louisiana, where this project was conceived. The editors would therefore first like to acknowledge Mother Nature for generously providing the adversity—including a tree which crashed through one of their living rooms during Hurricane Gustav in 2008—that challenged us to persist, as did so many other Louisianans in these times, and to see our project through. In a similar vein, several funding agencies, here to remain anonymous, contributed by denying our grant applications for a conference which was to provide the original basis for this volume. The application process itself was constructive, however, in that it drove us to identify and contact a distinguished group of some 25 scholars who saw the value of our comparative study and agreed in advance to come to Baton Rouge. Out of this group, a core of contributors emerged who were willing to continue, by their own means if necessary. We owe to them our profound thanks.

Since several members of this core taught at Georgetown University, we agreed to convene there voluntarily for a workshop in 2008 in order to share and exchange comments on our draft papers. This was immensely helpful in contributing to whatever coherence the volume as a whole possesses. We would especially like to acknowledge the generosity of the Theology Department at Georgetown, including Joseph Murphy and Anh Q. Tran, for hosting this meeting and making our stay there a comfortable and rewarding one. Professor Peter C. Phan was also especially supportive, even though he could not attend.

Others who contributed to our efforts include various colleagues at each home institution and the anonymous reviewers for Berghahn Books, not to mention their editorial staff, whose professionalism and patience we also appreciated. The artist in residence at Louisiana State University's unique Department of Geography and Anthropology, Mary Lee Eggart, is responsible for much of the book's visual appeal.

The project was initially conceived by David Lindenfeld, a historian. Miles Richardson, an anthropologist, was brought in at an early stage of the application process. He wishes to express his gratitude for the opportunity to participate.

Baton Rouge, Louisiana
June 2010

 INTRODUCTION

BEYOND CONVERSION AND SYNCRETISM

David Lindenfeld and Miles Richardson

It takes no special discernment to recognize that vigorous interactions among heterogeneous religious traditions play an important role in today's world. Such interactions can be seen as an inevitable by-product both of the accelerated movement of peoples and of the increasing volatility of information transfers that have taken place since the middle of the twentieth century. It should further come as no surprise that such cross-religious meetings can sometimes be emotionally charged and even incendiary, fuelling the violent clashes that make the headlines — although the positive gains in interreligious dialogue that arise from this same situation are less likely to receive public attention. Nevertheless, any public discussion of religious issues and terms has the potential to be hotly contested, as its participants become swept up in the ongoing struggles to maintain personal and collective identity while coping with an increasingly interdependent and cosmopolitan world.

Such trends naturally have their impact on the world of academic scholarship, where the tempo of change is customarily slower. Western academics find themselves holding on to their hats, so to speak, amidst the currently accelerating winds of religious interaction. For example, the Christian scholar Andrew F. Walls, commenting on the well-known demographic shift of world Christianity from the northern to the southern hemisphere, wrote that "it is safe for a European to make only one prediction about the ... African Biblical theology we all talk about: that it is likely either to puzzle us or to disturb us."[1]

To be sure, the study of Christianity as a global phenomenon has not remained static since Walls wrote those words in 1994. Missionary history, for example, is coming to be recognized as a prime site, rich in source materials, for the study of cross-cultural religious interactions — rather than largely being by, for, and about Western missionaries, as it was in the past.[2] And in African studies in particular, there has been a healthy cross-fertilization of anthropological and historical approaches to missionary activity, thanks in part to the work of Jean and John Comaroff.[3] Nevertheless, there remain in our view some serious conceptual roadblocks to the study of such interactions. These stem in no small part from the lingering associations of missionaries with colonialism and its legacies—associations still capable of generating considerable heat. Thus historians can point to many examples where missionaries worked at cross-purposes from colonial officials, but such dissonances were not always apparent to the indigenous peoples, who were likely to view missionaries and colonial officials as part of the same wave.[4]

All of this has profound implications for the vocabulary we have at our disposal to talk about cross-cultural relationships. If postcolonial and subaltern scholarship originally tended to view these primarily in dualistic terms, such as domination and resistance, hegemony and identity, this was soon seen as too simple and gave way to a variety of terms expressing some kind of ambivalent combination—as the Comaroffs put it, "that curious mix of consent and contestation, desire and disgust, appropriation and accommodation, refusal and refiguration, ethnicization and hybridization—subsumed in the term 'the colonial encounter.'"[5] In our view, it is this "curious mix" which is capable of more precise treatment. Moreover, as the Comaroffs also recognized, the study of such encounters is inextricably tied to the meaning of "conversion" and points to a needed complexification of that term.

This is where we hope the present volume makes a meaningful contribution. It looks at the ways in which different indigenous peoples have responded to the intrusion of foreign Christian missionaries into their worlds, and offers a number of case studies with an eye to identifying strategies and processes by which this negotiation typically takes place. Its aim is to point to a more nuanced and differentiated picture of such interchanges than is conveyed by terms presently in use. We have chosen to focus on the words "conversion" and "syncretism" as the take-off points for our discussion, partly because both terms have acquired a great variety of uses which need unpacking, and also because both have occasionally become lightning rods, so to speak, for impassioned public controversy in different parts of the world.

The desirability of such terminological refinement can be demonstrated, we believe, by looking at several scholarly disciplines and how they currently deal with religious interaction. The three disciplines we consider in this introduction—namely history, anthropology, and religious studies—are all represented in this volume.

Among historians, religion has been receiving increasing attention since the end of the Cold War, at least as far as Europe is concerned.[6] Moreover, economic globalization has stimulated the growth of one particular sub-discipline, namely world history, which has emerged as a research field as well as a teaching subject. Thanks to such works as

William McNeill's *The Rise of the West* and Immanuel Wallerstein's *The Modern World-System*, world historians do possess a narrative structure and theoretical framework to discuss patterns of trade, technological diffusion, and the like. But, as Patrick Manning has observed in his recent survey of this field, "[I]t is remarkable, in contrast, how little discussion of religion appears in the world history literature for recent centuries."[7] Manning offers two explanations for this state of affairs: first, a continuing preference among historians for secular explanations—seeing religious expansion, for example, as part of political or imperial history; second, the tendency to treat religious history as local history or as part of area studies rather than as a topic for global connections. We would further add: the relative paucity of theoretical models for religious interaction which would enable historians to make these connections—a paucity which may be due to lack of communication among disciplines where such models might be found.

It would seem that missionary history is a topic which lends itself to the development of such models, as well as to a narrative of globalization. Indeed, one might be tempted to view the broad contours of missionary history as parallel to, or even incorporated within, Wallerstein's framework of the modern world system. Wallerstein views capitalism as emanating out from certain "core" regions to the "periphery" (and "semi-periphery"), which provide the surplus labor to enrich the core. Older missionary histories typically portray their subjects in a similar manner, as fanning out from metropolitan centers in Europe and the United States, spreading Christianity and "civilization" to the far corners of the world. Yet the recent work on missionary interactions at the local level to which Manning refers, and on which this volume draws, points to quite an opposite picture of the actual transmission, one in which the bulk of evangelization is carried out by indigenous agents rather than by Westerners. An authority on Christianity in India, Robert Eric Frykenberg, states, perhaps with some exaggeration, "Not a single major movement was ever initiated by a foreign missionary."[8] Yet India serves as an example of how Christian "conversion" is seen today as a threat to Hindu identity—to the point of being subject to restrictive legislation.[9]

Turning to anthropology, that field has been transformed in the last quarter-century, thanks in large part to the post-colonial and postmodernist sensibilities that have pervaded the social sciences and the humanities in the same period. Anthropologists, no less than missionaries, have been implicated as agents of imperialism. More profoundly, the postmodernists' suspicion of grand narrative and hegemonic discourse, and their consequent inclination to view socio-cultural formations as constructions, fictions, or inventions, have eroded anthropologists' earlier beliefs in the authenticity and stability of the cultures they set out to study. This has led in turn to a celebration of cross-cultural mixing, whether known as hybridity, briocolage, creolization, or syncretism—all terms which tend to be used interchangeably and none too precisely.

One anthropologist, Charles Stewart, has argued that, of all these terms, "syncretism" is the most serviceable and deserves to be used as a general label for such intermixing—at least as far as religious interaction is concerned.[10] He bases his argument on the commonsensical claim that no culture is an island, and that borrowing and mixing have always gone on. Thus, people have practiced syncretism even when they were unaware of it or sought to deny it—as they not infrequently did. Yet in order to accommodate the variety of moves that take place under that label, Stewart presents syncretism as an extremely chameleon-like concept, changing coloration depending on who is using it. Thus, syncretism may assume positive connotations in some parts of the world (such as with Hindu nationalists in India who see the multiplicity of gods and spirits as a good thing) and negative ones in others (such as among Afro-Brazilians and Cubans, as Joseph Murphy's chapter makes clear). It may mean different things depending on whether it is pronounced by people in positions of authority or by those resisting such authority. Even within anthropology itself, syncretism was viewed positively in the United States, where Melville Herskovits saw it as abetting the integration of African-Americans into the melting pot, and negatively among British social anthropologists, who tended to accept the missionaries' pejorative evaluation of the term as applied to African religions.[11] Certainly Stewart is interested, as are we, in elucidating the processes by which different peoples negotiate the conflicting pulls of mixing and identity. But he claims that, aside from the broad generalization that syncretism exists, how it works simply varies from local case to local case. Certainly there is no arguing with the individuality of such cases and the need to do justice to that individuality. In attempting to go beyond syncretism, however, we are reaching for intermediate levels of generalization that suggest typical patterns that arise in certain situations—not in a deterministic sense, to be sure, but as an aid to sorting out cases that appear to be quite different but nonetheless share common features.

Stewart readily admits that opposition to syncretism in the name of cultural authenticity or purity is an equally pervasive pattern (although syncretism can also serve these ends, as in the Indian example). As a consequence, syncretism tends to be no less a contested term than conversion. The sensitivity of the subject among Afro-Latin populations in Cuba and Brazil, as portrayed by Murphy, stems from their having been forced, as slaves, to adopt Catholic saints as they struggled to preserve their African *orisha* deities. Practitioners today often reject the label of syncretism to characterize their religion, as it connotes for them and many others impurity and confusion. These devotees see their faith as pure, a heroic preservation of African spirituality now free to shed its Christian veneer.

But beyond this, the term "syncretism" also has racial overtones which heighten the level of contestation. Brazilians had their version of the melting pot, namely that true Brazilian-ness represented an amalgamation of the three "races" of the country—Indian, European, and African. But beneath the surface was the assumption that such amalgamation was actually a process of "whitening." In other words, syncretism was fine as long as it did not become too African.[12] Hence the further negative connotations of the term for Brazilians of African descent. Nonetheless, Murphy's research suggests that syncretism in Latin American cultures is not dead or dying: despite the protests, many continue their devotions to Catholic saints and *orisha* deities with equal fervor.

The contested aspect of syncretism becomes especially evident when we turn to the third discipline, religious studies. The definition of syncretism given in the *Evangelical Dictionary of World Missions* puts it concisely: "The replacement or dilution of the essential truths of the gospel through the incorporation of non-Christian elements."[13] Christian suspicion that its distinctive message could only be adulterated by the inclusion of foreign elements dates back to the third century.[14] One way in which recent Christian scholars have handled the obvious contradiction between this belief and the undeniable historical fact of admixture over time is to say that not all incorporations are conscious, and that the label of syncretism should apply only to those that lead to religious contestation.[15] These same scholars acknowledge, however, that such contestation is inseparable from the realities of power, and the term has been readily available to anathemize the beliefs or practices of any group that is seen as outside the mainstream (rather like the terms "cult" or "sect").[16] The recent trend among Catholics and Protestants towards ecumenicism and dialogue has by no means eliminated this tendency. A good example, cited by Stewart, is the language of the Second Vatican Council, which called for a willingness to adapt the divine message to the distinct practices of local cultures—but within limits. In the language of the council, "[T]hanks to such a procedure, every appearance of syncretism and of false particularism can be excluded, and Christian life can be accommodated to the genius and the dispositions of each culture."[17] By the same token, the negotiations within the World Council of Churches in the 1970s, which led to embracing interfaith dialogue, were marked with hesitations based on fear of syncretism.[18]

Nevertheless, there are signs, emerging again from local studies, that point beyond the limits of this language of anti-syncretism among religious activists. To cite one example, Edward Zehner, in his 2005 study of Protestant Evangelicals in predominately Buddhist Thailand, shows that these anti-syncretic Protestants are actually willing to tolerate a wide range of indigenous practices, as long as they do not violate certain basic Christian principles. His examples are worth quoting at length:

> Evangelical anti-syncretism—which remains strong—is not simply a blanket resistance to local cultural inputs. Rather it entails resistance to some inputs while embracing others… These days most evangelicals have little problem with tolerating differences in ritual form, as long as the underlying meanings remain the same. They don't care where the church meets … and they might not even insist on meeting on Sunday, if another day works better. It does not matter if the Eucharist … is celebrated with bread, matzo, wheat crackers, rice crackers, or pieces of yam … It does not matter if baptism is conducted in a river, a lake, a bathtub, a pool, or a concrete block tank constructed in the pastor's back yard … On the other hand, affirmation of certain core doctrines becomes important regardless of their local comprehensibility.[19]

In other words, adaptations of world religions like Christianity or Islam to local conditions are *selective* in what their practitioners accept and what they reject—just as are local responses to world religions. This is true regardless of whether this selection goes under the name of syncretism or anti-syncretism. Selectivity may be seen as a strategy by which parties in religious interaction negotiate a position between traditions which otherwise appear to be incommensurable. This gives us one key to developing a new vocabulary. In discussing religious interactions, one does well to regard not only what is brought together, but also what is left out.

Many of the essays in this volume also highlight the creativity and inventiveness of these combinations. For some, the term syncretism already conveys this dimension; for others, it is insufficient. Other terms like "creolization" or "hybridity," which are often used synonymously, bring out this aspect more prominently. Murphy sees creolization as suggesting a more extended process over time, allowing for multiple combinations and recombinations of diverse elements. Other scholars have turned to spatial metaphors: it is interesting that an ethnohistorian, Richard White, writing about colonial North America, and an Indian postcolonialist literary critic, Homi Bhabha, arrived independently at the same notion: that of a "middle ground" or "third space" to express the creative aspect of cross-cultural encounter. In both cases, this space was borne of the uncertainties of colonial power operating in a strange and alien place, which required that both sides create something new in order to communicate. For Bhabha, the postcolonial situation continues this uncertainty, which he views as neither a polarized "clash of civilizations" nor an easygoing, tolerant multiculturalism, but as a realm of engagement of genuine, often incompatible differences which he labels "hybridity."[20]

Needless to say, these terms have not escaped criticism, often on grounds similar to that of syncretism. As an ethnic term as well as a linguistic one, creolization is more literally chameleon-like than syncretism: Its referents change color depending on the ethnicity of those in or out of power.[21] Anthropologist Aisha Khan stresses the aspect of wishful thinking characteristic of both hybridity and creolization, which she labels "teleological optimism": Such mixtures are generally regarded as good, as if this were the only type of cross-cultural interaction that takes place. As with syncretism, these terms can sometimes be used to mask real inequalities which persist.[22] Sylvia Frey provides a good illustration of this in her essay on African-American Catholics in nineteenth-century New Orleans. In that setting, "creoles" are defined as free people of color, people who saw themselves as constituting an elite. Frey notes how they resisted identification with the slave population (or the ex-slave population after 1865).

A few further words of clarification on the scope and approach of this volume are in order. The cases are all drawn from what can be called the Age of European Imperialism, beginning with the Spanish conquest of the Americas and lasting well into the twentieth century. They all involve Europeans or peoples of European descent extending their control over others, more often than not with the aim of transforming them culturally and spiritually as well as dominating them politically and economically. We use the term "indigenous" to refer to the peoples who were the targets of this outreach. This is admittedly a broader use of the term than is customary, although its exact definition is anything but settled.[23] Perhaps the most notable deviation from the usual meaning is that we include not only inhabitants of a country that was conquered or settled by Europeans or their descendents, but also peoples who were uprooted and resettled by the processes of conquest and enslavement (such as the Yoruba in Cuba). Such target peoples encompass a wide range of types of societies—whether measured in terms of oral or written traditions, rural or urban economies, etc. What these disparate groups nevertheless have in common, we believe is a sense of agency even under conditions of foreign domination, and inventiveness and resiliency in shaping their religious responses.

The collection is divided into two parts. The essays in Part I by Saurabh Dube, C. Mathews Samson, Elizabeth Elbourne, and Richard Fox Young focus on conversion and reflect the increasing sophistication in the use of the term since Robert W. Hefner's collection *Conversion to Christianity* was published in 1993. The cases discussed range from central India to the Guatemalan highlands, colonial South Africa, colonial New York, and northern Sri Lanka. Part II deals with alternative ways of conceptualizing cross-cultural interaction, including syncretism but going well beyond it. The essays, by Joseph Murphy, Anh Q. Tran, David Lindenfeld, Sylvia Frey, and Anne Keary, discuss cases in Cuba, Vietnam, Qing China, colonial Nigeria, New Orleans, northwestern America, and eastern Australia. These pieces are introduced in greater detail in the sections that follow. The reader will notice, however, that the division between the two parts of this volume is not airtight or rigid—the chapters invariably reflect the interrelatedness of conversion processes and the combinations of indigenous and foreign elements that accompany them.

This volume has been a collaborative and interdisciplinary effort. The approaches of the contributors reflect the three disciplines mentioned above, and the editors David Lindenfeld and Miles Richardson are a historian and anthropologist, respectively. The discerning reader can probably sense some differences in their approaches in the two sections that follow. But we hope this will prove to be a stimulating rather than a jarring read.

CONVERSION AND ITS COMPLEXITIES (*Miles Richardson*)

The chapters of this book highlight the great variety of attitudes, moves, and meanings that come under the label "conversion." For some, conversion is encapsulated in the experience of a transformative moment in time; for others, it is an extended process. Conversion can occur individually or collectively. Some interpreters see the "turning" of conversion as basically a rupture with the past, while others stress its continuities with one's previous tradition. Some convert for utilitarian reasons; for others, sincerity is all. Conversion of indigenous religions to Christianity, from the standpoint of Christian practice, may proceed through liturgical sacraments, as one finds in Catholicism, or by personal testimony, which predominates in Protestant churches. In the latter case, frequently the individual stands before the congregation to proclaim that he or she has renounced a previous life of erroneous practices and now wants to live a new life in the Lord Jesus. This verbal narrative, even as the person struggles to recite it, assumes a familiar style recognizable to the community in which the individual dwells. Regardless of the emotional turmoil experienced, the telling quickly shapes itself into a distinctive type of discourse recognizable as a conversion narrative. Thus when we strive to understand what has transpired, we must remember that such conversion narratives are first and foremost words. As words so often do, they claim to represent reality, but also their speakers want us to believe in the authenticity of the experience. Thus they often have a rhetorical function which may overwhelm the representational function.

Among the radical, evangelical groups, people in the Southern Baptists constantly tell one another of their first encounter with the Lord. They must convince one another that they are speaking from the heart. Consequently, they may dramatize the two stages of conversion. First, they speak of their life of sin and the wrongs they thoughtlessly committed against themselves and their loved ones. Then, they switch to the moment when they heard the voice of the Lord and to the peace that flowed through their hearts, the "peace that passeth all understanding," and to the new Christian life of bounding goodness they now lead. Thus, when we hear or read of a person's conversion, we must pay attention to the rhetorical features.[24]

In Saurabh Dube's presentation of the movement of western Christianity into colonial central India we see the conversion narrative at the emotional apex of the encounter between the two religions, Christianity and Hinduism. Dube reports the accounts of two individuals, Ramnath Bajpai and Johann Purti. I choose the short, autobiographical account of Purti for further comment. The imprint of the narrative starts with Purti immediately announcing that he is a Christian, but one who was constantly at odds with his father's suggestions for an occupation. After telling of his consistent failure to find a satisfactory position he abruptly writes, "Within the course of 3 years ... I lost my 3 dear children." This amazingly short, flat statement of loss of his children tracks the conversion narratives in the southern United States. Even more familiar is Purti's telling of his dramatic discovering of God's plan for him. Purti opens his Bible in a random fashion, and 2 Timothy, verse 2 appears before his astonished eyes. Upon reading, he says, "O God, Thou art victorious," and then proceeds to an exemplary life of service. In my childhood in East Texas, I heard of people discovering God's wishes in this exact manner. I even tried it myself, but with no results.

Apart from evangelicals using the Holy Word in an iconic manner, this account of Purti in its very flatness and everydayness allows Dube, in his excellent manner, to offer "vernacular translation" as a most fitting term for the process by which people, overcome by a powerful, foreign religion, make it part of their everyday life—thereby conquering the conquerors.

C. Mathews Samson also gives examples of two people recounting their conversion experiences in his essay based on field work in Guatemala. Both are Maya (Mam) and consequently both were born Catholic, but both had converted to Presbyterianism, and both felt the impact of the newly arrived Pentecostalism, a much more ecstatic, less liturgical faith than Presbyterianism. The first narrative is an account of an older man, who some years back celebrated his 45th anniversary of becoming, in current terminology, a Christian, as distinct from being the Catholic that he as child became through the sacrament of infant baptism. He narrates his conversion as stemming from a growing doubt in his childhood faith. He recounts that he asked the person who presented him the New Testament, which he read without revelation, "How does one believe in the Lord Jesus?" The person directed him to a small Presbyterian chapel by the town's market. He tried to enter but knowing no one, he turned away in shame and fear. But he returns and this time a friend recognizes him and waves him inside. Then, instead of the glorious moment one would expect from the conversion narrative, he raises his hand presumably in response to a question such as "Who wants to accept Jesus Christ as their personal savior?" and the Mestizo, a Spanish-speaking, non-Mayan preacher congratulates him. This illustrates that, in some cases, the *action* of conversion precedes the inner conviction and gives it direction. Here the deed comes before the word. This may be a trace of the Catholic tradition of the region, despite the fact that the conversion is to Presbyterianism.

Both Dube's and Samson's essays show that, however dramatic the moment of conversion may sometimes be, such moments are invariably part of a larger process. Both also emphasize the costs that conversion frequently brings with it in cross-cultural settings. Each presents a case in which the convert provokes his father's fury. The Brahmin convert Chaube bears a large scar where his father struck him with an iron rod; his wife and child were taken from him. In the case of the Mayan, the emotional turmoil of the conversion comes later when his father ejects him from his home because the father believes the missionaries have replaced him as his son's father.

In her masterful accounting of coercion and conversion in two different corners of the European colonial presence among indigenous people, Elizabeth Elbourne provides us with rich material on how the colonial powers manipulated Christianity among the Mohawk in North America and the Khoekhoe in southern Africa to assist them militarily in their ongoing conflicts with their neighbors.

Conversion narratives were not recited among the Mohawk, for they became Christians through the Anglican ritual of baptism, which, although it does not claim the sacramental power of the Catholic rite, provides transition into Christianity without the dramatic emotional upheaval. Here one needs to insert a cautionary note: Although conversion narratives are absent in the sources consulted, additional research may uncover some, a possibility made likely by the presence in the neighborhood of the evangelist Jonathan Edwards. The Khoekhoe, on the other hand, found their way to Christianity through the medium of the Reform Movement. In her earlier work, Elbourne describes the rich tradition of reciting conversion narratives among the Khoekhoe Christians. I wonder how, given their conscription as solders, the Khoekhoe managed their military action while at the same time surrendering themselves to mercy of the Lord—"the Lord" of their colonial masters. Presumably, they accomplished this juggling through the power of conversion narratives. In negotiating their position as allies to the British, the Mohawk perhaps saw Christianity as a mechanism for strengthening their allegiance. In any case, as Elbourne tells it, they seemed to "prefer a hands-off approach to missionaries" and maintained an interest in liturgy, ritual and sacred text, and they sought baptism for their children. In contrast, the Khoekhoe become disillusioned with the British and rebelled. In their rebellion they promoted a millenarian Christianity to incite themselves against their former masters.

The co-option of Christianity for the purposes of military attacks constitutes an old, sad tale in the history of the faith. When Christianity became the religion of the Roman Empire in the fourth century, perhaps at that time it became militaristic. We need to recall the actions of St. James, the patron saint of the Spanish. In assisting their struggle to evict the Muslims from their land, in a flash of lightening St. James would appear before the Spanish astride a rearing white stallion, wielding his sword. In this manifestation, the former apostle to Jesus became Santiago de Matamores, St. James the Moor Slayer. Nonetheless, the soaring tones of the Beatitudes in Jesus' Sermon on the Mount reminds us even now that "[b]lessed are the peacemakers for they shall be called the children of God" (Matt. 5:9). On closer inspection a dialectic between warriors and peacemakers can be found in many cases of protracted Christian "conversion." A good example can be found in Elbourne's earlier work on the Khoekhoe: During a rebellion in 1850, rebels and loyalists quoted passages of the Book of Isaiah advocating war and peace respectively.[25]

Our discussion of conversion and its complexities has not spoken of the most complex of all, and that is collective conversion. One immediately recalls the introduction of Christianity into the western hemisphere, with the Spanish friars accompanying the conquistadores' *entradas* and converting thousands of indigenous people through the sacrament of baptism. Cynics, Christian or otherwise, might be crude enough to sneer at such accounts. Sylvia Frey, in her chronicling of the religious sisters' baptism of the babies of slaves in colonial New Orleans through the sacrament, admits that some spoke derisively of "cradle Christians," but she goes on to add that the sisters acted as sponsors of the babies, and some had as many as twenty-five godchildren. I think we can assume that the godmothers attended to the Christian welfare of their charges.

The proof that colonial collective conversion need not entail a diminution of religious sincerity or dedication may be seen in the lives of people today in Latin America. When I was in Colombia doing fieldwork in 1961–1962, a friend remarked, "I am a good Catholic but I don't like priests." His uncle, who seldom went to mass, explained his true faith was in the Virgin of Carmen. And to show how she cared for him he recounted the night when she protected him from the police's finding of the load of contraband cigars he had in his wagon.[26] Subsequent research in Costa Rica, Honduras, Guatemala, Mexico, and Peru continued to indicate the depth of popular faith among ordinary people who tell one another they will return from their journeys, "Si Dios quiere" ("If God so wills"), and setting off, they crossed themselves before a church they may have never entered.

Finally, the topic of "conversion"—in quotes—is the centerpiece of what is probably the most widely discussed theory of cross-cultural religious interaction in use today, particularly as far as the so-called world religions are concerned. This is the theory of anthropologist Robin Horton, based on his fieldwork in West Africa and which first appeared in 1971. Our collection contains a novel and insightful interpretation of Horton's work, by Richard Fox Young who applies it to certain situations in South Asia. The nub of the theory is based on a contrast between the "microcosm" of a traditional society, as in a village, and the "macrocosm" of a wider world which sooner or later impinges on it. Each of these levels has deities or spirits which tend to it: the "lesser deities" of the village and the "supreme being" of the wider world. The more one is drawn into the macrocosm, the greater the appeal of the supreme being. This, Horton claims, will happen regardless of whether Christian or Muslim proselytizers happen to be present. They are merely the catalysts for a development that occurs *within* the framework of indigenous religion.

Horton's own label for his approach is "intellectualist," by which he means that African religions should be viewed as "theoretical systems intended for the explanation, prediction, and control of space-time events"—in other words, religion is primarily a means of adapting to the challenges of this world rather than the next.[27] To a Protestant schooled on the centrality of salvation, this may appear to be a maverick view. But Horton strongly suggests that it is nineteenth- and twentieth-century Euro-American Protestantism that might be the maverick, in abandoning explanation-prediction-control for what he calls "the religion of communion," i.e., conceiving the relationship to God as a purely personal one.[28] In any case, Horton is far from the first anthropologist to conceive of non-Western religion as a primarily intellectual venture. Edward Burnett Tylor, often heralded as the father of anthropology, viewed the origin of religion in the efforts of early thinkers to marshal the evidence available to them to formulate a belief in spiritual beings from which, through further elaborations, became gods.[29] Somewhat later, an admirer of Tylor, Paul Radin wrote in his *Primitive Man as Philosopher*[30] of a category of myths whose unfolding came about as a result of a mind at work. More recently, Stewart Guthrie, in his book, *Faces in the Clouds: A New Theory of Religion*,[31] argues that the propensity for people to explain the surrounding human environment in anthropomorphic language is the core of religious thought. He draws both on Tylor and Horton in presenting religion as the human mind at work.

Young does not minimize the widespread criticism of Horton's boldly simplifying approach, which sometimes leaves one wondering how this theory continues to exercise its enchantment on subsequent generations of scholars. Perhaps its very falsifiability is the source of its ongoing fascination—it is a theory that one loves to shoot down. Yet, as Young reviews its reception among South Asian specialists, there appear to be sufficient if scattered grains of truth brought to light by its ability to keep the discussion going. Young finds such a case in a Tamil location on the northern tip of Sri Lanka. There a gifted missionary linguist worked on a translation of the Bible into Tamil. Arumukam was not a professed Protestant, and in fact he turned against Christianity to promote "Shaivism" in which he declared Shiva as one true God. He worked hard to rid the community of all autochthonous, non-Sanskritic divinities, including the Catholic saints and the Virgin Mary. In other words, Young notes, Arumukam promoted what Horton would call cognitive reorganization, which proceeded apace without Christianity. Young contends that Shaivism and its process of monolatry is a worthy example of the Intellectual Theory.

The novelty of Young's contribution lies in his pushing Horton's uncompromisingly intellectualist model to its logical conclusion—and thereby beyond the necessity of conversion itself. For if Christianity here is merely the catalyst and accelerator of changes occurring within an indigenous worldview, then it makes sense that the outcome is a new view of Shiva rather than of the Christian God or Christ. In this way, he shows how the issues raised by missionaries and the conversion process are inseparable from the issues raised by the term syncretism—how one combines the new and the old, the indigenous and the foreign.

SYNCRETISM AND ITS ALTERNATIVES (*David Lindenfeld*)

Merriam-Webster's *Collegiate Dictionary* (10th ed., 1999) defines syncretism as "the combination of different forms of belief or practice." As such, the application of syncretism to the study of cross-cultural religious interaction is virtually limitless—but not very helpful as an analytical tool. Nevertheless, syncretism is a term widely used in the history of ancient religions. "An immemorial and abundantly documented phenomenon," Mircea Eliade writes in his *History of Religious Ideas*, "syncretism had played an important part in the formation of Hittite, Greek, and Roman religions, in the religion of Israel, in Mahayana Buddhism, and in Taoism, but what marks the syncretism of the Hellenistic and Roman period is its scale and its surprising creativity."[32] From a greater distance of time, it is possible to view the actual mixing and merging of deities that occurred in the ancient world—a luxury that is often denied to students of more recent history. On the other hand, the essays presented here offer a view into the microscopic workings of religious interaction, often at the level of thick description, which reveal strategies and processes that are not necessarily found in accounts of older syncretisms.

To begin, it is clear that religious encounters, more often than not, take place between unequal parties. While examples of missionaries accompanying or following in the wake of conquistadores spring immediately to mind, there are probably more examples where the balance of power is in favor of the natives—where only a few missionaries have entered an area and are largely at the mercy of their hosts. Especially in the early stages of such encounters, an indigenous culture is likely to incorporate only a limited number of features from the missionary religion, while preserving its basic patterns and values more or less intact. It can happen, however, that over time an indigenous culture is modified by external influences to such a degree that it comes to resemble the foreign culture, or at least to identify with it. This is more likely to occur among limited sectors of the indigenous population than for the whole. Thus one terminological revision suggested by these essays is to reserve the label "syncretism" for interactions where the inputs from both cultures are somewhat in balance, while finding new names for situations in which either the indigenous or the foreign culture tends to predominate.

A case of dynamic balancing between heterogeneous cultural inputs is presented by Joseph Murphy in his chapter on Shango and Santa Barbara in Cuban (and Cuban-American) Santería. Following the ground-breaking lead of Herskovits in seeking to explain the relationship between African deities and the Christian saints, Murphy neither dismisses Santa Barbara as a veneer of Christianity nor lingers long on the African origin of Shango. Rather he rejoices in the various messages and the creativity that Cuban Santería conveys. One can view the interactions among the cult members in celebrating Shango in words, and the actions, and artifacts as constituting a performance now, and this contemporary performance reveals to us an androgynous Shango, with Santa Barbara not a veneer but a shining forth as Shango's femininity. The combination is as much an invitation to continuing ambiguity and paradox as it is a stable resolution or synthesis of two traditions.

For other, less balanced situations, the terms *selective inculturation* and *selective acculturation* suggest themselves. Neither, however, is problem-free, because of usages that have been previously established for them. Thus inculturation has become the term of choice to describe the evangelical outreach of the Catholic Church since Vatican II, although its roots go far deeper.[33] This use of inculturation implies that missionaries, whether foreign or native, are the primary agents of change. We would propose, however, an additional meaning which views inculturation as primarily an indigenous activity that extends well beyond that of evangelism, namely that of selectively incorporating foreign elements into one's own matrix, which nevertheless remains recognizably dominant.

Anh Q. Tran's chapter on *The Conference of Representatives of Four Religions,* an eighteenth-century Catholic "dialogue" in Vietnam, shows the first type of inculturation at work: The anonymous author seeks to show that the religious newcomer, Catholicism, is not foreign to the previously existing Vietnamese religions of Confucianism, Taoism, and Buddhism. Nevertheless, there are limits to this compatibility; the Catholic

Church had already rejected ancestor worship by this time. Tran makes clear that the work is not a genuine dialogue, but an apologia for Christianity. Tran's chapter demonstrates that the predominantly "exclusivist" orientation of Christianity at the time, which saw itself as superior to the other religions even while building on them in part, was quite different from the popular Vietnamese outlook, which tended to accept elements of the three Asian religions and blend them with their folk practices. Inculturation in this case, then, was not a two-way street, despite the fact that the author was a native Vietnamese, writing in the vernacular language.

Examples of the second meaning of inculturation may be found in Anne Keary's chapter, which compares indigenous peoples' initial encounters with missionaries in eastern Australia and the Pacific northwest. Thus the Australian Awabakal people, upon meeting the English missionary Threlkeld, perform their version of English hymns, combined with a dance, "in accordance with an indigenous custom of learning and passing on new songs." And in North America the headmen of the Nimiipu took particular delight in telling Bible stories as a way of enhancing their own authority.

An extreme form of selective inculturation in the second sense may be called *concentration of spirituality*. In these cases, not only are the foreign incorporations limited, but they are used to sweep away large portions of the indigenous religion as well, thus focusing on a few divinities rather than many. The Judeo-Christian-Islamic injunction against idolatry and graven images has served as a powerful tool in this respect. Nevertheless, the indigenous cultural pattern still remains unmistakably dominant. David Lindenfeld's comparative study of the Taiping Rebellion in nineteenth-century China and the Aladura praying churches among the Yoruba in southwest Nigeria presents instances of this pattern. Both movements swept away statues, temples, fetishes of the old religions, while still presenting a religion far removed from that of the missionaries. It should be noted that cross-religious interaction need not always be the instigator of such spiritual housecleanings: There are numerous examples within a given religious tradition, whether labeled indigenous or otherwise.[34] The Protestant Reformation springs immediately to mind. The effect of such simplifications seems to be that of energizing the practitioners by focusing their attention on a few elements. The word "purification" is often used in this connection.[35] This further helps explain why, in many cases, ascetic behaviors such as fasting, renunciation of alcohol, and restriction of sexual activity accompany this pattern. Another source of such energizing is millennial expectation, which may be considered a form of concentrated spirituality insofar as one believes that one's own time is of surpassing religious importance in all the ages in history. This energizing enters into many cases of what Anthony F. C. Wallace called "revitalization movements," in which charismatic leaders emerge to reform a culture that is in crisis. Wallace's study of the Seneca prophet Handsome Lake, which Elizabeth Elbourne discusses briefly in her chapter, served as a prototype for this concept.[36]

Another example of concentrated spirituality may be found in Richard Fox Young's chapter. His discussion of "pantheon simplification" in northern Sri Lanka shows that, under the repeated impact of Protestant preaching of "*the* one true God," the Tamils applied this reasoning to their own Hinduism, elevating Shiva at the expense of lesser Hindu deities.

The term *acculturation* suggests the opposite of inculturation, namely change to or toward a foreign model. Yet its usage is no less problematic. It was the preferred term of American anthropologists in the early twentieth century to refer to cultural mixing in general. Herskovits used it along with syncretism. Yet despite the subtlety of his analyses, the term came to be seen as having an implicit subtext, namely that of assimilation to a predominately European cultural model, much as we saw in the Brazilian case.[37] Thus it has become dated, as demonstrated by the fact that it merited an article in the 1968 *International Encyclopedia of the Social Sciences*, but not in the 2001 *International Encyclopedia of the Social and Behavioral Sciences*. Still, some term is needed to denote the cases where groups are drawn to and identify with a culture that is not their own. Frey's portrait of an African Catholic female religious order in eighteenth- and nineteenth-century New Orleans presents us with a clear example, one of Francophone identification. Frey cites documents from the order in French as late as 1894. She points to education as a focal point of the order's activities, which constituted "the principal arena for the evangelization of the black New Orleanians." Whenever the topic of education appears in missionary literature, it generally means Western education; the acceptance and appeal of missionaries as teachers thus serves as an indicator of acculturation. Frey's narrative also poignantly conveys the fact that acculturation came at a cost: As the American racial divide widened in the late nineteenth century, the African-American Catholics lost status and bargaining power. Frey's work is also innovative when it comes to gender: She documents not only the preponderance of women in missionary roles, but also how this qualitatively affected the means of conversion, e.g. through serving as godparents to slave children.

A different approach to the question of cultural and religious interaction is suggested by Dube in this volume with the concept of *vernacu-*

lar translation. This terminology is considerably less problematic than that of inculturation/acculturation, because it resonates simultaneously with the interest in languages and texts in postmodernist and postcolonialist literature, which Dube draws upon, and with a dominant motif in recent religious studies, particularly Christian missionary scholarship. Andrew Walls puts translation at the heart of the Christian message when he writes, "Incarnation is translation. When God in Christ became man, Divinity was translated into humanity as though humanity were a receptor language."[38] Moreover, *vernacular* translation has been seen as basic to Christian missionary work ever since Paul began spreading the word to the Gentiles. In his influential book *Translating the Message*, the African theologian Lamin Sanneh asserts that "the recipient culture is the authentic destination of God's salvific promise and, as a consequence, has an honored place under 'the kindness of God,' with the attendant safeguards against cultural absolutism."[39] A good example is the anonymous Vietnamese Christian presented in Tran's essay. He carefully seeks to calibrate Christian teachings on honoring one's earthly and heavenly father with East Asian notions of ancestor worship. Implicit in this evangelical notion is that translation is not static; the act of translation itself modifies the message, a point which Dube also makes with respect to the indigene. This, be it noted, gets us rather far from the ordinary notion of translation as an attempt at being faithful to the original. Indeed, the word "reinterpretation" may be a more accurate synonym for translation in this sense.

This point is underscored by Dube's case study of conversion in central India. He presents two accounts of a conversion of a Brahman, one by a missionary, the other by the convert's son. Each one fashions a narrative of the conversion that is in accord with his respective worldview. One is struck by how little overlap there is between them. The comparison points to the fact that one cannot overemphasize the importance of selectivity when discussing interaction as translation.

Anne Keary's chapter, juxtaposing missionary and indigenous perspectives in her focused comparison of a North American and an Australian colonial encounter, provides further illustrations of this point— and of the sheer multivocality of translation processes in even the most delimited of cases. Her essay brings out the fact that translation is always a double process: Both missionary and indigene are translating, interpreting what they perceive to be the other's worldview in terms of their own. Moreover, she shows that these interpretations are conditioned by a number of variables. There are, for one, the *epistemological structures* which the colonizers and indigenes already possess and which tend to generate stereotypes about the other. Her examples reveal, however, that the dynamic relationships among the factors of colonization, structures, and stereotypes work very differently in the two cases: The lack of well-established colonial structures in the Australian case when compared to the North American ironically allowed for more extensive cross-cultural contact between missionary and native. In addition, there are the *agendas* which the different parties—settlers, missionaries, and natives—bring to the encounter, and these may coincide, converge, or diverge. All of these factors affect not only the translation process itself, but also the attitudes that the parties bring to that process, their degree of self-consciousness about it. In the end, Keary's study—like Dube's—convinces us of the fragility of translation processes.

If translation breaks down, or threatens to, there is the alternative of *dialogue*, which also occurs in Keary's essay. This is a form of religious interaction that has attracted great interest in the latter part of the twentieth century. One can view interreligious dialogue as incorporating vernacular translation but necessarily going beyond it. In other words, each side must make the effort of interpreting another's faith in terms that one finds comprehensible. But this cannot be the final step; rather the goal is to understand the other in the other's terms—to de-vernacularize, as it were. By the same token, dialogue does not necessarily imply transformation of one's own religious point of view, or the expectation that one will transform the other. In short, this complex act of translation has the opposite goal of missionary translation.[40] It can lead to the realization of *convergence*, when the two sides recognize they share the same principles.

A further alternative to vernacular translation is what anthropologist William K. Powers has dubbed *dual religious participation,* i.e., the practice of two religions simultaneously. This would refer, for example, to professed Christians who participate in baptism and communion, yet continue to consult indigenous healers or diviners when the need arises. Powers developed the idea from his work with the Oglala Sioux and sees it as quite distinct from syncretism.[41] For the Sioux, the pattern developed as a direct result of white interdiction: During the years in which most traditional rituals were prohibited, from 1883 to 1934, the only way of preserving them was to carry them on in secret. But afterwards, this pattern held as well, even after the traditional religion was revived in the 1960s and 70s.

In the volume's first part, Samson presents a comparable case when he discusses pluralism among the Mayans in Guatemala: The country is largely Christian, but Mayan spirituality has been kept alive and is undergoing a revival. Samson shows how Mayan religion is coming out in the public sphere, as witnessed by a book-signing in an urban hotel.

Although not as systematically researched, the practice of dual religious participation is probably quite widespread in many cultures. J.D.Y. Peel also finds it among the Yoruba in Nigeria, not so much among the Aladuras as among those who attend the missionary churches.[42] The concept might also serve as a model for so-called secular cultures of modern Europe, as people who do not think of themselves as religious nevertheless participate in certain religious holidays (Christmas, Easter) and may want to get married in a church.[43]

To conclude, one might ask how these different terminologies fit together, if at all? We are certainly not suggesting that they occur in a particular sequence, or even one at a time.[44] It would seem, however, that some describe short-term processes and others apply to more extended ones. Thus inculturation generally occurs during the early stages of cross-cultural religious contact, when knowledge and information about the foreign religion is fragmentary and partial. Concentration of spirituality, in the cases presented here, is also an immediate response, given the presence of a charismatic leader or leaders. But given the right type of organization, it can become an enduring feature, as with the Aladuras. Acculturation, by contrast, generally presupposes prolonged exposure. The same might be said of syncretism, at least as Murphy presents it. Translation and dialogue, on the other hand, necessarily operate at both immediate and long-term levels, as Keary's chapter clearly demonstrates. Translators are needed at the initial stages in order to achieve elemental understanding, however fragmentary. A good translation, however, presupposes knowledge of the whole language, which comes with time, not just with learning isolated sets of words. At the same time, we should guard against teleological optimism and the assumption that good translation inevitably will occur. Dual religious participation might be a long-term alternative.

Our terminological arabesques ultimately point to the lack of finality of any such conceptual schemes, and to the endless creativity that culture-mixing exhibits. The irreducibility of these mixtures to explanation on the purely economic or political plane bears witness to the spiritual dimension of human existence, the pondering about who we are and how we fit into the broader scheme of things—an activity that has probably been in existence since the emergence of the early hominids some 3 million years ago. Perhaps the word that best illustrates this pondering is discourse, in its broadest sense. We are constantly addressing each other through word, gesture, or artifact about how it is that we, you and I, are. Religious discourse thus seems to be an integral and indispensable part of this activity called culture. Religion in its multitudinous accents seemingly constantly refreshes itself in providing us with assurances that this path or that other is the true one we must pursue.

Notes

1. Andrew F. Walls, *The Missionary Movement in Christian History: Studies in the Transmission of Faith* (Maryknoll, NY, 1994), 11.

2. See, e.g., Andrew Porter, *Religion versus Empire? British Protestant Missionaries and Overseas Expansion, 1700–1914* (Manchester, UK, 2004), 1–7; Ussama Makdisi, *Artillery of Heaven: American Missionaries and the Failed Conversion of the Middle East* (Ithaca, 2008); Dana L. Robert, *Christian Mission: How Christianity Became a World Religion* (Chichester, UK, 2008).

3. Jean Comaroff and John Comaroff, *Of Revelation and Revolution: Christianity, Colonialism, and Consciousness in South Africa*, 2 vols. (Chicago, 1991, 1997). For a critical discussion, see the review essays in *The American Historical Review* 108, no. 2 (2003): 434–78.

4. Peter van der Veer, *Imperial Encounters: Religion and Modernity in India and Britain* (Princeton, 2001), 23. In a companion volume to the *Oxford History of the British Empire*, titled *Missions and Empire* (Oxford, 2005), editor Norman Etherington characterizes the relationship between the two as "unfinished business."

5. Comaroff and Comaroff, *Revelation and Revolution* 2: 22.

6. See David Lindenfeld, "The Christian Religion in Modern European and World History: A Review of *The Cambridge History of Christianity, 1800–2000*," *History Compass* 6, no. 6 (2008): 1426–38.

7. Patrick Manning, *Navigating World History* (New York, 2003), 248.

8. Robert Eric Frykenberg, "Christian Missions and the Raj," in *Missions and Empire*, ed. Norman Etherington (Oxford, 2005), 117 (cf. Etherington's statement, 7).

9. Arpita Anant, "Anti-Conversion Laws," *The Hindu*, 17 December 2002, http://www.hindu.com/thehindu/op/2002/12/17/stories/2002121700110200.htm (accessed 8 June, 2011).

10. Charles Stewart, "Syncretism and Its Synonyms: Reflection on Cultural Mixture," *Diacritics* 29, no. 3 (1999): 40; Charles Stewart, "Problematizing Syncretism," introduction to *Syncretism/Anti-Syncretism: The Politics of Religious Synthesis*, ed. Charles Stewart and Rosalind Shaw (London, 1994), 2.

11. Stewart, "Syncretism and Its Synonyms," 46–51.

12. Ibid., 47–48. For a fuller account, see Josué A. Sathler and Amós Nascimento, "Black Masks on White Faces: Liberation Theology and the Quest for Syncretism in the Brazilian Context," in *Liberation Theologies, Postmodernity, and the Americas*, ed. David Batstone et al. (London, 1997), 95–122.

13. Quoted in Edwin Zehner, "Orthodox Hybridities: Anti-Syncretism and Localization in the Evangelical Christianity of Thailand," *Anthropological Quarterly* 78, no. 3 (2005): 592.

14. Jerald D. Gort, "Syncretism and Dialogue: Christian Historical and Earlier Ecumenical Perceptions," in *Dialogue and Syncretism: An Interdisciplinary Approach*, ed. Jerald Gort, et al. (Grand Rapids, MI, 1989), 37–38.

15. André Droogers, "Syncretism: The Problem of Definition, the Definition of the Problem," in Gort et al., ed., *Dialogue and Syncretism*, 14, 20; Dirk C. Mulder, "Dialogue and Syncretism: Some Concluding Observations," ibid., 206.

16. Droogers, "Syncretism," 16; Mulder, ibid., 204.

17. Quoted in Stewart, "Syncretism and Its Synonyms," 53.

18. Robert B. Sheard, *Interreligious Dialogue in the Catholic Church Since Vatican II* (Lewiston, NY, 1987), 163, 235–56, 245, 251–52.

19. Zehner, "Orthodox Hybridities," 593.

20. Richard White, *The Middle Ground: Indians, Empires and Republics in the Great Lakes Region, 1650-1815* (Cambridge, 1991); Homi K. Bhabha, *The Location of Culture* (London, 1994), 36, 38, 217.

21. Stewart, "Creolization: History, Ethnography, Theory," in *Creolization: History, Ethnography, Theory*, Charles Stewart, ed. (Walnut Creek, CA, 2007), 8. On the transmutations of the term in Louisiana, see Gwendolyn Midlo Hall, *Africans in Colonial Louisiana: The Development of Afro-Creole Culture in the Eighteenth Century* (Baton Rouge, LA, 1992), 157–58.

22. Aisha Khan, "Good to Think? Creolization, Optimism, and Agency," *Current Anthropology* 48, no. 5 (2007): 653–56.

23. See Ken S. Coates, *A Global History of Indigenous Peoples: Struggle and Survival* (New York, 2004), 1–15.

24. Miles Richardson, *Being-in-Christ and putting death in its place: An anthropologist's Account of Christian performances in Spanish America and in the American South*, Baton Rouge, LA, 2003.

25. Elizabeth Elbourne, *Blood Ground. Colonialism, Missions, and the Contest for Christianity in the Cape Colony and Britain, 1799-1853* (Montreal, 2002), 364–65.

26. Miles Richardson, *San Pedro, Colombia: Small Town in a Developing Society* (Prospect Heights, IL, 1986).

27. Robin Horton, "African Conversion," *Africa: Journal of the International African Institute* 41 (1971): 94. Another version of the "intellectualist" account, based largely on the theories of Max Weber, may be found in the introduction to *Conversion to Christianity: Historical and Anthropological Perspectives on a Great Transformation*, ed. Robert W. Hefner (Berkeley, 1993), 3–44.

28. Horton, "African Conversion," 96.

29. E. B. Tylor, *Primitive Culture*, 2 vols. (London, 1873).

30. (New York, 1957).

31. (Oxford, 1993).

32. Mircea Eliade, *A History of Religious Ideas*, 3 vols. (Chicago, 1978, 1982, 1987), 3: 277. For a survey, see Carsten Colpe, "Syncretism," in *Encyclopedia of Religion*, ed. Mircea Eliade (New York, 1987), 14: 218–27.

33. For a review and commentary on this sometimes confusing terminology, see Peter C. Phan, *In Our Own Tongues: Perspectives from Asia on Mission and Inculturation* (Maryknoll, NY, 2003), 3–10.

34. See, e.g., Willy De Craemer, Jan Vansina, and Renee C. Fox, "Religious Movements in Central Africa: A Theoretical Study," *Comparative Studies in Soci-*

ety and History 18, no. 4 (1976): 466; and Danilyn Rutherford, "The Bible Meets the Idol: Writing and Conversion in Biak, Irian Jaya, Indonesia," in *The Anthropology of Christianity,* ed. Fenella Cannell (Durham, 2006), 240–65.

35. Cf. Walter E. A. van Beek, ed. *The Quest for Purity: Dynamics of Puritan Movements* (Berlin, 1988). The collection includes studies of Calvin's Geneva, the New England Puritans, the Wahabbi movement, the Fulani Jihad, the Iranian Revolution, as well as the Taiping Rebellion and twentieth-century Communism.

36. Anthony F. C. Wallace, "Revitalization Movements: Some Theoretical Considerations," *American Anthropologist* 58, no. 2 (1956): 264–81; and *The Death and Rebirth of the Seneca* (New York, 1972).

37. Edward H. Spicer, "Acculturation," in *International Encyclopedia of the Social Sciences,* ed. David L. Sills (New York, 1968), 1: 21. See also Stewart, "Syncretism and Its Synonyms," 49–51.

38. Walls, *Missionary Movement,* 27.

39. Lamin Sanneh, *Translating the Message: The Missionary Impact on Culture* (Maryknoll, NY,1989), 31.

40. For an overview of the dialogue process, see the essays in Gort et al., ed., *Dialogue and Syncretism,* particularly those of Maurice Friedman (76–84) and Dirk C. Mulder (203–11).

41. William K. Powers, "Dual Religious Participation. Stratagems of Conversion among the Lakota," in his *Beyond the Vision: Essays on American Indian Culture* (Norman, OK, 1987), ch. 5. See also Raymond J. DeMallie and Douglas R. Parks, Introduction to *Sioux Indian Religion. Tradition and Innovation,* ed. Raymond J. DeMallie and Douglas R. Parks (Norman, OK, 1987), 14.

42. J.D.Y. Peel, "Syncretism and Religious Change," *Comparative Studies in Society and History* 10, no. 2 (1968): 129.

43. Writing in 1978, sociologist David Martin observed that 90 percent of Spanish workers baptized their children and the same number expressed anticlerical sentiments. See *A General Theory of Secularization* (New York, 1978), 259.

44. For a work that utilizes the multiple strategies of "syncretism, convergence, and dualism," see Susan Neylan, *The Heavens Are Changing: Nineteenth-Century Protestant Missions and Tsimshian Christianity* (Montreal, 2003).

PART I

CONVERSION AND ITS COMPLEXITIES

1

Conversion, Translation, and Life-History in Colonial Central India

Saurabh Dube

This essay explores the interplay of conversion, translation, and life-history embedded within processes of evangelical entanglements between Euro-American missionaries and central-Indian peoples. It focuses on autobiographies and biographies of converts to Christianity in the Chhattisgarh region of central India, especially accounts written between the 1920s and the 1940s. Here, the exact ordinariness and the very details of these texts — mediated by procedures of vernacular translation — reveal the writings as key registers of evangelical entanglements.

OVERTURE

In 1868 the Reverend Oscar Lohr of the German Evangelical Mission Society initiated evangelical work in Chhattisgarh. Over the next eight decades, six missionary organizations — the German (later American) Evangelical Mission Society, the American Mennonites, the General Conference Mennonites, the Disciples of Christ, the Methodists, and the Pentecostal Bands of the World — conducted the evangelical enterprise there. Aided by paternalist institutions such as Christian villages, hospitals, and orphanages, conversions to Christianity grew haltingly, primarily through ties of family and kinship among lower-caste and *adivasi* (or indigenous) groups. On the one hand, the converts continued to understand missionary injunctions and to interpret evangelical truths through the grids of quotidian cultures. These peoples participated in the making of a vernacular and a colonial Christianity, crucially drawing in the energies of their Western, evangelical benefactors and turning them into, at once, witting accomplices and hapless victims. On the other hand, the mission project itself unraveled through contradictory connections with colonial cultures. Such processes in central India were intimately tied to those of congregations and churches in Midwestern America. The missionaries had to leave India after its independence.

In 1947 there were only around 15,000 Protestant Christians in a population of 7 million in Chhattisgarh. At the same time, in independent India, as under imperial rule, the social and political significance of Christian converts has exceeded their numerical unimportance.

Christianity and conversion are politically loaded and fiercely contended terms in India today. There are severe problems with the ways in such questions are posed, arguments conducted, and battles fought—in public and academic arenas. On the one hand, in both domains debate and discussion continue to be haunted by a pervasive fault-line: Either the missionary is cast as the crafty agent of colonial rule, *or* the evangelist is projected as the lofty benefactor to the native. Both overlook the fact that mission projects at once *elaborated* as well as *questioned* colonial power. On the other hand, the converts themselves are either understood as historical villains who betrayed their earlier faith for material gains, *or* they are seen as historical victims who converted to Christianity in order to escape poverty and to gain social mobility. Once more, each side overlooks the fact that the converts could conceptually translate the message of Christianity through their own meanings and practices, in order to create rather particular, vernacular, regional-Indian forms of Christianity.

My wider research project on evangelical entanglements addresses such problems by focusing on three broad, overlapping processes. First, it discusses the interweaving of missionary efforts and converts' practices with principles of caste-sect and dynamics of village life. The contentious admixtures shaped the missionary enterprise and a vernacular Christianity. Second, the project considers the connections and contradictions between the missionary project and imperial power and between a vernacular (Indian) Christianity and colonial cultures. Such fraught linkages underlay critical expressions of modernity, evangelism, and empire on the ground. Third and finally, the study explores wide-ranging expressions of community and nation in the wake of conversion. These underscore controversial issues of the so-called "majority" and "minority," politics and religion, and the citizen and the convert, especially in independent India. It is in these ways that I engage and extend the recent historical anthropology of Christianity and colonialism across different continents. This scholarship has pointed to: first, the contradictory location of the mission project in the fabrication of colonial cultures;[1] and second, the place of such contradiction and contention in the shaping of various forms of vernacular Christianity.[2] Unsurprisingly, given its twin bases in anthropology and history, my study conjoins archival research in extensive missionary repositories with field work in central India and the Midwestern United States.

STIPULATIONS OF CONVERSION

The autobiographical and biographical materials that I discuss in this chapter narrate the life-histories of individual converts to the Christian faith in colonial India.[3] On the one hand, all too often, particularly in social science literature, Christian conversion in non-western contexts appears as an essentially collective endeavor, opposing it to the image of the solitary Saul who sees the light in understandings of conversion in western arenas. Here modular understandings construe conversion as a search for meaning in front of the onslaught of modernization/modernity in remote non-western theatres. Such schemes tend to bracket the distinct experiences of the events and processes of conversion on the part of particular persons, especially their notions of lives and histories. On the other hand, Pauline propositions and psychological prototypes regarding conversion tend to present it as an exclusively individual act, also intimating a solitary trajectory. Here the lone seeker transfers to a new, primary religious affiliation through a judicious choice among distinct and competing faiths, and then acts upon this choice through sincere personal belief and committed membership of community in Christ. At the basis of such understandings are meta-historical and meta-cultural assumptions regarding action and understanding, conversion and Christianity. These two apparently opposed orientations can incline toward discounting what is salient and specific about life histories in the wake of conversion.

None of this should be surprising. In everyday and academic arenas, pervasive conceptions of conversion – as an individual event or a collective endeavor – are bedeviled by two overlapping difficulties. First, they remain rooted in common sense European connotations of the category. Second, they turn conversion into a self-contained analytical apparatus and a self-generative descriptive domain. It is in this way that the event of conversion is widely understood as intimating a singular life and indicating an exclusive history for the convert, individually and collectively. Such conceptions require staying with longer, thinking through farther, exactly because they carry immense force. Their story lines are simple and seductive. Their familiarity invites belief and elicits agreement. After all, from the presence of the self-determining actor to the resonance of universal history, the stipulations of the subject and the norms of narrative articulated by these understandings are variously constitutive of the modern condition. For our purposes, at stake here are wide-ranging issues of how conversion and life-histories might be rethought, especially as entailing procedures of translation.

Most conversions to Christianity in colonial central India came about through networks of extended kinship, further involving bonds of caste and sect, and the prospects of a better life under the paternalist economies of mission stations. Yet, people also converted in other ways, variously negotiating ties of kith and kin, caste and sect. Indeed, even those Christians whose conversion was effected through conduits of kinship were not simply figures of a singular, collective logic. In each case, conversion provided a resource for the distinct plotting of lives, the different telling of histories. This is revealed by the writings discussed in this chapter. The accounts were at once shaped by colonial verities and marked by vernacular attributes. Although apparently formulaic in nature, they engage and exceed the *telos* of dominant narratives of conversion to Christianity. The accounts imbue such exclusive story lines with their own notations. Here conversion and life-history appear as processes and practices of translation, involving the entangled work yet the unequal labor of the convert and the missionary. They reveal that at the core of colonial histories and evangelical entanglements lay the complex making and unmaking of historical forms, social identities, ritual practices, mythic meanings, narrative forms, and vernacular translations.

TERMS OF TRANSLATION

Beginning with the issue of the impossibility of translation, which I have discussed elsewhere, the subject of translation is a vexed one.[4] My point here is merely that, as George Steiner's "abundant, vulgar fact," translation is possible because it happens, and it happens all the time in social worlds.[5] Indeed, it is precisely the routine performance and the quotidian practice of translation that have found critical considerations in recent times.[6] To begin with, in debates on cultural translation there has been keen recognition of what Talal Asad has described as the "inequality of languages."[7] Such inequality also implies inequity, the two together inscribing and re-inserting asymmetries of languages and idioms, knowledge and power in the name of a neutral science and in the guise of an authoritative translation. All of this has led to distinctive bids toward a critical-creative practice of translation in history and anthropology.[8] It has also encouraged critical scholarship to emphasize that processes of translation were central to the elaboration of colonial cultures, instituting distinct forms of colonizing power and eliciting diverse practices of colonized subjects.[9] Indeed, in the articulation of Christianity and colonialism, as Vicente Rafael has argued, by "setting languages in motion, translation tended to cast intentions adrift, now laying, now subverting the ideological grounds of colonial hegemony."[10] Here was dialogue and distinction that secured and subverted colonial power and missionary authority by construing these through familiar referents and unfamiliar premises.

At this point, it is important to clarify my use of the category *vernacular translation*. The notion at once builds upon and departs from Vicente Rafael's imaginative discussion of Spanish colonial and Christian translation among the Tagalog people of the Philippines. Now, for Rafael, translation refers to certified practices involving clerical-colonial renderings of the Word and its attendant tools and texts into the vernacular. He describes the Tagalog "response" to such processes as "vernacularization."[11] In contrast, my own focus concerns non-certified procedures of translation set in motion among Indian Christians in the wake of evangelization and translation initiated by the Euro-American missionary. It is such procedures that I call vernacular translation. Put differently, vernacular translation does not simply indicate the linguistic rendering of texts and works from the English language into vernacular idioms. Rather, it equally refers to procedures of the *transmutation* of distinct categories and discrete concepts. These procedures lay between the interplay (and inequality) of languages, between the exchange (and inequity) of idioms, ever on the cusp of the English and the vernaculars, incessantly straddling and scrambling the boundaries and horizons of the original and the translation.

Understood in this fashion, the practices of vernacular translation that underlie the accounts discussed herein inhabited the interstices brought into existence by the "separation between the original message of Christianity ... and its rhetorical formulation in the vernacular" by missionaries in colonial India. Indeed, as we shall soon see, the missionaries themselves could not escape the force and reach of vernacular translation.[12] And so, procedures of vernacular translation often constrained the universalizing assumptions of a colonial Christianity in British India. Yet, they did this not so much by turning away from its totalizing impulses as by imbuing these with an excess of meaning, a surplus of faith. In other words, vernacular translation illuminates Indian renderings of Christianity and empire but not simply as a response to—which is to say, never ever split apart from—the Euro-American evangelist and colonial power.[13]

GROUNDS OF WITNESS

From the very beginnings of the missionary project, lowly, native workers of the mission played a critical role in the expression of evangelical entanglements. I have shown elsewhere that the early Euro-American evangelists were pressed for time and strapped for money. Hesitant in the primary language, Hindi, they were unsure of the regional vernacular, Chhattisgarhi. Here trained native Christians provided the way forward for the evangelical enterprise. Yet, the perceptions and practices of the Indian evangelical workers could also exceed the interests and expectations of the missionaries, critically shaping patterns of evangelical entanglements, including the designs of a vernacular Christianity.[14] It is the writings concerning such Indian evangelical operatives that are the subject of this essay.

The first Indian workers of the mission arose from among the ranks of the original lower-caste converts in Chhattisgarh, who were taught and trained by the missionaries.[15] At the same time, for the work of evangelism, the other means of acquiring workers—primarily as preachers, and later pastors—consisted of drawing in the energies of the occasional, often upper-caste, literate convert to Christianity within the region.[16] This was the case with Simon Ramnath Bajpai, a Brahman, who began his vocation as a teacher, then became an evangelist, and was finally ordained into the Ministry. The mission also engaged the services of trained employees of missions from outside Chhattisgarh. This was the case with Pandit Gangaram Chaube, a "native evangelist" with the Church Missionary Society in Jabalpur, who was brought to the village of Bisrampur as a catechist of the German Evangelical Mission Society in April 1872.[17] Gangaram Chaube was to be followed by other catechists and pastors who were trained at different missions in north India and then recruited to work in Chhattisgarh. Together, such were some of the preconditions for the work of witness and the labor of the life-history of the Indian evangelical workers that are unraveled in the account below.

AN EXEMPLARY CONVERT: A MISSIONARY'S WITNESS

I begin with two biographical accounts of the Reverend Ramnath Simon Bajpai, one written by his son David Bajpai and the other drafted by the missionary Theodore C. Seybold.[18] Here is how the missionary's narrative opens:

> One of the earliest entries in the baptismal registry in the archives of the Evangelical and Reformed Mission in Raipur, C. P., India, reads as follows: "Ramanth Simon Bajpai, about 22 years old, baptized May 6 1882, by Andrew Stoll. … Ramnath the Brahmin became, as a follower of Jesus Christ, a member of the Church and served to win many, mostly Untouchables, with whom formerly he could never have so much as associated; now those from among them who became Christians became with him fellow-members of the body of Christ."[19]

This description—and the account that follows it—casts the very distinctiveness of the life of Ramnath Bajpai as inextricably intertwined with the history of the evangelical mission in Chhattisgarh, the one luminously reflecting the other. Inserted into the living organism that is the Church the exemplary figure of this Brahman convert to the Christian faith marks a break with the dead past of India, which has separated the upper-caste from the untouchable, pointing to the horizon where the unity of India's peoples lies. The authoritative terms of the missionary's narrative are next carried forward through an invocation of the trials and tribulations faced by the young Ramnath Bajpai. The chief hurdles in the path of Ramnath are imposed by the burden of caste, denying him paternal bonds and fraternal ties, quotidian kinship and Christian affinity. Kith and sons forsake him. Attempts are made to separate from his only friend, the lone missionary, and his spiritual father, the one Master. Ramnath's story is envisioned in the mirror of the Apostles. Indeed, Ramnath "himself confessed that the pressure was so great that at one time he almost yielded; and he would then humbly say: 'How very appropriate that the name of Simon was given to me, for like Simon Peter I was tempted to deny my Lord. But God saved me from this great sin.'" Like Simon Peter, Ramnath Bajpai stands at the head of his flock.

If this story line is framed by the living presence of the Church, the dead hand of caste, and the struggles endured by the Apostles, the narrative as a whole is articulated by the critical trope of conversion. Yet, such transformation of faith comes with its own twist. Theodore Seybold does not equate the conversion of Ramnath with his institutional acceptance of the Christian faith, the event of his baptism. Rather, the missionary locates it long, long before, in the phenomenal transformation that came upon Ramnath, when he miraculously met the pioneer missionary in the Chhattisgarh region: "At the time of his conversion Ramnath was a student in a normal school in Raipur as he wanted to become a teacher. While there he and other students came to hear of a missionary who had come into the area and who seemed to be fulfilling the prophecy of an old Indian leader who predicted that a white teacher would come to them and lead them into an understanding of the truth. So he went to visit this missionary, the Rev. Oskar Lohr, and was very much impressed by what he heard and by what he read in the tracts and booklets given him by his new friend." Note that the missionary unequivocally situates Ramnath's conversion at the time when he was a student in school. The conversion came about when he met the missionary Oscar Lohr, "who seemed to be fulfilling the prophecy of an old Indian leader who predicted that a white teacher would come to them and lead them into an understanding of the truth."

Theodore Seybold's simple statement carries immense import. A tale current in the late nineteenth and early twentieth centuries in Chhattisgarh told of how Ghasidas, the first guru of the Satnami caste-sect, had prophesied that he would be followed by a *topi-wallah sahab* (hat wearing white man) who would deliver the Satnamis. The story became salient lore for the Euro-American missionaries and Indian Christians in the region, and an article of faith for the Satnami converts to Christianity. Elsewhere, I have shown how this tradition was shaped through the pooled resources of Satnami myths, missionary stories, and converts' tales. The tradition was then authoritatively inscribed in official histories of the mission and the Church in Chhattisgarh.[20] My point here is that if the missionary Seybold seized upon this myth to imbue it with a distinct resonance, it was precisely because the story carried critical connotations for his narrative of an exemplary convert, his account of the formative conversion of Ramnath Bajpai.

In the lore of Christian communities and evangelical missionaries in Chhattisgarh, the extraordinary prophecy of Guru Ghasidas and its miraculous fulfillment by Oscar Lohr constituted the motive force behind the first conversions in the region. Such was the strength of this lore that the missionary Theodore Seybold could not escape its implications while writing in the mid twentieth century of an early and exemplary convert to Christianity. To plot the life of a pioneer upper-caste convert, a connection had to be made between ancient prophecy, Oscar Lohr, and Ramnath Bajpai. It followed that in the missionary's account the story regarding the prophecy was robbed of its specificity, simultaneously widening and narrowing its range of address. The palpable figure of Ghasidas was rendered simply as "an old Indian leader." The prophecy itself did not concern just the Satnami community, but all the people of Chhattisgarh. At the same time, the divination really came true with the consummate convert, Ramnath Bajpai.

I have indicated earlier that singular understandings of conversion tend to overlook the textures and temporalities of myths, histories, and narratives that are constitutive of evangelical entanglements. In the testimony of Theodore Seybold, the conversion of Ramnath was exclusive in nature, based on the image of the solitary Saul who saw the light, intimating a novel trajectory of faith and life. At the same time, in this account the very terms of an immaculate conversion were acutely forged through the force of rumor and the strength of prophecy. This is to say that distinctive entailments of myth, history, and narrative—themselves turning on processes of vernacular translation—broke upon the missionary's description of Ramnath's life-history. Thus, a most singular rendering of conversion was yet enacted through the wide-ranging formations of meanings embedded in processes of evangelical entanglements.

AN EXEMPLARY CHARACTER: A SON'S TESTIMONY

This brings me to Ramanth's life-history that was written by his son, David Bajpai.[21] The account follows a different direction from the missionary's narrative. Thus, very early in the account David Bajpai writes:

> Before making the decision [to convert] he [Ramnath] met another Brahmin, Pandit Gangaram Chaube, who showed him a large scar on his head. Several years previously when he [Gangaram] decided to become a follower of Christ his father became so furiously angry that he struck him on the head with an iron rod causing a deep wound. His wife and child were taken away from him; and as persecution continued he sought refuge (1873) in Bisrampur with Rev. O. Lohr, the first pioneer missionary in Chhattisgarh. Missionaries and other friends who knew my father very well verify the fact that he [too] was brave and fearless.

It only follows that David Bajpai's account based on a rather particular blueprint, one involving the biography of an exemplary character, itself inflected by the lore of the learned Brahman. Here, Ramnath's preparation for his eventual religious transformation is not governed by a rupture with caste, a break with Hinduism, an encounter with a missionary, or a spiritual experience in the image of Christian conversion. Instead, a distinct narrative propels Ramnath toward his encounter with Christianity. This story is based upon Ramnath's already distinguished ancestry, at once Brahmanical and martial, as also his own intellectual prowess as a student:

> He [Ramnath] was especially proficient in Hindi and Sanskrit. Among the religious books of the Hindus he had particular preference for the Ramayan, and could repeat long portions of it from memory. Hindus invited him to their homes in order to have him read the shastra to the group assembled there. Prominent and wealthy Hindus would grant him gifts of money and cloth for serving them in that way. His way of reading the Ramayan was so pleasing that Zamindars [landlords] and Rajas [petty Chieftains] in and around Raipur would also invite him.

This portrayal is rooted in the widespread lore of the learned Brahman conquering all with his liturgical abilities and scholarly propensities, so that he finds high office in a royal court. The tale that follows is founded on Ramnath's own spiritual experience as envisioned in the mirror of Hindu *darshan* (vision/envisioning of divinity). Indeed, it is only after he is thus primed and presented that Ramnath Bajpai can sally forth to consummate his manifest, Christian destiny.

Not surprisingly, David Bajpai's later description of his father's "change of faith" is less the litany of a miraculous spiritual transformation and more the mapping of an everyday religious turn. On the one hand, Ramnath is portrayed as the ideal convert who judiciously compares competing faiths to discover the truth for himself. If the encounter with the Gospel reveals the limits of Ramnath's earlier religious certainties, he nonetheless reads it with a "critical, yet open mind." On the other hand, Ramnath's breach with Hinduism is founded upon the Bible, quite literally. In a context where the missionaries at once cast native converts as "equals in the Kingdom of God" and yet treated them as children struggling to grasp rational thought, a surplus of belief in the Bible was often an article of faith for Indian Christians. Taken together, Ramnath's commitment to the Gospel builds upon his prior propensities and draws in his present faculties, compelling him to reason while capturing his emotions, winning his heart as well as his head.

Ramnath is not just a mimic man or an acute double, simply envisioned in the evangelical mirror, in the likeness of the missionary. In David Bajpai's account, Ramnath's sincere character and self-commitment to the Bible put him on par with the missionaries, while distinguishing his persona from their personalities. It follows that in contrast to the missionary Seybold's more linear account of Ramanth's change of faith, David Bajpai's narrative of his father's conversion traverses a jagged trajectory. In the missionary's tale, a single string binds Ramnath's conversion with his baptism—his formative change of spiritual orientation with his formal entry into the Christian church—where each step is marked by a breach with the past. The son's story exceeds the life of the convert as a reflection of the history of the mission.

For one part, as we have noted, Ramnath's upright character and his self-commitment to the Word—on par with the missionary, yet innately different—seemingly surmount all obstacles in his path to conversion and lead Ramnath inexorably toward his entry into the community of Christ through baptism. But there is also more to the picture. In David Bajpai's description of his father's life, Ramanth's "former Hindu friends" sought to dissuade him from visiting the missionary Andrew Stoll, and when arguments failed they pelted him with stones. Instead of getting angry and retaliating against those who harassed him in public spaces by reporting their actions to the police, Ramnath bore all insults patiently, using such "occasions as opportunities" to inform his assailants of the truth of Christianity. Only after the final assault launched by his Brahman kith and his immediate kin, did Ramnath realize that "such unjust treatment would make it impossible for him to remain at home among his family and relatives." It dawned on him that "like other converts before him, he would not long be tolerated among his own people, would be disinherited and put out of caste." He asked himself: "Where shall I go? Where shall I eat?" Now Ramnath "felt compelled to seek a place of refuge among the Christians." His fears were assuaged by the assurance of Andrew Stoll that so long as the missionary had something to eat, so would Ramnath. On 6 May 1882, Ramnath was "received into the Christian Church by baptism and given the name Simon." This example shows that that binds of caste and kin constitute more than hurdles that must be deftly overcome by the enquirer-into-convert; rather, they also bear a distinct gravity, a discrete force. It is Ramnath's realization of the rupture with these ties and the fear this engenders that lead him to seek refuge among Christians, and to convert through baptism—as a last step, a final resort.

Taken together, these conjoint movements in David Bajpai's biographical account of his father's conversion were governed by and acutely expressed the stipulations of vernacular translation. Indeed, his writing did not merely supply details to a prior blueprint provided by the missionary. Rather, it populated the narrative of his father's life with a different resonance, underscoring how two stories of one life reveal the divergent conjunctions between conversion and life-history, mediated by translation.

DRAMA AND DISCONTENT:
A TALE OF AN *ADIVASI* CHRISTIAN

Despite their differences, both the narratives that I have discussed were founded on the mutual premise that the life they were recounting embodied distinction. Such distinction barely required noting, but acutely demanded description. At the same time, few autobiographical accounts embedded in the evangelical encounter could similarly take for granted the distinctiveness of their own lives. Here the uncommon and the unremarkable had to be conjured and construed; the distinctive and the routine had to be reckoned with and sorted out. Such is the case with the writings of native evangelical workers, elicited by missionaries in the 1920s and 1930s, possibly for publication, and the life stories of Indian Christians, which I collected in the late 1990s, for the purpose of research. Mired in the common and the quotidian, in various ways these narratives dramatized the ordinary as the remarkable, and pursued the uncommon in the everyday. In the case of all these narratives, it would be much too facile to present the lives they narrated as all-of-a-piece. Mindful of a warning issued by Arthur O. Lovejoy more than fifty years ago, this would be to ignore the "inner tensions— the fluctuations and hesitancies between opposing ideas or moods" that run through such accounts.[22] The attempt of these narratives was to revealingly dramatize the very commonness of the lives of their protagonists. Such dramatizations provided the accounts with an end, but they could not resolve the "fluctuations and hesitancies" at the heart of the story and the finish of the tale. Indeed, the dramatizations were themselves constituted by the tensions of the accounts. In different ways, such narratives juxtaposed contrary ideas and images, contending thoughts and tendencies. They revealed their protagonists as being wrong and right, quarrelsome and correct, discontented and honest. Here, an acute contrariness can run through several of these accounts, and opposing tendencies can underwrite many of these tales. Such "inner tensions" escape and exceed authoritative apprehensions of conversion that project an exclusive and harmonious life of the convert.

As an illustration of what I have been arguing let me turn to the "Life Story of Johann Purti," which was first drafted by J. Purti and then typed by a missionary in April 1934.[23] Here is how the "Life Story of Johann Purti" begins:

> Sandu Purti was a Munda farmer in Kotna village 7 miles East of Khanti Sub-Division and Police Station in Ranchi Station. After Sepoy Mutiny in 1857 he became a Christian and was named Samuel Purti in baptism when he was a young man. He had three children[,] Kushalmay, Yakub and Boaz. I am the youngest son of his oldest son Kushalmay Purti. My grand father possessed some farms in Ulihatu too, 12 miles East from Kotna. I was born [on] 4th April 1890 in Ulihatu and was brought up in the same village. (1)

At the beginning, through an emphasis upon geographical detail and historical chronology, Johann Purti establishes his ancestry and the fact that he was born a Christian. Here there is no rhapsodic or tortured tale of religious transformation. A simple sentence suffices: "After Sepoy Mutiny in 1857 he [Purti's grandfather] became a Christian and was named Samuel Purti in baptism."[24] Next, the account quickly covers Johann's initial lack of interest in attending school, his appreciation of learning upon moving to a boarding school, and his return home in the middle of the last year of high school after discovering that his father was borrowing money for his education.

None of this is remarkable, hardly preparing us for the change of note that suddenly follows:

> After leaving school my father asked me to join the Theological Seminary but I refused, telling him that one who wanted to be a padre should join because I looked down on the padres. Then my father asked me to learn

the work of petition writer in the court but I said to him that one who would tell a lie and would rob the poor, should go to the court. Then my father asked me to get a position in the railway or in the Forest Department. I answered him that one who wanted to be a vagabond should join these two lines. Then my father asked me what I wanted to do. I told him I would be a farmer. Outwardly he assented but inwardly he wanted that I should change my mind. So he began giving me very hard works. I was working with servants as servants. I was working so hard that it changed my mind. I went to a relative who was a doctor with the intention to learn the work of a compounder [a doctor's assistant who mixed medicines—or compounds—until a few decades ago] but I was not satisfied and wanted to go to a great hospital for which I asked a recommendation from the Principal of my school. (1–2)

This unusual passage introduces us to the critical devices shaping Johann Purti's autobiographical account, which together constitute a curious amalgam. First, the narrative is entirely cast as that of a life seeking an occupation, an existence stalking a vocation. Second, recalcitrance toward paternal authority, refusal of paternalist power, runs through the text. Third, a perpetual note of dissatisfaction afflicts the protagonist of this story, which is also the basis of his recalcitrance. Fourth, the sources of this discontent often lie in the nature of the occupation ahead of Johann Purti, and in the hardships such work entails, which teach him a lesson. Yet, the roots of this discontent equally constitute an existential condition. Fifth, abrupt changes of mind as much as God's guidance lead our protagonist in his choices of career. Sixth and finally, such tropes—concerning the salience of occupation, the place of recalcitrance, and the presence of dissatisfaction—pattern the entire narrative, driving it toward its resolution. Here the critical forms are the vocation of a padre and the work of a compounder. Yet, like the narrative itself, the resolution too is unstable.

Having pre-empted the nature of the narrative ahead, let us cycle back to the nitty-gritty of Johann Purti's life story. After receiving Johann's letter, the Principal sends him a letter of recommendation, also inviting him back to the school, offering to pay for the former pupil's education "if desired again." When Johann goes and meets the Principal, the benevolent, paternalist figure provides the assurance that he would personally write to the Civil Surgeon of the "great hospital" in Ranchi about a compounder's position, and in the meanwhile gives Johann "a light work of clerk in his office." Presumably Johann Purti had refused the Principal's offer of returning to school, but now another opportunity presents itself, of resuming education to enter God's work: "One day he [the Principal] asked me placing his hand on my shoulder 'Will you dear chap, learn Theology?'" Johann's recalcitrant response is characteristic: "I threw his hand away say 'no.' From that day he never asked me like again." Soon after Johann refuses his Christian calling, a letter comes from the Civil Surgeon stating that there is no vacancy for a compounder in the hospital. But such is Johann's investment in the idea of becoming a compounder that he even considers training for the position at the Leper Asylum in the town of Purulia, a place of hardship, a far cry from the "great hospital"—a consideration that he does not put through into practice (2).

Instead, not much later, Johann returns to the Principal, once more with the thought of asking him again to write a recommendation letter to the Civil Surgeon of the Government Hospital. But on his way a change comes upon Johann's mind quite by itself, explained only by the direction it points to: "I told him that I would read in the Seminary." The astonished Principal asks him to return in a few hours, when he reminds Johann that he would have to "learn 4 years in the Seminary." But Johann is equal to the challenge: "I replied I would learn for 7 years. From that day I began studying in the Seminary." At the same time, Johann's education toward the service of God does not lead to his own happiness. When he finishes at the seminary, it is 1915, World War I has begun, the German missionaries have been sent away from India, and there is no work for the seminary-trained Johann in his own church. Only after reading an advertisement in his church newspaper, more than a year later, at the end of 1916, does Johann find employment as a catechist in Bisrampur.

Johann remains at the pioneer mission station in Chhattisgarh for four years, but we can only wonder if he is actually satisfied with his life there. For as soon as he comes across an advertisement for the position of a compounder in the service of the National Missionary Society in the princely state of Rewa, something happens: "My mind again revolted and I went way and joined the N. M. S. [National Missionary Society]." Yet, joy and contentment are not to be had by him even now: He writes that he was "sorry I was not made a compounder but was made a private tutor and pedagogue of the Prince of Sohagpur. In their company I spent five year[s]. I suffered a great loss there. Within the course of 3 years there I lost my 3 dear children" (2–3).

Soon the National Missionary Society is forbidden to conduct "public Christian work" in the region by the ruler of Rewa. Johann is once more "placed in a dilemma": "The N.M.S. called me for work in Jharsaguda and Dr. J. Gass [of the American Evangelical Mission Society] called me for work in the Kalahandi State." What is Johann's way out of his predicament? "I submitted myself to God for guidance and he sent me back to Raipur." While in Raipur, the missionary J. Gass informs him that the congregation at Bisrampur want him as their pastor. Not unlike his answers to his father and the school Principal when they ask him to learn theology, Johann tells Gass that he is "not willing" to take up the position. The missionary suggests that Johann "pray and think over it then to reply." Now, a mellow Johann comes home and decides that he would do "what God wished" (3–4).

The moment of revelation, the most dramatic event in his discontented life, is upon Johann Purti:

> I opened the Bible and 2 Tim. 2 came out to my eyes and I began reading. I thought the book opened by itself, it is not of any great consequence. I closed it. Second time I decided that this time whatever may come out I must abide. This time 1 Tim. 4:12 came out. I sat silent and said 'O God, Thou art victorious." Next day I told Dr. J. Gass that I would go to Bisrampur. I was licensed as a pastor in 1927 and ordained Feb. 23, 1930. I am now a compounder of the greatest physician Jesus. (4)

How are we to read this resolution, which of course bears upon the entire, prior narrative? The fact that Johann Purti's story follows a pattern of constant struggle leading to an eventual realization in the Truth of Christ suggests that it perhaps reflects the life of a saint, or that it possibly follows the tale of an exemplary Christian figure. However, after talking with scholars of Christianity, delving into the hagiographies of the Early Christians and the Church Fathers, I have yet to make the connection. Something else is at work here.

Recall that when he first opens the Bible, trying to decide whether he should become a pastor, Johann's eyes alight upon 2 Timothy 2:2–6. This is what he would have read:

> You then, my son, be strong in the Grace that is Jesus Christ. And the things you have heard me say in the presence of many witnesses entrust to reliable men who will be also qualified to teach others. Endure hardships with us like a good soldier of Christ Jesus. No one serving as a soldier gets involved in civilian affairs—he wants to please his commanding officer. Similarly, if anyone competes as an athlete, he does not receive the victor's crown unless he competes according to the rules. The hardworking farmer should be the first to receive a share of the crops.

Now, the messages to be "strong" and to bear the truth to "reliable men" carry immense import for Johann's vocation ahead as a pastor. At the same time, the advice to "endure hardships" and to be "hardworking," the admonition against getting "involved in civilian affairs," and the injunction to play according to the rules seems to speak poignantly not only to Johann's possible future but also to his discontented past: from Johann's recalcitrant nature to his quest to become a compounder, which lead to constant dissatisfaction, abrupt moves, and several hardships in the story of his life.

Yet, this is not all. For a little later, under the description of "A Work man Approved by God," immediately after learning of the need to cleanse oneself of ignoble purposes in life, Johann would have read:

> Flee the evil desires of youth, and pursue righteousness, faith, love and peace, along with those who call on the Lord out of a pure heart. Don't have anything to do with foolish and stupid arguments, because you know they produce quarrels. And the Lord's servant must not quarrel; instead, he must be kind to everyone, able to teach, not resentful. (2 Tim. 2:22–25)

It is hardly surprising that both the poignancy and prescience of these words startled Johann. And so he opened the book again, where 1 Timothy 4:12 told him:

> Don't let anyone look down on you because of you are young, but set an example for the believers in speech, in life, in faith and in purity.

Taken together, these passages possibly directed Johann to confront his past of "foolish and stupid arguments" (and of the consequent "quarrels" both inner and outer), to come to terms with his "young" life of 37 years, and to go forth into pastoral labor. And so, the resolution of the testimony of Johann Purti struggled and reckoned with his history, intimating and endorsing his future. Indeed, Johann's past and future stood conjoined in the declaration that he was "now a compounder of the greatest physician Jesus": Now his own worldly desire stood spiritually realized quite as the prior wishes of his father, the school principal, and the missionary J. Gass—that their ward serve the Lord—appeared finally fulfilled.

Yet, as indicated earlier, it will be much too facile to present Johann Purti's narrative as all of a piece. For this will be to ignore exactly the "inner tensions—the fluctuations and hesitancies between opposing ideas or moods," underscored by Lovejoy, that run through Johann's account. Of course, such attributes are no monopoly of Johann's tale, finding discrete expression in other Christian life-histories. At the same time, the "inner tensions" do appear strikingly in Purti's story. This should not surprise us. After all, Johann's attempt was to revealingly dramatize the very commonness of his life. Such dramatization provided the narrative with an end, but it could not resolve the "fluctuations and hesitancies" at the heart of the story and the finish of the tale. Indeed, the dramatization was itself propelled and contained by the constitutive tensions of the account.[25]

And what of the end of Johann's story? It is not only that the transformation that follows Johann's encounter with passages of the Book loses some of its motive force because obedience to God's command

had also characterized his life earlier. It is also that the resolution itself—
Johann's becoming a compounder of the greatest physician Jesus—is
not simply joyous, but equally accompanied by a note of discontent.
For at the very moment Johann makes this declaration, he also recalls
that he was "willing to be persecuted in Kalahandi which means black
earthen pot." Similarly, now in Bisrampur there are "difficulties and
persecutions not only from non-Christians but even more from Christians who are not loyal and do want to listen to the admonitions of God's
Word" (4). It bears mention that these difficulties are tied to the struggle
launched in the early 1930s by the Bisrampur congregation against the
missionaries and their pastor, Johann Purti. This struggle, conducted
in an evangelical idiom, had its beginnings in a case of adultery between Rebecca, a "virgin Christian girl of Bisrampur," and Boas Purti,
Johann's uncle and the *lambardar* (official-in-charge of landed property)
of the mission-owned village of Bisrampur. Equally, such persecution is
betokened by the pointlessness of arguments and quarrels described by
the fragments of the Bible that Johann encountered. Yet, my point is that
the appearance of "difficulties and persecutions" at the very moment of
the resolution of Johann's tales are bound as well to the contrary moods
and textures that characterize his entire narrative.[26]

To be sure, the pointed nature of Johann's story of a life in search of
a vocation are very much those of a Christian in colonial India. Born
into an adivasi family that had converted to Christianity in the mid
nineteenth century, Johann's acquisition of education led him to negotiate the choices of occupation that were open to an Indian Christian in
the early twentieth century. At the same time, this should not obscure
two inter-related points. On the one hand, the decisive commonness of
Johann's autobiography, including his attempts to dramatize his life-
story that only underscore its pathos, militate against the melodrama
implied by authoritative versions of conversion. On the other hand, the
acute contrariness that runs through Johann's narrative, the opposing
tendencies that underwrite the tale, these inner tensions escape and
exceed the exclusive life of the convert insinuated by dominant conceptions of conversion. Once more, these varied attributes and distinct
movements that characterize Johann Purti's account are each illustra-
tive of and intimately embody procedures of vernacular translation.

CODA

In discussing the autobiographies, biographies, and other writings of Indian evangelical workers, this essay has sought to show the limitations

of authoritative apprehensions and commonplace conceptions of conversion, which imbue lives and histories of subjects of religious change with relentless singularity. At the same time, I have not proceeded by sharply separating the vernacular attributes of an Indian Christianity from its colonial connections, barely discussing, for example, the continuities between prior faiths and an indigenous Christianity. Such connections and differences are ever salient, but they never constitute pristine, pure verities. Indeed, to imagine and institute an unsullied, heroic, minority faith is to share ground with propositions regarding radical rupture as constitutive of conversion, already given, always there. Mere oppositions assiduously reverse yet acutely reflect the objects of their critique. As an alternative, in this essay I have focused on the details and the dynamics of accounts of a Euro-American evangelist and Indian Christians, their drama and their divergence, their exact surplus of faith and their own renderings of conversion. My analytical wager concerns ways of reading that explore the distinction and difference of these narratives, at once vernacular and colonial, simultaneously contrary and common. It is in this spirit, too, that I have spoken of such accounts as shaped in crucibles of vernacular translation.

The point is not one of substituting the category of conversion with that of translation, vernacular or otherwise. For assiduously turning our backs to suspect categories—that are heuristically aggrandizing and which might even appear as analytical nightmares—does not lead to their inevitable excision or inexorable exorcism. All too often, such categories—from "culture" and "tradition" to "conversion" and "modernity"—are at once concepts and entities, indeed concepts-entities. They powerfully inform and poignantly inhabit the worlds not only of scholar-analysts but of everyday subjects, from converts to their enemies. Here, the challenge is to revisit and rethink the terms and textures of conversion—and those of syncretism—through other critical filters, in this case hinging on procedures of vernacular translation.

As a *word*, conversion—to become (or be born as) the member of a new faith—carried exclusive connotations mainly in the writing of the missionary Theodore Seybold. Yet, even this most singular rendering of the conversion of the Brahman Ramnath came with its own twist, split and shaped by the force of the wide-ranging making of myth and narrative, history and legend at the core of evangelical entanglements, entailing attributes of vernacular translation. As an *event*, conversion was described in inherently different ways, shored by procedures of vernacular translation, in the narratives explored in this essay. As a *resource,* conversion allowed life stories of Indian Christian to be plotted in distinct manners, quite as these accounts usually remained rooted in the common and the quotidian, the twin processes shored up by vernacular translation. On the one had, the precise diversity, difference, and distinction at the heart of these tales exceed the singularity of lives entailed by dominant designs of conversion. On the other hand, the very commonness of these life stories, including efforts to dramatize their constitutive terms, militates against the melodrama implied by inherited imaginings of conversion. Together, throughout this essay, my interpretive wager has turned on the submission that the notion of vernacular translation allows us to capture such difference and diversity— and commonness and contrariety—at the core of everyday attributes of conversion and converts, as cultural categories and historical subjects.

Notes

This essay forms part of a larger project on evangelical entanglements, straddling central Indian histories and Midwestern American pasts, in the nineteenth and twentieth centuries. The project is embodied in several past and forthcoming publications—some of which I draw upon in this chapter—as indicated in the notes below. At the same time, the writing of this essay was made possible by a fellowship from the John Simon Guggenheim Memorial Foundation, New York, for my research on "Christianity, Colonialism, Conversion, 1860-2005." I am grateful to the Foundation for the award, the Department of Anthropology at Johns Hopkins University for a visiting professorship, and to the editors of this volume for their comments.

1. For central India, I have discussed such questions in Saurabh Dube, *Stitches on Time: Colonial Textures and Postcolonial Tangles* (Durham, NC, 2004). Concerning other studies see, for example, Webb Keane, *Christian Moderns: Freedom and Fetish in the Mission Encounter* (Berkeley, 2007); Ussama Makdisi, "Reclaiming the Land of the Bible: Missionaries, Secularism, and Evangelical Modernity," *American Historical Review* 102 (1997): 680–713; Ussama Makdisi, *Artillery of Heaven: American Missionaries and the Failed Conversion of the Middle East* (Ithaca, 2008); Nicholas Thomas, "Colonial Conversions: Difference, Hierarchy and History in Early Twentieth Century Evangelical Propaganda," *Comparative Studies in Society and History* 34 (1992): 366–89; Walter Mignolo, "On the Colonization of Amerindian Languages and Memories: Renaissance Theories of Writing and the Discontinuity of the Classical Tradition," *Comparative Studies in Society and History* 34 (1992): 301–30; Jean Comaroff and John Comaroff, *Of Revelation and Revolution*, 2 vols. (Chicago, 1991, 1997); Jean Comaroff and John Comaroff, "Christianity and Colonialism in South Africa," *American Ethnologist* 13 (1986): 1–22; John Comaroff, "Images of Empire, Contests of Conscience: Models of Colonial Domination in South Africa," *American Ethnologist* 16 (1989): 661–85; and David Scott, "Conversion and Demonism: Colonial Christian Discourse on Religion in Sri Lanka," *Comparative Studies in Society and History* 34 (1992): 331–65. See also J.D.Y. Peel, "'For Who Hath Despised the Day of Small

Things?': Missionary Narratives and Historical Anthropology," *Comparative Studies in Society and History* 37 (1995): 581–607; Ann Stoler, "Rethinking Colonial Categories: European Communities and the Boundaries of Rule," *Comparative Studies in Society and History* 31 (1989): 134–61; Frederick Cooper and Ann Stoler, eds., *Tensions of Empire: Bourgeois Cultures in a Colonial World* (Berkeley, 1997); and Vicente Rafael, *Contracting Colonialism: Translation and Christian Conversion in Tagalog Society under Early Spanish Rule* (Ithaca, NY, 1988).

2. I discuss the contours of a vernacular Christianity in central India in Saurabh Dube, *Untouchable Pasts: Religion, Identity, and Authority among a Central Indian Community, 1780-1950* (Albany, NY, 1998). Concerning other sites see, for example, Keane, *Christian Moderns*; Joel Robbins, *Becoming Sinners: Christianity and Moral Torment in a Papua New Guinea Society* (Berkeley, 2004); Matthew Engelke, *A Problem of Presence: Beyond Scripture in an African Church* (Berkeley, 2007); Fenella Cannell, ed., *The Anthropology of Christianity* (Durham, NC, 2006); Birgit Meyer, *Translating the Devil: Religion and Modernity among the Ewe in Ghana* (Trenton, NJ, 1999); Pier M. Larson, "'Capacities and Modes of Thinking': Intellectual Engagements and Subaltern Hegemony in the Early History of Malgasy Christianity," *American Historical Review* 102 (1997): 968–1002; Paul Stuart Landau, *The Realm of the Word: Language, Gender, and Christianity in a Southern African Kingdom* [(Portsmouth, NH, 1995); Geoffrey White, *Identity through History: Living Stories in a Solomon Islands Society* (Cambridge, 1991); Dube, *Stitches on Time*; Robert Hefner, ed., *Conversion to Christianity: Historical and Anthropological Perspectives on a Great Transformation* (Berkeley, 1993); and Comaroff and Comaroff, *Revelation and Revolution*, vol. 2. See also, Peel, "Day of Small Things"; Rafael, *Contracting Colonialism*; Derek Peterson, "Translating the Word: Dialogism and Debate in Two Gikuyu Dictionaries," *The Journal of Religious History* 23 (1999): 31–50; Diane Austin-Broos, *Jamaica Genesis: Religion and the Politics of Moral Orders* (Chicago, 1997); David Smilde, *Reason to Believe: Cultural Agency in Latin American Evangelism* (Berkeley, 2007); Susan F. Harding, *The Book of Jeremy Falwell: Fundamentalist Language and Politics* (Princeton, 2000); and Rebecca J. Lester, *Jesus in Our Wombs: Embodying Modernity in a Mexican Convent* (Berkeley, 2005).

3. The arguments of this section draw upon Saurabh Dube, *Native Witness: Colonial Writings of a Vernacular Christianity*, manuscript of book in progress, n.d.

4. For a wider elaboration of the issues discussed in this section see Saurabh Dube, "Conversion to Translation: Colonial Writings of a Vernacular Christianity," in *Enchantments of Modernity: Empire, Nation, Globalization*, ed. Saurabh Dube (New Delhi, 2009), 133–67.

5. George Steiner, *After Babel: Aspects of Language and Translation* (London, 1975), 250.

6. See especially Willis Barnstone, *The Poetics of Translation: History, Theory, Practice* (New Haven, CT,1993).

7. Talal Asad, *Genealogies of Religion: Disciplines and Reasons of Power in Christianity and Islam* (Baltimore, 1993), 171–99.

8. Dipesh Chakrabarty, *Provincializing Europe: Historical Thought and Postcolonial Difference* (Princeton, 2000), 17–18. See also Naoki Sakai, *Translation and Subjectivity* (Minneapolis, MN, 1997).

9. See, for example, Rafael, *Contracting Colonialism;* Larson, "'Capacities and Modes of Thinking'"; and Peterson, "Translating the Word." See also Johannes Fabian, *Language and Colonial Power: The Appropriation of Swahili in the Former Belgian Congo, 1880–1938* (Cambridge, 1986); and Walter Mignolo, *The Darker Side of the Renaissance: Literacy, Territoriality, and Colonization* (Ann Arbor, MI, 1995).

10. Rafael, *Contracting Colonialism,* 21.

11. Ibid., xi, 21, and passim.

12. Ibid., 20–21.

13. I elaborate these considerations of vernacular translation by reading the catechist's chronicles alongside the Bible and different missionary writings in English and Hindi in Dube, *Native Witness.*

14. See, for instance, Dube, *Untouchable Pasts;* Dube, "Conversion to Translation"; Dube, *Stitches on Time;* and Saurabh Dube, "Traveling Light: Missionary Musings, Colonial Cultures, and Anthropological Anxieties," in *Travel Worlds: Journeys in Contemporary Cultural Politics,* ed. Raminder Kaur and John Hutnyk (London, 1999), 29–50.

15. M. M. Paul, *Chhatisgarh Evangelical Kalasiya ka Sankshipt Itihas* (Allahabad, 1936), 8–9; Theodore Seybold, *God's Guiding Hand: History of the Central Indian Mission, 1868–1967* (Philadelphia, 1971), 28–29.

16. Paul, *Chhatisgarh Evangelical Kalasiya,* 9.

17. The missionary Andrew Stoll was later to write of him: "Still very active at 60 years of age, he preaches in the villages and in the city day after day. Once a proud young Brahmin, the Spirit of Christ has transformed him into a friend and a brother of the lowliest of the low. His example has often strengthened my faith" (cited in Seybold, *God's Guiding Hand,* 29).

18. Theodore Seybold served as a missionary in Chhattisgarh between 1913 and 1958. For nine years he frequently met Ramnath Bajpai. Seybold lived for a long time in the home of the Missionary Jacob Gass; Ramnath was the head catechist working under Gass and was often present in the missionary's home. Few biographical details are forthcoming about David Bajpai. For a wider discussion of the life-histories explored in this essay, see Saurabh Dube, "Witnessing lives: Conversion and Life-history in Colonial Central India," in *Ancient to Modern: Religion, Power, and Community in India,* ed. Ishita Banerjee-Dube and Saurabh Dube (New Delhi, 2008), 259–90.

19. Theodore Seybold, "The Reverend Ramnath Simon Bajpai," typescript, n.d., 84-9b Bio 52, Eden Archives & Library, Webster Groves, MD (hereafter EAL), 1. Except when indicated, all the quotations from this text are from the first page.

20. Dube, *Untouchable Pasts.*

21. David Bajpai, "My Father—Rev. Simon Ramnath Bajpai," typescript, 1945, 84-9b Bio 52, EAL.

22. Arthur O. Lovejoy, cited in Stephen Kern, *The Culture of Time and Space 1880-1918* (Cambridge MA, 1983), 10. Of course, Lovejoy was speaking of the reading of texts—an emphasis that I feel bears extension to the narratives of lives.

23. Johann Purti, "Life Story of Johann Purti," typescript, 1934, 84-9b Bio 52, EAL. The citations of page numbers of this account appear within parenthesis in the text that follows.

24. Indeed, "conversion" does not appear as a dramatic or miraculous event in any of the life-histories written or narrated by Christians in Central India that I consulted for this paper. This is true of various autobiographical accounts of women and men in Chhattisgarh today. It also holds for narratives written in the colonial period. If contrary tendencies characterize David Bajpai's story of his father's conversion and Johann Purti narrates the event of his grandfather's becoming Christian as an undramatic fact, even those accounts in which conversion was accorded centrality told the tale in rather low-key ways. For example, consider the life story of the catechist Loknath Timothy, written in the late 1920s. Loknath's family members were among the earlier converts to Christianity in Chhattisgarh, and the first of his two-page narrative concerns these times. At the beginning he tells us: "In a village 12 miles from Bisrampur, Jangir I was born July 12, 1864. Father's name (after Baptism) Adam, mother's name Eve." After this Loknath describes the networks of kinship that led his entire family, Satnami by caste, to move to Bisrampur, the land they were given to settle there, and their eventual "confirmation" as Christians by the missionary Oscar Lohr. On the one hand, there is no rancor or persecution that greets Loknath's family when they decide to move to Bisrampur. Rather, the proprietor of their ancestral village entreats them not to leave their land, promising them a comfortable life there. On the other hand, in addition to the strength of kinship, the family's turning to Christianity appears as a consequence of the contented community that was to be found in Bisrampur. Taken together, there is nothing theatrical about this narrative of conversion, and its unremarkable representation speaks for itself. Similarly, in the autobiography of M. M. Paul—a native evangelist, later a "national" missionary—the conversion of his father and uncle, "Tiwari Brahmin[s]," is a critical part of the narrative, occupying more than a page of the one and a half page typescript. Yet, the circumstances and the event of conversion are not described as a magnificent melodrama of religious transformation. Instead, they are presented in an entirely matter-of-fact manner as a story of gradual change of faith, from the meeting of the two poor but religious Brahmans with itinerant Christian speakers, to their sustained contact with missionaries, to the bitterness they face from the community, to their escape to a big city and their conversion there, all rendered in a quotidian key. Loknath Timothy, "Autobiography of Old Catechist Loknath (Hindi idioms retained)," typescript, 1928, M. P. Davis Papers, EAL, 1; M. M. Paul, "Autobiography of M. M. Paul, Head Catechist at Mahasamund," typescript, n.d., 84-9b Bio 52, EAL, 1-2.

25. The precise terms of its dramatization and the exact form of its contrariness distinguish Johann's tale from other life-histories within the evangelist encounter. Here the contrast with the writings of Theodore Seybold and David Bajpai is abundantly clear. Equally, other accounts often represented the distinction of a life by seeking out the remarkable in the common, whether it was Loknath Timothy establishing in his life story that he was an earlier convert to Christianity in the region and describing a fight in which the missionary Andrew Stoll and he were both injured; or it was M. M. Paul highlighting the conversion of his Brahman father; or it was older, Mennonite women—met during fieldwork—telling their tales as a succession of life-stages: birth, childhood in a home or an orphanage, courtship under the supervision of the missionary

"mama," marriage overseen by the missionary "papa," employment, and the death of the husband, all punctuated by extraordinary events such as famines and floods. Even when there were attempts to dramatize the narratives, these followed the rehearsals of Mennonite principles or Christian codes being upheld at different moments of lives and stories.

26. For a detailed reading of this conflict, see Saurabh Dube, "Paternalism and Freedom: The Evangelical Encounter in Colonial Chhattisgarh, Central India," *Modern Asian Studies* 29 (1995): 171–201.

2

CONVERSION AT THE BOUNDARIES
OF RELIGION, IDENTITY, AND POLITICS
IN PLURICULTURAL GUATEMALA

C. Mathews Samson

Wading into the waters surrounding discourse in the social sciences
and the humanities in regard to syncretism and conversion is a risky
task. The terms as well as the frameworks surrounding them are mul-
tireferential, and taking seriously the "beyond" in the title of this volume also reveals something of a dual optic at work in the literature
addressing syncretism in the Americas. To some degree the literature
even tracks along geographic lines. Two recent edited volumes provide
the outlines of a debate that is more complicated than can be fully addressed here. Nevertheless, in *Reinventing Religions*, co-editors Sidney
Greenfield and André Droogers survey the cases in Afro-Latin American and Caribbean contexts from Brazil to Trinidad and flatly state that
"syncretism is still a useful term for examining the results of contact
between peoples and cultures," while "[r]evitalization, on the other
hand, no longer seems to be of analytic utility. The meanings attributed
to syncretism, however, … have become the subject of a lively debate
based more on the theoretical orientation of the student than on the
reality being studied."[1]

Alternatively, a shift in focus to Native North America and Oceania
reveals a more congenial engagement with revitalization perspectives
and the movements they seek to describe. Revitalization movements,
as exemplified by the Ghost Dance in the former case and cargo cults in
the latter, typically respond to the shock of cultural intrusion through
imaginative recastings of native identities. In his introduction to *Reassessing Revitalization Movements*, Michael Harkin argues that such

> movements, which may apparently isolate (in the case of nativistic move-
> ments) or connect cultures and groups, are simply one of the most obvi-
> ous and obviously transcultural mechanisms by which groups attempt
> to articulate with the outside world. At the same time, such articulations
> have profound resonance on the individual, who feels threatened and

insecure in a changing world and who may fall back into a contemplation of the nature of history and time, to the temporal aporia.[2]

Although taking a both/and instead of an either/or perspective on this apparent divide, here I situate conversion to historical Protestantism among a segment of the Maya population in Guatemala's western highlands within a transcultural frame shaped by the renewal of ethnic identity in the present. This framing shows the Maya responding in processual fashion not only to the forces of modernization and globalization but also to rhythms of community and local culture as they have claimed social and political space within the nation-state since the beginnings of the Maya Movement in the mid 1980s.[3] In this light, conversion is shown to take place within an even more comprehensive structure, one reflecting the extant cultural and religious pluralism that has been more forthrightly acknowledged since the end of Guatemala's civil conflict in 1996. An ethnographic approach is uniquely situated to ascertain the outlines used for defining conversion in particular cases and to reveal how the formation of self-identity transcends the demands of both dogma and tradition.

CONCEPTUALIZING RELIGIOUS CHANGE IN THE AMERICAS

Context is significant, if not everything, in terms of the contrasts between these two perspectives regarding syncretism and revitalization. Placing them side by side shows a common acknowledgment that in addressing such issues, and (by extension) issues of conversion, we are dealing with socially constructed processes that embody the tension between personal and group agency. Conversion takes place in between forces and processes structured by historical circumstances and local responses to those circumstances. This "in-between" space is where an ethnographic approach to conversion has the potential to reveal some of the tension inherent in elucidating the meaning of conversion — or the meaning embodied in any particular experience of conversion — and in linking conversion to individual and communal experiences with larger social forces.

Despite their summary dismissal of conceptualizations of religious change centered on revitalization, Greenfield and Droogers (and various authors in their work) do propose different theoretical stances for approaching specific cases of syncretism — praxis theories, cognitive anthropology, local/global interfaces, and even economic and entrepreneurial approaches.[4] Such overarching theoretical perspectives resonate as well with other work being done on religion in the Americas, particularly that of Manuel Vásquez and Marie Marquardt, who in their work *Globalizing the Sacred* delineate a series of "analytical tools" to be considered in analyzing religious change: glocalization, deterritorialization and reterritorialization, transnational religious networks, hybridity and nonexclusionary identity, and borders and borderlands.[5] In some ways, the broader concerns in employing these framing devices can be seen specifically in their discussion of hybridity as "a useful conceptual device to understand multiple, fluid, and often contradictory religious identities and practices that have proliferated with globalization. Hybridity points to 'how newness enters the world,' and specifically how cultures become the locus for multiple contestations, for creative resistance and appropriation."[6]

The nexus of contestation, resistance, and appropriation provides a point of orientation for those who seek to cross the boundaries of scholarly disciplines and religious traditions when analyzing the very personal experience of conversion in the lives of individuals and communities. At the same time, Harkin, again addressing revitalization, posits religious change in culture and history in a way that provides grounding for the more fluid approach to conversion and cultural change indexed by terms like hybridity and globalization:

> There are thus two poles to the concept of revitalization. ... [I]t fulfills a human psychic need to cope with the basic temporal aporia common to all people but which becomes foregrounded in times of crisis. ... [I]t is inflected by specific cultural and historical forms. To focus solely on the former is to run the risk of ignoring the ethnohistorical specificity. To focus solely on the latter is to ignore the similarities of such movements across time and place and their rootedness in certain recurring human dilemmas, albeit ones that are particularly prone to be felt during historically parlous times. The preferred interpretive strategy is thus dialogic, as the phenomenology is as well.[7]

At issue in this essay is precisely a concern for such ethnohistorical specificity and dialogue. The ethnographic perspective points toward the *how* of what people are up to when they are being religious rather than initially giving attention to the *why*. Moreover, practice approaches that show the individual engaged at the concrete intersections of local practice with global forces work well with dialogic approaches that emphasize voicing and agency when indigenous peoples reflect on religious change and missionization not only in Mesoamerica but throughout the Americas.

Although it is nearly forty years old, and far from uncontested,[8] one cue for integrating practice with ethnography comes from Clifford

Geertz's seminal essay on ethnography as "thick description." Geertz argues that "the aim of anthropology is the enlargement of the universe of human discourse," and enlargement is accomplished by understanding that "culture is not a power ... it is a context . ...." By engaging that context, the implication is that "[u]nderstanding a people's culture exposes their normalness without reducing their particularity."[9] Beyond such description however, the context itself is often power-laden, and Sherry Ortner's description of her initial attraction to practice theory is helpful in bridging the distance between context and agency—or in this essay the space between the process of conversion and the potential convert. In her words, "the production of the world through human practice ... seemed new and very powerful, providing a dialectical synthesis between 'structure'(or the social world as constituted) and 'agency' (or the interested practices of real people) that had not previously been achieved. Moreover, the idea that the world is 'made—in a very extended and complex sense, of course—through the actions of ordinary people also meant that it could be unmade and remade."[10]

While little attention is given to any kind of crisis precipitating conversion in the cases considered here, there can be no doubt about the "recurring human dilemmas" addressed in the narratives. Issues of the immediate consequences of conversion and the need to see oneself as still connected with ancestors who partook of a radically different cosmology foreground the interpretation. Yet, they do so in ways that open the consideration of the meaning of conversion to broader contexts, practically demanding that attention be given to those who have made different kinds of decisions—given the plurality of options facing indigenous peoples (and all of us) in the present. While primary attention is given here to culture, this approach is consistent with that of historians such as Susan Neylan, who in writing of conversion among the Tsimshian of the North Pacific Coast of Canada opts to study what she calls the "proselytizing-conversion experience." She argues that "'[c]onversion' was rarely absolute. Religious beliefs were interpreted through one's culture context and necessitated a blurring of boundaries between spiritual systems in order to construct meaning."[11]

ETHNOGRAPHIC APPROACHES TO CONVERSION AND THE GUATEMALAN CONTEXT

The boundaries considered in Guatemala exist not only between Protestantism and Catholicism but also between Christianity and persisting expressions of a Maya practice and cosmovision with roots in Mesoamerica stretching back to at least three millennia before the Spanish invasion. But religion, while integral to community life and local expressions of identity, is not seen here as determinative for social processes. So the interface between religion and ethnicity and the way in which each articulates with other arenas of social interaction become central for understanding conversion in Guatemala. Key to this consideration is the recognition that the predominantly rural 22 Mayan language communities in Guatemala currently comprise perhaps 50 percent of the total population of the country of 13,500,000 and continue to lag behind the Mestizo population in indicators of social and economic well-being.[12] Religion, in a context of ethnic tension and socio-economic stress, might best be thought of as a social resource that plays out differentially depending upon how beliefs and practices are situated in daily life. This is not, however, to capitulate to a kind of crisis-solace or deprivation theory of the role of religion in the lives of converts; rather, it situates the ethnographic analysis of conversion within the perspective of "lived religion" that includes meaning, including theology, and the social and political conditions that inform decisions made in the religious facet of a person's life.[13]

An appreciation of the dynamics of conversion in Guatemala begins by taking into account two waves of evangelization in the past five centuries—the first beginning with the Spanish invasion led by Hernan Cortés's lieutenant, Pedro de Alvarado, in 1523, and the second with the formal arrival of a Presbyterian missionary, John Clark Hill, in 1882. Hill arrived at the invitation of Liberal president and "strongman" Justo Rufino Barrios in 1882 after an appeal to the Presbyterian Board of Foreign Missions. It also bears noting that in the face of these evangelization projects there was neither a unified Maya identity nor a single polity in the pre-Colombian territory comprising present day Guatemala. If the various Maya groups in the region have historically shared a common mother language and aspects of a broader cultural tradition that include common foodways and modes of social organization, local religious practice has been very much tied to the landscape and particular ways in which the sacred inheres in both the land and the community.[14]

For this essay, the vantage point of conversion to historical Protestantism becomes a lens for gaining a more nuanced perspective on the meaning of Maya identity, Maya-ness, when it is infused with strains of a religion with only 125 years of history in Guatemala. No doubt the story is one of colonialism and the imposition of a new religion on an indigenous and Catholic landscape as part of a missionization project that Virginia Garrard-Burnett has called "spiritual manifest destiny."[15]

At the same time, it is a story of adaptation and renewal as the Maya have incorporated the new belief systems into their own worldview, and at times even Mayanized the evangelizer's religion in what can be considered a process of "interculturation."[16]

Beyond the historical currents of evangelization, two aspects of social and cultural change also need to be taken into account in an effort to contextualize conversion narratives and conversion careers in contemporary Guatemala.[17] First is the shift in Guatemala's religious landscape over the past five decades. According to a 2006 survey of adults age 18 and older by the Pew Forum for Religion and Public Life, current religious affiliation is reported as 48 percent Catholic, 34 percent Protestant, and 15 percent unaffiliated.[18] This is a sea change from figures as late as 1960 when Protestants, beginning from the formal and official presence of Presbyterians in 1882, composed perhaps a total of 5 percent of the Guatemalan populace.[19] Startlingly, the report also indicates that some 60 percent of the entire country might actually be "renewalist"! A more complete accounting for religious diversity in the present moment would require taking into account the diversity of practices within both the Catholic and Protestant communities—as well as a multiplicity of indigenous practices ranging from what is often referred to as a syncretic version of Catholicism and Maya traditions ("folk" Catholicism) to contemporary manifestations of Maya spirituality, often simply labeled *costumbre* as a way of emphasizing continuity with the past practices of Maya communities. Some practitioners of *costumbre* eschew any evidence of Christianity in their practice.[20] Returning to the Christian population for the moment, beyond the aggregate numbers, it is striking that more than 60 percent of Catholics and some 85 percent of Protestants are characterized as "renewalists," a cover term the report uses to include both charismatic and Pentecostal Christians "because of their common belief in the spiritually renewing gifts of the Holy Spirit."[21]

The second crucial piece of information is the push for the recognition of cultural pluralism that became more open in the years leading to the signing of the so-called "firm and lasting" peace accord that put an end to a 36-year civil conflict in Guatemala on 26 December 1996. I was in the Constitutional Plaza that day, and an umbrella group called the Coordination of Organizations of the Maya People of Guatemala passed out fliers that articulated the concerns of the majority Maya population in those days when the future seemed bright and somewhat hopeful:

> The signing of the peace puts an end to the armed conflict, but not the end to the cause that gave rise to it. Instead, these causes remain intact, affecting the great Majority of the Maya Population, especially the Maya

people who keep in their memory and in their daily living the effects of almost 500 years of colonialism exercised by those who continue to hold the political, economic, and cultural power in Guatemala. The period of the signing of the peace will consist in changing the unequal forms of relationships between Guatemalans for a more just form—democratic and pluralistic, within a pluricultural and plurilingual state in Iximulew Guatemala.

This is a powerful statement of hope in the possibility of reconciliation in the wake of civil conflict.[22] It also represents the thrust of concerns for the *reivindicación* (recovery or revindication) of Maya culture and identity embodied in the Maya Movement, which, as noted earlier, seeks to put the Maya community's demands for cultural and political rights on the agenda of the state.[23] Beginning in the 1990s the recognition of Maya religious practices became a prominent part of the movement both at the local level and in terms of the push for respect for indigenous culture that received impetus in the international arena in the form of Convention 169 of the International Labor Organization. Within Guatemala, the Accord on the Identity and Rights of the Indigenous Peoples that was approved in March of 1995 as a side agreement leading up to the final peace accord "includes various paragraphs that refer to the respect, valorization, and promotion of [indigenous] spirituality, its practitioners, and for sacred places."[24]

Yet, the truth is that on many levels the peace process has not gone well for the nation as a whole.[25] From the Maya perspective, there is a continual struggle to put representatives in Congress even as there has been little success in fielding candidates at the presidential and vice-presidential levels, although representation in municipal-level politics is a fertile field for looking at Maya adaptation and resistance to the demands of the state. While the political arena as such is beyond the scope of this essay, in what follows, I address issues of conversion at the local level with fragments of two conversion narratives before returning briefly to the role of religion in the nation-state as a way of pointing to spaces of analysis that are opened by ethnographic perspectives on conversion and syncretism.

CONTENTIOUS CONVERSIONS

The narratives here were collected in the late 1990s among Mam speakers in the *municipio* of San Juan Ostuncalco (population 41,140 in 2002) in the western highlands of the department of Quetzaltenango. The Mam are currently the fourth largest Maya group in Guatemala with more than 600,000 people in the western region of the country extending to the Mexican border with Chiapas. The community as a whole is more geographically isolated from national affairs than more well known groups such as the K'iche' and the Kaqchikel who have figured prominently in Guatemalan historical accounts since the beginning of the Spanish invasion in the sixteenth century and continue to have more access to opportunities for work and education in urban zones. Much of the leadership of the contemporary Maya Movement also comes from the Kaqchikel and K'iche' communities.

Such cursory descriptions are, of course, generalizations, and highland and lowland Maya communities share aspects of a common cultural

Map 2.1. | *Highland Guatemala and primary areas of majority Maya population. Drawn by Mary Lee Eggart.*

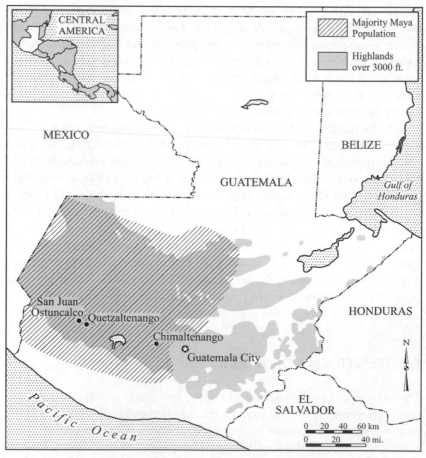

tradition rooted in language and worldview in southern Mesoamerica in Mexico, Guatemala, Honduras, and Belize. As well, Maya from the *municipios* of the western highlands have migrated to the United States over the last three decades to escape violence or to increase the economic well-being of themselves and their families. New housing construction, frequently of more than one storey, is often pointed to when traveling through the area as evidence that the owner or a family member has traveled to El Norte. In several years since the turn of the millennium, remittances (*remesas*) have been the largest single source of foreign income for Guatemala, although climates of stricter enforcement of immigration laws in the United States may have an impact on this pattern in the near future. At the community level, many Mam continue to maintain a connection to the land by maintaining their own cornfields (*milpas*) even when dedicated to working as laborers for others or to other activities such as craft production or professional careers such as teaching or working for NGOs in the region. Multiple economic strategies are common among Maya families throughout the country, and a significant number of women still dedicate themselves to weaving activities, although much of it is for domestic use within the household.

Illustration 2.1. | *Market plaza in San Juan Ostuncalco from mayor's office. Photo © C. Mathews Samson.*

San Juan Ostuncalco has been the center of Presbyterian evangelical efforts among the Mam since at least 1911, although established missionary presence in the *municipio* begins with the arrival of a resident missionary couple in about 1923. On the western extreme of a large valley that includes Quetzaltenango on the east, the *cabecera* sits at an altitude of some 8,200 feet above sea level, virtually at the edge of the steep, narrow escarpment running from the highlands to coffee country in the more temperate zones to ranch territory closer to the littorals near the Pacific coast. San Juan recorded a population increase of around 24 percent between the censuses of 1994 and 2002.[26] The town also had an indigenous population in excess of 80 percent in 1994, compared with a figure of just under 60 percent for the department as a whole.

Missionary practice has a complicated legacy, including several individuals with connections to the Presbyterian community who occupied mayoral posts in Ostuncalco and surrounding communities beginning in the early 1990s. Such political involvement challenges stereotypes of Latin American evangelicals as apolitical and supportive of conservative political agendas that support status quo politics even in the context of human rights violations.[27] Moreover, the individuals in these positions in the wake of elections in 1999 and 2003 indicated a strong desire for community service and even expressed their desire to serve in such positions with language of fulfilling a calling, language with resonance in both evangelical and Maya discourse.[28] The Ostuncalco context provides evidence of the increasing religious pluralism throughout the western highlands wherein residents are routinely engaged in a range of community activities with others who do not share their particular religious orientation. Without a doubt, this diversity (as well as the disparaging discourse frequently directed toward those engaged with either Maya practices or Catholicism as idol worshipers) has created conflict in a number of communities throughout Mesoamerica; nevertheless, while not ignoring the negative aspects of missionary activity, ethnographic engagement with local communities provides a fertile field for the consideration of the meaning of pluralism for individuals and for local level political and social interaction.

My initial objective in the field work on which this essay is based was to engage Mam Protestants in conversation regarding the relationship between evangelical religion and Maya spirituality. Beyond a concern with "traditional practices" or *costumbre* among a group of people, in time another significant issue came to the fore: Does conversion imply that a person has completely left a prior worldview or identity behind?[29] And beyond the focus on the individual convert, a second issue confronts those who deal with Protestant conversion in particular, especially given Protestantism's emphasis on the individual and some sense of a personal relationship with Jesus leading to salvation. Despite tension between Maya religious practice and the practices of Maya Catholicism in Mesoamerica, both Maya spirituality and the Maya-Catholic practices emphasize communal harmony and connections with the transcendent that more readily embody the mystical presence of creative forces in beings such as mountain spirits or saints than does the rationalistic word-based theology of historical Protestantism.

In this sense it is legitimate to ask whether or not conversion results in a kind of Weberian disenchantment of the world as the convert is at least potentially cut off from his or her past and culture and thrown into the new worldview of the evangelical community, whose members are focused on the Word as a point of orientation for belief and practice.[30] Such a shift in orientation reflects a change in what Edward Fischer refers to as "cultural logics" or the "dynamic, shared predispositions that inform behavior and thought."[31] Rather than determining the limits of action, such logics "lend a sense of regularity and continuity to behavior through post hoc analysis."[32] With this observation in mind, the tension we encounter in the examples that follow might be seen as a struggle between different kinds of orientation to the world. The space of disenchantment when one is brought into discourse-based, rational religion predicated upon speaking the language of salvation can nevertheless also become a space for the reconstitution of meaning, a re-enchantment that continues to search for a sense of continuity with what has gone before.[33]

Here I consider two contrasting conversion narratives that demonstrate some of the outlines for understanding conversion in the Guatemalan context. Both are personal accounts — one presenting conversion as a radical break with the past embodied in the family and aspects of community tradition, and the other a more tension-laden account wherein the convert tries to make sense of conversion in cultural terms by considering what a changed worldview might mean for Maya identity in the family network both in the past and the present. The essential tension is between elements of *costumbre* and the demands of the new faith on the convert. In both cases this tension is manifest within the context of perceptions regarding the family and family connections within the boundaries of the reorientation of worldview demanded by conversion. Generational shifts are also embedded in these narratives, although this aspect will not be addressed at length here. It is instructive, nevertheless, to note that generational conflict has been dealt with extensively in the literature on Guatemalan communities where attempts by the Catholic Action movement to purify traditional Catholic practices often pitted new cadres of better-educated youth against the community wisdom of the elders who were the leaders of the past.[34]

CONVERSION AS BREAKING WITH THE PAST

The first case involves the man who, at the time I interviewed him, was the oldest living Mam Presbyterian minister. When I interviewed him in 1998, he was a couple of years removed from a celebration that had marked the fiftieth anniversary of his conversion to Protestantism from what would be considered at least a nominal Catholicism. Mesoamerican evangelicals often refer to the time before their conversion as the time "before I was Christian." Converts themselves often employ this discourse as a way of differentiating themselves from their former way of life before conversion. While the phrasing certainly contrasts with the ecumenical discourse of historical Protestants in North America, it is indicative of the contested field of discourse that conversion represents in Central America and Mexico.[35]

The larger interview in which I engaged him suggests no real dissatisfaction in his pre-conversion life in a rural area outside of the urban center of Ostuncalco. Conversion for him seemed to be mostly related to finding some kind of truth in the face of competing dogmas as the local context became more pluralistic. A friend gave him a copy of the New Testament, which he read a little, but without much understanding. He reported trying to dedicate an entire day to reading the Testament with the friend: "But I didn't last," he said. He lasted half a day and began to understand a little, although "according to what I thought, I was a good Catholic and wanted to be a good Catholic," he said. He wanted, however, "to know the truth," and he and his friend only read together. Then he says, "I set out to pray without knowing what praying was." After nearly three weeks, he began to understand a prayer that he had prayed as a Catholic. He began to understand that the prayer was speaking about the death of Christ and recited the last section of the prayer from memory:

Oh Lord, I offer you my life
and deeds and works
for the satisfaction of my sins.
I confess your goodness
that gives me the grace
for the merit
of your precious blood
until the end of my life.

Although he asked, he never received an answer about whether truth was in Catholicism or evangelicalism, but he did begin to understand that the prayer was speaking about the death of Christ. Then he recounts the story of his conversion:

> So that was when I made my decision to accept Christ. I asked that same person who had arrived with the Bible, or the New Testament, how does one believe in the Lord Jesus Christ? He told me, "Well, go to the church over there in San Juan, in this place, in that side of the market there. ... And enter the church without any kind of fear, enter the church and sit down and when they make the invitation, then you raise your hand and say that you're going to accept Christ. ..." I set out, when Sunday came, I came from there and came to San Juan, but I couldn't go in. I couldn't enter the church; I stayed in the door, but I felt something. Something of shame, something of fear. There wasn't anyone to invite me in. From there I returned. ... Rather, I went back home. Another Sunday I went again, and the same thing happened. Then, it wasn't the same, but I stayed there standing in the door. Since I had gone to work in the *fincas*, I knew a man named Agustín Romero, and this Agustín, when he looked toward the door, when he saw me, made a sign with his hand for me to enter and told me to come in. So I had self-confidence to enter.

The conversion is a simple matter of raising his hand and being congratulated by the Mestizo pastor. Then he recounts the story of not knowing how he felt about his new situation, coming into contact with a prominent missionary couple in the area who hired him to help with some writing and translation in Mam, and the legalization of his marriage. His wife was ill during the legalization of the marriage, but she was transported by the missionaries to the mayor's office to answer questions. The conversion and the growing relationship with the missionary couple became a source of conflict during the illness, and eventually his father threw the son out of the house that he himself had helped construct on his own property in line with patrilocal residence patterns for newly-married Maya couples. The minister did not initially believe that his father would actually throw him out of the house; yet, if the father was breaking with tradition by evicting the son, the precipitating factor was the tension wrought by the conversion and the new relationships it engendered. He continued:

> But he told me a second time, so I asked him, "So papá," I said, "You really are speaking seriously?" "Yes," he said, "Yes, I'm speaking seriously." "Okay," I said, "Are you going to tell me who my father is." I said to him, "Are you going to tell me who my father is?" "I am, but since you have disobeyed me, for that I am not your father. Get out!" So I said, "Forgive me, father. You are my father, you." He repeated, "Go and acknowledge as your parents those you have loved." "Look, papá," I said,

"They are not my parents, you are my father, first God and you." "Yes," he said, "but because you disobeyed me now I'm not your father." "Okay, so it is," I told him. "Are you going to give me a month to remain in this little house, one month I ask you." … "Okay," he told me. I asked God to help me find a place to make the house.

There is more to this story, just as there are a number of ways to analyze the process of conversion discussed in these excerpts. The convert eventually finds himself preaching in a rather itinerant fashion, sees converts among his immediate family and community, and even achieves some degree of reconciliation with his father, who never is actually said to have converted. Yet, the primary theme is conversion as a break with past traditions and even with family members who represent the older traditions and lifeways. At the same time, through the conversion of siblings, one of whom seems to have converted earlier and re-converted at the prompting of the minister, the latter is able to begin a congregation in the local community.[36] He also, apparently because they had taught him to write to some degree in the Mam language, becomes an assistant to the missionaries. This eventually leads to the possibility of further education, which leads in turn to his ordination, although I have no information about that event. It is noteworthy that it was his conversion that was celebrated during the 1990s and not his ordination.

A less obvious but significant issue is the role of people from other cultures—a Ladino preacher and missionaries (identified as North Americans in the narrative)—as those who are the bearers of the new tradition. There is something simultaneously powerful and disturbing about the convert's father identifying the missionaries as the new parents as he throws the son out of his house. The central point of tension is the family network and the authority of the father within Mam culture. While conversion itself is an individual affair, in the convert's generation and succeeding generations, family is often reconstituted in the new religion practices, and many small congregations are constituted as extensions of one or several families within a particular community. It is significant that the children of this minister remained active to varying degrees in the local evangelical community, now into the fifth and sixth decades of their lives, and one son even became the *alcalde* (mayor) of Ostuncalco in the early 1990s. Some might see in this evidence of what has been called a Protestant uplift, which gives more credence to the Weber thesis about the material and social benefits of conversion. A more interesting issue for the ongoing study of conversion is that of increasing pluralism in religious practice and trust gained within segments of the larger community when an evangelical can be elected to the highest local office in an area that is still predominately Catholic. Even then, such examples of coexistence are not uniformly harmonious, and one of the issues to be investigated was the negative attitude of the local priest toward the young evangelical mayor.

Beyond the family and community dynamics, however, there is in this case a harkening to a cosmovision in which the ancestors play a key role in grounding community identity and traditions that tie families to each other in the Mam worldview. The new belief system chosen by the son irreparably breaks this link, and the son will have to find a new home away from his family and the land that symbolizes interconnectedness in Maya cosmology.

CONVERSION AS INCORPORATING TRADITION

The second narrative presents a contrasting approach to conversion, including a degree of reflexivity that is likely not possible in the immediacy of conversion. This case involves a Mam Presbyterian minister who was about 40 years old and who came of age during the 1970s while struggling with family problems related to a marginal economic situation and conflict his father was involved in with other members of the community. This minister also endured military service and experienced aspects of the repression in one of Ostuncalco's neighboring communities, Concepción Chiquirichapa. Though not mentioned here in a direct way, Bible reading was ultimately an important aspect of this man's conversion in a context where his family engaged at different times both local shamanic traditions and local spiritists in attempts to confront his mother's persistent illnesses and the father's attempts to provide for the family, even at one point dedicating himself to fabrication of the local home brew before landing in jail after yet another conflict.

This minister represents a strongly biblical and Calvinistic approach to evangelicalism, and he is concerned about Pentecostal influences on the theology and practice of Presbyterianism in the highlands. He does deal with Mam cultural issues through linguistic training and Bible translation, and he is very interested in theological education. In several interviews with this minister, I felt that I did not have much luck in persuading him to talk about Maya spirituality and how it related to his evangelicalism. I often interviewed him in the company of a younger Mam layperson who was active in youth ministry and an elder in a local congregation. This latter man represented a Mam perspective much more informed by life in a small urban area than was so for the many pastors who had stronger roots in the countryside. While both men be lieved that Maya shamans had power, they were much more focused on the power of Jesus Christ to overcome the deleterious effects of the activities of *brujos* or witches, who are still credited with the power, it seems, to kill. In fact, the minister credits a local shaman with having bewitched his mother in a series of events leading to her death. The sense of power and transcendence infusing life is palpable in listening to the tape again, and the minister expresses a strong belief that an-other outcome might have been possible if his mother's faith had been in Jesus.[37]

In a sense, I am taking a step back from such issues to look at the ho-rizon of conversion and the way in which it plays out in a person's sense of place in the world. An ongoing concern in my research has had to do with the persistence of Maya culture or religious perspectives within the lives of people who participate in Protestant communities instead of remaining involved with the traditions of *costumbre* in the Ostun-calco area. One morning, I became frustrated with lack of information I had gathered in relation to this rather unfocused research question, and I asked him directly, "Do you believe that you in one way or another still personally manage aspects of Maya religion? In any manner?" He replied with an answer that revealed a unique way of coming to terms with his evangelicalism and with an ancestor who had been quite im-portant in his life, a *tartarabuela* or great-great-grandmother:

> … In my case there is a need for more information in terms of the concept regarding faith. The last time I was remembering some of what my great, great grandmother said, right? But one thing I'm remembering is that she said that in the case of the Maya priests, as they call them now, she said this is more recent. Likewise, she said that which is Catholic, that which is evangelical, is not of us. That came when the white people came, the Spaniards. And she said that they are not our people; they are our ene-mies. Along with all this [came] imposition of what is foreign—that there are priests, that there has to be mass in the church, that one has to go to school, all of that. And the evangelical churches aren't of us, she said. Only, this was brought later. Speaking of the Maya priests, or as it is said in Mam *aj k'ab'*, I don't say that what they do is not ours, but it is recent as well. Except before we have this teaching that our parents and we [our-selves] have to respect God and keep with us the idea that God is present wherever we are—whether we are in the house, in the road, at work. But the idea given by the Maya priests is that we have to go to worship God in the mountains … that one goes to worship in front of a rock, she said. But God is not the rock, she said. God is not there, but in all places. So in one sense, I believe that, yes, this is within Christian faith. It is possible that, yes, we are practicing part of what they practiced, right?
>
> …

Later when I had just begun to read the Bible, I remembered what she had told me. But a lot of what she said, I found in the Bible. [In] the case of respect, I found in the Bible that you have to have that, respect for parents, right? In the Bible it says that as well, "Honor your father and mother." And there is one God, the God, Father God. In Mam ... *el mero anciano,* the real elder, right? But the concept is one. ...

So I think that in some way, yes, among the people here before, there was a concept, a more clear concept of God; and perhaps religion was like that as well, with a faith in God like that in the time of Abraham. We don't know. Unfortunately, we don't have that information. ... But the manner in which she spoke, in light of reading the Bible, I came to a consciousness that she, while she was here on the earth, was carrying a faith in the Kingdom of God.

And really, I came to believe ... I came to believe that, yes, she also died, but she was not lost.

When I initially looked at this narrative, I examined the way in which this minister tried to bridge the gap between cultures— between the evangelical identity and the need to do away with past religious or spiritual traditions in the face of conversion.[38] Further reflection reveals that there is more at stake in his response to my question. Even the reference to his *tartarubuela* (great-great grandmother) tells us that we are dealing with a rather unique discourse. The discourse is not formally that of a *testimonio* or a direct autobiographical accounting of conversion and its meaning. Rather, it can be placed in the category of a kind of personal mytho-history. The speaker simultaneously embraces a personal spirituality even while seeking to transcend the personal (and the personally spiritual) and reconcile some of the ethnic and racial tensions that so shape culture and society in Guatemala. The discourse shows us one way in which Mam Maya Protestants can provide us with a clearer picture of the relationship between power and meaning in situations of cultural contact and conflict. The emphasis here, however, is not on the conflict so much as it is on the creative aspects of integrating personal and group identity, smoothing out troubling edges in the process.

In the post-conflict situation through which Guatemalans are living, there may well be good reasons for embracing the universalizing tendencies of the Christian discourse recounted by Presbyterian missionary-turned-anthropologist David Scotchmer when he says that

the new kinship system, while essentially redefined around the gospel and experienced within the church as an institution, shows features of exclusivity, rights, and obligations common to any family. Protestant conversion within the Mayan culture makes little sense without an understanding of the social and theological shift represented by participation and membership within this extended family.[39]

The reference here is to new modes of kinship, not to ethnicity or ethnic identity as such. One of the visible signs of this kinship is the simple convention of using terms like *hermano* or *hermana* (brother or sister) in greeting one another at church-related activities. At the same time, it is clear that even new relatives will not be embraced from outside of the particular personal, communal, and cultural circumstances through which converts embrace evangelical practices. If sometimes a person has to leave home, kin, and country to make a new life, Maya cosmology may dictate that on some level they take the ancestors with them. Far from a disenchantment of the world, the continuing presence of the ancestors in such discourse reveals an unavoidable personal engagement with conversion that does not fit linear narratives usually associated with missionization. The world is given new meaning, re-enchanted with the presence of those who in some narratives of conversion might be forever lost or outside the circle of hearth and home symbolized by the new family ties. Conversion itself becomes a process almost demanding a blurring of boundaries that simultaneously remains rooted in place and experience as shifting worldviews and cosmology are negotiated and reconstituted over time.[40]

CONCLUSION: A VIEW TOWARD PLURICULTURAL ENGAGEMENT WITHIN THE NATION

Changing the scale of analysis might seem to beg the question of conversion, but the rawness of the tensions as well as the extant cultural and religious pluralism in Guatemala make it a stimulating place to work, a place where one needs to keep one eye focused on local continuity and change and the other firmly trained on larger political and social interactions. These interactions take place in the Maya Movement as it seeks provide a space for the renewal of ethnic pride in a new generation that did not live under the daily threat of violence as their parents did. In addition, human rights and NGO communities are searching for models for reconciliation and social sustainability as the excitement of the peace process dissolves in a present fraught with anxiety and an unclear path into the future. To be sure one also needs to keep an eye trained on electoral processes at the national level and the way in which they provide a type of mimesis for social tension in particular places within Guatemala and even in transnational space—when one considers the continuing traffic between local communities and the North that seems to be little diminished despite the current political climate regarding immigrants in the United States.

One of the issues I wanted to research during my field season in the summer of 2007 was taken off the agenda when I was handed a Guatemalan newspaper on my flight from Miami to Guatemala City. Harold Caballeros, perhaps the most prominent neo-Pentecostal minister in the country, was barred from running for the presidency by the country's Tribunal Supremo Electoral (TSE) because of a technicality surrounding his party's late filing of a document in the run-up to election season. Caballeros is not Maya, and his party was called *Visión con Valores* (Vision with Values)—in Spanish, ¡*VIVA!* As noted below, neo-Pentecostalism remains largely an urban, elite-based phenomenon, and it is important to note that Caballeros has long been a proponent of spiritual warfare, a doctrine that frequently links Guatemala's social problems to some degree with indigenous religious practices of the past, practices understood to be pagan and even demonic.[41]

On another front, the winning candidate, after three tries, was Alvaro Colom, a center-left candidate running on the ticket of the National Union of Hope (UNE). Colom is from an elite family with ties to the political and social oligarchy in the country. Part of the implication here is that he is Ladino or Mestizo in the common parlance of most of Latin America. Colom is also widely known to have credentials as a Maya priest, the general import of which is that he apprenticed as a shaman at some juncture and continues to make it known that this is an important aspect of who he is. There are plenty of questions to be raised here, but the significant point is that apparently in some evangelical circles he was not welcomed for exactly that reason. Moreover, Colom spelled backward for some translates in Spanish to Moloc, a deity in the Hebrew scriptures who was considered a source of idolatry for the Hebrew people.[42] In a Latin American country where the first evangelical president was accused of genocide in the early 1980s and the second resigned in disgrace and landed in exile after trying to dissolve congress in the early 1990s, these kinds of stories cannot be ignored in trying to understand the meaning of conversion and religious change of the magnitude experienced over the past three decades. After all, some people saw evangelical president number two as playing King David to the first president's King Saul.[43] The Biblical text is embodied in the lives of figures who play out their public roles on the national stage, and it lives on in the life trajectories of those who seek to follow its teachings.

Class and ethnicity remain part of the story, and one of the critiques of neo-Pentecostal discourse has been not solely the way its teachings are pitched to the elite classes of society but also the very nature of the prosperity gospel it proclaims. This is a gospel that does in many ways appear to uphold the status quo in a country that has one of the most inequitable distributions of wealth in the world. One's position in society can be interpreted as a sign of blessing. Yet, even here the ethnographic caution is that neo-Pentecostal influence through the media and through the sense of mission growing out of its teaching extends to people in all sectors of society. Ethnographic interpretations of neo-Pentecostal practice are best positioned within studies directed toward making sense of what a pluricultural society in Guatemala will look like as the twenty-first century progresses.

Another experience from the summer of 2007 demonstrates the multiple dimensions in which the interplay between religious traditions manifests itself in Guatemala; one might even consider it to be sign of re-enchantment in process. Such re-enchantment, or reconfiguration of meaning, emerges in part from the legacy of what continues to be referred to as the culture of violence in Guatemala today. Some of those voices I hear in the field talk about *convivencia*, best translated for our purposes as living together across lines of ethnic and religious heterodoxy. But Latin Americans also talk about the *imaginario*, a concept somewhat inadequately translated as "the imaginary," one that reflects the possibility of a new world coming into being. With those ideas in mind, scholars working in Mesoamerica have much to learn from the Maya worldview, which informs us that it is important not only to bring the ancestors into a new space and time but also to look for signs of balance, harmony, and equilibrium in the midst of social changes that none of us can escape. In contexts of violence and massive cultural change, as reflected in the historical imposition of new religious traditions or in the reconstruction of meaning in the life of the convert, historical memory and *testimonios* (the act of recounting the stories of individuals and peoples) augment those other discourses (religious and secular) that daily define us in both our commonality and particularity. Pluralism itself becomes a resource for re-enchantment rather than a threat.

So it is that Maya religious practices will continue play a key role in the definition of Maya-ness on the Guatemalan national stage in addition to the imagining of new ways of being within the Mesoamerican context. During the course of my research in 2007, I attended a book presentation in a downtown hotel in the midst of the hustle and bustle of the city's afternoon rush hour traffic. While the event was not held amid the glitter in Guatemala's "Zona Viva," it was, nevertheless, attended by some several dozens of people, primarily Maya interested in the projection of a Maya agenda into the political process. The book in question was concerned with political parties in the national elections and their stance in regard to Maya issues, specifically the concerns of Maya women.[44] As an educational event, the presentation of the book was combined with commentary from two critics and a time for questions fielded from the audience. Arriving a couple of minutes late, I was handed a program as I entered the meeting hall, and I immediately noticed that the assembled were turning toward the four cardinal directions as a Maya spiritual guide (a priestess in this case) lit candles and opened the event with an invocation that was noted as part of the program. Following the presentations, with everyone ready for refreshments in the way that most Guatemalan communal events seek to evoke something of the sacredness of conviviality, there was a "closing of the invocation." I was struck by the ecumenical tone of the prayer and how in many ways it would not have been out of place in one of the rural evangelical *templos* that I have spent a fair amount of time in over the past decade.

No doubt this experience reflects more than the pluralism of contending expressions of religion inscribed on the landscape of contemporary Guatemala. From the sacred mountains, caves, lakes, and archaeological sites of the Maya, to the prominent and ever-present Catholic churches situated on the plaza of cities and villages; and from the brightly colored evangelical *templos* in urban *barrios* and rural settings far from urban centers, to the 12,500-seat "megafrater" building of the Fraternidad Cristiana, the boundaries of religion and religious prac-

Illustration 2.2. | *Invitation to the inauguration of the 12,500-seat auditorium of the Fraternidad Cristiana in Guatemala City. Courtesy of Fraternidad Cristiana de Guatemala.*

Una iglesia cristiana para la familia

No se pierda la oportunidad

de asistir a la inauguración del Mega-Auditórium en Ciudad San Cristobal 27 de mayo de 2007

tices are not only blurred but negotiated. Even a mural can be found in the National Museum of Ethnography and History that acknowledges Guatemala's pluralism. Although it begins with the creation according to the *Popol Wuj* and recapitulates the persistence of Maya ethnicity and religion in the last frame, intermediate scenes depict some of the current influences on Guatemalan identity and culture—evangelicals, Mormons, Jews, and Muslims all make an appearance.

The book presentation was a cultural event that projected Maya identity and Maya spirituality into public space in a manner that would have been difficult only a few years before. Questions of ethnicity were integrally linked with spirituality and the power gained by a sense of political presence in a place where in the not-too-distant past, Maya people in customary dress—and, without a doubt, prayers offered to the four directions—would have been considered decidedly out of place. To move beyond abstract discourses of conversion and syncretism, one begins with an emphasis on the continuing need for people to find a place from which to act within the world, a need to blur (and perhaps cross) boundaries in the continuing struggle to renew a sense of self and community. For Maya Protestant converts, the past is not simply left behind, and space has to be made for the ancestors who may yet speak again in unimaginable places.

Acknowledgments

I am grateful to David Lindenfeld and Miles Richardson for the invitation to participate in a project that gave me the opportunity to revisit some of my work while considering the perspectives of new colleagues during our two meaningful days together in Georgetown. The University of Alabama Press gave me permission to quote from my work *Re-enchanting the World: Maya Protestantism in the Guatemalan Highlands* (Tuscaloosa: The University of Alabama Press, 2007). Most of what I have incorporated here comes from chapter 5 in that volume.

Notes

1. Sidney M. Greenfield and André Droogers, "A Symposium," Introduction to *Reinventing Religions: Syncretism and Transformation in Africa and the Americas* (Lanham, MD, 2001), 18.

2. Michael E. Harkin, Introduction to *Reassessing Revitalization Movements: Perspectives from North America and the Pacific Islands* (Lincoln, NE 2004), xxiv.

3. On ethnic renewal movements, see Joane Nagel, *American Indian Ethnic Renewal: Red Power and the Resurgence of Identity and Culture* (New York, 1996).

4. André Droogers and Sidney M. Greenfield, "Recovering and Reconstructing Syncretism," in *Reinventing Religions*, 32–37.

5. Manuel Vásquez and Marie Marquardt, *Globalizing the Sacred* (New Brunswick, NJ, 2003), 49–64.

6. Ibid., 58–59.

7. Harkin, Introduction to *Reassessing Revitalization Movements*, xxiv–xxv.

8. The most direct critique in this regard is Talal Asad, "Anthropological Conceptions of Religion: Reflections on Geertz," *Man* 18 (1983): 237–59.

9. Clifford Geertz, "Thick Description: Toward an Interpretive Theory of Culture," in *The Interpretation of Cultures* (New York, 1973), 14.

10. Sherry B. Ortner, "Updating Practice Theory," in *Anthropology and Social Theory: Culture, Power, and the Acting Subject* (Durham, NC, 2006), 16–17.

11. Susan Neylan, *The Heavens Are Changing: Nineteenth-Century Protestant Missions and Tsimshian Christianity* (Montreal, 2003), 17.

12. Population statistics for the Maya are a topic for debate. I use the 50 percent number as the lower side of estimates from Maya scholars and activists who claim that the government statistics undercount them and, in the extreme case, perpetuate the assimilation of the Maya as a political policy. The 2002 census reported that 39 percent of the population was Maya—4,411,964 out of a total population of 11,237,196. Together with the Maya population in Mexico, Belize, and Honduras, the total Maya population in Mesoamerica reaches 6,000,000, and possibly as high as 8,000,000.

13. See Meredith B. McGuire's edited volume *Lived Religion: Faith and Practice in Everyday Life* (New York, 2008).

14. See Richard Wilson, *Maya Resurgence in Guatemala: Q'eqchi' Experiences* (Norman, OK, 1995), for an example of this involving mountain spirits, also called the *duenos* or owners, or in the Q'eqchi' language *tzuultaq'a*. Translation issues abound here, and these figures are often called "Earth Lords," although the literal translation of *tzuultaq'a* is "hill-valley," a term that shows the link between conceptualizations linking the natural world and the transcendent. On this point, see the brief discussion in James E. Brady and Wendy Ashmore, "Mountains, Caves, Water: Ideational Landscapes of the Ancient Maya," in *Archaeologies of Landscape: Contemporary Perspectives*, ed. Wendy Ashmore and A. Bernard Knapp (Malden, MA, 1999), 126–28. Abigail E. Adams, "Making One Our Word: Protestant Qéqchi' Mayas in Highland Guatemala," in *Holy Saints and Fiery Preachers: The Anthropology of Protestantism in Mexico and Central America*, ed. James W. Dow and Alan R. Sandstrom (Westport, CT, 2001), 205–33, provides a fascinating discussion of how this aspect of Maya cosmology is reflected in the construction of a Protestant church building or *templo*. See also Abigail E. Adams, "Appropriating Maya Land, Labor And Spirituality: Germans in Guatemala, 1860–1945," paper presented at the Biennial Meeting of the Society for the Anthropology of Religion (Phoenix, 2006).

15. Virginia Garrard-Burnett, *Protestantism in Guatemala: Living in the New Jerusalem* (Austin, TX, 1998), 23–24.

16. I am making a leap here from the concept of inculturation, which implies a restatement of the dominant religion in terms of the language and worldview of those who are incorporating it into their lifeways. Interculturation is a conscious taking into account of the mutual influence of cultures (and religions) upon each other and represents another step in the process of dialogue when cultures come into contact. On inculturation and "Protestant Mayanized theology," see Garrard-Burnett, "Inculturated Protestant Theology in Guatemala," in *Theology and the Religions: A Dialogue,* ed. Vigo Mortensen (Grand Rapids, MI, 2003), 97–107.

17. The term "conversion career" is taken from Henri Gooren, "Conversion Careers in Latin America: Entering and Leaving Church among Pentecostals, Catholics, and Mormons," in *Conversion of a Continent: Contemporary Religious Change in Latin America,* ed. Timothy J. Steigenga and Edward L. Cleary (New Brunswick, NJ, 2007), 52–71.

18. Pew Forum for Religion and Public Life, *Spirit and Power: A 10-Country Survey of Pentecostals* (Washington, D.C., 2007), 80, http://pewforum.org/publications/surveys/pentecostals-06.pdf (accessed 13 November 2009).

19. Gooren, "Conversion Careers," 181.

20. The preferred term for Protestants on the ground in Mesoamerica is *evangélico* (evangelical). It shifts the focus toward practices related to the biblical text while setting up a contrast with Catholic emphasis on the Mass and religious imagery, which many evangelicals consider to be a form of paganism.

21. Pew Forum, *Spirit and Power,* 1. The work of Clifford Holland with PROLADES (Programa Latinoamericano de Estudios Sociorreligiosos) in Costa Rica shows similar tendencies in terms of affiliation: 56.9 percent Catholic, 30.7 percent Protestant, and 12.4 percent none/other. See "Table of Statistics on Religious Affiliation in the Americas and the Iberian Peninsula," http://www.prolades.com/amertbl06.htm (accessed 3 June 2010). Sources of the statistics for each country are provided there. Interestingly, the "none/other" category is highest in Central America among all the regions of Latin America. Panama is an exception to this generalization, and Honduras is shown there as having the highest percentage of Protestants at 36 percent while El Salvador comes in at 34.4 percent. In the United States, the "none" figure is put at 8 percent.

22. Even the term reconciliation is contested by some who look at issues of the construction of civil society and the meaning of historical memory after the war. See Elizabeth Oglesby, "Educating Citizens in Postwar Guatemala: Historical Memory, Genocide, and the Culture of Peace," *Radical History* 97 (2007): 97 n. 42.

23. Víctor Gálvez Borrell and Alberto Esquit Choy, *The Mayan Movement Today: Issues of Indigenous Culture and Development in Guatemala,* trans. Matthew Creelman (Guatemala City, 1997).

24. José Roberto Morales Sic, "Religión y Espiritualidad Maya," in *Mayanización y Vida Cotidiana: La Ideología Multicultural en la Sociedad Guatemalteca,* ed. Santiago Bastos and Aura Cumes, 3 vols. (Guatemala City, 2007), 3: 267. It should also be noted that within the Maya Movement are people belonging to all of the religions mentioned in this essay. Religion, as distinct from culture, becomes a space for some conflict depending upon how one defines Maya iden-

tity. Both Catholics and evangelicals who participate openly in Maya ceremonies are sometimes criticized because "for a long time the ceremonies have been stigmatized as acts of 'witchcraft' or 'sinful acts'" (ibid., 278). Translations from this source are my own.

25. Violence and citizen insecurity remain intractable problems in the face of impunity and a weak judicial system. These problems are largely linked to the unequal distribution of wealth and the inability of the economy to absorb the large numbers of people entering the work force each year. They are exacerbated by gang activity and drug running, as Guatemala has become a transhipment zone in the context of the "war" on drugs and the confrontation with what have been referred to as "occult powers" that are understood to have links to criminal elements within society as well as to the military. Workers for human rights in a number of areas continue to receive threats for speaking out, and the specter of femicide (*femicidio*) has arisen in which some 5,000 women have been brutally murdered since early in the 2000s.

26. This extrapolation comes from comparing with figures from the 1994 and the 2002 censuses. I initially accessed the latter numbers online, but they are no longer available for easy access. The web site for Guatemala's Instituto Nacional de Estadistica is http://www.ine.gob.gt/.

27. This was the longstanding view of the results of Protestant missionary activity, particularly from the left during the difficult years of the national security state and revolutionary movements of the late 1960s and extending into the 1970s and 1980s. Protestant groups were often criticized for being extensions of political agendas emanating from the United States. More nuanced analyses beginning in the 1990s have challenged this view with a perspective that seeks to demonstrate how various Protestantisms have become indigenous to the Latin American context.

28. See C. Mathews Samson, "From War to Reconciliation: Guatemalan Evangelicals and the Transition to Democracy, 1982–2001," in *Evangelical Christianity and Democracy in Latin America,* ed. Paul Freston (New York, 2008), 81–84, for a discussion of these issues.

29. *Costumbre* at its most basic level implies "custom," and the use of the term leads toward a more practice-oriented approach to the study of religion (and culture) in Mesoamerica. The term itself is difficult in that it often refers to an aspect of Maya Catholicism that focuses on care for the saints in religious sodalities called *cofradías,* part of the *cargo* system whereby members of the community fulfill both religions and civic roles over the course of their lifetimes. *Costumbre* is rooted in place and a sense of a shared communal identity, and for that reason the term increasingly refers to Mayan spiritual or religious practices that downplay Catholic connections altogether. Today the preferred terms are Maya spirituality and Maya religion. These practices often center on various kinds of ritualistic fire ceremonies in which offerings and other sacrifices are presented for the purpose of maintaining communal and spiritual harmony. The fire itself is also read as a form of divination. A common goal of these activities is to put the individual on the proper road appropriate to his or her destiny as revealed in the characteristics linked to the day of a person's birth. This is not fate but rather a notion of being (and living) in harmony with one's essential nature.

30. The focus on "the Word" here resonates most clearly with historical Protestantism and non-Pentecostal evangelicals. It is no accident that the standard historiography of the promotion of Protestant migration to various places in Latin America in the last half of nineteenth century links Protestantism to perceived benefits of modernization such as literacy and technological advancement. Pentecostalism is only now receiving some of the attention it deserves, given its predominance within the Latin American Protestant community. One of the more interesting considerations is whether or not spirit-based Pentecostalism, with its emphasis on the gifts of the Holy Spirit, represents a stronger connection with a type of mysticism than does historical Protestantism. There seems to be little question that this is the case, but continued research into the connection with the numinous is warranted before making the connection too forthrightly. Additionally, on brief field trips to Guatemala during the summers of 2008 and 2009, in several Pentecostal settings I observed considerable preaching and praying in communal fashion but no actual speaking in tongues. While some Presbyterians in the Mam context often expressed concern about the Pentecostalization of their liturgy, one can argue that there is also a rationalization of Pentecostalism taking place in the face of globalization and the transnational movement of peoples and ideas across increasingly porous boundaries.

31. Edward F. Fischer, *Cultural Logics and Global Economics: Maya Identity in Thought and Practice* (Austin, TX, 2001), 15.

32. See John D. Early, *The Maya and Catholicism: An Encounter of Worldviews* (Gainesville, FL, 2006) for an extended description of Maya cultural logics, especially the idea that Maya ceremonies are about keeping a covenant as much as they are about sacrifice.

33. An example of an evangelical context where speaking in the appropriate manner is the substance of conversion is provided in Susan Harding, "Convicted by the Holy Spirit: The Rhetoric of Fundamental Baptist Conversion," *American Ethnologist* 14 (1987): 167–81. For a detailed ethnographic analysis of the construction of images of Christ through words, particularly among Southern Baptists, and the juxtaposition with the use of symbols in Spanish America, see Miles Richardson, *Being-in-Christ and Putting Death in Its Place: An Anthropologist's Account of Christian Performance in Spanish America and the American South* (Baton Rouge, LA, 2003).

34. Barbara Tedlock, *Time and the Highland Maya*, rev. ed. (Albuquerque, NM, 1982); Kay B. Warren, *Symbols of Subordination: Indian Identity in a Guatemalan Town* (Austin, TX, 1989); Robert S. Carlsen, *The War for the Heart and Soul of a Highland Maya Town* (Austin, TX, 1997); Ricardo Falla, *Quiché Rebelde: Religious Conversion, Politics, Ethnic Identity in Guatemala*, trans. Phillip Berryman (Austin, TX, 2001).

35. This language plays out in some interesting ways. For years I have noted stickers with Catholic images on the door or small windows of homes informing would-be evangelizers that the inhabitants of the home are Catholics. While beyond the strict bounds of Mesoamerica, on a visit to Nicaragua in October of 2008, I saw a sticker with a prominent image of the Virgin of Guadalupe that informed outsiders that the inhabitants were Christians—in effect reasserting Catholics' claims to be included under that label.

36. The issue of the durability of conversion, and people leaving churches out the back door complicates analysis of conversion as well as the process of gathering statistics on conversion to evangelicalism in Latin America. For helpful framing of these issues, see Edward L. Cleary, "Shopping Around: Questions about Latin American Conversions," *International Bulletin of Missionary Research* 28 (2004): 50–54; and Timothy J. Steigenga, "Religious Conversion in the Americas: Meanings, Measures, and Methods," *International Bulletin of Missionary Research* 34 (2010): 77–82.

37. While outside my concerns here, the evangelical connection made between sorcery and Satan or the devil should not be overlooked in either a literal or a metaphysical sense. Of course, the tension between different experiences of reality is a significant part of what is at stake in these kinds of confrontations involving different religious or spiritual traditions.

38. C. Mathews Samson, "Interpretando la identidad religiosa: la cultura Maya y la religión evangélica bajo una perspectiva etnográfica," *Memorias del Segundo Congreso Sobre el Pop Wuj* (Quetzaltenango, Guatemala, 1999).

39. David G. Scotchmer, "Symbols of Salvation: A Local Mayan Protestant Theology," *Missiology* 17 (1989): 304.

40. This processual view of conversion is consistent with the notion of "conversion as a continuum" posited in Timothy J. Steigenga and Edward L. Cleary, "Understanding Conversion in the Americas," in *Conversion of a Continent*, 3–32 (New Brunswick, NJ, 2007). Their skepticism about unitary market models of conversion (on either the supply or the demand side) or the possibility of pegging particular aspects of political and social change to conversion is essential in my view.

41. This rhetoric was central to his thinking in Harold Caballeros, *Victorious Warfare: Discovering Your Rightful Place in God's Kingdom* (Nashville, TN, 2001), although this perspective does not seem central to his current political discourse, which has increasingly become more sophisticated and to some degree pluralistic. For VIVA's stance on issues related to indigenous peoples, see Luis Rodolfo Ochoa and Byron Garoz, *Origen, Ideología y Propuesta de los Partidos Políticos Inscritos en el TSE, 2007* (Guatemala City, 2007), 87–89.

42. For further information see Francis Gigo, "Moloch," in *The Catholic Encyclopedia,* 15 vols. (New York, 1911), http://www.newadvent.org/cathen/10443b.htm (accessed 30 November 2008).

43. See Samson, "From War to Reconciliation," 88–89, for commentary on this discourse as it pertains to Guatemala's neo-Pentecostal community.

44. Ochoa and Garoz, *Origen, Ideología y Propuesta.*

3

CHRISTIAN SOLDIERS, CHRISTIAN ALLIES: COERCION AND CONVERSION IN SOUTHERN AFRICA AND NORTHEASTERN AMERICA AT THE TURN OF THE NINETEENTH CENTURY

Elizabeth Elbourne

The nature of the relationship between Christian missions and European imperialism is a question that has preoccupied not only critics of missions but also not a few historians of Christianity in the British empire—even if the history of Christianity clearly cannot be contained within the bounds either of the history of missions or of empire.[1] A critical point that emerges from much of this literature is that the relationship of missionary activity to empire surely varies by time and place, among other things according to the stage of imperial conquest and the degree of power available to colonized groups. I suggest in this chapter that conversion to Christianity in a frontier zone often had different implications for colonized peoples than conversion in a settled colonial state. A second key point is that Christianity's relationship with colonialism did in fact matter deeply, but converts nonetheless often took up Christianity and transformed it from within, sometimes using Christianity in turn to combat colonialism or slavery. Despite the seeming optimism of this broad conclusion, which might argue for limits to the "colonization of consciousness" (in Jean and John Comaroff's trenchant phrase),[2] European proponents of Christianity did often in fact argue that conversion would create loyal subjects of empire, while powerful contemporary critiques of cultural colonialism certainly suggest that debate over the meaning of Christianity is not closed.[3]

In this essay, I seek to contribute to this discussion in two ways with attention to case studies drawn from the British Empire in southern Africa and in northeastern North America from the late eighteenth to early nineteenth centuries. I want first to suggest that despite the currency of debate over missions and empire, insufficient attention has been paid to the role of the military, that key colonial institution, and of interaction between colonized peoples and the military in the domain of religion, particularly in the period before the mid nineteenth century when past and current military officers (including naval officers) were often the backbone of colonial administrations.[4] Paying more attention to the military, as well as to the coercive power of settler militias, sheds light on both the spread of Christianity and resistance to it. For example, military officers sometimes tried to promote Christianity in order to foster imperial loyalty, even if they were frequently at odds with missionaries, while potential converts sometimes feared Christianity because they associated it with military service. Secondly, and more broadly, however, negotiating with Christianity in frontier zones, particularly at times of warfare or potential warfare, changed the dynamics of conversion for indigenous peoples. Historians of religion might valuably pay more attention to the violence of frontier zones in white settler colonies and ask how this affected the reception of Christianity. In other words, imperial coercive power mattered, even when the coercion was not overt. This seems a useful corrective to more overtly intellectualist accounts, even as taking account of the imperial context and of the looming threat of violence also illuminates the intellectual reception of Christianity.

To explore these broad themes, in this essay I compare the interaction between Christianity, imperial militaries and alliance politics in contested borderlands between New York and Six Nations territory in the period of the American revolution, and along the frontiers of the Cape Colony in the early nineteenth century, with particular attention to the Kanienkehaka (Mohawk) and other Six Nations groups in the first instance and to the Khoekhoe in the second. Two caveats: I am not attempting to examine the full panoply of reasons for conversion by members of either society (which in both cases stretch back into the seventeenth century) but rather to broaden a conversation that is already very rich. Secondly, the current discussion focuses far more on men than on women, but I hope a gendered analysis nonetheless yields useful insight into ideas about masculinity and into particular pressures on men.

Christianity in a frontier society was never neutral. It bristled with the language of conquest and of salvation; it allowed access to new power; it threatened the end of other kinds of power. Coded in multiple ways, Christianity was tied to power both sacred and material, even if it also promised relief from the kingdoms of this world. In this context, conversion could never be solely what missionaries anticipated: the product of a naked encounter between the individual soul and God. Even in less charged contexts, the genre conventions of conversion stories were not always experienced as expected in societies that did not necessarily share emotions or ideas such as a conviction of innate sinfulness, seen by many evangelical missionaries as essential prerequisites for experiencing grace.[5] Evangelical theories of conversion did not reflect the lived reality of "conversion" in actual complicated, messy encounters, underscoring the difficulty of understanding social and religious change in the language of missionaries only—even if many converts did nonetheless come to share particular languages and theologies of conversion. As we will see with particular force in the case of the Six Nations, in tense and potentially violent contested spaces, indigenous peoples needed to think through carefully the meanings of relationships in one form or another with Christianity.

My own earlier work on the Khoekhoe on the eastern frontier of the Cape Colony in southern Africa has highlighted for me how complicated the relationship is between coercion and consent in violent societies, and thus how difficult it is to discuss conversion—in theological theory a supreme act of independent choice—as part of a relationship with coercion, violence and colonial power, without being reductive in turn.[6] I began to work on the Haudenosaunee ("people of the longhouse" or Iroquois) in northeastern North America because I was interested in British Christian humanitarian networks in the late eighteenth and early nineteenth centuries and their interaction with the Haudenosaunee, among other indigenous groups. This hardly makes me qualified to discuss Haudenosaunee spirituality in depth over time, but it has nonetheless created an opportunity to observe both parallels and striking differences in uses that different groups attempted to make of Christianity in colonial situations both characterized by violence, militarization, and the incorporation of indigenous men into colonial military structures. Despite important structural differences, not least both the greater degree of power available to North American groups and the major wars between Europeans fought in the region, looking at North America through a comparative lens highlights the potential utility of a more extended analysis of Haudenosaunee spirituality with attention to the interaction between Christianity and military and political pressures.

The Khoekhoe converted in large numbers in a context in which they had previously been excluded from full civic membership on the basis of religious claims and indeed often coerced into slavery in all but name; this entailed in the first instance a military alliance at the turn of the century with the incoming British against the Dutch speakers of the earlier colonial period. However inadvertently, this brought the Khoekhoe, with their relatively limited room to maneuver, into the British army (and eventually towards large-scale disillusion with the British). In a different situation, the Mohawk, like other Six Nations groups, often attempted to negotiate with Christianity without ceding to it, and to play different versions of Christianity off against one another, reflecting their military interaction with competing European powers. At least some among the Anglican Mohawk (Kanienkehaka), key allies of the British during the American Revolution whose ranks numbered more Christians than any other Six Nations group in the Anglophone sphere of influence in the late eighteenth century, used Christianity in part as a way to broker bargains, hoping for an exchange of military loyalty and spiritual alliance for the protection of land.

In both southern Africa and northeastern America the British Empire depended heavily on indigenous soldiers, as did many other European powers and merchant companies that faced one another across the globe.[7] Armies and militia on the one hand, and Christian missions on the other, provided two possible and sometimes overlapping routes for the integration, however reluctant and partial, of indigenous men into colonial structures. In the Cape Colony the Dutch East India Company created a corps of Khoekhoe soldiers that would be inherited by the British and that would serve in every major frontier war on the mobile and contested frontiers of that colony until the soldiers themselves rebelled in 1850. In eighteenth-century North America, the competing French and British empires leaned heavily on their indigenous allies, even though these warriors saw themselves precisely as allies and not as dependent subjects.[8] Well after the final defeat of the French during the Seven Years War (1756–1763), the British sought to use indigenous allies as a bulwark against rebellious white settlers, while American rebels looked for Amerindian support during the revolution.[9]

Relationships between the British military and indigenous soldiers were often very fraught, forged as they were in traumatic and violent circumstances. They shifted in response to the degree of indigenous resistance to the imposition of imperial control. Indeed military allies could morph into armed and well-informed enemies with surprising ease—and a leitmotif of British attitudes to their allies was often fear.[10] It seems a fair generalization nonetheless that Christianity was introduced in uneasily conquered territories with frontiers in flux, at the same time that enormous pressure was placed on indigenous men to serve in some capacity in the British military establishment, or alternatively, from the direction of indigenous societies themselves, to take up arms against the invaders, or, from settlers, to serve in militias and raiding parties, often against other indigenous groups. Christianity and the politics of military alliance were closely linked from the outset.

Like loyalty, conventional Christian practices might be rapidly dropped or transformed in different political circumstances and yet still be meaningful to adherents. Neither "alliance" nor "conversion" was a one-way street: Indigenous peoples often had more flexible views of both than did, say, British missionaries. At the same time, the army also provided a locus of cultural interaction, albeit in very unequal and violent circumstances. Finally, the military context is one of a number of factors helping to explain the deep divides within a number of communities over the costs and benefits of Christianity: Christianity was dangerous, as well as potentially salvific, and its sacred power could destroy as well as save.

THE KHOEKHOE AND THE SAN IN THE
LATE EIGHTEENTH-CENTURY EASTERN CAPE

Formal European ownership claims in what became known as the Cape Colony date to 1652, with the establishment of a refreshment station by the VOC (Dutch East India Company) on land occupied by both hunter-gatherers and by nomadic cattle herders. In 1795 the Dutch East India Company temporarily ceded the Cape to the British in the face of advancing French armies and popular uprisings in the Netherlands. In 1801 the British relinquished the Cape to the newly formed Batavian Republic under the Treaty of Amiens. In turn, the Batavians returned the Cape to Britain in 1806, to be confirmed in 1814 at the end of the Napoleonic Wars.

Nomadic groups on the frontiers of Dutch settlement suffered severely in the Dutch period. Work by some superb scholars, including Richard Elphick, Nigel Penn, and Susan Newton-King, paints a grim picture of competition over labor and resources in the frontiers of settlement in the absence of strong central authority with a will to impose order. Even in the aftermath of conquest, many frontier farmers were physically abusive to their laborers, of whose untrammeled liberty, as Newton-King persuasively argues, they were often afraid, seeing Khoisan laborers as the "enemy within."[11] The Khoekhoe and the San (see below) were not, then, unlike the Six Nations, perceived as crucial military allies. What they had that settlers wanted was land and labor. While the frontier remained open, warfare raged relatively unchecked, and cycles of revenge killings created a climate of violence and fear.

On both the northern and eastern frontiers settlers at various points in the seventeenth and eighteenth centuries waged genocidal warfare against hunter gatherers known collectively as San (although the relationship and overlap between San hunters and Khoekhoe cattle herders is a hotly disputed topic), while also attempting to incorporate people of Khoisan (Khoekhoe and San) descent into frontier society as laborers and sexual partners. Commando raids usually killed men, and sometimes killed women, but often brought back young children and sometimes women to be incorporated into the web of dependents on white farms. There was a trade in children, although its full extent is hard to judge. By the end of the eighteenth century there was a large "mixed" population, largely with white fathers and Khoekhoe and San mothers. Not all of these children were the product of coercion, but the vulnerability of farm women made exploitation a fact of life. A web of local custom, including "apprenticeship" and "vagrancy" legislation, kept Khoisan people tied to white farms. Male dependents often had to serve themselves on commandoes against people defined as "bushmen" (or San), and white farmers were often accompanied by *agterryders*—boys or young men who would ride behind the farmer and carry his gun. Many people of at least partial Khoisan descent left the areas of white settlement to create new settlements beyond colonial frontiers, bringing with them, when they were able, guns and horses and contributing to the considerable regional disruption in the interior. Many white colonists defined themselves as *christemensch* and Africans as heathen. Passage into the white community might take place through the baptismal font: Robert Shell argues convincingly, for example, that mixed-race children could be considered part of the white community if the father were to have them baptized and acknowledge himself as the father.[12] All of these dynamics were further complicated by the fact that the Cape was a slave-holding society, despite the fact that frontier farmers were usually too poor to depend on slaves, and that VOC employees themselves had limited degrees of freedom.

In this context, as I have argued elsewhere, converts struggled to define themselves as the true Christians and used their own versions of Calvinist Christianity to support claims for better treatment. To claim Christianity was in itself a means of claiming status. At the same time, mission stations, especially those of the London Missionary Society, played central material roles in providing areas of refuge, and many Khoisan farm workers left their masters to join mission stations.

An important point of contrast with the Haudenosaunee is that it was a change of imperial masters, linked to warfare and instability in the European state system, that created a context in which Christianity could play this explosive role. On the one hand, more expansive evangelical versions of Christianity were increasingly influential at the Cape even before the end of the VOC overlordship, and the Moravians had resumed mission work among the Khoisan of the western Cape by 1792 (reviving a brief 1737–45 mission).[13] On the other hand, the dynamics of frontier Christianity changed most dramatically with the advent of new players, opening the door for indigenous people to try to play off the local Dutch against the incoming British. From 1799 to 1801 complicated warfare raged in the Eastern Cape among the Xhosa, white settlers, and Khoekhoe (including Khoekhoe dependents who fought with their masters, as well as rebel Khoekhoe who left their masters to join with the Xhosa in their conflict with the aggressively encroaching colony). The British found themselves the targets of attempted allegiances by some Khoekhoe who saw the British trying to subdue rebellious Dutch speakers. It was in this confused and explosive situation that the first stations were founded.

THE KANIENKEHAKA AND THE HAUDENOSAUNEE

If late eighteenth-century settlers in southern Africa often sought to exclude Khoisan peoples in frontier zones from the community of Christians, even as white farmers incorporated Khoisan dependents into their households, late eighteenth-century imperial administrators in northeastern North America struggled in contrast to attract indigenous peoples to their own particular versions of Christianity in the hope of bolstering military and diplomatic alliances with politically independent peoples who still held land. Although clearly there were significant intellectual and cultural differences between these very diverse peoples, profoundly affecting their interactions with Christianity, different colonial situations also created different underlying structures. In particular, the fact that political dynamics in northeastern North America were influenced by the presence of competing empires meant that the relationship claims contingent on "conversion" had a different political—and therefore military—weight for indigenous peoples. Empires had more powerful presences in North America than in eighteenth-century South Africa, and indigenous people therefore had more scope to try to play imperial powers off against one another, or settlers against metropoles, or one denomination against one another. They were not necessarily successful, but a wider range of strategies was nonetheless available. Here I will look briefly at uses of Christianity by the Mohawk, the closest military allies of the British in the late eighteenth century in the region that is now New York state, in order to illustrate the different dynamics in a different colonial situation, with some contrasting examination of Seneca ambivalence in a political context in which alliance seemed less advantageous.

Both the Mohawk and the Seneca were members of the eighteenth-century league known as the Six Nations, which united several nations of the Haudenosaunee. Its center of power lay in what is today known as upper New York State although groups ranged widely across northeastern North America, and there were and are significant Mohawk groups in what is now Quebec. The Mohawk in Quebec, who had moved there in the seventeenth century, became enmeshed in different alliances marked by allegiance to the French, but remained in close contact (despite disputes) with their Six Nations kin. The Six Nations consisted in the late eighteenth century of the Mohawk or Kanienkehaka, Seneca, Tuscarora, Oneida, Onondaga, and Cayuga. This alliance was cemented through family ties, diplomacy and religion. Members shared a common lifestyle based on a mixed economy that involved both agriculture and hunting and gathering. Before and during colonial conquest they relied on extensive hunting grounds in the hinterland of particular settlements; settler colonialism was thus a significant threat to their economic lifestyle and to worldviews and cultural practices that arguably depended at least in part on access to land. Scholars suggest that Iroquoian peoples saw a seamless link between different elements of the spirit and the material world, that they emphasized relationships between the component parts of these worlds, and that they sought through a wide variety of rituals and daily practices to ensure harmony between these component parts, including themselves. Kinship relationships thus played a very important role in the linked diplomatic and spiritual life of Iroquoian peoples. So too did rituals designed to harness and control the sacred power immanent in all things. These included medicine society rituals, such as those carried out by members of the "false face" society, who sought out the causes of illness while wearing sacred masks carved from trees by each healer. Associational culture was, as this suggests, a significant part of Six Nations religious activity. Anthony Wallace distinguishes between "rituals of thanksgiving and hope" and "rituals of fear and mourning," both of which he sees as "cathartic ways of handling existential frustration" in societies that tended to value reticence in other contexts.[14]

From the early seventeenth century onward, Iroquoian peoples had been no exception to the rule that the indigenous peoples of North America needed to navigate among competing European powers—the Dutch, the French, the Spanish and the British—maintaining economic relationships while attempting to preserve political independence.[15] As Jeremy Adelman and Stephen Aron suggest, the Great Lakes region of the northeast might be described as "borderlands," defined in their terms as a region between empires in which indigenous peoples were enabled to work as brokers as long as relative stalemate in European power relations persisted.[16] Adelman and Aron build on Richard

White's concept of a "middle ground," a term White famously uses to describe the Great Lakes region between 1660 and 1815 as a zone of relative indigenous autonomy.[17] Shifting his gaze from the Algonquian peoples who were the main focus of White's work to the more eastern Six Nations of New York and Canada in the 1770s, on the eve of revolution, Alan Taylor prefers to see the land of the Haudenosaunee as "divided ground."[18] By the 1770s, in the aftermath of Pontiac's rebellion, and the Treaty of Fort Stanwix in which the Mohawk controversially allocated large tracts of land occupied by their dependent allies to whites, the region of New York was awash in land-hungry settlers, and some of the remaining territories of the Iroquois were already within the provincial boundaries of white New York.[19]

There were Haudenosaunee peoples on both sides of the frontier between the British and the French, including substantial settlement near Montreal, just as there would be Haudenosaunee peoples on both sides of the eventual Canadian/American frontier. A central theme of the very rich and extensive research on their alliances with imperial powers as well as with each other is the need to survive by playing one imperial power against another.[20] Even the New York Mohawk chose imperial partners with very considerable reluctance in order to serve their own ends and as part of a much longer history of long-distance diplomacy in a mobile world, as well as a more local history of struggles over land. Some did in the end nonetheless forge a relationship with the British that would be memorialized in the concept of a covenant chain.[21] By the late eighteenth century, the two principal remaining Mohawk villages in the New York region, Canajoharie and Tiononderoge, were surrounded by white settlers and compelled to interact both with Albany and the British imperial state, through the figure of the high-living Indian superintendent, Sir William Johnson.

In the meantime, Iroquoian people within the ambit of New France had a long and complicated history of interaction with French colonists, including fur traders, settlers, and Jesuit missionaries, further complicated by extended warfare with other indigenous groups. The seventeenth-century Mohawk experience was marked by conquest by the French, catastrophic death rates from European-introduced diseases (notably smallpox), and wide-ranging warfare in which the Mohawk attempted to replenish their ranks through what Daniel Richter and others describe as "mourning wars," as well as to establish and maintain regional hegemony in rivalry with the French. In mourning wars, communities tried to replace dead members by capturing members of other communities in warfare; captives might be either put to death in order to assuage the grief of mourners, or else incorporated into Haudenasaunee society. Richter claims that with the catastrophic death rates of the early seventeenth century, mourning wars accelerated and became increasingly destructive and dysfunctional, plunging the region into further damaging conflict.[22]

In this maelstrom, it may not be surprising that some were interested in exploring the sources of French power, as Allan Greer suggests, and turned to elements of Catholicism, despite great opposition from others who saw Christianity as a source of danger.[23] A substantial number of Iroquoian people living in what is now the New York region made decisions in the seventeenth century to migrate into the territories of New France, where they established villages that would be missionized by Jesuits and Sulpicians, including Kahnawake, outside what is now Montreal; the lands on which these villages were located were seen by the Haudensosaunee as their own to begin with, however. According to Denis Delâge, the Iroquois had experienced such high death rates and incorporated so many captives that their societies were highly multicultural by this stage; Delâge argues that those who left to form new communities in New France were largely of captive stock, and thus more attracted to the use of new religious beliefs to remake new communities than so-called "old stock" Kanienkehaka, who tended to remain in core Mohawk territory in modern-day New York. Settlement in French territories and the adoption of Catholicism entailed significant pressure on converts to fight with French. Delâge suggests that the French saw military service by these converts as a form of service to the state, while the Mohawk themselves probably saw it as a token of alliance.[24]

Six Nations peoples were thus no strangers to the interaction between diplomacy and cultural practices. The Six Nations were themselves a confederacy maintained by elaborate diplomatic practices in which shared ritual, such as the ceremonies of condolence that opened meetings, played an important symbolic role. Within communities, war captives, or at least their children, had the possibility of becoming Haudenosaunee through adopting Haudenosaunee practices; this was significant in an environment in which (as was the case in southern Africa) power was linked to the capacity to accumulate people. By the late eighteenth century, the Six Nations, by now very small groups compared to the influx of white settlers into the northeast, had long experience as cultural brokers and diplomats in a polyvalent world. It is not surprising that they were conscious of denominational difference, in some cases interested in using Christianity to diplomatic ends and apparently frequently theologically flexible.

CHRISTIANITY AND ALLIANCE: PERSPECTIVES FROM SOUTHERN AFRICA

In the late eighteenth-century and early nineteenth-century Cape Colony, the politics of allegiance worked differently than was the case in the northeastern American borderlands. Rather than competing to attract indigenous peoples to various forms of Christianity, many frontier settlers in fact feared conversion by their dependents. Christianity guarded the frontier between white and heathen status, and between the dominant and the servile. From a very different direction, administrators often worried that the wrong kind of Christianity would produce a rebellious local population. At the same time, men such as Dundas, the governor of the Cape in the 1790s, or Colonel Collins, the author of an 1809 report on the San, clearly thought that correctly-run mission stations (like a well-run regiment) might civilize and pacify unruly Khoekhoe or San populations, and restrain them from waging war on colonists.[25] The politics of using Christianity as a means to interact with the "white" population were thus charged and difficult to navigate for people of Khoisan descent. To claim to be Christian was an important way to claim status and to denigrate in turn the inadequate Christianity of many white settlers. At the same time, Christian subjects of the colony were expected to render military service, and it was anticipated that Christian subjects would not rebel. This was a different power dynamic overall than that experienced in the late eighteenth and early nineteenth centuries by the Six Nations, despite the real parallels between dispossession and land theft, and the use of violence against indigenous peoples by white settlers in both contexts. In ways parallel to North America, however, in spite of the fact that Khoisan military support was certainly less crucial to state policy than was the case in North America, all three of the administrations that ran the Cape from the late eighteenth to early nineteenth centuries pressed the Khoisan to serve as soldiers. In the context of widespread labor coercion, including extensive corvée labor for the white community, the Khoisan had less choice than the Six Nations about whether to cooperate with colonial militaries, and were less able to convert an offer of military allegiance into a bargaining chip. Nonetheless, I would suggest that Khoisan men used Christianity to attempt to broker better relations with the British state—albeit at the cost of military allegiance—both as militia members in highly contested frontier zones and as soldiers in the Cape Corps.

In order to understand Khoekhoe availability to serve as soldiers, it is important to underscore that in the late eighteenth and early nineteenth centuries men were usually already involved in violent interaction in some capacity. Settlers put pressure on their indigenous dependents to provide militia service. Beyond the Cape, trading and raiding groups often competed to survive, often through violent conflict.[26] Newton-King has shown that at least some Dutch-speaking farmers on the colonial frontier used their Khoekhoe dependents, usually bound to farms by complex webs of vagrancy and apprenticeship legislation and the capture of families, as military servants on commando raids against the "Bushmen" (or San), thus incorporating the Khoisan into the operation of colonial militia. In this context Khoisan men witnessed and indeed were probably forced to participate in many atrocities. One young boy, Andries Stoffels, later a fervent Christian convert, attested that these sights greatly affected him in later life.[27] Some farmers called out on commando duty would in fact send their Khoekhoe "servants" instead. During the brutal frontier warfare of 1799 to 1801, most of these "farm servants" deserted their masters and fought for their freedom; those who remained often had to fight against the so-called rebels. There is evidence of internecine warfare on many levels, the damage from which must have run deep.

Settlers committed many atrocities against the Khoisan, of whom they were often afraid, even when they were working as household dependents; a telling parallel is with the kind of violent abuse meted out in slave-holding societies upon the bodies of household slaves. It is critically important to distinguish between the actions of settlers and those of the coerced male dependents of those settlers, whose own families were often held hostage and who were brutally treated themselves. Nonetheless, it still seems significant to an understanding of trauma that some fought on the settler side when atrocities were committed. Many of those who carried out acts of violence would have been captured themselves as young children. Newton-King estimates that about one eighth of so-called "Hottentot" dependents on white farms on the eastern Cape frontier in the late eighteenth century were war captives, almost all of whom would have been women or captured as very young children, since men were almost always killed on commando.[28] This certainly introduces the issue of child soldiers and the psychological costs of this phenomenon. Men who had fought each other, and their families, ended up living together on mission stations and later on the Kat River settlement. Many Khoekhoe-descended men, often with Khoekhoe mothers and white fathers, fanned into the interior of southern Africa if they could flee the conditions of the frontier. Their knowledge of, and access to, guns and horses made them able in their turn to dominate indigenous peoples of the interior, including the Tswana who were subject for a while to Griqua hegemony in the southeast, and the Nama in the southwest. This hegemony was often bolstered by claims to cultural superiority through a knowledge of Christianity, as indeed members of emigrant communities provided a core of regional associate mission workers for the London Missionary Society.

As I have suggested elsewhere, this context of extreme trauma, coercion and violence may have made many Khoekhoe people more receptive to cultural change and to the adoption of Christianity, which appeared to provide an explanation for suffering. Protestant evangelical Christianity, so oriented to sin, suffering, and redemption, very possibly provided an outlet for the expiation of guilt. Be that as it may, the commando system was marked by a resolute refusal on the part of many settlers to admit Khoekhoe people to Christianity: The Khoekhoe were household dependents but they were kept in different status categories, defined among other things by lack of access to Christian baptism. This was different from the later British administrative model, according to which Christianity would facilitate the incorporation of indigenous people into the military, as well as into local militia structures to be used against the Xhosa (as the frontier, and the locus of frontier violence, shifted). In each of the four frontier wars between 1801 and 1853, the colonial state called disproportionately on the Khoekhoe to furnish men for militias, as a proof of the same loyalty on the basis of which Christian converts were claiming equal rights.

In addition to this type of employment of people of Khoekhoe and San descent on commando raids and in militia, there was a regiment based in Cape Town that employed primarily Khoekhoe soldiers, and that also played a key role on frontier warfare. This was first formed in 1781 by the Dutch East India Company (VOC), then in charge of the Cape Colony in the context of its mercantile activities in southern Africa, and south and southeast Asia. The original regiment was limited to so-called "Bastard Hottentots," or people of mixed white and Khoekhoe descent (who continued to be known as "basters" well into the nineteenth century). In 1801 the incoming British administration formed a 735-member corps of Khoekhoe soldiers as a British line regiment, as V. C. Malherbe documents.[29] "The Hottentot is capable of a much greater degree of civilization than is generally imagined, and perhaps converting him into a soldier may be one of the best steps towards it," commented the new governor of the Cape Colony, Lord Macartney, to Henry Dundas in 1799, reflecting the view that military service was a way of creating closer cultural linkages between the "savage" and the "civil" that would also be reflected on northeastern American frontiers.[30]

A telling debate in 1803 between the then-Batavian governor-general Jan Willem Janssens and the head of the London Missionary Society mission, Johannes Theodorus van der Kemp, brought out tensions associated with conversion and military service. During the Batavian interregnum Janssens felt that English missions were subversive of Dutch authority and ordered Van der Kemp and his colleague James Read confined to Cape Town, away from their rural station of Bethelsdorp. Janssens was a military man, who had his eye firmly on military defenses in the context of the ongoing European war; Van der Kemp also had an earlier military background, having served in the army of William of Orange that was opposed to the Batavian Patriots. Before being summoned to Cape Town, Van der Kemp and Read filed complaints that the army was holding conscripted men after the expiration of their terms. Janssens complained in turn that the missionaries were encouraging desertion and insubordinate behavior among soldiers in the corps. He further contended that the Hottentots were treated like European soldiers and could not expect special privileges. He could not discharge soldiers even if their terms had expired, while Holland and its colonies were still at war, noting that "a great number of European soldiers are in those circumstances and not a one attains his discharge." Janssens urged Van der Kemp instead to teach obedience to Khoekhoe soldiers according to Christian dictates. Some Christians were in fact better soldiers than their fellows and forged better relationships with their white officers: "I have had the honor to mention by a former opportunity to your reverends, that the Men from Bethelsdorp conducted themselves particularly well, the officers confided more in them, as there were some among them who appeared to have made some advance in their religious instruction, and gave many outward evidence thereof." Nonetheless, more recently these very men had become "ringleaders" to "mislead others to disorder"; furthermore, "in practicing their irregularity, in the obstinate perseverance in the same, they called out the name of Mr. Vanderkemp not in the way of lamentation, but in the tone of provocation," according to Janssens.[31] This short vignette underscores official uncertainty about whether Christianity made men better soldiers; at the same time, it hints at ways in which converts were enabled to be more defiant, under very difficult circumstances.

At first the British imperial administration at the Cape Colony, re-taken from the Dutch in 1806 and ratified in 1814 at the Treaty of Amiens, was similarly wary of the evangelical Christianity preached by the mostly working-class and nonconformist envoys of the London Missionary Society and tried to restrict missionary activity.[32] Over time, however, as the society grew more respectable and Christianity was increasingly used as a justification for colonial expansion, administrations generally shifted to seeing Christianization as a less ambiguous precursor to military loyalty. This sometimes meant that missionaries had to fight against being viewed by the colonial state as military recruiters for fear of community resistance. In 1814, for example, William Anderson, the LMS missionary to the Griqua (groups of mixed but dominantly Khoekhoe ancestry, many of whose members had fled the formal bounds of the Cape Colony) was ordered by the Cape administration to deliver a quota of soldiers to the Cape Regiment from his mission of Griquatown. The Griqua were furious and many abandoned the mission. A large number explicitly rejected missionary governance at Griquatown and trekked to found a new trading and raiding community on the Harts River, many declaring that they had "given up all religious worship" or even testifying to their "aversion" to Christianity.[33] At the same time, by at least the 1830s, Christianized Griqua had developed their own militia system and defined citizenship (or *burger* status) in part by the obligation to provide militia service.[34] Control over conscription, linked to Christian status, thus became a focal point for political struggles.

The Cape regiment was not, however, the most onerous of the demands of the colonial state upon Khoekhoe men. After 1828, under Acting Governor Bourke, the state shifted to a policy of putative legal equality between "white" and "Hottentot" with the passage of Ordinance 50. This created equality under the law for free people at the Cape, among other things abolishing the obligation for "Hottentots" to carry passes. The government also opened land for Khoekhoe settlement in the Kat River valley (claimed by the Gonaqua Khoekhoe but more recently captured from the insurgent Xhosa under Maqomo). In exchange for land, the Khoekhoe were to act as buffers between the white colony and the Xhosa. The settlement was indeed burnt three times during subsequent frontier wars, and the inhabitants lost a great deal of property. First to be called out and last to be allowed to return home, Khoekhoe men served the Cape Colony during the bitter wars of 1834–35 and 1846 at considerable personal and community cost.

THE POLITICS OF CHRISTIAN ALLEGIANCE IN THE NORTHEASTERN BORDERLANDS

In northeastern North America, a number of eighteenth-century imperial administrators also assumed that a shared religion would strengthen white-native alliances. This view was echoed, albeit far more warily,

by both indigenous opponents and proponents of some form of coop-
eration with imperial power. The Mohawk whose lands bordered and
overlapped with the lands of New York provide a particularly significant case study as they were closely associated with the policy of the
"covenant chain," for the most part maintaining (despite deep internal
controversy) a military alliance with the British during the late eighteenth century.[35] Complex local politics favored the emergence of anglophile leaders who were able to exploit relations with British Indian
superintendent Sir William Johnson to present themselves as intercul-
tural brokers and thus carve out new spheres of influence. Hendriks,
who visited Britain in 1710 posing as a sachem as part of a visit of four
"Indian kings" and Joseph Brant, brother of Johnson's mistress, a visitor to Britain in 1776 and in 1786, and a military ally of the British during the American revolution in the hope of protecting Mohawk lands,
both managed to play this role. Both adroitly deployed the idioms of
both Mohawk and white diplomacy, including the exchange of cultural forms such as clothing.[36] For Brant, adherence to Anglicanism was
among other things a way of brokering a relationship with the imperial
metropole over the heads of local settlers with whom inhabitants of two
key Mohawk villages were both in intimate daily contact and yet also at
odds over land. The evidence also suggests, however, that community
adherence to Christianity ran deeper than a straight materialist account
would suggest.

Daniel Richter's important work on late seventeenth- and early eighteenth-century Protestant missionary work among the Mohawk Iroquois of the upper New York region argues that they were conscious
of, and wary about, the political implications of Christianity. Those who
remained in New York had rejected the move to Canada to follow the
Jesuits. They were in this early period interested in the power of Christianity, and responsive to some elements of Christian experience, but
they were, with justification, cautious about handing power to missionaries or to the imperial administrators with whom missionaries were
in contact.

The first person to seek for Protestant Mohawk converts, almost 75
years after initial trading contacts between the Dutch and the Mohawk,
was Dutch Reformed minister Godfridius Dellius from Albany. Dellius
claimed 200 converts but saw his mission collapse in 1699 when it was
revealed that he had been defrauding converts into ceding him land.
Local ministers Johannes Lydius (Dellius' replacement) and Bernardus
Freeman continued to preach occasionally to the Mohawk until Lydius'
death in 1710. Many Mohawk had themselves baptized. Nonetheless,
when in 1712 the Anglican SPG sent William Andrews to the village

of Tiononderoge (next to Fort Hunter), he would last only seven years before the SPG abandoned the mission, claiming that despite baptisms the approximately 360 residents of the village were heathens, "and Heathens they will still be."[37]

Despite the SPG's conviction that the mission was a failure, Richter contends that the Mohawk Protestants were demanding that it exist on their terms, rather than rejecting it outright. They were interested in Christianity because it resonated with their own conviction that the world was filled with spiritual power. Like many Khoekhoe, the Mohawk seem to have seen Christian missionaries as figures of power with whom alliances could be advantageous, if properly managed.[38] As Richter eloquently put it:

> Alliances that unified individuals, king groups, villages and nations increased the spiritual power of all concerned; conversely, actions that divided people weakened them. To the extent, then, that links to a Protestant missionary and his religious practices strengthened ties to the English of New York and elsewhere, they increased Mohawk spiritual—and temporal—power. To the extent a missionary brought disunity to Iroquois villages, however, he produced opposite results.[39]

Other Six Nations villages besides Tiononderoge refused to listen to missionaries or even allow them to visit, while even the Tiononderoge Mohawk preferred that Andrews stay in the Fort and not come to the village, and they refused to force their children to go to school. They did not express guilt and repentance in the sense expected by evangelicals, but they did want a minister to carry out life-stage rituals. The Tiononderoge Mohawk did not see Christianity as exclusive, and most continued to carry out a variety of "Iroquois" practices, such as consultation with shamans. Although Andrews felt that they were not Christians, when SPG missionaries returned to the area in the late 1720s they discovered a core of fifty-odd Mohawk who were instructed in Christianity and they found that most people had had themselves and their children baptized.[40] Lay readers played an important role in maintaining an independent Mohawk Christianity. In 1746, for example, after SPG missionary Barclay was transferred to New York, he arranged for the society to pay Mohawk readers to read prayers on Sundays.[41]

While it is clear that Anglicanism among the Mohawk was maintained internally throughout the eighteenth century, it is unclear from the existing record whether the majority adhered to Christianity and what that Christianity looked like. Nor is it possible to recapture easily the oral ways in which Christianity was transmitted, and transformed. Throughout the eighteenth century, the Mohawk nonetheless cultivated a *public* allegiance to Anglicanism, symbolized by the preservation of sacred objects, as well as by Bible translations. This public allegiance had important political implications.

In 1710, a group of four men claiming to be "Indian kings" visited London and were received by Queen Anne. It is unclear what the status of these men really was; as Eric Hinderaker argues, they appear to have been posing as sachems, with the support of local agent Peter Schuyler and an anglophile Mohawk faction, in order to nudge the British and some of the Mohawk themselves into a closer relationship.[42] They were nonetheless indubitably successful in cementing a linked military and religious alliance. The New England Society for the Propagation of the Gospel agreed to send a missionary, while Queen Anne donated silver communion vessels to the community. The silverware may well have been taken by those members of the Six Nations who wanted some form of relationship with the British as both seal and symbol of a verbal agreement, consonant with the exchange of wampum belts in order to confirm and commemorate agreements between different parties. This was also in line with the exchange of gifts that typically sealed diplomatic alliances. As Alan Taylor argues, the eighteenth-century Haudenosaunee almost certainly put more stock in verbal agreements than in written documents. The material objects that marked such exchanges would have had particular political value—perhaps especially objects such as communion vessels that were used to enact ceremonies on a regular cyclical basis. Certainly, Queen Anne's silverware was valuable to the Mohawk. As the American Anglican minister Reverend Pilkin commented in 1878 (also of course reflecting Anglican myth-making), "[T]hey have today the large solid silver communion service given them by Queen Ann [sic] which they carried with them together with their church bell and church furniture across the wilderness to their new home."[43] After being buried before the trek and then carried to Canada the communion vessels were split in 1788 between those establishing a new settlement at Grand River under Joseph Brant's leadership and those moving to Tyendinaga, and are still kept in churches in these respective settlements.[44] Communion vessels might have had particular weight as guarantors of land, the key issue for the Mohawk in the wars of the eighteenth century,

Snatches of stories about church bells suggest that the church bell was another important symbol of identity and by extension that Christianity was valuable to the eighteenth-century Mohawk. William Johnson had an Anglican church constructed at the Mohawk settlement of Canajoharie in 1769, in the hope of consolidating relations with his closest indigenous allies; it is telling that his earlier construction effort at the village had been a fort. Confusing stories circulate about this bell.

It was the subject of a story told by W. L. Greene, a descendant of the white family that moved onto Upper Castle land after the expulsion of the Kanienkeha. Greene informed historian Lyman Draper of the local story that soon after the settlement of the place by "the Dutch" (by which he may have meant Germans), the "Indians came one night to steal the bell," making off with it suspended on a rail. They forgot to remove the clapper, however, and were betrayed by the ringing of the bell which "aroused the sturdy Dutchmen from their sleep," and obliged the Mohawk to drop the bell into the Mohawk River "at the fording place now called 'Christie's reef.'"[45] Nathaniel Benton told a similar story in 1856 in his *History of Herkimer County*. He more convincingly placed the attack on the bell, however, during the American Revolution, claiming that the bell was "highly regarded by the Indians" and they took it in the night and hid it from the "German population in the neighborhood," only to be betrayed once again by the sound of an unattached clapper.

Another story about a stolen bell is discussed by Taaiaike Alfred in the collection *Captive Histories*.[46] A New York white woman, Mrs. E. A. Smith, collected a story from Kahnawake in 1882 recounting that the Mohawk participated in a famous French-Indian raid of the Massachusetts settlement of Deerfield in 1704 (at which some fifty settlers were killed) in order to get back a bell that rightfully belonged to Kahnawake, this time from English settlers; the bell in this story had been commissioned by the Jesuits for the church at Kahnawake and was desired by the Catholic Mohawk. Mrs. Smith's friend "Alexandre" said the story was unlikely. Instead Alexandre confided that the *true* story about the bell currently in the church was that it had been given by King George IV to a delegation of Mohawk chiefs from Kahnawake including Alexandre's father: "[T]he visitors were very kindly received and when leaving were requested to name some present they would like to take home as a keepsakes, one chose a large violin, another a big brass kettle for maple sugar, and my father suggested that we needed a new church bell." Once again, the bell functioned as a sign of alliance.[47] In all these stories and memories, the bell served a mnemonic function beyond its utilitarian role as time keeper and marker of divine service.

From an imperial and settler perspective, competition for Mohawk religious allegiance was long-standing in the region well before the revolution. Jonathan Edwards, the important nonconformist divine, left an interesting description of efforts by Albany settlers to coax a large group of Mohawk to move back to a largely Mahican praying town, Stockbridge, in order to be instructed in the Christian faith and to send their children to school, after having decamped in the face of military conflict and financial scandal. Edwards describes a full council meeting on the topic in 1757 (in keeping with Six Nations diplomatic convention) in the midst of the Seven Years War. The Mohawk spokesman informed the Albany representatives that they "put these honourable gentlemen in mind, how the English had failed of those things that they had encouraged them with the hopes of heretofore; and they desired that now nothing might be said but what should stand, and be made good ..."[48] The Church of England, which was, in Edwards' words, "very jealous of the Mohawks, being very opposite to their coming hither," made Abraham, a leader in the movement to align with Stockbridge, a reader in the church and gave him a salary of five pounds a year. Abraham took the position and the salary. Edwards nonetheless reported that Abraham claimed to officiate among his people while exhorting them to go to Stockbridge for instruction. He supposedly said

> that there they live in darkness, but here is light; that he knows but very little, and can teach them but little, but that there are those that can give them vastly greater degrees of knowledge. And on this account he suffers a sort of persecution from some opposers among his people who ridicule his zeal, and oppose the Indians coming hither, and tell him and others that the English will fail and disappoint them.[49]

Religious allegiance was clearly a form of social, and potentially of political, allegiance. It is also clear that men like Abraham sought to play one religious group off against another, just as the Six Nations struggled on the wider stage to play one European nation off against another. The wider context, however, is that during the Seven Years War, Mohawk warriors ultimately fought against one another on the side of the French and the British with tragic effects; the battle of Lake George saw particularly devastating blows to an already shrinking base of Mohawk warriors. The longstanding, if internally controversial, alliance of the Mohawk with the British ultimately also bore bitter fruit in the aftermath of the American Revolution. After the brutal struggles ignited in New York by the revolution, the American patriots expelled many of the Mohawk from their lands in modern-day New York State. The exile to Canada left behind the remnants of destroyed houses, burnt fields, and the ruins of an Anglican mission station. "There is still standing at the mouth of the Scholarie Creek," wrote the former rector of St. Peter's Church, Albany, Thomas Pilkin, "a strongly built stone house that is all that remains of the *Fort Hunter*. It was the residence of the Chaplain and the Center of a great missionary work. When erected it was on the frontier and looked out on the unbroken wilderness that stretched as far as the St. Lawrence."[50] Looking back to the Seven Years War, Pilkin was typical in making a link between religious and military alliance. "In that house," he continued, "many a scheme was planned by Sir William Johnson and others in our struggle with the French for the possession of New York. I believe that the *Fort Hunter* mission, which was wonderfully successful so that at one time there was not an unbaptised person, man, woman or child among the Mohawks had more to do than any other thing in defeating the French."[51]

This was very much a British perspective, not a Mohawk one. It illustrates, nonetheless, the mingling of religious and military objectives in the minds of many white administrators and settlers by the end of the eighteenth century. Indian superintendent Sir William Johnson provides a prime example. The largest landowner in New York at his death in 1774 and a substantial slave-holder, Johnson performed a delicate balancing act in cultivating allegiances with the Mohawk, whom he saw as key to the Six Nations confederacy, from whose lands he himself benefited, and from whose ranks came his principal sexual partner, Koñwatsiãtsiaiéñni, also known as Mary or Molly Brant (and largely commemorated today under the latter name).[52] Johnson was the scion of a Catholic family in Ireland. Nonetheless, he used Anglicanism to set himself up as a major landowner and source of patriarchal authority. Although he sent a number of young Six Nations men to be educated by the nonconformist Dr. Wheelock (founder of what would eventually become Dartmouth College), he withdrew his particular protégé Joseph Brant (or Thayendanegea), Mary's brother, in order to ensure that he ended up an Anglican.[53] Despite not following Christian orthodoxy in his private life, Johnson sponsored church building and acted as local patron of the Anglican church among the Six Nations. In the turbulent run-up to revolution in 1771, for example, Johnson attempted to prevent Oneida Christians from petitioning Boston ministers for a church and urged them to apply to the King instead (meaning that they would have become Anglican rather than nonconformist). According to the young Presbyterian missionary Samuel Kirkland's second-hand (and doubtless biased) report of an account given by Oneida headmen, Johnson tried to convince them "that these Boston people are a seditious & Rebellious people, great enemies in government. That they killed their king [meaning Charles I] & then were obliged to flee for their lives ... That the King's Ministers were not so rigid as these New England Ministers. That they would baptize all Children & grown people too without asking so many questions &c &c ..."[54] In 1771, then, Johnson was still trying to appeal to the desire of a Six Nations group for some access to Christianity but in a form that would maximize local control.

For many British people, in contrast, Anglicanism implied fealty to the British state; it was certainly resisted by white settlers in Johnson's ambit on that basis. It is difficult to know what being an Anglican meant to an official such as Johnson but it was doubtless tied to the maintenance of hierarchy. In the context of the Mohawk Valley, Anglicanism was the religion of the elite; here, as elsewhere in the northeast, nonconformist resentment of elite Anglican control played a significant role in revolutionary politics. Adherence to Anglicanism was traditionally identified by British conservatives with loyalty to the British constitution. Daniel Claus, Johnson's German-born son-in-law and deputy agent to the Iroquois in Canada (after Johnson's 1774 death and the outbreak of revolution), was entirely typical in lamenting in 1782 the weakened position of the Anglican church in Quebec after the post-revolution influx of loyalists, forced as the church was to give way to "dissenters and papists." Deploying typical High Church language, Claus looked for God's deliverance of His "trusty militant church" from both internal and external enemies.[55] Claus also complained angrily to the Society for Propagation of the Gospel in 1782 that English fur traders from Québec took a Catholic missionary and a Catholic "Indian Mass book" with them to promote the fur trade: Anglicanism, rather than any other form of Christianity, must be promoted among indigenous peoples.[56]

For their part, late eighteenth-century Mohawk Christians continued to maintain Christianity on their own terms and seemingly to prefer a hands-off approach by missionaries. Thus in 1775, at a difficult and extended meeting between Six Nations and American representatives, Mohawk sachem Abraham, speaking for the Six Nations, appealed to the rebels not to send away SPG minister John Stuart. While his arguments (in that charged context) were designed to show that Stuart was not a political menace to the patriots, they probably also reflected Mohawk views of the role of a missionary:

> We would likewise mention our father the minister who resides among the Mohawks, and was sent to them by the King. He does not meddle in civil affairs, but instructs them in the way to Heaven. He absolutely refuses to attend to any political matters, and says they do not belong to him [...] It would occasion great disturbance was he to be taken away. The King sent him to them, and they would look upon it as taking away one of their own body.[57]

The Mohawk maintained an interest in liturgy, ritual, and sacred text: these were elements of the sacred power of Christianity that did not always require mediation by white priests, arguably provided a route to salvation without behavioral control, and could potentially co-exist with other forms of access to sacred power. During the American Revolution, for example, refugee Mohawk, compelled to flee to Canadian territory after their expulsion from their territories in New York, requested a missionary from the Society for the Propagation of the Gospel to replace Stuart, who was after all held prisoner by the Americans; according to Daniel Claus, they wanted a minister to serve their needs by baptizing children and performing marriages and funerals. This was, however, only an occasional need, and these ceremonies could be clustered together. Although they needed an ordained person to carry out certain sacraments, Claus' letter indicates that the Mohawk had clearly been maintaining Anglican practice and religious education on their own initiative, and that two Mohawk men had been running a school in New York.

Translating sacred texts into Mohawk was an important component of this approach. Indeed, both white and Mohawk family members of the Johnson-Brant faction used the translation of Christian texts into Mohawk as a way to consolidate their own power, as well as to shore up an independent Christianity among the Mohawk. In 1780, when the bulk of the New York Mohawk were already refugees, Claus wrote a primer for teaching in the Mohawk language, as well as dispatching Mohawk-language prayer books to refugees.[58] The primer is revealing, suggesting a Christianity that required linkage to the Anglo-American world of text, but which could be maintained independently by a convert community. This mirrors, in my opinion, the efforts of the Brant faction to remain militarily allied but politically independent.

The primer consisted of word lists in English and Mohawk.[59] It also included several catechisms and prayers that would have helped Mohawk instructors work with children under their care. The first catechism, "A Short Scripture Catechism for Children, which will serve to explain to them many Principal Persons contained in the Scriptures," listed notable characters of the Bible in a way that stressed stories rather than theology ("Q. Who was NEBUCHADNEZAR? A. The proud King of Babylon, who run [sic] mad and was driven among the Beasts, lived with them and eat [sic] Grass, and grew hairy all over his Body").[60] The traditional Church of England catechism for children followed. Reflecting Anglican theology, the catechism emphasized the sacraments, opening with questions about baptism and the role of godparents:

Question: What is your Name?
Answer: N. or M.
Question: Who gave you this Name?
Answer: My Godfathers and Godmothers in my Baptism; wherein I was made a member of Christ, the child of God, and an inheritor of the kingdom of Heaven.[61]

Perhaps it is not surprising that so many Mohawk sought baptism for their children and that the role of godparent was an important one. The primer also included a very lengthy "morning prayer for the Master and Scholars" in Mohawk and a similar evening prayer service, both of which would have enabled the schoolmaster to function in the role of priest. Mohawk chief Kanonraron (Aaron Hill) wrote to Claus in 1782 that his translation was invaluable, implying, in fact, that without such texts it was difficult to keep people from straying. "Brother, we render you our highest Thanks and most heartily salute you as many of us are Christians & proselytes, it is entirely owing to you that Christianity is upheld amongst us," wrote Hill. "[T]he Good Spirit from above must have inspired you to compose the little Books of Instruction, we are now all supplied with new Books, was it not for [your?] being alive, we should be miserable, as we know of no person whatsoever in the Indian Service able to undertake the Task."[62]

Key British ally Joseph Brant not only translated the Gospel of St. Mark but also many prayers and rites of worship. The 1787 gospel translation was prepared under the patronage of George III while Brant was in the UK for a second visit in 1785–6, and the volume was expensively and attractively bound. The frontispiece showed the interior of a chapel with portraits of the king and queen and two bishops, as well as Six Nations figures receiving the Bible. Many years later, Brant's daughter Elizabeth would in her turn translate parts of the Bible into English; these too were presented to the monarch, in this case Queen Victoria. For his part, Joseph's protégé and adoptive nephew John Norton translated the Gospel of St. John into Mohawk for the British and Foreign Bible Society, an event memorialized in a window in the 1843 chapel built by the Mohawk community at the Bay of Quinte.

This does not mean that all members of the community adopted Christianity but more minimally that the public symbolism was important to community leaders. This is particularly clear in the case of Joseph Brant, whose allegiances were carefully considered and performed, and whose family links with an Anglican elite predisposed him to both Anglicanism and freemasonry. Once the revolutionary war broke out, a persistent allegiance to Anglicanism reflected Brant's military stance. He clearly presented himself as a Christian in London in 1776. James Boswell, for example, wrote a short account of Brant's visit in which he described Brant as an exemplar of the rise of the Mohawk to Christianity and civilization, in contrast to the "wild" chiefs who had visited in 1710.[63] Brant was also a Freemason, having received Masonic degrees during this 1776 voyage—both a token of allegiance to the Johnson family and a means of access to a shared military culture.[64]

I think it is possible that for many among the late eighteenth-century Six Nations, certain practices might be adopted in part as a form of alliance, possibly with political connotations, but these adaptations were not a final "conversion," even though they were certainly not meaningless. Nor were different customs mutually exclusive, despite the claims of Christian denominations to possess final versions of truth. Members of the British military in fact sometimes had a similarly flexible and politically-informed view of custom. Arnaud Balvay argues that in New France, French soldiers often acquired "native" tattoos, while at the same time baptismal records reveal Mohawk soldiers receiving baptism, often with white fellow soldiers as sponsors. Balvay speculates that these habits may have been cultural symbols of alliance, creating, in the case of baptism, important pseudo-kin linkages.[65] There were many white "rangers" who fought with Brant, or with other indigenous warriors, in the revolutionary wars and followed him as their leader; they adopted Indian dress and war cries.[66] So too did many in the British army more widely during the Seven Years War.[67] Custom marked identity but was not immutable, and the sharing of cultural markers might shore up a warrior culture.

As for Brant, he spent a great deal of effort before and after the war tending his reputation in increasingly difficult circumstances. His biographers convey the sense that he grew increasingly angry and disillusioned by the end of his life. Indeed, the Anglican bishop John Strachan suggested in 1819 that John Stuart had told him that Brant had lost his originally sincere faith in Britain back in the 1770s, but the truth of this is difficult to know.[68]

What this brief account of the Mohawk does not capture is intellectual debate about Christianity and the meaning of conversion or indeed negotiation among different meaning systems. This is clearly a very rich field; the charged political context surely lent an edge to internal debates. For example, a sense of intense contestation emerges from the diaries of Samuel Kirkland, an important Presbyterian missionary who tried to establish a mission to the Seneca in the mid 1760s with little success, and then worked among the more receptive Oneida, whom he worked to dissuade from joining the British during the American Revolution.

A couple of examples of self-conscious reflections on Christianity and power will have to suffice. In 1772 the Oneida themselves pronounced in favor of the greater community autonomy afforded, in their opinion, by Anglicanism and Catholicism. According to an orator speaking to Kirkland for sachems and warriors of the towns of old Onoide and Kanonwaroharie, a sacramental approach to Christianity, including baptism, was preferable:

Our Minds are filled with anxiety & concern. The Reason is this: you white ppl. tell us two different Commands [of] God, as tho' God had two minds. Indeed, to speak plainly as things appear to us, the Gospel [of] God, or Jesus Good News has become two, & those widely differg [from] each other. *One*, we formerly heard by our first teachers, we mean the Ministers that were sent & came among us. Their Voices all agreed as one, although some [of] them came [from] ano[ther] quarter, Viz, Canada, who were [of] a different language, yet both taught the same thing, at least they were so near alike that in our opinion they were one, & we think that we may with propriety & justice call them *one & the same thing*. But you Fa[ther] hv come to us with a new Commd [of] God, altoe[ther] new, ano[ther] Gospel.[69]

Tagawaron continued (at least in Kirkland's rendition) that "our first Ministers" (by which he meant both Jesuits and Anglicans) were "very fond" of baptizing children as desired, teaching that delay was dangerous. Similarly, if any adult wished to become a Christian and "be made holy," then "he must look out a Man" from among the people, "to give him a N[ame], learn the Lords prayer, creed, & 10 Comd & confess [his] Sins & then he was baptized without any objections, & a bottle or two [of] Rum given by the God-father to drink [his] health." In contrast, Kirkland refused to baptize many children and shut up the "way to Heavn" or made it "narrow." Indeed, some had been frightened from an initial resolve to seek baptism by the long and severe examination that Kirkland required and had returned to their "old practices." The community preferred a more open route to God: "We don't think that your way is wrong, nor do we say the old way is wrong, but both right. However we hv chosen the old."[69] Like the Mohawk, these village elders appear to have been seeking a version of Christianity that was under their own control, a critical strategy in the complex world of the borderlands.

Among the Seneca, Kirkland encountered more explicit rejections of the political implications of Christianity. In council debate in 1765 among men (women's councils would have surely contributed as well in less recoverable ways), one of the strongest opponents of the missionary, "Captain Onoonghwandekha," described how the recent death of a villager with whom Kirkland had lodged delivered a warning. The "white people's book," he said, was "never made for Indians. Our great Superintendent Thaonghyawagon, [i.e.,] Upholder of the Skies gave us a book. He wrote it in our heads and in our minds and gave us rules about worshipping him. ..." He continued that if the Seneca were to accept the book they would become "a miserable abject people" who would no longer be warriors. "How many remnants of tribes to the East are so reduced, that they pound sticks to make brooms, to buy a loaf of Bread or it may be a shirt," he said. "The warriors, which they boasted of, before these foreigners, the white people, crossed the great Lake, where are they now? Why their grandsons are all become *mere women*."[70] This was a significant epistemological debate that involved competing views of causation and that doubtless influenced ways of thinking about Christianity. Overall, however, military and colonial context surely exacerbated a parallel intellectual move to the alliance politics I have been examining above, namely the development of the idea of different customs and beliefs attached to the bodies of particular peoples.

DISILLUSIONMENT AND THE REINVENTION OF CHRISTIANITY

In southern Africa, many Khockhoe converts became disillusioned with the British, who were not perceived as having kept their end of colonial bargains. In "Mlanjeni's war" of 1850, the formerly loyal troops turned against their colonial masters. The Khockhoe rebellion against the colony began with a mutiny by Khoekhoe troops in the Cape Corps, spearheaded by the most overtly Christian. Indeed, early plans for mutiny were discussed under the cover of prayer meetings, suggesting among other things the power of alternate associational cultures in providing possibilities for resistance. A millenarian version of Christianity was espoused by many rebels, as prophecy was turned to the ends of liberation.[71]

The Khoekhoe rebellion sharpened for many administrators and settlers a fear of the Christianized soldier that was part of a widespread reaction against the claims to equality of Christian indigenous people in British settler colonies. In the midst of the 1850–53 frontier war, the lieutenant-governor of the Cape Colony, George Cathcart, reflected that the Khoekhoe were more dangerous enemies than the Xhosa: "These are much more mischevious and dangerous from their far superior progress in civilization, natural intelligence, and their skill in horsemanship, and the use of arms; and they are headed by very able leaders."[72] Christianity had become a source of danger, not necessarily a sign of alliance; it was also clearly out of both settler and missionary hands.

This is not the place to re-tell the story of the Khoekhoe rebellion of 1850–53. What I do want to do, however, is to throw into relief the parallel processes of debate, disillusionment, and willingness to use a variety of sources of spiritual power among the Six Nations at the turn of the century, many of which were also by this stage disillusioned allies as the military situation shifted and colonial states no longer required indigenous support. Many among the Six Nations experienced a need to reconstruct their traditions and identity in the face of profound colonial challenges, as the full extent of land losses and loss of power became clear in the wake of the consolidation of white boundaries and the continuing influx of white settlers. Prophetic teachings were one response, as was the drive to unite scattered groups.[73] On the wider Amerindian stage, the best-known pan-Indian leader was the part Shawnee, part Creek Tecumseh whose half-brother Tenskwatawa mobilized prophecy to the ends of the movement. One striking feature of such debates was the conceptualization of religion as a form of ethnically-specific tradition, coupled, however, with a broadening of ethnicity to include a widening circle of people of native descent. As was the case of Christianity in southern Africa, prophetic visions had the ability to recreate, or even to create, unity and to assist a reconceptualization of the people that could work on both political and spiritual levels.

Towards the end of the American Revolution, American troops drove the Haudenosaunee from their lands in New York. At the treaty negotiations, the British betrayed their Six Nations allies and allowed the Americans to keep Six Nations territories (the loyalist Six Nations received less extensive lands at Grand River and the Bay of Quinte of Upper Canada in return). At the turn of the eighteenth century, as the physical conditions of the Haudenosaunee worsened and as more and more lands were lost to whites, the Seneca prophet Handsome Lake died, was revived, and spoke a vision he had received while dead (or so it was subsequently told). As did many in similar colonial situations, he called for the purification of the people, through an end to witchcraft and sexual immorality, as well as a renewal of faith and purpose. I am not sufficiently knowledgeable to comment on this complicated and vibrant ongoing tradition. I do want to make the more focused suggestion, however, that Handsome Lake's preaching after his visions, repeated annually by his adherents, articulates a sense of parallel white and native religious traditions that would also become apparent in South Africa in the context of bitter political struggles. Handsome Lake called for a renewal of Six Nations spirituality in the face of serious challenges to the community and what he saw as internal decay.

Arthur C. Parker, the Seneca archaeologist who was the amanuensis of the written version of the Code of Handsome Lake dating from 1913, recorded Sosondowa (Edward Cornplanter), who was taught the words and tradition by Henry Stevens, who had been taught by Blacksnake, who had been taught by Handsome Lake (Ganiodaiio). According to Sosondowa (probably in the translation of the Six Nations Baptist lay preacher William Bluesky), "Now this happened a long time ago and across the great salt sea, odji'ke?da:gi'ga, that stretches east. There is, so it seems, a world there and soil like ours" where so many people swarmed that "they crowded upon one another and had no place for hunting." Among the great queen's servants was "a young preacher of the queen's religion, so it is said." The "great queen" asked the preacher to "clean some old volumes which she had concealed in a hidden chest. So he obeyed and when he had cleaned the last book, which was at the bottom of the chest, he opened it and looked about and listened, for truly he had no right to read the book and wanted no one to detect him. He read. It was a great book and told him many things which he never knew before. Therefore he was greatly worried. He read of a great man who had been a prophet and the son of the Great Ruler. He had been born on the earth and the white men to whom he preached killed him. ..."[74]

After telling a version of the story of Jesus, the account continues that the young preacher became worried when he realized that his God "was not on the earth to see" and felt he had been deceived by his teachers. His teachers told him to seek for God on the earth, but instead he found Hanisse'ono, the evil one, disguised as a great lord in a castle of gold, and the preacher took him to be God. According to the account, the evil one said to him, "'Across the ocean that lies toward the sunset is another world and a great country and a people whom you have never seen. Those people are virtuous, they have no unnatural evil habits and they are honest. A great reward is yours if you will help me. Here are five things that men and women enjoy; take them to these people and make them as white men are. Then shall you be rich and powerful and you may become the chief of all great preachers here.'" The gifts were a "flask of rum, a pack of playing cards, a handful of coins, a violin and a decayed leg bone." When they were given to the people of America by the whites, the gifts made them trade their land for baubles and become immoral and impoverished. To rescue them from their misery the Creator sent Gaiwiio, the word.

This version of a foundation myth, it seems to me, contextualizes Christianity as the religion of the Queen and calls for a revival of Haudenosaunee tradition but it does not see the two as mutually exclusive. It calls for new religious forms to respond to colonialism rather than Christianity. It also suggests that an evil form of religion was responsible for colonial degradation, and that a right version might overcome it. At the same time, the vision of Handsome Lake hints that the very process of colonialism nurtured a sense of cultural relativism and of the possibility of mutually compatible but parallel religious traditions. In some ways, colonialism fostered theological flexibility, rather than the dualism of the classic conversion narrative.

CONCLUSIONS

This brief survey suggests that it is helpful, if difficult, to think about coercion in a broad sense, without creating reductionist or simplistically materialist accounts. For example, context compelled awareness among potential converts of the implications of different *kinds* of Christianity, and a desire to negotiate among them, not least because different colonial powers were often associated with different forms of Christianity. Violence also created a need for people (especially converts) to control Christianity—perhaps through distancing, the selective use of its techniques, or through the choice of one interpretation over another. The material context, in other words, had emotional and intellectual implications.

The experiences of the Khoekhoe, Mohawk, and Seneca were not atypical. If missionaries rapidly accompanied (and preceded) the expansion of imperial frontiers, imperial activity in this period was at the same time characteristically accompanied by relatively chaotic open frontier zones of military struggle, power imbalance, and cultural exchange. Material opportunities for indigenous people through the route of traditional economies usually worsened, even if new imperial economies provided economic opportunities such as soldiering. Despite great variations in degrees of indigenous freedom and negotiating power, ranging from Brant's family alliances to the coercion applied to Khoisan captives, partially Christianized communities were still subject to enormous pressure to fight with imperial armies. Communities tried to use the politics of Christianity to their own ends, among other things in order to negotiate in difficult situations: the Mohawk to obtain respect and to protect land in working through the politics of alliance, the Khoekhoe in order to present themselves as equal in worth (or superior) to whites and as entitled to freedom. Many people of Khoekhoe descent also took both colonial military techniques and Christian identity claims beyond white colonial territory as they carved out new spaces in a fluid, contested, and often violent interior. In both situations, imperial administrators often had military backgrounds. They frequently looked at Christian converts as potential soldiers, hoping that Christianity would instill virtues of obedience and loyalty. In both cases, versions of prophetic religion ultimately helped fuel anti-colonial resistance as well as new forms of accommodation to colonial realities.

Finally, I would suggest that the very experience of serving in armies, of cultural exchange in a military context and of long-distance military struggles on contested colonial frontiers all contributed to a degree of cultural relativism, perhaps especially in the case of the Mohawk, and, paradoxically, opened the door to the use of religion and the idea of "tradition" as tools for the reinvention of the self. There is a great deal that is not known about this process. To bring together military and religious history does, however, enable us to pose questions about the relationship between what are too often seen as distinct spheres and in so doing also to rethink the concept of conversion.

Notes

1. Norman Etherington, ed., *Missions and Empire* (Oxford, 2004), Brian Stanley, *The Bible and the Flag: Protestant Missions and British Imperialism in the Nineteenth and Twentieth Centuries* (Leicester, 1990); Andrew Porter, ed., *The Imperial Horizons of Protestant Missions, 1880–1914* (Grand Rapids, 2003); and Andrew Porter, *Religion versus Empire? British Protestant Missionaries and Overseas Expansion, 1700–1914* (Manchester, UK, 2004).

2. Jean Comaroff and John Comaroff, *Of Revelation and Revolution: Christianity, Colonialism and Consciousness,* 2 vols. (Chicago, 1991, 1997), 1: 26, 199; Jean Comaroff and John Comaroff, "The Colonization of Consciousness in South Africa," *Economy and Society* 18 (1989): 267–96.

3. See e.g., Roland David Chrisjohn and Sherri Young, *The Circle Game: Shadows and Substance in the Indian Residential School Experience in Canada,* rev. ed., (Penticon, B.C., 2006).

4. C. A. Bayly draws attention to the importance of former officers who had served in the Napoleonic wars to early nineteenth-century colonial administration: C. A. Bayly, *Imperial Meridian: The British Empire and the World, 1780–1830* (London, 1989).

5. As Daniel Richter puts it nicely in considering seventeenth-century Natick conversion narratives, "[T]he structure of any conversion narrative was rooted in Calvinist teachings about how God's grace worked in people's lives." *Facing East from Indian Country: A Native History of Early America* (Cambridge, MA, 2001), 118. Compare also David Bebbington's discussion of conversion in his *Evangelicalism: Comparative Studies of Popular Protestantism in North America, the British Isles and Beyond, 1700–1900* (New York, 1994).

6. Elizabeth Elbourne, *Blood Ground: Colonialism, Missions and the Contest for Christianity in Britain and the Eastern Cape, 1799–1853* (Montreal, 2002).

7. Tony Ballantyne, *Between Colonialism and Diaspora: Sikh Cultural Formations in an Imperial World* (Durham, NC, 2006); Peter Way, "The Cutting Edge of Culture: British Soldiers Encounter Native Americans in the French and Indian Wars," in *Empire and Others: British Encounters with Indigenous Peoples,*

1600–1850, ed. R. Halpern and M. Daunton, 123–48 (Philadelphia, 1999). For French comparisons, see Myron Echenberg, *Colonial Conscripts: The Tirailleurs Sénégalais in French West Africa, 1857–1960* (Portsmouth, NH, 1991); and Arnaud Balvay, *L'Epée et la Plume: Amérindiens et soldats des troupes de la marine en Louisiane et au Pays d'en Haut* (Québec, 2006).

8. For example, Stephen Brumwell, *Redcoats: The British Soldier and War in the Americas, 1755–1763* (Cambridge, 2002), 162–90; and D. Peter MacLeod, *The Canadian Iroquois and the Seven Years War* (Toronto, 1996).

9. Barbara Graymount, *The Iroquois and the American Revolution* (Syracuse, NY, 1972); and Alan Taylor, *The Divided Ground: Indians, Settlers, and the Northern Borderland of the American Revolution* (New York, 2006).

10. Nigel Penn's work on Khoisan-Dutch relations on the northern frontiers of the Cape Colony illustrates this fluidity between ally and enemy in microcosm. *Forgotten Frontier: Colonist and Khoisan on the Cape's Northern Frontier in the 18th Century* (Athens, OH, 2006).

11. *Masters and Servants on the Cape Eastern Frontier, 1760–1803* (Cambridge, 1999).

12. Robert Shell, *Children of Bondage: A Social History of the Slave Society at the Cape of Good Hope, 1652–1838* (Hanover, NH, 1994). On the overall picture, see Penn, *Forgotten Frontier;* Elbourne, *Blood Ground;* Newton-King, *Masters and Servants;* and V. C. Malherbe and Richard Elphick, "The Khoisan to 1828," in *The Shaping of South African Society, 1652–1840,* ed. Richard Elphick and Hermann Giliomee, rev. ed., 35–50 (Middletown, CT, 1989).

13. On the general history of Moravian missions in South Africa, see Bernard Kruger, *The Pear Tree Blossoms: A History of the Moravian Missions in South Africa, 1737–1869* (Genadendal, South Africa, 1966).

14. Anthony F. C. Wallace, *The Death and Rebirth of the Seneca* (New York, 1970), 50.

15. Denys Delâge, *Bitter Feast: Amerindians and Europeans in the American Northeast, 1660–1664* (Vancouver, 1993; orig. pub. as *Le pays renversé,* 1985).

16. Jeremy Adelman and Stephen Aron, "From Borderlands to Borders: Empires, Nation-States, and the Peoples in Between in North American History," *American Historical Review* 104 (1999): 814–41.

17. Richard White, *The Middle Ground: Indians, Empires and Republics in the Great Lakes Region, 1650-1815* (Cambridge, 1991).

18. Taylor, *Divided Ground.*

19. Ibid., 11.

20. Richter, *Facing East from Indian Country,* esp. 151–80; Jon Parmenter, "At the Wood's Edge: Iroquois Foreign Relations, 1727–1768" (Ph.D. thesis, University of Michigan, 1999); Barbara Graymount, *The Iroquois in the American Revolution* (Syracuse, 1972); Daniel Richter, *The Ordeal of the Longhouse: The Peoples of the Iroquois League in the Era of European Colonization* (Chapel Hill, NC, 1992); Taylor, *Divided Ground;* Isabel Kelsay, *Joseph Brant, 1743–1807: Man of Two Worlds* (Syracuse, 1984); Denys Delâge, *Bitter Feast;* Roland Viau, *Enfants du néant et mangeurs d'ames* (Montreal, 1997); and Barbara Mann, *Iroquoian Women: The Gantowisas* (New York, 2000).

21. On the long-standing history of the concept of the covenant chain, see Richter, *Ordeal of the Longhouse.*

22. Daniel Richter, "War and Culture: The Iroquois Experience," *William and Mary Quarterly* 3, no. 40 (1983): 528–59.

23. Allan Greer, *Mohawk Saint: Catherine Tekakwitha and the Jesuits* (Oxford, 2005); Karen Anderson, *Chain Her by One Foot: The Subjugation of Women in Seventeenth-Century New France* (London, 1991); and James Axtell, *The Invasion Within: The Contest of Cultures in Colonial North America* (New York, 1985).

24. Denys Delâge, "Les Iroquois chrétiens des 'reductions', 1667–1770: I. Migration et rapports avec les Français," *Recherches Amérindiennes au Québec* 21 (1991): 59–70.

25. Penn, *Forgotten Frontier;* "Major R. Collins' Report," 30 May 1808, in *Records of the Cape Colony,* ed. G. M. Theal, 36 vols. (London: 1897–1905), vol. VI.

26. On structural processes that led to the formation and reformation of polities, see, inter alia, Norman Etherington, *The Great Treks: The Transformation of Southern Africa, 1815–1854* (London, 2001).

27. James Read, biography of Andries Stoffels reprinted in Josiah Bassett, *Life of a Vagrant* (London, 1836).

28. *Masters and Servants,* 116–49.

29. V. C. Malherbe, "The Khoekhoe Soldiers at the Cape of Good Hope: How the Khoekhoen Were Drawn into the Dutch and British Defensive Systems, to c. 1809," *Military History Journal* 12 (2002), http://samilitaryhistory.org/vol123vm .html (accessed June 25, 2011).

30. Ibid.,

31. J. W. Janssens to J. T. van der Kemp, Cape of Good Hope, 28 February 1805, School of Oriental and African Studies, London, Council for World Mission archives, London Missionary Society papers, South Africa Incoming Correspondence, Box 3, Folder 1, Jacket A.

32. In the late 1810s and early1820s, for example, the governor Charles Somerset, later accused of financial mismanagement and corruption, refused to give licenses to LMS missionaries to travel beyond the then-boundaries of the Cape Colony.

33 Martin Legasick, "The Northern Frontier to c. 1840: The rise and decline of the Griqua people", in *Shaping of South African Society,* ed. Elphick and Giliomee, 384–390. On Griqua identity and history: Linda Waldman, *The Griqua Conundrum: Political and Socio-Cultural identity in the Northern Cape, South Africa* (Oxford, 2007); Robert Ross, *Adam Kok's Griquas* (Cambridge, 1976).

34. For example, "De grondstellingen en wetten van het District Philippolis (18 November 1833)", in Karel Schoeman, *Griqua Records: The Philippolis Captaincy, 1825–1861* (Cape Town,1996), 3.

35. On the difficulty of maintaining neutrality, see Caitlin A. Fitz, "Suspected on Both Sides: Little Abraham, Iroquois Neutrality and the American Revolution," *Journal of the Early Republic* 28 (2008): 299–335.

36. Tim Shannon, "Dressing for Success on the Mohawk Frontier: Hendrik, William Johnson, and the Indian Fashion," *William and Mary Quarterly* 3, no. 53 (1996): 13–42.

37. Daniel K. Richter, "'Some of them … would always have a minister with them': Mohawk Protestantism, 1683–1719," *American Indian Quarterly* 16 (1992): 472, citing William Andrews to SPG Secretary, 17 April 1718, Records of the Society for the Propagation of the Gospel: Letter Books, XIII, 319.

38. Compare Johannes Theodorus van der Kemp's early reception by the Xhosa chief Nqika, who asked the missionary to make it rain while also slaughtering an ox in keeping with Xhosa custom. J. T. Van der Kemp, "An Account of the Religion, Customs, Population, Government, Language, History, and Natural Productions of the Caffaria," *Transactions of the London Missionary Society*, vol. 1, 432–507 (London, 1804). I am drawing here on Janet Hodgson's term "sacred power." "A Battle for Sacred Power: Christian Beginnings Among the Xhosa," in *Christianity in South Africa: A Political, Social and Cultural History*, ed. Richard Elphick and Rodney Davenport, 68–88 (Los Angeles, 1997.

39. Richter, "'Some of them …'," 473.

40. Ibid.

41. John Wolfe Lydekker, *The Faithful Mohawks* (Cambridge, 1938), 60.

42. Eric Hinderaker, "The 'Four Indian Kings' and the Imaginative Construction of the First British Empire," *The William and Mary Quarterly* 3, no. 53 (1996), 487–526.

43. Thomas Pilkin to Lyman Draper, 13 March 1878, Wisconsin Historical Society, Madison, Draper Papers, Series F, vol. I, 140ff.

44. Information about the division of Queen Anne's silver is from the web site maintained by the Mohawk of the Bay of Quinte/Kenhteke Kanienkeha, www.mbq-tmt.org, accessed 25 November 2008.

45. W. L. Greene to Lyman Draper, Danube, New York, 4 January 1878, Draper papers, Series F, vol. 2, 43 ff.

46. Evan Haefeli and Kevin Sweeney, eds., *Captive Histories: English, French and Native Narratives of the 1704 Deerfield Raid* (Amherst, MA 2006); for further comments on the bell story, see the review by Dale Miquelon, h-france.net/vol7reviews/miquelon2.html (accessed 10 June 2011).

47. Mrs. E. A. Smith, "The Story of the Bell, 1882," in *Captive Histories*, 220.

48. Jonathan Edwards, Stockbridge, to Hon Thomas Hubbard of Boston, 31 August 1757, copied in Draper Papers, series F, vol. 1, 45 ff.

49. Ibid.

50. Thomas Pilkin to Lyman Draper, Detroit, 13 March 1878, Draper Papers, Series F, vol. 1, 140.

51. Ibid.

52. The most recent biography of Sir William Johnson is by Fintan O'Toole, *White Savage: William Johnson and the Invention of America* (New York, 2005). Barbara Graymount's biography of Koñwatsiãtsiaiéñni (Mary Brant) in the *Dictionary of Canadian Biography Online* (Toronto: University of Toronto Press, 2000) includes a useful bibliography.

53. See James Axtell, "Dr. Wheelock's Little Red Schoolhouse," in *The European and the Indian: Essays in the Ethnohistory of Colonial North America*, ed. James Axtell, 87–109 (New York, 1981), on Wheelock's school; and Taylor, *Divided Ground*.

54. Walter Pilkington, ed., *Journals of Samuel Kirkland* (Clinton, NY, 1980), 6.

55. National Archives of Canada (NAC), SPG papers, C Canada (pre-diocesan), Box 1: Daniel Claus to SPG, Montreal, 9 October 1782.

56. "What opinion must not the Canadians have of the English to see them sacrifice the Honour of their Religion to Gain and procuring to themselves a continuance of Trade by fixing a wandering Indian Nation to a certain spot [by?] giving them a place of worship, & a papist priest when with that Nation a protestant would have answered as well?" National Archives of Canada (NAC), SPG papers, C Canada (pre-diocesan), Box 1: Daniel Claus to SPG, Montreal, 9 October 1782.

57. Abraham Yates, jun, "Proceedings of the Commissioners to treat with the Six Nations of Indians," *Documents Relative to the Colonial History of the State of New York* (Albany, 1853–1887), vol. VIII, pp. 621–3; see also Lydekker, *Faithful Mohawks*, 143.

58. NAC, SPG papers, C Canada (pre-diocesan), Box 1: Daniel Claus to SPG, Montreal, 1782.

59. The words were divided into lists by the number of syllables, rather than being translations of one another. Daniel Claus, *A Primer, for the Use of the Mohawk Children, To acquire the Spelling, Reading and Writing of their own... Waerighwaghsawe Iksaongoenwa Tsiwaondad-derighhonny Kaghyadoghsera* (Montreal, 1781), 4–18.

60. Ibid., 27.

61. As cited in ibid., 33.

62. NAC, SPG papers, C Canada (pre-diocesan), Box 1: Aaron Hill to Daniel Claus, Niagara, 1 September 1782, original and translation enclosed in Claus to SPG, 9 October 1782.

63. *London Magazine*, July 1776.

64. Taylor, *Divided Ground*, 65–66.

65. Balvay, *L'Epée et la plume*.

66. E.g., J. Long, *Voyages and Travels of an Indian Interpreter and Trader in the Years 1768–1788* (Chicago, 1922; orig. pub. London, 1791).

67. Way, "Cutting Edge of Culture."

68. Kelsay, *Joseph Brant*; [John Strachan], "Life of Captain Brant," *Christian Recorder*, May, 1819, no. 3, 106–112 and June, 1819, no. 4, 145–151.

69. Pilkington, ed., *Journals of Samuel Kirkland*, 73–74 (2 March 1772). The brackets are Kirkland's own.

70. Ibid., 24 (7 April 1765). Interestingly, the head sachem, Kirkland's sponsor in the village, argued that the death of the warrior was not necessarily the product of witchcraft or other maleficent influences: Sometimes things happened simply because they were the will of God, or a product of human actions.

71. Elbourne, *Blood Ground*, 345–76. Among a rich literature on millenarian and prophetic movements and their use against colonialism, see Michael Adas, *Prophets of Rebellion: Millenarian Protest Movements against the European Colonial Order* (Chapel Hill, NC, 1979); Gregory Dowd, *War Under Heaven: Pontiac, the Indian Nations and the British Empire* (Baltimore, 2002).

72. George Cathcart to Sir John Pakington, Fort Beaufort, June 21, 1852, reproduced in British Parliamentary Papers, 1852–53 [1635] Vol. LXVI, "Correspondence with the Governor regarding the Kaffirs and the recent Rebellion," 120.

73. Compare Gregory Dowd, *A Spirited Resistance: The North American Indian Struggle for Unity, 1745–1815* (Baltimore, 1992).

74. Arthur C. Parker, "How the White Race Came to America and Why the Gaiwiio Became a Necessity," related by So-Son-Do-Wa', *The Code of Handsome Lake* (Albany, NY: 1913), 16.

🪷 4

Horton's "Intellectualist Theory" of Conversion, Reflected on by a South Asianist

Richard Fox Young

In these pages, I am arguing—counter-intuitively, some might think—that the "Intellectualist Theory," a theory of conversion formulated by social anthropologist Robin Horton to account for the phenomenal growth of Christianity in Africa, is actually better at doing the very opposite: explaining why reconversion back to traditional religions could (or does) occur. As a South Asianist, I have concluded that grappling with Horton, an Africanist, opens up possibilities for testing his hypothesis in new and constructive ways. In being so persuaded, I have hardly any allies; with the exception of Richard Eaton, whose work on the Nagas of the Northeast Highlands I discuss, the interest Horton elicits from South Asianists has been almost negligible. Here, I want to contest that unwarranted sense of South Asian exceptionalism; unlike Africa (where reversion to traditional religions rarely happens), South Asia offers an abundance of cases for testing a theory like Horton's, if, that is, my guerrilla reading of it (as it were) turns out to be correct.

And so, under my first heading, "Intellectualist Theory as 'Cognitive Reorganization,'" I talk about "pantheon simplification" as a way of describing the changes that Horton sees occurring in African cosmologies as they collide with or are impinged upon by Christianity (or Islam, as the case might be). Following that, I review the rather checkered reception the Intellectualist Theory enjoys among my tribe of scholars under the heading "Is Horton a Good Fit for South Asia?" I suggest that he might indeed be quite a good one when I adduce a particular nineteenth-century case study from the North of Sri Lanka under the heading "A Shaivite Cosmological Upgrade?" Lastly, in "Postscript on Comparative Possibilities," I draw attention to additional cases from South Asia, Hindu primarily but also Buddhist, where a Hortonesque analysis, necessary adjustments considered, appears to be potentially apropos.

One does not need to be an Africanist to be familiar with Robin Horton's work on conversion. Horton's Intellectualist Theory, now celebrating half a century of durability (its antecedents go back to the 1960s), enjoys the distinction of being called "the classic treatment of African conversion." So says Philip Curtin in his influential book, *The World and the West.*[1] As of now, the Social Science Citation Index lists some 100 items that refer to Horton's seminal essay of 1971, "African Conversion," which appeared in *Africa*, a rather obscure journal at the time; topping the SSCI's current listings is an article fresh off the press (at this writing) from a leading professional periodical, the *Journal of the American Academy of Religion.*[2] It helped that Horton formulated his original hypothesis about conversion at a time when historians and social scientists felt anxious about catching up with demographic data that showed Christianity's center of gravity shifting from the northern to the southern hemisphere, mostly to Africa. The timing was ripe and a guarantee, of sorts, that the Intellectualist Theory would ride the burgeoning wave of interest in African Christianity. And, since understanding Christianity is indispensable to an understanding of modern Africa, that wave is unlikely to crest anytime soon. It stands to reason, then, that Africa will continue to be the primary testing ground of the general theory Horton developed.

Over time, however, Horton's readership has diversified. The attention he garners is no longer limited mainly to Africanists; the phenomenology of conversion is of widespread interest, and while some scholars welcome the explanatory models he constructs, others wince and find them flawed. Later, I allude to the kinds of criticism the Intellectualist Theory typically provokes, some of which I share. Still, Horton is hard to avoid. You might focus on Roman conversion to Hellenistic Judaism in late antiquity[3]; on the conversion of Germanic peoples in the medieval Carolingian empire[4]; on Mayan conversion to Catholicism during the Spanish conquest of Mesoamerica[5]; on the conversion of the Cree and other indigenous peoples of New France[6]; or, to carry this on a little longer, you might focus on the African Diaspora of the American South and British Caribbean[7]; the conversion of Chinese immigrants in the U.S.A. today[8]; the conversion of Orthodox Christians to Pentecostalism in contemporary Addis Ababa[9]; or conversion to Protestantism in the highlands of post-war Vietnam[10]: Chances are that Horton will have an influence on how you think and talk about conversion, whether you simply genuflect in his direction or not. It seems obvious, but here I must add that parallel demonstrations are no proof of a theory's validity.[11]

On the whole, South Asianists take to Horton less avidly than other regional specialists who study conversion. One reason may be that Christianity is not indispensable for understanding South Asia's modern history the way it is for Africa's; the number of scholars mobilized for such a purpose therefore bears no comparison. There are exceptions, and I discuss them under a later heading. Another reason—the main deterrent to portability—is a questionable sense of South Asian exceptionalism. Horton himself spoke ambivalently about comparing Africa with South Asia, phenomenologically, and seems to have felt that Hinduism would surely be the undoing of his explanatory model.[12] Under my first heading, where I summarize the Intellectualist Theory, we shall see what Horton thought an African cosmology looks like. I suspect, though, that he was wrong about South Asia. And so, under another heading, I adduce my own work on Protestant Christianity and Tamil Shaivism in nineteenth-century Sri Lanka as evidence that might buttress Horton's hypothesis that much of the action most worth watching in conversion actually takes place cognitively, within religious cosmologies. Still, I have no interest in validation, and in the end I suggest a few refinements that might clarify ambiguities of theory and terminology that Horton tolerated, to the detriment of his model. One such ambiguity I must mention right away: Horton distrusted the word "conversion" and usually placed inverted commas around it, but without being really clear as to why[13]; to him, it was weighted down with all the wrong connotations—rejection, replacement, and substitution. This was not what he saw happening, even in traditional African societies that were being increasingly identified demographically as Christian.

INTELLECTUALIST THEORY AS "COGNITIVE REORGANIZATION"

For a respected ethnographer who lived in West Africa most of his professional life and did his early work on the Kalabari of the Niger Delta, Horton sounds awfully abstract and totalizing when he first lays down the groundwork for the Intellectualist Theory, in 1971.[14] Roundly criticized,[15] he mobilized a vast amount of ethnographic expertise in defense of the Intellectualist Theory in subsequent essays.[16] These, however, concern us less; in any event, his interests shifted toward Islam, while his explanatory models began to lose their salience in the midst of so many parallel demonstration cases.

Doing justice to the elegance and economy of Horton's thesis about African traditional religions is not easy, but rationality, reflexivity, and resilience are the main features that stand out in his discussion: Instead of being doomed to extinction when confronted by Christianity (in an extra-African form of it, propagated by foreign missionaries), African cosmologies "rationally adapt" themselves (or, better, their believer/practitioners do) in response to changes in their environment. This happens in ways that are typical of "cognitive reorganization"[17] in being conscious and deliberate, premeditated and purposeful, instead of haphazard or ad hoc. As Horton later clarified,[18] in the face of mounting criticism: "Where people confront new and puzzling situations, they tend to adapt to them as far as possible in terms of their existing ideas and attitudes." Or, as some astute commentators, Terence Ranger and Isaria Kimambo, affirmed: "People do not just scrap their religions systems but seek to modify them."[19]

Still, rates of adaptability differ, and Horton's ideal-typical cosmology therefore consists of two extremes. At one end are the people groups that inhabit the microcosmic world of self-sufficient agrarian communities. For purposes of explanation, prediction, and control (viz., of "real" world events), they look to "lesser beings" (ancestors, spirits, etc.), whom they perceive as being more involved in their affairs than any presumptive "supreme being" (Olorun or Chukwu, say, for the Yoruba and Igbo, respectively). Unless the equilibrium of the microcosm is disturbed, Horton argues, the "supreme being" remains no more than tacitly acknowledged.[20] At the other end are the more mobile people groups (pastoralists, traders, etc.) who enter into or inhabit the macrocosmic world. There they are exposed to a variety of translocal influences, for good or ill. For them, a "supreme being" who remains merely tacit no longer suffices; here, Horton invokes Weber's concept of rationalization (defined as bringing belief into alignment with experience, or the attribution of causality to a single divinity). To such macrocosmically-oriented people groups, Horton attributes a predisposition for conversion.

Note, though, that instead of rejecting the indigenous cosmology and replacing it with an exogenous substitute, macrocosmically-oriented people groups appropriate the idiom (cultic and theological) of a religion like Christianity but without betrayal of their own indigenous cosmological orientation. What happens next is neither pantheon liquidation nor pantheon substitution but rather pantheon simplification (entailing the enhancement of, say, Olorun or Chukwu, at the expense of lesser beings who are simply demoted and inferiorized, not eliminated). Horton thus argues that a cosmological upgrade precipitates a change in African religion that gets it onto a monolatric trajectory. In pre-Christian Africa, changes like these were "already in the air," he says, because microcosms were always and everywhere being sucked into macrocosms. The upshot of the Intellectualist Theory has got to be Horton's startling contention[21] that in this process Christianity cannot be singled out as the cause of conversion but only as a "stimulator" or "accelerator" of it, which anyway was underway already. In short, however one might feel about Christianity (or Islam, as he elsewhere argued) being thought of as a kind of host organism for a parasitic relationship with African traditional religions, Horton makes a compelling case for thinking of Christianity as an African religion. This opens up a new conversation about (Christianity's) Africanization as a process that occurs instead of, or alongside, (Africa's) Christianization.

This is not the place to rehearse the whole catalogue of complaints that scholars level against the Intellectualist Theory—they are legion. Yes, it seems overly-generalized, although skeletal, I suppose, is what a macrocausal theory has to be; I agree, too, that it hollows out the religions it must inevitably name and characterize (Is Christianity only about "communion" with a "supreme being"? Are the "lesser beings" of African traditional religions only invoked for reasons of explanation, prediction, and control?); and I sympathize with scholars who feel uneasy about Horton's reductionisms, which are unapologetically dehistoricized. Logically, even the Weberian insistence on rationalization seems misplaced; after all, why pantheon simplification instead of pantheon complexification (by which I mean proliferation of "lesser beings," for which historical evidence exists)? For all that (and much more), Horton reinvests African traditional religionists with an agency all their own, and in this respect I submit that he was remarkably prescient, historiographically. Back in the early 1970s, African Christianity was still being written about as if it were only a chapter in Euro-American mission history. Here, Horton was being unorthodox, as Ranger recognized (whose remarks on the Intellectualist Theory are the first on record that I know of):

> What Horton does is to widen out the issue [of African Christian history]. It is not enough, he implies, to show that African religious belief was a factor at particular points in the Christian history of Africa; to show, as we now can, that the initial reception of Christianity in different African societies depended partly upon the religious situation in those societies as well as upon the political and economic situation. ... Over and above that, so Horton argues, we must see the total process of conversion and of the diffusion of Christianity as a phase *in a specifically African religious historiography*.[22] (emphasis added)

Ranger was right about Horton being cutting edge—and yet, agency is never utterly absolute and unconstrained, whether that of indigenous African peoples or that of exogenous powers and principalities (merchants, missionaries, militaries). This, then, is one way I find the Intellectualist Theory deficient and to be in need of refinement; for it strikes me as being crucial to its credibility that indigenous voices be heard on the role of agency in conversion. Theoreticians do not ordinarily listen for that, and Horton will therefore be of little avail in that endeavor.

Besides, on its own terms, the idea itself of "cognitive reorganization" still needs to be unpacked. Is it all that obvious that being religious is the same thing as having a systematized set of articulated beliefs that one can step back from, reconsider, and then reorganize as need arises? Au contraire: For those who reject Horton's interiorist bias, as Robert Hefner does (Hefner worked on conversion in Javanese society), "[c]onversion is rarely the outcome of intellectual appeal alone."[23] At most, then, Horton sheds some helpful light on why people convert to Christianity (because of a precipitating cause such as the implosion of a microcosm) but none at all as to what it then means to be a convert. We need to think of conversion as a social-cum-cognitive process, like Rita Smith Kipp who found among the Batak Protestants of Indonesia that "a convert's new identity may at first be lightly worn and only dimly understood. What being a Christian ... means is then rethought and renegotiated over the years."[24] Actually, the field research I know of just will not support the idea that converts ever really think about conversion the way the Intellectualist Theory claims they do. The findings of Elizabeth Isichei from the Jos Plateau of Nigeria are a case in point, and that comes pretty close to home for Horton. The data she collected in the late 1970s from still-surviving first-generation Yoruba Christians confirms that the heart's needs almost always trump the mind's; often, they are simply the fiercely urgent needs of, for instance, having sufficient salt in one's diet (gratis, at mission stations), rest on the Sabbath from agricultural labor, and relief from the high cost of tribal initiations and ritual sacrifice (necessitating a frequent outlay of fowl).[25]

And so, while I agree with anthropologist Joel Robbins[26] about the possibility of "détente" between the utilitarian and intellectualist approaches[27] and feel that rehabilitating the word "adhesion" would enrich the lexicon we use for analysis (too much weight being carried by the word "conversion"), when all is said and done I am still left with the impression (which I share with Robbins[28]) that Horton has begged an important question: Why, actually, do converts convert, if all the necessary cosmological upgrades are in place already (or, potentially)? Would it not work better for the Intellectualist Theory if one could adduce in its defense examples of African people groups who remain in, or reconvert to, their own indigenous religions once they undergo "cognitive reorganization"? While it would seem that the Intellectualist Theory was designed to explain this very sort of thing, what we get instead is a theory that purports to explain conversion to Christianity. Indeed, to my knowledge, cases of revitalization and reconversion have rarely been reported since Ranger pointed out, long ago,[29] that Horton's thesis found confirmation of sorts in the rise to prominence of Mwari, the "supreme being" of surviving southern Shona traditionalists, around the same time that Zimbabwe was rapidly Christianizing, demographically. When such cases are reported (e.g., Aguilar on the Waso Boorana of Kenya[30]), the causes are unrecognizably Hortonesque. That is why, rather counter-intuitively, I am now going to argue that while Africanists may have thought up a good theory, South Asianists are the ones who have the cases—or might.

IS HORTON A GOOD FIT FOR SOUTH ASIA?

When South Asianists have been unusually tepid about the Intellectualist Theory and Horton himself doubts its explanatory value outside Africa, convinced already that India would always be a theater of "pure contrast" to Africa, to say that I suspect them all of being wrong makes me feel more than a little Lone Ranger-ish. Not that Horton elicits no interest; he most certainly does. Among the South Asianists I know of who listened in on the debate among Africanists over the Intellectualist Theory was Raj historian Robert Frykenberg (University of Wisconsin, Madison) who worked on the Horton model in a doctoral seminar in the late 1970s, only to conclude that "as soon as one tries to apply it [to South Asia], complications arise."[31] One of the most formidable that occurred to Frykenberg comes out of what I have diagnosed already as a misplaced sense of South Asian exceptionalism. Thrown by Horton's description of the "basic African cosmology" and failing to recognize it as an abstraction of the Weberian ideal-type that nowhere exists in nature, Frykenberg understandably balked at the thought of any South Asian cosmology being as simple as the one for Africa that Horton constructed (having only two tiers, it seems insufficiently hierarchical). Anyway, South Asianists nowadays are more alert to the dangers of theorization based on dubious essentializations and less fixated on finding a model cosmology that fits all sizes (of, say, Sanskritic Hinduisms of the "Great Tradition" and vernacular Hinduisms of the "Little Tradition"). Contextually adjusted, the models one might construct for South Asian theisms would probably differ the least from Horton's at the low end inhabited by "lesser beings," but the most at the high end occupied by various "supreme beings." South Asia, after all, is no stranger to competing, sectarian monolatries.

Another historian who has worked assiduously on conversion in South Asia but with more optimism about Horton's adoptability and greater openness toward his adaptability is Australian Geoffrey Oddie (University of Sydney), who initially had the same sense of South Asian exceptionalism that Frykenberg evinced.[32] Later, Oddie invoked Horton in a study of conversion in nineteenth-century Bengal where members of a Vaishnava sect called the Kartabhaja (found mainly among Hindus of the marginal castes) had become Christians in numbers that were quite large for an area where conversion was infrequent or rare. Whether Oddie invoked Horton in recognizably Hortonesque ways seems debatable, however; surely, Horton is emptied of analytic significance when all that he is made to stand for is summed up in the commonplace that "pre-Christian ideas" such as *bhakti* (theistic devotionalism centered on an avatar of Vishnu) play "an important role in conversion."[33] For that, we do not need the Intellectualist Theory, which turns the whole notion of conversion to Christianity on its head. The same volume carrying Oddie's essay has one by George Oommen on the nineteenth-century conversion to Christianity of the Pulaya, a marginal caste community found in Travancore (South India). In this, Oommen openly questions Horton's relevance, but, apparently, without really knowing why and with the same indifferent grasp of the Intellectualist Theory. Misled like Frykenberg by Horton's ideal-typical model, Oommen cannot imagine anything so simplistic being of help in understanding Pulaya conversion. Besides, Oommen knows the intricacies of Pulaya cosmology so intimately that he wants to save them from reductionists like Horton; he therefore concludes that the Pulaya "converted in spite of the pre-existing belief system."[34] This is the kind of analytic deadlock—each scholar's invocation of Horton canceling the other's out—that makes a person wonder, Might Horton be a better "fit" for the analogues of African traditional religions in South Asia than for the religions we refer to as Hindu, whether Sanskritic or vernacular, Brahminical or Dalit.

Earlier, when I said that Christianity was not as indispensable for understanding modern South Asia as it is for Africa, I did not mean to imply that Christianity had no purchase anywhere in the region. That would be false, nowhere more so than among the Nagas and other Highland peoples of the North East where any notion of India as Hindu seems utterly absurd. Demographically, India is Christian here, even though the populations are too small to make a difference, nationally. Highland Christianity, Richard Eaton claims, has become a Naga religion, and in proof of this Eaton (who participated in the Frykenberg seminar I mentioned) offers an elaborate, fine-tuned Hortonesque analysis—perhaps the most elaborate and fine-tuned on record—that in certain respects outdoes anything Horton himself attempted. Missionization among the Naga followed on the heels of annexation and colonization in the late nineteenth century, but with unequal rapidity among the three lineage groups Eaton studied, the Ao, Sema, and Angami. Though each had been subjected to similar macrocosmic disturbances (precipitated, for instance, by a government ban on headhunting and the church's on alcohol), only the Ao and Sema responded with much alacrity to the changes in their environment. Largely Christian now, the Angami lagged far behind. This is the kind of conundrum the Intellectualist Theory was meant to crack, and Eaton accordingly attributes the varying rates of conversion to contrastive cosmologies that predisposed the more macrocosmically-oriented Ao and Sema to conversion, just as Horton predicted.[35] When, however, Eaton speaks of pantheon liquidation (he writes there of this as the fate suffered by "the entire lower tier of lesser spirits"),[36] then the analysis seems so theory-driven as to exceed what even Horton would have felt was warranted. Were it so, one wonders how the Pentecostalization of the Highlands could ever occur, which nowadays is proceeding apace. Still, instead of gossamer webs, Eaton offers an analytically astute, thick-description case study that helpfully poses problems having to do with "cognitive reorganization" in distinctively Hortonesque ways: "[W]ho, in the meeting of two cultures," he asks, "is actually changing whom? And what, in the end, is actually changing?"[37]

A SHAIVITE COSMOLOGICAL UPGRADE?

And yet, while such questions are helpful, the either/or in which Eaton frames them makes the outcome look suspiciously predetermined. Be that as it may, the Naga conversion case is as good as it gets, unless you adopt the revisionist reading of Horton that I am an advocate of — that he does better at explaining "conversion from" than "conversion to"; or, alternatively, that what the Intellectualist Theory contributes to is a better angle on the appropriation processes by which Christianity (viz., the Euro-American, missionary-initiated variety) becomes African, say, or Nagamese. That being so, the kinds of cases that are going to be illuminated by the Horton model will not be found either in Africa, where ex post facto testability is a foregone conclusion (the evidence having long ago been "overlaid by Christian activity," as Ranger avers),[38] or among the South Asian conversion phenomena of the Highland kind. More promising are cases where reconversion from Christianity occurs in places — plentiful enough, I think — where Christianity itself can be adduced as a catalyst for an upgrade in the indigenous cosmology.

One such case I know of personally and have written about,[39] where huge amounts of catalytic activity occurred before the mid 1800s when the really interesting interreligious interaction gets going, is the stem-shaped peninsula called Jaffna atop the mango-shaped island of Sri Lanka (to use an indigenous geographical metaphor). In the infinite gradations between microcosm and macrocosm, Jaffna Tamils were rather more cosmopolitan than isolated, on the whole (naturally, its population cohorts were involved in varying degrees in the South India/ Indian Ocean macrocosm); religiously, the peninsula was predominantly Shaivite. A turnstile, as it were, for traffic between the island and the mainland (barely fifty miles away), the peninsula was strategically located and therefore attractive to Europe's maritime powers, the Portuguese, Dutch, and British (successively). Having worked in and on Jaffna before I came to know of Horton, I have long felt a need to reexamine my findings in light of his.

In the mid 1500s, Augustinians, Dominicans, and Jesuits began constructing coral-hewn churches (incredibly durable), which they filled to capacity until the mid 1600s; then the Dutch arrived and made the Catholic churches Reformed churches, which they also filled to capacity; until, that is, the British arrived in the late 1700s—with Americans in their wake—who made them Anglican or Wesleyan, Congregationalist or Presbyterian. Ecclesiastical records confirm that virtually the whole population became "civil rite" Christians, Catholic first, then Reformed, for utilitarian reasons. While some caste communities remained staunchly Catholic (Karaiyar fisherfolk, for example), others—Vellalas in particular, who are Jaffna's landowning, cultivator caste—returned to their temples once the British dismantled the draconian Dutch policies that fostered hypocrisy. However messily and mercilessly, Christianity had been around for years, change had been in the air without being manifest in any "cognitive reorganization" of the indigenous cosmology in ways that made reconversion an attractive proposition. The Catholic cosmology that came from Portugal was as densely inhabited by "lesser beings" as Jaffna's own homegrown variety.[40] And, under Holland, the severely aniconic faith that came to Jaffna arrived before Protestant missions had even been thought of in Europe, which was why the Reformed Church was all but indifferent to all things Hindu even though public life had to be formally Christian. For a more radically disenchanted Protestantism, implacably opposed to any and all involvement in "lesser beings" for purposes of explanation, prediction, and control, we can skip over the centuries for a closer look at the last missionary period, the Anglo-American one. More than the Luso-

Dutch, it exemplifies an illuminating observation by anthropologist Stanley Tambiah (himself a Sri Lankan Tamil):

> Judaeo-Christian monotheism is honour bound to declare any concep-
> tion of a cosmos, in which man and transcendental entities share certain
> similar properties and capacities, and can have relations of reciprocity,
> exchange and even coercion, and in which objects and forces that exist
> apart from and anterior to them can be employed, as not only polytheistic
> but also magical and pagan.[41]

Where there should have been around a hundred thousand Protestants in Jaffna when the new wave of missionaries repossessed the
fifty (or so) buildings the Dutch Reformed Church had abandoned
twenty years previously (in 1796), no Tamils were found at all, only
Burghers who had stayed behind. The hemorrhage had happened almost overnight, and in the interregnum between ecclesiastical occupa-
tions, a spurt in temple construction was evident. The church I know
best, in the hamlet of Batticotta (in Vattukkottai, eight miles from Jaffna
town), had had some 2,500 parishioners under the Jesuits when it was
"Our Lady of the Ascension" for around 150 years; and for almost as
long under Dutch *predikaants* (ministers), it had maintained that same
high number. The Americans, however, had to open schools before anyone would darken the church door. At this, the newcomers were quite
good, imparting useful knowledge in the sense that it was well adapted
to colonial needs. Actually, the response was overwhelmingly positive,
number-wise; Vellalas, anxious to reconsolidate their domination over
Jaffna, were avid patrons. Indeed, without the much-needed transfu-
sion from the schools, whether Protestantism could have been resusci-
tated at all seems an open question. The question would return again
at mid-century when Tamil Shaivites realized that missionaries were
not the only ones who could open schools of the kind that upwardly-
mobile Vellalas would attend.

Having to condense, I can only mention what transpired inside the
peninsula's Protestant schools, although missionaries always and everywhere seemed to be on message in the lanes and byways and bazaars of
Jaffna, wherever they could tell people about the one true God. In tan-
dem with rising literacy (Tamil and English), a burgeoning tract literature came into existence; although anti-Hindu, such tracts were widely
read, there being little else in print that a literate person could read.
One that the Americans used extensively was called *Blind Way* (*Karuttu
vari*), which pretty much says in advance that the contents are going to
be polemical—and they are. Trained at institutions such as Princeton,
the Congregationalists and Presbyterians who went out to Jaffna had

soli Deo gloria and other Reformation dicta ringing in their ears. So conditioned, and knowing only a kind of street-smart ethnography, they were unable to appreciate how "reciprocity, exchange and even coercion"[42] could be worthy of the worship due to the one true God. It had not escaped their notice that "lesser beings" in the Tamil pantheon were sometimes called "blind deities" (*karuttut teyvam*) for failing to heed a person's needs, in spite of being praised and prayed to. Feeling honor bound, missionaries drew upon a rich traditional lexicon to heap scorn upon *anekeshvaravadis* (polytheists, or "believers in many deities"), and came up with new epithets of their own for "pagan" and "heathen" (e.g., *ajñani*, which translates literally as "ignorant," or "unknowing."[43]

"[W]ho in the meeting of two cultures," Richard Eaton asks us to ask, "is actually changing whom?" Though I was put off by what I heard missionaries saying (about cholera epidemics, for instance), the evidence simply was not there that would discount missionary agency entirely or turn what happened in Jaffna thereafter into a hollowing out of Christianity in a way remotely similar to what the Intellectualist Theory tells us to expect. Most certainly, Tamil sensibilities were offended and grievances festered. A more civil discourse would have been nice. Analytically, however, the important developments were those that occurred gradually over the years within the indigenous cosmology. However irritating, all that harping on the one true God was heard, taken to heart, and internalized. Of the many Vellalas who received a Christian education, the one who almost single-handedly turned the tables on Christianity in Jaffna and precipitated the mass reconversion movement of the mid 1800s was a product of Wesleyan schools who became a renowned Tamil scholar, Arumuka Pillai (1822–1879). Later called Navalar ("Silver-Tongued"), Arumukam was born into the family of a middling official in the erstwhile Dutch administration, someone who had therefore been at least a nominal Christian and was acculturated to the colonial milieu.

Though not a professed Christian, Arumukam worked for years with a gifted missionary linguist on a Tamil Bible translation (now known as the "Navalar Bible"), and the knowledge thus acquired made him a formidable adversary when (for reasons still uncertain) he began to publicly oppose the missionaries he had worked with for so long. Earlier, when I found it helpful (as I still do) to think of Arumukam as a Hindu Protestant or Protestant Hindu, and interpreted the changes he introduced into Tamil Shaivism as Protestantization, I was less aware than I was after I read Horton that a good deal of "cognitive reorganization" was occurring within the indigenous cosmology and that it could not be so accounted for. I had found signs of Protestantization in

Illustration 4.1. | *Arumuka Navalar of Jaffna, Shaivite Hindu revivalist. Drawn by Mary Lee Eggart.*

Arumukam's expository preaching on Tamil sacred texts (*piracankam*, which in pre-Navalar Jaffna had been limited to recitation). On these occasions, Arumukam drummed into the heads of his Vellala audiences the dictum of *soli Deo gloria* that "There is but one God," and that God is none other than Shiva. To him, being a person of dharmic rectitude meant not only being a practicing Shaiva (wearing *vibhuti* or sacred ashes, using *rudraksha* prayer beads, reciting the *pañcakshara*, "Glory be to Shiva") but also being a believing Shaiva: or, as his catechism states, "Shivaism [sic] is the religion which holds Shiva as Supreme Being." And I knew that Arumukam was as hard as the missionaries on what he considered cultic laxity, that he "cleansed the temple" (as it were), conducting a relentless crusade to rid Jaffna of all autochthonous, non-Sanskritic divinities, which meant no more prayers to Kannakiyamman (a very popular Jain goddess), to Muslim peers, Catholic saints, or the Virgin Mary.

Still, Horton helped me see that it would have been too facile to simply write this all off as Protestantization; cosmologically, in having made Shiva Jaffna's uncontested apical deity, Arumukam precipitated the kind of pantheon enhancement I have already differentiated from pantheon liquidation, substitution, and complexification. In being Hortonesque, it was monolatric and not, strictly speaking, a monotheistic upgrade at all. It was, however, all that many Vellalas needed in order to feel differently about being Hindu, for reconversions to occur, and for the reconverted to have the temerity to fling back at the missionaries the same abuse that had taunted them. In this meeting of cultures, it could now be asked who the *anekeshvaravadis*—polytheists—really were: After all, which entity of the Trinity did Christians believe is the apical one—the Father, the Son, or the Holy Spirit? And yet, Arumukam had imbibed so much of Christian piety that he could sound downright Providentialistic about the missionaries who had been so irksome: Had Shiva not brought them to Jaffna to "chastise" the people and goad them into becoming better Shaivites? Here, then, we have an indigenous voice—sounding unmistakably theological—on macrocau-

---

Illustration 4.2. | *The mission school in Jaffna, ca. 1848, when Arumuka Navalar left it to reconvert Tamil Christians to Shaivite Hinduism. Drawn by Mary Lee Eggart.*

sality, and it throws Horton's most daring contention into doubt, that "cognitive reorganization" would have occurred even in the absence of Christianity and that Christianity could only have made the change occur faster than otherwise. Alone, this neither disproves the Intellectualist Theory nor means that one would want to see Horton's analytic usefulness trivialized or limited just to Africa where the model originated. Indeed, without it, one might not see as clearly that the main change agents are usually or always indigenous and that much of the action most worth watching in conversion occurs, phenomenologically, within the indigenous cosmology, whatever it might be.

POSTSCRIPT ON COMPARATIVE POSSIBILITIES

Having reached my conclusion under the heading above, here I only make brief comments about other cases from South Asia that Hortonists might work with. First, though, I hazard a generalization and say that pantheon enhancement has long been a regular feature of Hindu sectarianism. Still, it was not until the early nineteenth century, in contexts which could be described as "microcosmically-challenged," that cosmological upgrades helped precipitate movements of resistance to missionary Christianity, bringing disaffected Hindus back into the fold, as it were. Such movements usually arose inside metropolitan India (making the Jaffna case an especially early and interesting exception). A prime example is the Brahmo Samaj, founded in Calcutta (Kolkata) by the Bengali reformer Ram Mohun Roy (1772–1833).[44] Ram Mohun's theistic monism (or, monistic theism—his Bengali writings turn the normally neuter brahman into a masculine noun) probably exemplifies a kind of pantheon eradication, unlike the pantheon enhancement that we saw in Jaffna. Also distinct and complex are the accelerants of cognitive changes that Ram Mohun effected, which include but are not exhausted by Christianity (mediated through the English Baptists of Serampore, among others). Islam, too, was another important environmental influence, but most Hortonesque of all were perhaps India's own traditions of religious and philosophical reflection. All such possibilities (theism, polytheism, monolatry, monism, etc., etc.) were familiar from antiquity and had been debated already, rigorously; in this view, the increasingly cross-cultural, polyglot, and multireligious circumstances of Bengal galvanized—and most certainly accelerated—a reinvigoration of the same traditions to which Ram Mohun was heir.

Still, for all their interest, India's reform movements are not the primary example I want to introduce. This one also comes from my pre-

Horton days,[45] from the South of Sri Lanka where Sinhalese Theravada Buddhism interacted with missionary Christianity in similar ways, politically, and over the same centuries as Tamil Shaivism did in the North. Cosmologically, however, Horton's categories might have to be stretched almost to the breaking point, for there is perhaps no religion so de-theocized as the monastic, nirvanically-oriented Theravada of the Great Tradition. By its norms, nothing probably sounds more ludicrous than pantheon enhancement, whether monotheistic or monolatric. Much historical light has been thrown on this by Alan Strathern[46] during the earliest period of Sinhalese interaction with Portuguese Catholicism. Strathern finds evidence there of a Theravada-derived "transcendentalist intransigence" toward monotheism that helps account for the initial resistance of Sinhalese royalty to conversion. As in the North, however, so in the South, where interaction with the more severely disenchanted varieties of Protestantism catalyzed a kind of pantheon enhancement at the level of the more karmically-oriented, non-monastic Buddhism of the Theravada Little Tradition. There, missionary criticism of the "lesser beings" of the indigenous cosmology (populated by Hindu divinities, Muslim peers, Catholic saints and the Virgin Mary) catalyzed a reaction that set in motion a process of Protestantization not unlike the one I have described for the North. The most obvious structural difference is that the Buddha was made to reign uncontested as the apical figure of the cognitively reorganized pantheon. While this puts a new twist on *soli Deo gloria*, all the elements of a Hortonesque analysis appear to be present. Naturally, the case I refer to has to be understood in terms of its own historical specificity. Besides Protestants, one would have to take into account the involvements of foreign Theosophists (Henry Steel Olcott, Helena Petrovna Blavatsky, et al.), for they were totally antipathetic to Little Tradition Theravada.

Notes

1. Philip D. Curtin, *The World and the West: The European Challenge and the Overseas Response in the Age of Empire* (Cambridge, 2000), 125.

2. Mika Vahakangas, "Ghambageu Encounters Jesus in Sonjo Mythology: Syncretism as African Rational Action," *Journal of the American Academy of Religion* 76 (2008): 111–37.

3. Alan F. Segal, *Paul the Convert: The Apostolate and Apostasy of Saul the Pharisee* (New Haven, CT, 1990).

4. Carole M. Cusak, *Conversion among the Germanic Peoples* (London, 1998).

5. Nancy M. Farriss, *Maya Society under Colonial Rule: The Collective Enterprise of Survival* (Princeton, NJ, 1984).

6. F. Morantz, "In the Land of the Lions: The Ethnohistory of Bruce G. Trigger," in *The Archaeology of Bruce Trigger: Theoretical Empiricism,* ed. R. F. Williamson and M. S. Bisson, 142–73 (Montreal, 2006).

7. Sylvia R. Frey and Betty Wood, *Come Shouting to Zion: African American Protestantism in the American South and British Caribbean* (Chapel Hill, NC, 1998).

8. Fenggang Yang, *Chinese Christians in America: Conversion, Assimilation, and Adhesive Identities* (University Park, PA, 1999).

9. Abbebe Kifleyesus, "Flaunt Fancy for Christ's Celebrity: Pentecostal Proselytisation and Identity Formation in Addis Ababa," in *Ethiopia and the Missions: Historical and Anthropological Insights,* ed. V. Böll, et al., 123–40 (Münster, 2005).

10. Philip Taylor, ed., *Modernity and Re-Enchantment: Religion in Post-Revolutionary Vietnam* (Singapore, 2007).

11. Theda Skocpol and Margaret Somers, "The Uses of Comparative History in Macrosocial Inquiry," *Comparative Studies in Society and History* 22 (1980): 191.

12. Robin Horton and J.D.Y. Peel, "Conversion and Confusion: A Rejoinder on Christianity in Eastern Nigeria," *Revue Canadienne des Études Africaines* [Canadian Journal of African Studies] 10 (1976): 484.

13. Robin Horton, "On the Rationality of Conversion, Part II," *Africa: Journal of the International African Institute* 45 (1975): 394.

14. Robin Horton, "African Conversion," *Africa: Journal of the International African Institute* 41 (1971): 85–108.

15. Humphrey J. Fisher, "Conversion Reconsidered: Some Historical Aspects of Religious Conversion," *Africa. Journal of the International African Institute* 43 (1973): 27–40. A tenacious critic, Fisher elaborated his position in "The Juggernaut's Apologia: Conversion to Islam in Black Africa," *Africa: Journal of the International African Institute* 55 (1985): 153–73, and in "Many Deep Baptisms: Reflections on Religious, Chiefly Muslim Conversion in Black Africa," *Bulletin of the School of Oriental and African Studies* 57 (1994): 68–81.

16. Horton, "On the Rationality of Conversion," 219–35, 373–99.

17. "Cognitive reorganization" is a helpful term I borrow from Morantz, "In the Land of the Lions."

18. Horton and Peel, "Conversion and Confusion," 482.

19. Terence O. Ranger and Isaria N. Kimambo, eds., *The Historical Study of African Religion: With Special Reference to East and Central Africa,* (London, 1972), 15.

20. Horton leaves us to imagine for ourselves how a microcosm's collapse facilitates its conversion. Here, I suggest African literature as a way of filling in the blanks. *Le Pauvre Christ de Bomba* [The Poor Christ of Bomba], published in 1956 by Mongo Beti of Cameroon is an outstanding novel (trans. Gerald Moore, (Oxford: Heinemann, 1971)) that opens a literary window onto the processes Horton depersonalizes for the sake of crafting his general theory. The novel is pervaded by a sense of impending crisis (from the indigenous point of view) that comes from knowing that a remote, unmissionized region—the country of the Tala people—is about to be opened up to commerce and "civilization" by the French colonial administration. Here we see the macrocosm impinging,

violently, on the microcosm. Fr. Drumont, a fictionalized Catholic priest who despairs of ever being able to convert the Tala, is informed of the project by a civil servant named Vidal, a Faustian figure and notorious Afrophobe. Their dialogue, which I condense, has them cross paths when Fr. Drumont is itinerating in the Tala country. With grim humor, Beti brings to life an inconvenient truth that the Intellectualist Theory dehistoricizes and underemphasizes—that colonialism and Christian missions sometimes acted in concert:

> Fr. Drumont: It's only the people on the main roads who make good Christians. The ones hereabouts are extremely refractory.
>
> M. Vidal: Father, did you really say that only those on the main roads make good Christians?
>
> Fr. Drumont: Yes, why?
>
> M. Vidal: Then rejoice, Father, and cast your cares away! Soon you will have both your road and your flock. Good news, eh?
>
> Fr. Drumont: Are you off your head?
>
> M. Vidal: Listen, Father. The tour I'm making now is just the curtain-raiser for a really big project. We are going to drive a road right through the Tala country. … Isn't that interesting news?
>
> Fr. Drumont: Will you have machines?
>
> M. Vidal: Machines, pah! What do we want machines for? Good heaven, would that be worth our while? … Your palmy days have come again; you'll have hordes of faithful converts. (34–35, passim)

21. Horton, "African Conversion," 104.

22. Ranger and Kimambo, *The Historical Study of African Religion*, 22.

23. Robert W. Hefner, "Of Faith and Commitment: Christian Conversion in Muslim Java," in *Conversion to Christianity: Historical and Anthropological Perspectives on a Great Tradition*, ed. Robert W. Hefner (Berkeley, CA, 1993), 110.

24. Rita Smith Kipp, "Conversion by Affiliation: The History of the Karo Batak Church," *American Ethnologist* 22 (1995): 871.

25. Elizabeth Isichei, ed., *Jos Oral History and Literature Texts*, 6 vols. (Jos, Nigeria, 1981).

26. Joel Robbins, *Becoming Sinners: Christianity and Moral Torment in a Papua New Guinea Society* (Berkeley, CA, 2004), 87.

27. The "détente" Robbins envisions, lucidly if also idealistically, is this:

> [The Intellectualist Theory] has a difficult time accounting for the very early stages of conversion, those in which people first engage the new religion with very little sense of what it might provide them by way of intellectual resources. Since Christianity is unlikely to appear as fully coherent on people's first encounter with it, one imagines that motives other than strictly sense-making ones probably sustain those early contacts. … Good at explaining the initial impetus toward conversion, the utilitarian approach gives way to the intellectualist one when it comes time to explain why in some cases people stay with the new religion and come to engage it deeply. Conversely, the intellectu-

alist approach, weak when explaining people's initial interest in world religions, can leave this job to the utilitarian theory without consigning itself to irrelevance. This détente suggests a two-stage model of conversion, one in which utilitarian concerns eventually give way to intellectualist ones as people come to understand the religion they are converting to. (Ibid., 86–7).

Now, to bring this into conversation with literature once again, see the Cameroonian novel, *Poor Christ of Bomba* (n. 20, supra). This will have the hapless people of Tala flock to the Church thinking that being baptized will keep them from being conscripted for corvée labor, as their lives are soon to be disrupted by a road the French are building into the remote region they inhabit. This, though, only explains why they convert to Christianity, not what it means to be a convert, and while the novel depicts the whole affair as mordantly and risibly as possible, there are certainly believers among the Tala who, as Robbins would say, "stay with the new religion and come to engage it deeply" (Robbins, *Becoming Sinners*, 87).

28. Ibid., 339, n.2.

29. Terence O. Ranger, "African Conversion," review of Horton, *Africa* (1971), and M. L. Daneel, *The Background and Rise of Southern Shona Independent Churches* (The Hague: Mouton, 1971), *African Religious Research* 1 (1973): 41.

30. Mario I. Aguilar, "African Conversion from a World Religion: Religious Diversification by the Waso Boorana in Kenya," *Africa: Journal of the International African Institute* 65 (1995): 525–44.

31. Robert Eric Frykenberg, "On the Study of Conversion Movements: A Review Article and a Theoretical Note," *Indian Economic and Social History Review* 17 (1980): 136.

32. Deryck Schreuder and Geoffrey Oddie, "What is Conversion? History, Christianity and Religious Change in Colonial Africa and South Asia," *Journal of Religious History* 15 (1989): 496–518.

33. Geoffrey A. Oddie, "Old Wine in New Bottles? Kartabhaja (Vaishnava) Converts to Evangelical Christianity in Bengal, 1800–1845," in *Religious Conversion Movements in South Asia: Continuity and Change*, ed. Geoffrey A. Oddie (Richmond, UK, 1997), 72.

34. George Oommen, "Strength of Tradition and Weakness of Communication: Central Kerala Dalit Conversion," in Oddie, *Religious Conversion Movements in South Asia*, 93.

35. To conserve space, I have elided from my overview of Horton and Eaton their important discussion of God's indigenous names in Africa and among the Naga. Historically, many traditional religionists identify the "God" spoken of by Christian missionaries with their own indigenous "supreme being." Naming the Divine thus has enormous implications, missionally (and, of course, theologically). While this worked out well for the Ao and Sema, inept linguistic choices hampered the progress of conversion among the Angami. Little of this, however, carries over into my discussion of Protestant Christianity and Tamil Shaivism. Not for connotation but for denotation (i.e., perfectly good, unobjectionable names, like Shiva, had already been taken), personal names were

eschewed for the Divine. In any case, Indic lexicons are rich in terms for "god" and "God." In the North of Sri Lanka in the nineteenth century, the favored missionary term was *Katavul,* from Tamil.

36. Richard M. Eaton, "Comparative History as World History: Religious Conversion in Modern India," *Journal of World History* 8 (1997): 259.

37. Ibid., 244.

38. Ranger, "African Conversion," 44.

39. Richard Fox Young and Subrahmaniam Jebanesan, *The Bible Trembled: The Hindu-Christian Controversies of Nineteenth-Century Ceylon* (Vienna, 1995).

40. On contemporaneous Spanish Catholicism in Mesoamerica, see Farriss, *Maya Society under Colonial Rule,* 294ff.

41. Stanley J. Tambiah, *Magic, Science, Religion, and the Scope of Rationality* (Cambridge, 1990), 7–8.

42. Ibid., 8.

43. In Special Collections at Princeton Theological Seminary, there is a manuscript sermon from Jaffna in Tamil, c. 1823, by Henry Woodward (1797–1834), the first graduate from Princeton to become a missionary anywhere, which blames the *ajñani* for an outbreak of cholera.

44. On Roy, see Wilhelm Halbfass, *India and Europe: An Essay in Understanding* (Albany, NY, 1988), 197–216.

45. Richard Fox Young and G.P.V. Somaratna, *Vain Debates: The Buddhist-Christian Controversies of Nineteenth-Century Ceylon* (Vienna, 1996).

46. Alan Strathern, *Kingship and Conversion in Sixteenth-Century Sri Lanka: Portuguese Imperialism in a Buddhist Land* (Cambridge, 2007), and "Transcendentalist Intransigence: Why Rulers Rejected Monotheism in Early Modern Southeast Asia and Beyond," *Comparative Studies in Society and History* 49 (2007): 358–83.

 Part II

SYNCRETISM AND ITS ALTERNATIVES

5

SANTA BARBARA AFRICANA:
BEYOND SYNCRETISM IN CUBA

Joseph M. Murphy

The notion of syncretism has a long history in the interpretation of the religions of the African diaspora. Pioneering ethnologists such as Raymundo Nina Rodriques in Brazil and Fernando Ortiz in Cuba were employing the term in the early decades of the twentieth century to account for the co-existence of African and Catholic elements in the spiritual lives of their fellow citizens of color.[1] In an influential paper of 1937 called "African Gods and Catholic Saints in New World Negro Belief," American anthropologist Melville Herskovits highlighted one of the most striking of these religious juxtapositions. He wrote of the "tendency of native peoples who have had long contact with Catholicism to achieve a syncretism between their aboriginal religious beliefs and the doctrines and rituals of the Church," exemplified by Afro Latins who:

> ... in responding to the acculturative process, have succeeded in achieving, at least in their religious life, a synthesis between aboriginal African patterns and the European traditions to which they have been exposed.[2]

This view of syncretism or synthesis as the primary explanatory category for the study of Caribbean and Afro-Latin traditions dominated the field for the next fifty years.[3] More recently however the paradigm has come under criticism from both scholars and practitioners themselves. Scholars have seen Herskovits's characterization of syncretism as overly mechanistic, and as undervaluing individual creativity and agency in favor of larger, impersonal forces of acculturation.[4] The religious products of the encounter between African slaves and European enslavers that Herskovits attributed to "the acculturative process" have been seen to imply socio-determined transitions to a dominant, Western cultural system. Beliefs and practices of African origin were therefore seen as cultural "survivals," lingering behind an inexorable process of Westernization. The acculturative model of Afro-Latin syncretism thus was seen to fail to recognize the retention of African traits as active resistance on the part of the enslaved, valorizing African ways of knowing as powerful weapons against the dominating culture. In Andrew Apter's words:

> ... Herskovits's syncretic paradigm highlights the limitations of American liberal scholarship... it privilege[s] adaptation and accommodation over opposition and contradiction ... his understanding that such culturally embodied imponderables [e.g.: African religious symbols] persisted as retentions because they resisted change. Clearly, this notion of resistance is passive, attributed elsewhere to "the force of cultural conservatism."[5]

A second concern on the part of scholars with the syncretism model for the study of Afro-Latin religion concerns the simplification of cultural sources to two: European and African.[6] Closer attention to history reveals that each of these cultural precedents is itself a loose arrangement of traits from a bewildering variety of sources. The preferred model therefore might be creolization, repeated reintegrations of cultural traits to form new entities. Afro-Latin religions therefore are not so much syncretisms of African and European elements as creole constructions of elements from overlapping constructions of the past. What is "African" and what is "European" is no longer fully, or at least easily, identifiable in the revalorizations of the meaning of religious symbols over quite short periods of time.[7]

Since the 1980s an increasing number of practitioners of Afro-Latin religions have written defenses of their traditions, objecting to the term syncretism as demeaning and misleading. They have seen that the label "syncretistic" has been a term of disparagement when used by religious authorities. For those who are committed to the purity and excellence of their tradition, the label syncretistic implies impurity and mongrelization. They rightly note that the obvious cultural mixtures that have gone into the development of the Christian tradition rarely cause Christians to think of their religion as syncretistic, so the purpose of the term can only be to denigrate and marginalize the traditions born in the Caribbean.

Priests of Afro-Latin religions are suspicious of the term syncretism for another reason, one that combines the scholarly critique about agency with their own concerns about purity. They argue that far from being mixed, their traditions are essentially African and that the Christian elements observed by outsiders are camouflage to protect African worship from persecution. Priests and priestesses of Afro-Latin religions deliberately used deception to hide their veneration of African spirits behind a facade of Christian symbols. Rather than passive converts to Christianity, or confused "syncretists," they were active agents in the preservation of their African traditions against determined efforts by Christian authorities to destroy them. In the translated words of distinguished Candomblé priestess Mãe Stella of Bahia, Brazil: "Our ancestors, for the sake of not being massacred, were obliged to syncretism. This is what we want to stop doing ... we are beyond the time to hide our religion."[8]

Finally we can see a revival of interest in the category with the work of anthropologists Charles Stewart and Rosalind Shaw. For them the term syncretism, and its reactive companion anti-syncretism, mark vital processes of identity formation and social border construction. They write: "[R]ather than treating syncretism as a category—an "ism"—we wish to focus upon *processes* of religious synthesis and upon *discourses* of syncretism. This necessarily involves attending to the workings of power and agency."[9]

It may well be impossible to rescue the term from the history of disparagement it connotes. Several scholars have advocated abandoning the term altogether. Yet the controversy around "syncretism" indicates to me that something important in the study of religion is at stake, not the least of which is the problematic category of "religion" itself. In this paper I would like to revisit the idea of "syncretism" as an explanatory category in the study of Caribbean religions and more particularly within the tradition most popularly known as Santería. I will look at one so-called syncretism, the now classic one between an African god and Catholic saint, specifically an *orisha*-spirit called Shango and the Catholic Santa Barbara. I argue that this well-established correspondence between *orisha* and saint is a conscious, thoughtful strategy on the part of enslaved and liberated Africans in Cuba to organize their religious experience in a meaningful way. The correspondence of Shango and Santa Barbara allowed Afro-Cubans to layer their social, cultural, and religious lives in fulfilling and sustaining ways under extraordinary duress. Rather than a simple disguise or camouflage in an age of religious oppression, I believe that the *orisha*-saint correspondence extends and enhances the social and spiritual possibilities for their devotees. I will begin with a discussion of the devotions to *orisha* Shango in Africa and in Cuba, move to the veneration of Santa Barbara in Cuba, examine the correspondence of the two in Santería practice, and conclude with the implications for the utility of "syncretism" as an explanatory category for the correspondence.

SHANGO IN AFRICA

Oral histories locate Shango in the distant times of human origins after the creation of the world.[10] He was the son of Orañyan founder of the

Yoruba city of Oyo which became the capital of a great West African empire in the seventeenth century. In at least one reckoning Shango was the son of Oduduwa, the divine ancestor of the Yoruba people. Shango is usually considered the fourth *alafin* or "owner of the palace" of Oyo and its most revered hero. There are many stories of Shango's bravery in battle and his extraordinary powers. As a master horseman he led the Oyo cavalry to important victories in the consolidation of Oyo's hegemony over much of Yorubaland. At the empire's height in the eighteenth century, Oyo controlled large areas of what is now Nigeria and Benin, and many kings paid tribute to the *alafin*. The city was famous as a commercial center and its trade routes spread west to Ghana, north to the Islamic states of Kano and Bornu, and south to the lucrative European markets on the Atlantic coast. Oyo cavalry was unrivaled in the region and made for swift communications and rapid military responses across the empire. Shango was reputed to be Oyo's greatest horseman, and his skills reflected the lightning speed of the kingdom's power.

Yet there is also a persistent strain of ambivalence in the Shango story, and there are still more accounts of his powers being tested, misused, and rejected. The most well-known of these was recorded by a nineteenth-century Yoruba historian who took the English name of Samuel Johnson.[11] He writes that Shango was as famous for his supernatural powers of attracting lightning as for his military skills. Shango could direct fire out of his mouth to consume his enemies and bring lightning down on those he judged to be evil-doers. During one demonstration of his lightning charms he inadvertently set the Oyo palace ablaze, killing many of his wives and children. In despair he abdicated his throne and set off for Nupeland to the north where his maternal grandfather ruled. Johnson notes that in some versions Shango decided himself to abdicate out of remorse, while in other accounts he was forced to step down by "a strong party in the state." As he left for Nupeland those loyal to him attempted to dissuade him from leaving, but he violently attacked them for their interference. Johnson writes:

> He was said to have caused 160 persons to be slain in a fit of anger, of those who were showing much concern and over-anxiety on his behalf, and who would prevent him by force from carrying out his resolve.[12]

After this, all his party deserted him, and in despair Shango hanged himself at the nearby town of Koso. Apparently many people of Oyo repented their denial of Shango and, on visiting Koso, brought back the news that he had not hanged but instead underwent an apotheosis into an *orisha*, a divine being. His principal shrine was established at Koso and a priesthood was ordained there to revere his memory and carry out his divine will. Shango now rules from heaven as the master of thunder and lightning and is venerated throughout Yorubaland.

Other stories of Shango's fall carry similar themes of ambivalent power and ambiguous fate. In one he is challenged by one his generals who had taken for himself one of Oyo's tributary states and mastered a charm that was impervious to Shango's fire. He came to Oyo in triumph to demonstrate his power over Shango by having a large fire built at the Oyo market and hurling himself into it. Untouched by the flames he declared, "All the fire of this town [Oyo] cannot touch me. Abdicate your throne or I will drive you out of this town."[13] Defeated, Shango left Oyo accompanied only by his loyal wife Oya. Again, it is said that he hanged himself in the forest and ascended to heaven on a golden chain. Oya organized his followers to sing, "Oba Koso" a Yoruba pun meaning "The King at Koso" and "The King did not hang himself."

The denial of hanging is addressed in yet another version where Shango is said to have entered the forest after quarrels within his palace and complaints of tyranny from without. When his followers came searching for him they heard his voice from afar saying, "I will not come back to you: I will now rule you unseen."[14]

The combination of royal and supernatural powers makes Shango a compelling and dreadful figure in Yoruba mythology. The French ethnographer Pierre Verger recorded Shango's devotees singing at a ceremony for the great *alafin*:

He dances savagely in the courtyard of the impertinent
He sets fire to the house of the man who lies.
Owner of the destroying ax,
He sounds his maracas like iron handbells.[15]

Another song recorded by Ulli Beier praises Shango:

Shango is the death that drips *to, to, to,*
Like indigo dye dripping from a cloth.
Shango is the death that kills money with a big stick.
He is the lightning flash
Wrapped in a cloak of death.[16]

Shango's priests offered the divine *alafin* sacrifice and prayer and acted as his mediums in ceremonial states of trance. When the ritual conditions were appropriate Shango was said to "ride" his priests and priestesses like a horse (*elegun*), "mounting" their bodies and directing them to do his will. In ceremonial trance Shango priests and priestesses would incarnate the royal *orisha*, exhort their congregations, and prophesy and heal. Mounted by their deity they were variously called the "eyes," "wives," and "horses" of the orisha king, mediums to his presence throughout his earthly realm.

The veneration of Shango, and these themes of royalty, warfare, fire and lightning, ambiguous power, apotheosis, and spirit mediumship, were carried to a new world when his priests and priestesses suffered mass enslavements beginning in the late eighteenth century.

SHANGO IN CUBA

The successful revolution in Haiti and the liberation of its enslaved population in the first decade of the nineteenth century had far-reaching consequences for the Yoruba. At the moment that European investors were seeking vast new investments in sugar cultivation, the Yoruba were beset with civil strife. Hundreds of thousands of Yoruba men, women, and children were displaced by the disintegration of the Oyo empire and sold as slaves to work in the burgeoning sugar mills of Cuba. Between 1821 and 1860, some 375,000 Africans were brought to Cuba, and by 1850 nearly 35 percent of them might have been designated Yoruba.[17] The arrival of such large numbers of Yoruba in such a relatively short period of time transformed Cuba's ethnic mosaic and ensured that the Yoruba were a lasting cultural presence on the island. Though over one hundred different African ethnicities have been documented in Cuba, only a few were able to sustain themselves throughout the ordeal of slavery and its aftermath.[18] Through their trial and rebirth in Cuba, Yoruba traditions have achieved a preeminence throughout the Afro-Atlantic world.

The Yoruba of Cuba were known as Lucumi and their traditions today are still often referred to as *la regla lucumi* (the Lucumi order). The Lucumi language was spoken throughout the island and Lucumi institutions were recognized in nineteenth-century Havana and Matanzas. The most public of these were chartered assemblies known as *cabildos africanos*, mutual aid societies organized by people from the same *nación* or ethnic group in Africa.[19] Fernando Ortiz documented fourteen different African *naciónes* among the *cabildos* of Havana at the end of the nineteenth century with the Lucumi, once again, preeminent.[20] The *cabildos africanos* provided financial legal assistance, health care, funeral services and recreational opportunities for their members and families. In many cases they acted as savings banks where members could raise the funds to purchase their freedom and that of other members. This orientation toward independence and freedom took on other dimensions in that the *cabildos* were often at the center of active resistance to the government and the slave system. One of the earliest and best known Afro-Cuban resistance movements was organized at a Havana Lucumi *cabildo* and called *Cabildo Shangó Terdún.*[21] In 1812 a well-planned uprising of enslaved and free people of color was exposed and the *cabildo* leaders put on trial. Their avowed goals according to the records were "to abolish slavery and the slave trade, and to overthrow colonial tyranny and to substitute the corrupt and feudal regime with another, Cuban in nature, and without odious discriminations."[22]

The name *Shangó Terdún* can be roughly translated as "Shango is the Thunder Stone,"[23] and the connection between the powers of the royal *orisha* and the struggle for freedom was likely made by the conspirators. Historian Philip Howard writes:

> From Shangó they received special spiritual powers by heredity. It is possible that their belief in Shangó may have prompted them to engage in conspiracy, thinking that the god might protect them as they plotted to make war on Spain.[24]

The conspiracy failed but the name *Shangó Tedún* continued to inspire Afro-Cubans in resistance to their enslavement and struggle for civil rights. There were several other *cabildos* that took up the name in the nineteenth and twentieth centuries, honoring the memory of Afro-Cuban resistance and the patronage of the Shango.[25]

Allied with their economic and political functions, the *cabildos* also offered religious opportunities to their members. The great Cuban folklorist Lydia Cabrera notes that Afro-Cuban priests of Shango in the mid twentieth century remembered "Changó Terddúm" with pride and traced their descent in Shango's priesthood through the old *cabildo.* Parenthetically Cabrera notes that *cabildo Changó Terddúm* was known by another name, *cabildo de Santa Bárbara,* indicating a devotion to one of the most popular Catholic saints of the island. Many of the *cabildo* leaders had served as militiamen and, as Santa Barbara was known to be much respected in the military, it may be through their influence that Shangó Tedún took on this saintly patroness.

Many of the *cabildos* were also *cofradías,* religious brotherhoods sanctioned by the Catholic Church and dedicated to the veneration of a Catholic saint. It was a matter of law that all slaves carried to the island be baptized as Roman Catholics, and most civic rights and duties were legitimized by the Church. On a popular level, nearly every person, place, and thing was identified with a patron saint, and the *cabildos* followed suit. On the feast days of their heavenly patrons and on other major festivals of the Church, the *cabildo* members would process through the streets of the cities carrying an image of their saint.

This concern for both Catholic and African traditions can be seen in the by-laws of a Havana *cabildo* called *El cabildo africano Lucumi*. The *cabildo* was reorganized in 1839 under the patronage of Saint Barbara with a banner of scarlet and white. In its regulations the *cabildo* agreed to march in all the festivals and offer dances "prohibiting the interference of drum rhythms that are not of its [Lucumi] *nación*." Annually on Saint Barbara's feast day of 4 December, the *cabildo* agreed to sponsor a solemn Mass at a church and on the following day a requiem Mass for deceased members with an ensuing procession.[26]

Here we see a concern for the exclusive preservation of Lucumi drum rhythms and dances brought together with the public veneration of Santa Barbara. Shango's distinctive colors of red and white are corresponded with those of Santa Barbara. The Lucumi were developing a means to maintain Shango devotions while participating in the public and Catholic religious life of Cuba.

Though the Oyo empire was dissolved in the maelstrom of the Atlantic slave trade, Yoruba religious traditions took root in Cuba through the veneration of Shango. Art historian David Brown speaks of a "shangoization" of Yoruba religion in Cuba, whereby the rites of initiation and manifestation of different Yoruba *orishas* were reorganized along the model of Shango's royal installation.[27] Calixta Morales, one of Lydia Cabrera's senior teachers in the religion of the *orisha* deities, told the folklorist: "[T]o make an *orisha* is to make a king."[28] She is saying that to initiate a devotee into the mysteries of most of the major *orishas*, he or she must be "crowned" in the tradition of the royal house at Oyo. Thus devotees of *orishas* such as Obatalá, the Ifé king of purity, Yemayá, the ocean mother, Ochún, the river healer, and Oya the stormy warrior, are all initiated into the mysteries of their deities according to the rites of Shango. The initiate is seated on Shango's mortar throne and called "*iyawó*" or "bride" of the *orisha*. The concept of initiation as royal installation, and the relationship between human and *orisha* as one of bride and spouse, shows the power of Shango traditions and its priests to mold all others in the new world of Cuba. Historian Miguel Ramos, himself a Shango priest, has documented the largely successful efforts of priests descended from such Havana *cabildos* such as *Changó Tedún* to create an Oyo-centered orthodoxy in the diaspora. By the force of "Havana's ordination mandate," only those crowned on Shango's mortar and presented to his sacred *batá* drums could be considered authoritative priests of his or her *orisha*.[29]

The very heart of *orisha* veneration in Cuba owes its impetus to the worship traditions of Shango. It will be recalled that the messengers of the *alafin*, as well as the priests of Shango, were alternately called "wives" and "eyes" of the earthly and heavenly *alafin*. It was the priestly "wives" of Shango who brought the presence of the *orisha*, and by extension the presence of his earthly successor, into the corners of the empire by ceremonial spirit manifestation. "Possessing" his Oyo-trained medium priests, Shango could interact with his earthly subjects through his priestly "wives." He could bless or admonish them and offer them heavenly protection or chastisement. In the diaspora in Cuba this model of *orisha* worship became the central ceremony of *orisha* congregations throughout the island. Occasioned by Shango's sacred *batá* drums, most of the major *orishas* came to manifest themselves through their medium "wives" and made themselves present to inspire their devotees. Through the institutions of royal ordination and ceremonial spirit manifestation, Oyo and Shango reasserted their authority in diaspora. Ramos cites a sentiment common among *orisha* priests in Cuba, "Shango inventó la religión" (Shango invented the religion).[30] While this may be an something of an overstatement, it is apparent that Shango's priests and priestesses reinvented Yoruba traditions in the Americas and shaped them to meet the challenges of the harsh new world.

In Cuba, Shango's veneration required the delimitation of spaces and times where the *orisha alafin's* earthly presence could be localized in ceremonial forms. In the old *cabildos,* and today in many private homes of *orisha* devotees, a corner space is usually found for the construction of occasional altar displays which both conceal and reveal Shango's presence and tell his story in visual form.[31] At the center of every Shango altar are his sacred stones (*otan*) resting and concealed inside a lidded wooden bowl (*sopera* or tureen). The *sopera* bowl is often placed on a wood mortar, enthroned like the kings of Oyo. Overhanging and enclosing the space are red and white hangings of glittering cloth, the more sumptuous and bright the better to reflect the glory of the *orisha alafin*. The altar is Shango's throne, the space his court, the devotees who prostrate themselves before the stones, his courtiers. The *sopera* is often adorned with intricately-strung necklaces of red and white beads which are worn by the *orisha's* devotees on ceremonial occasions. It may be further draped with rich cloth *paños,* panels of satiny fabric which shroud the *sopera,* as a tabernacle for Shango in his stones. The altar space may be adorned further with ritual symbols of Shango: his *oché*—the twin-bladed thunder ax; his *ogués*—the beaded ram's horns; or arrayed on the floor before his throne might lie his sacred double-headed *batá* drums. The ax, horns, drums—even the arrangement of the hangings—suggest doubleness, twinness and thus balance.[32] Altar maker and *orisha* priest Ysamur Flores-Peña says that Lucumi altars "are earthly conceptualizations of each *santo's* heaven."[33] In the brilliant display Shango reveals himself in heavenly balance, his ideal state that stabilizes the imbalances of his powerful will.

At times of initiation or anniversaries of ordination, the floor before the altar may be spread with Shango's favorite foods: okra stew, ram, apples, and bananas. Surrounded by these offerings, the altar becomes a sanctuary before which the dance-dramas of Lucumi religion are performed. When a new initiate is ordained as a priest of Shango he or she is vested in a satin costume of crimson and white, each a unique creation of a master dressmaker. Shango wears distinctive three-quarter length short trousers called *chokotó* that are often hemmed in a crenellated pattern, like the battlements of a royal castle.[34] Magnificently costumed, the new priest of Shango, now his *iyawo* or bride, dances before the congregation to the rhythms of the *batá*. If Shango finds the dances, rhythms, foods, and regalia to his liking, he may descend to "possess" the *iyawo*, "mount" him or her, and manifest himself in the *iyawo*'s whirling body. Incarnated in his human medium, Shango comes to bless and reprimand, heal and prophesy for his subjects. Grasping his thunder ax, he brings down lightning to terrify the wicked and fight for the oppressed.

The allusion to castle crenellation in Shango's initiatory garments recalls us to the creolizing process in Shango's rebirth in Cuba. For the castle is a motif of Santa Barbara, and the connection between Shango and Santa Barbara is recognized in many Lucumi symbolic displays for Shango. Her chromolithograph is often affixed to the drapery or her image may be set atop the *sopera*. A widely-distributed photograph of a Shango altar shows a characteristic arrangement: wooden *sopera*, flanked by red-painted *ochés*, atop the inverted mortar; this time it is draped with a silkscreened cloth bearing a silhouette of the saint.[35] Anthropologist William Bascom saw a magnificent ceremonial machete made for Shango's altar on sale in Havana in the 1940s. Covered with cowries and red and white beads, the image of Santa Barbara could be found in the beadwork.[36] Art historian Robert Farris Thompson has called attention to the frequent use of castle-motifs in Cuban Shango altars, an appropriation of Santa Barbara's imagery for Shango's uses.[37] We turn now to see what these uses are, and how the Lucumi organize a complex religious life of many parts.

SANTA BARBARA MOUNTED

We have seen the Yoruba peoples, enslaved and scattered, employing a variety of strategies to survive and flourish in Cuba. Taking advantage of the relative freedom of association provided by the *cabildos*, Yoruba men and women reconstructed their sense of themselves through the development of their traditions of veneration to the *orishas*, the deities of Africa. We have seen, too, that part of the transformation of *orisha* traditions in the Americas involved the appropriation of Christian institutions and symbolism. At least one incarnation of *Cabildo Changó Tedún* was also known as *Cabildo Santa Barbara*, and its members likely participated in the public veneration of the saint on her 4 December feast day. It is interesting to ask why priests and priestesses of Shango chose Santa Barbara as their Catholic patroness and how they organized their African devotions to cohere with their Christian ones.

Santa Barbara has been one of the most popular saints in Christendom and her legend has been preserved since at least the seventh century.[38] Her story is set in the times of persecution surrounding the third-century reign of the Emperor Diocletian. Barbara is said to have been the daughter of a wealthy pagan named Dioscorus who imprisoned her in a tower, either to prevent her marriage or to keep her from the corrupting influence of Christianity. Somehow Barbara learned the elements of the Christian faith and her father denounced her to the Roman prefect. She was tortured and sentenced to death by beheading. Barbara's father himself carried out the sentence, but as punishment for such a terrible deed he was struck by lightning and consumed in fire. Church scholar J. P. Kirsch writes:

> The legend that her father was struck by lightning caused her, probably, to be regarded by the common people as the patron saint in times of danger from thunderstorms and fire, and later by analogy, as the protector of artillerymen and miners.[39]

Today the United States Army maintains an honorary society called the Order of Saint Barbara and its web site illuminates the connection between lightning and artillery:

> When gunpowder made its appearance in the Western world, Saint Barbara was invoked for aid against accidents resulting from explosions—since some of the earlier artillery pieces often blew up instead of firing their projectiles. St. Barbara became the patroness of the artillerymen.[40]

It is not difficult to see significant parallels in the stories of Santa Barbara and Shango. Each dies an ignominious death, yet brings death to family by lightning. Each associates lightning with retribution. Each is invoked for protection against such rough justice. And each is connected with the militancy of fire: Shango in his magic and lightning, and Santa Barbara in the force and danger of gunpowder.

The connections are even more apparent in the iconography of the saint. Santa Barbara is depicted in statuary and lithography as a beautiful young woman with unbound hair. She is bedecked with the regalia of martyrdom: crown, red cape, and royal palm. She often carries a sword to show the instrument of her martyrdom and a chalice and Eucharistic wafer to assure those who petition her that they will receive the sacrament at the time of death. In statuary she is accompanied by a miniature tower, often with three windows which recall her devotion to the Christian trinity. In lithography she is usually depicted standing before the tower, often with lightning coursing through the distant sky. In several images her crown is crenellated like a tower battlement, and in a Cuban postcard she stands before Havana's Morro Castle, guarding the entrance to the city's harbor. Each reinforces her connection with fortifications and the military.

The associations between Santa Barbara's imagery and Shango's seem abundant and apparent. Shango is a crowned king, the owner of a great palace. He is a armed warrior whose colors are red and white. He manifests in thunder and lightning and illuminates the great palm and *ceiba* trees. In many images of Santa Barbara the haft of her sword intersects with the hilt to resemble Shango's *oché*, his double-headed thunder ax.[41] Even the Eucharistic cup may be taken for a double-headed instrument, either the *oché* or a *batá* drum.

As so many Lucumi did not read it is likely that these iconographic associations furthered the identification of Shango and Santa Barbara to circles well beyond the literate leadership of the *cabildos*. By the mid nineteenth century it was apparent even to visitors to Cuba that the Lucumi had created associations between their *orishas* and the Catholic saints. Swedish traveler Frederika Bremer visited the *Cabildo de Señora Santa Barbara de la nación Lucumi Alagua* and witnessed a dancer

> … with a scarlet hat upon his head, and with a great number of glittering strings of beads round his neck, arms, and body, which was naked to the waist, from which hung scarlet skirts.[42]

Amid the displays of Catholic saints Bremer was quick to note the remains of the "superstition and idolatry of their native land."[43] At the turn of the twentieth century American visitor Irene Wright documents some of the specific correspondences with predictable Northern indignation:

> It was the most astounding confusion of heathenish and Catholic worship one could imagine: they sang in barbarous tongue to Christian saints, and to them they sacrifice white cocks occasionally; in the dances, which must have originated about African campfires, they flaunt yellow as the color of Our Lady of Cobre, white for Mary of Mercies, purple and green

Illustration 5.1. | *Birthday Altar (Trono) of Chango Ladé, Houston, Texas, 1989. © Tony de Quinzio. Courtesy of Mary Ann Clark.*

for Saint Joseph, and red for the favorite saint, protecting Durbara, each of whom has an African name. In honor of these respective patrons they wear copper, silver, bead and coral trinkets. The local Catholic church recognizes this same symbolism, in color and in ornament.[44]

In the early decades of the twentieth century Cuban Spiritualists had isolated "Seven African Powers" among the Lucumi *orishas* and created an image that is now ubiquitous in the Latin world. A widely-distributed chromolithograph depicts a chain of seven cameos of Catholic saints surrounding a image of the crucified Christ. Each image bears a text label below it that identifies the saint by the name of a Lucumi *orisha*. Our Lady of Ransom is labeled Obatala; Our Lady of Regla—Yemalla; Our Lady of Charity—Ochun; Benedict the Moor—Elegua; John the Baptist—Ogum; Francis of Assisi—Orula; and Santa Barbara is labeled Chango.

In the present many popular songs attest to the juxtaposition of saint and *orisha*. While the chorus chants "Que Viva Chango" in a salsa song by N. G. La Banda, the vocalist sings, "*Santa Barbara bendita, para ti surge mi lira, y con emocion se inspira, ante su imagen bonita*" (Holy Santa Barbara, for you my lyre sings, and it's inspired with emotion, in front of your beautiful image).[45] Another popular Cuban *salsero* Adalberto Alvarez sings: "*Desde la Africa vinieron y entre nosotros quedaron, todos aquellos guerreros; Y a mi cultura pasaron, Obatala es Mercedes, Ochun es la Caridad, Santa Barbara es Chango, Regla es Yemaya*" (From Africa they came and they stayed among us, all those warriors; And they passed into my culture, Obatala is Mercedes, Ochun is Caridad, Santa Barbara is Chango, Regla is Yemaya.).[46]

Perhaps the most intriguing correspondence between Santa Barbara and Shango can be found in many *botanicas*, religious goods stores in Latin neighborhoods throughout the United *States*. A spectacular example may be found at *Botanica Yemayá y Changó* in Washington, D.C.: a statue of Santa Barbara mounted on a horse, sword raised for battle. The nearly life-sized fiberglass sculpture is set in a niche all to itself surrounded by a dazzling array of red and white symbols of Shango. A shelf overhead bears a line of red candles. To Santa Barbara's right the shrine maker has fixed a beautiful beaded *oché*, the red and white pattern of the encrusted beads vibrating like zigzagging lightning. To her left hangs a horse-tail fly whisk, the *iruké*, a Yoruba symbol of royalty; its handle also shimmering with red and white beads. Draped about the horse's neck is a massive *collar de mazo*, a multi-strand beaded initiation necklace. The effect is rich, royal, and heavenly when we recall Flores-Peña's idea about the Lucumi aesthetics of divinity. The statue of Santa Barbara itself is raised on a dais so that the saint appears above

Illustration 5.2. | *Shrine to Santa Barbara-Shango, Washington, D.C., 2000. Photo © Joseph M. Murphy.*

us, looking down from her mount. The horse is supported by a pylon molded to look like a tree and in the base are cast in lifelike fiberglass offerings red apples, yellow bananas, and a red rooster. The floor of the base is wrapped in silver foil and surrounded by buckets of fresh red flowers.

Santa Barbara is depicted as a pale-skinned young woman, with long molded dark hair. She is dressed in a long white robe with a red mantle lying across her back. Sitting on her head is a golden crown and she is haloed with a gold metal nimbus. Her right hand raises the Eucharistic cup, filled with dollar-bill offerings. Her left holds the reins of the horse and her sword. She gazes ahead placidly. The final touch of this bright composition is the sculpting of the saint's small legs, set together over the left side of her mount, sidesaddle.

The mounted Santa Barbara statue is an engrossing study in mixed religious symbolism for any number of reasons. Here in the United States capital, a large, public shrine for Santa Barbara and Shango is an active devotional site. Fresh flowers and crisp dollar bills show that people are coming to the statue to petition the divinity for favor. The mounted female figure is white, pale, a picture of pious European virginity. Around her are signs of African royalty: *iruké* fly-whisks; *ochés;* and heavy, rich strands of beads. The symbols are unmistakably Shango's, appropriate to his initiation altars and *batá* drum dances. The shrine not only juxtaposes Shango's African accoutrements with Santa Barbara's sculptural styles, but blends the symbolism in mounting Barbara on horseback. In the hands of the Lucumi artist the aesthetics of Santa Barbara's portraiture are molded to reflect Shango's symbolism. Shango is remembered in oral traditions as a cavalryman and so, to reinforce his recognition through Santa Barbara's sculptural conventions, it is appropriate that Santa Barbara is mounted. And, as befits a saint and gentlewoman, she is sidesaddle.[47] The knowledge and praise of Shango's equestrianism meets Santa Barbara's gentility to form a uniquely creole construction.

There is an active pun at work as well. As a "divine horseman" Shango is known to "mount" his devotees in ceremonial spirit manifestation. As a rider directs a horse and puts it through its paces, so the *orisha* Shango "mounts" the body of his medium priests and priestesses. By showing Santa Barbara/Shango mounted, the relationship between horse and rider, and thus human and divine is displayed. This relationship between rider and mount has sexual connotations as well that are not lost on Shango's devotees. To be a mount of Shango is to be his "bride" at initiation and "wife" in attendance. The ecstasy of spirit mediumship, during which the devotee loses consciousness, can also be understood as the sexual union of human and the *orisha* who mounts him or her.[48]

Finally the great Santa Barbara/Shango statue begs a question that has been here all along. Why did the Lucumi, in seeking an iconogra-

Illustration 5.3. | *Santa Barbara Statue with* aro *ring of Shango's tools, Philadelphia. Photo © Joseph M. Murphy.*

phy and social context to venerate Shango, choose a woman to do so? There are plenty of male saints. If Shango is a warrior, often described as "muy macho," hyper-masculine, why choose the pale virgin Barbara? Would there not have been an obvious and irreconcilable discontinuity between the black, male god and the white, female saint?

The most usual explanation refers to the necessity for the Lucumi to disguise their *orisha* devotions from the police power of Church or state officials. In the early days of Cuban independence at the dawn of the twentieth century, the ruling elite was anxious to prove its "progressive" capacity for self-government and so launched a number of repressive campaigns against "brujería" or sorcery.[49] In this environment it was important for *orisha* devotees to insist that the Lucumi practices were Catholic. Fernando Ortiz records one such incident:

> The sorcerer Bocú defended himself skillfully before the tribunal that condemned him, saying that the altar that he had in his house was dedicated to a Catholic divinity, to Santa Barbara, and that, of course, he was not a sorcerer.[50]

Hiding *orisha* veneration from such harassment would seem a wise course and the saints might serve as effective camouflage. This view would see Lucumi participation in folk Catholicism as a cover, screen, or blind to deflect attention from their true religion, *orisha* veneration. Irene Wright, the American visitor to the *cabildo* cited above, speaks of the Lucumi "flaunting" the symbols of the Catholic saints, implying an insincere display. While Yoruba sculptural arts survived in Cuba in a number of striking examples; the plaster and paper images of the Catholic saints were at hand and relatively cheap. The Lucumi witnessed the veneration of the saints all around them and its conventions provided ready models for alternate and semi-clandestine devotions to the *orishas*. Still, why Santa Barbara and not another saint to disguise Shango? It could be her association with the military and the fact that early *cabildo* leaders were often military personnel. They may have brought their devotions to Santa Barbara back to the *cabildos* and then made the appropriate correspondences. It may be that the story of death by lightning and the petition for protection against it was too powerful an association to ignore. If the Lucumi were invoking Shango for protection against lightning when they were among themselves would it not be natural, not to mention politic, to invoke Santa Barbara when they were among others? The correspondence is certainly reinforced in the common colors. Wright saw the association of Catholic saint and *orisha* primarily by color, "red for the favorite saint, protecting Barbara." Santa Barbara's popularity in Cuba and her invariable portrayal in a scarlet cloak would make her the prime candidate to represent Shango's fiery red. With a niche for red-clad Santa Barbara in nearly every Cuban chapel there were multiple opportunities to represent Shango and thus the iconography of color could have been more important than that of gender. Historian of religion Mary Ann Clark argues that color symbolism is a primal marker of *orisha* identity in Lucumi iconography, more important than the anthropomorphic images of the saints. She writes:

> ... as human figures they [the saints] more closely approximate our anthropomorphized visions but they are in no way closer to the Orisha they represent than fruit, candles, bolts of cloth, sets of beads or natural phenomena.[51]

In choosing to represent elemental *orishas* by anthropomorphic saints it would appear that the Lucumi are following African iconographic conventions in the depiction of the *orishas* in Cuba. For it is rarely the deity and almost always the human medium who is portrayed in human form. *Orishas*, with the possible exception of Eleggua, are rarely imaged in anthropomorphic form in Yoruba art. The regalia of Santa Barbara and the other Catholic saints suggest the initiation vestments of the *iyawo*, the newly made "bride" of the *orisha*. It is likely that the vestments of the Catholic saints themselves were important influences in the development of Lucumi initiation clothing.[52] The white, female figure is thus not Shango "himself" but rather "Shango in manifestation" through the person of his priestly medium.

Finally the gender of the *orishas* have an interesting indeterminacy. Many stories of the *orishas* point to a time in the primordial past when they were of different genders.[53] This could be again an emphasis on their priests "in manifestation" as Shango or Obatala. Thus stories "when Obatala was a woman" could be historical markers highlighting the mythicized actions of Obatala priestesses in the past.

Shango in particular has a provocative capacity to manifest across genders. Among the Lucumi there is a much contested tradition that Shango has two natures: Changó macho (male) and Changó hembra (female). Shango priest Andres refers to "a belief in the religion" that "Shango is six months a woman and six months a man."[54] William Bascom heard a similar assertion when he asked Cuban devotees about the correspondence with Santa Barbara:

> ... the identification of Chango with a female led some informants to say that Chango changes his sex, is a hermaphrodite, or has distinct male and female manifestations. Most informants emphatically denied these views, and for many Chango is the epitome of machismo because of his many wives and love affairs.[55]

These "accusations" and denials represent an ongoing pattern in Shango veneration now brought into the realm of gender. As the impetuous king of Oyo who rides swift horses and swifter lightning, he is the paragon of masculine aggression and pride. The Lucumi count him handsome, fastidious, muscled like his *batá* drummers. In Africa, when he manifests himself in the bodies of his priests, they often wear women's clothing and hairstyles. Lorand Matory sees this transvestism as an important political and religious reflection of power relations in Oyo. Shango, the mighty *alafin* "possesses" his "wives" and so subjugates his people to his will. Matory writes:

> The cross-dressing of male possession priests in the Oyo-Yoruba context seems to represent … the male adoption of a style of productive and re-productive servitude attributed typically to the fecund wives of mighty husbands.[56]

This propensity of Shango to be portrayed as a woman is remembered in a famous Lucumi *pataki* divination story.[57] Shango was defeated in battle and pursued by his enemies to the house of Oya, his favorite wife. Oya came out to meet the surrounding army and consented to a search for Shango if they would allow her a few moments to get properly dressed. She hurriedly cut some of her hair to make a wig for Shango, dressed him in women's clothing and sent him through the enemy line with a company of women messengers. Thus Shango escapes his enemies by this "disguise" and lives on to rule though the form of womanly "messengers."

The ambivalence about Shango's gender is also recalled in some of his dance behavior where, in Shango priest Andres's phrase, "he has to prove that he's a man" by taking off his shirt. On at least one occasion he has been seen dancing with his *oché* ax between his legs to call attention to his masculine virility.[58] Yet again the theme of ambivalence is inescapable. Shango's veneration is so deeply defined by his detractors, doubters of his manhood or his divinity. He is forever required to prove his power, be it to the satellite states of Old Oyo, or the Oyo council, or the assemblies who invoke him.

This same interest in gender and disguise can be seen in attitudes about Santa Barbara. When asked about Santa Barbara's story the botanica owner said that in ancient times she had been a warrior and "hid as a man and fought many battles. She had the same job as Shango."[59] It seems that saints as well as *orishas* can hide themselves and manifest themselves in alternate genders. Through folk memory and ceremonial re-enactment, the Lucumi tradition is maintaining the power of Shango in particular and divinity in general to be more that it appears: to be something and something else again. "Shango means trouble," the *olorishas* say, and the ambivalence surrounding his power, his gender, and his divinity is preserved in his encounter with Santa Barbara. Shango is hiding behind Santa Barbara, manifesting through her, and alternating with her in a dynamic symbol of Lucumi religious life. The indeterminacy and ambivalence is a hallmark of the sacred. The divinity has the power to confound categories to the wonder and edification of its devotee. In Cuba, the mixed alternatives have been constructed out of Cuban social experience: African and the European; male and the female. The power of Shango and Santa Barbara is enhanced by simultaneity: that they are both the same divinity and a different one.

SYNCRETISM: THE OUTSIDE AND THE INSIDE

The decision on the part of the Cuban Lucumi to correspond Shango with Santa Barbara represents extraordinary religious creativity and resilience. Enslaved, stripped of the social and material supports of African religious life, Yoruba men and women in Cuba found a way to survive and flourish in the harshest of new worlds. The folk Catholicism into which they were thrust became a vehicle for the development of their traditions of Shango veneration and so shaped a complex religious world where *orishas* and saints could be both same and different.

We have spoken of the idea of that the saints acted as a kind of camouflage for the *orishas*, a survival mechanism on the part of the Lucumi in a strange and oppressive land. Forced by law into Catholic baptism, surveilled by Church and State, it made sense for the Lucumi to disguise their worship of the *orishas* in the face of persecution. In deceiving a hostile authority, the Lucumi can be seen as agents in taking control of their symbolic life and resisting the cruelties visited upon them. It is gratifying to think of the Lucumi outwitting their oppressors as a clever rabbit bests a stronger bear in a different African-American context.

The "hiding the *orishas*" thesis has been put forward by a number of authors and goes back to the earliest observers. Irene Wright, the American traveler cited above, referred to the Lucumi as "flaunting" Catholic imagery. Herskovits speaks of "devious reinterpretations" of European symbols by Africans in the Americas.[60] More recently the deception explanation has been reviewed and accepted by Andrés Pérez y Mena, who argues that Euro-centric researchers were themselves deceived by practitioners to believe that that the Catholic symbols at Caribbean altars were evidence of syncretism and that the saints were more important than they in fact were in the devotional life of *orisha* venerators.[61] Mary Ann Clark maintains from her extensive experience of *orisha* traditions in Houston that "*no hay ningún santo aqui*" (There are no saints here). She observes that the saints are not primary signifiers of the *orishas* but rather supernumerary ones. She writes:

> I ... suggest that among a wider range of goods that can be associated with the Orisha, the Catholic saints form not primary but secondary, substitutable signs. By focusing scholarly attention on the relationship between saints and Orisha we have over-valorized one set of secondary signs while disregarding many which are more basic.[62]

Many believers as well have seen the saints as unnecessary, if not corrupt, symbols in the religion. Earlier in this chapter, I cited one of the most distinguished *orisha* priestesses in the world, Mãe Stella of Bahia, Brazil, who has dedicated herself to a program of *contrasincretismo*. Oba Ernesto Pichardo writes in the mission statement of Church of Lukumi Babalu Aye, perhaps the foremost institution of *orisha* veneration in the United States: "Our culture and traditions are not a source of embarrassment that needs to be disguised through syncretism."[63] New York Yoruba priest Gary Edwards promotes a "Yoruba Reversionism" for practitioners in the Americas in which "Orisa concepts, where possible, should be returned to their original pre-slavery state minus the influence of the Catholic saints. ..."[64]

While the necessity to hide the veneration of the *orishas* should not be underestimated, it does not explain the resiliency and creativity of the *orisha*-saint correspondence. There is more at work in the correspondence of Shango and Santa Barbara than simple deception of colonial authority. Similar correspondences are found throughout the African diaspora, and they have persisted into relatively ecumenical times. They are not arbitrary, but thoughtful. Given the longevity and ubiquity of the association of Shango-Santa Barbara, it seems clear that the Lucumi were not organizing their participation in both *orisha* and saint veneration as "true" devotions hidden behind "false" ones, or, at least, as *only* true behind false. The masking of Shango by Santa Barbara has an ironic dimension, a double-entendre that means more than one thing to the devotees who maintain it.

Judith Gleason articulates a more nuanced view of the co-existence of the *orishas* and saints in Cuba when she writes that the correspondences are "based on intuitive kinship rather than happenstance." She speaks of a creative sense of "shared sovereignty. You acquire strengths from both, but don't get them confused."[65]

When master drummer Francisco Aguabella appears in the documentary film *Sworn to the Drum* he is shown playing *batá* drums at a ceremony for Shango. In the next scene he is lovingly decorating his castle-like Santa Barbara altar with red flowers, miniature *batá* drums and a white horse. He says: "Santa Barbara is *mi patrona* ... I don't work on Santa Barbara's day. I love this saint very much."[66]

Aguabella's devotion to Santa Barbara, like that of so many other Lucumi practitioners, appears to be a less a camouflage and more a form of his devotion to Shango, appropriate to certain levels of discourse and social experience. He does not seem to be pretending to venerate Santa Barbara, but rather venerating her as a representation of Shango.

Another great Afro-Cuban devotee is even more forthright in his defense of the place of the Catholic saints in his devotional life. Master drummer Felipe García Villamil speaks of the movement in the United States to purify Yoruba traditions of the Catholic saints:

> Here they want to eliminate the statues, well, they may do it if they want to, but we can't. If I find out that in Cuba they begin to do the same I'm going to protest, because that would be a lack of respect for our ancestors. What happened was that our ancestors used the statues to be able to manifest the power of their things, the stones were below those statues. Even if they were Catholic figures and at the time may have had no spirituality, our ancestors gave them a spirituality by using them the way they did. Then when we came along the saints were already there. We were born seeing that the Virgen de la Caridad del Cobre is Ochún. So how can they come now and tell us it isn't Ochún? Those things have roots that cannot be unearthed. Doing so would be mocking our ancestors.[67]

Garcia Villamil may be arguing the position of the "old guard" who grew up in Cuba with the Roman Catholic sacred canopy spread over its social life. As Miguel Ramos has argued the younger generation of orisha priests and priestesses are losing the "affinities" that Gleason spoke of in regard to the saints.[68] The saints no longer occupy the same place in contemporary society, Cuban or North American, that they did, and the movement to find new signifiers or return to antique ones will go on. There will continue to be orthodoxies and heterodoxies for those, in Gleason's words, "for whom revelation and relativism pose intolerable contradictions or, at the other end of the spectrum, by nativist or nationalist spokespersons struggling to erase residues of subordination."[69]

The organizing principle of the Lucumi appropriation of the saints can be seen in continuity with Yoruba patterns of religious symbolism. Melville Herskovits emphasized the West African paradigm of accumulation of devotions to spiritual beings, the readiness of West African peoples to add the deities of neighbors, conquerors and vassals to their pantheons.[70] From this perspective the Lucumi appropriation of Catholic saints is an extension of the Yoruba integration of deities from Dahomey or Tapa. Andrew Apter takes this point farther in seeing the African appropriation of conqueror's gods as a "counter-hegemonic strategy" to get power over them.[71]

In addition to appropriation of foreign spirits, Yoruba religion, like many African traditions, involves progressive initiation into secrets, or perhaps better, "mysteries" (*awo*). The practitioner is led by those who "have" the *orisha* into deeper levels of understanding of the meaning and power of *orisha* symbols. At each level of initiation the devotee discerns covert meanings that are known only to progressively restricted groups of initiates. Apter speaks of *imo jinle* "deep knowledge" available to powerful priests and priestesses that allow them to discriminate between overt and hidden truths.[72] In Shango veneration we learn that horses can be riders, wives can be husbands, women can be men, and saints can be *orishas*. The initiatory message is clear: What appears is not the whole reality, and beneath each level of understanding lies another one—"*mas profundo, mas profundo a la infinidad*" in the words of Cuban Ochún priestess Maria Galban.

The saints and *orishas* thus constitute a fascinating juxtaposition of outer and inner, cast in terms of initiatory knowledge and social experience. The saints are a level of *orisha*, a more visible and public way to represent the *orishas* in a complex and heterogeneous society. Santa Barbara is, then, the outer level, the outer face of Shango, appropriate to public, Catholic levels of discourse. Shango is "inner knowledge" appropriate to the more intimate world of Lucumi ceremony and aspiration. Santa Barbara is an extension of Shango into the creole world of the Americas, where his power can be more broadly represented, understood, and shared. Santa Barbara and Shango thus might be seen as different representations of the power of lightning at different levels of social and spiritual experience.

I will conclude with a brief return to our problem of syncretism. I believe what is interesting about the phenomenon that we call "syncretism" is not the fact of cultural mixture, which is present in every historical religious expression, but rather the way in which the mixture is organized. If the term is to be useful in describing religious phenomena such as the correspondence of Shango and Santa Barbara, I would like to attach to it certain qualifications that reveal the dynamics of Lucumi spirituality—the way in which Yoruba and Roman Catholic elements are mixed. I see in the "syncretism" of African god and Catholic saint three characteristics that may be present in other such syncretisms and that reveal the particular qualities of mixture that make Lucumi religion sensible to its devotees.

First, the syncretism of Shango and Santa Barbara is one of *juxtaposition:* The *orisha* and saint are placed side by side in thoughtful ways in space and time. They are deliberately organized in arrangements of higher and lower, inner and outer. They comment on each other, revealing new meanings of similarity and difference in their placement and structure. Second, the syncretism of *orisha* and saint is characterized by ambivalence: They are both valid ways of accessing the power of lightning, at once the same and different. Shango is at once an exemplar of justice and a overweening monarch; at once a *macho* man and a disguised women or wifely medium. And he is both a warrior and a virgin martyr. The meaning of Shango and Santa Barbara moves back and forth between and among these possibilities, producing a powerful tension, irony, and sometimes parody. Third, this juxtaposition and ambivalence has religious implications in the experience of *paradox*. In Mircea Eliade's formulation, religious symbols are *hierophanies*, irruptions of the sacred realm into that of the profane, the world of absolute being into the temporal and conditioned world we live in.[73] To express this extraordinary coming together, religious people use paradox in attempt to capture and experience the ineffable transcendence of the sacred world. The results are meaningful but non-rational, even impossible juxtapositions: the bush of Moses that is not consumed by its flames, the virgin mother of Christian devotion, the Indian Siva Ardhanisvara—the male god who is a woman. Shango-Santa Barbara is another expression of this paradox using the symbols of the Lucumi's complex social experience.

I think that these characteristics are present in other syncretisms in other cultural contexts as well. And a consideration of the juxtapositions, ambivalences, and paradoxes of other mixed symbolic formu-

---

Illustration 5.4. | *Altar cake for Santa Barbara-Shango, Alexandria, Virginia, 2005. Photo © Joseph M. Murphy.*

lations may yield insight into their meanings for their creators. The Indian, Nigerian, Chinese, Iroquois, Mayan, and other peoples represented in this volume are making arrangements of Christian and indigenous symbolic elements. These arrangements make sense in their local idioms and work to foster satisfying social and religious experiences.

For the Lucumi, the correspondence of Santa Barbara and Shango became the way to distinguish between their cultural and social identities as well as connect them. They could be both Lucumi and Cuban while maintaining a dynamic tension between the two. The juxtaposition of Santa Barbara and Shango in Lucumi ceremonial life reveals a creative response to a complex and difficult social environment as well as a subtle spirituality. The Lucumi recognize that the deity has more than one face, more than one manifestation, and rests always below what appears. The correspondence of *orisha* and saint allows the Lucumi to live in multiple worlds as citizens of Oyo, Cuba, and heaven.

Notes

1. Raymundo Nina Rodriguez, *O Animismo Fetichista dos Negros Bahianos* (Rio de Janeiro, 1935 [1906]); Fernando Ortiz, *Hampa Afro-Cubana: Los Negros Brujos* (Miami, 1969 [1906]).

2. Melville J. Herskovits, "African Gods and Catholic Saints in New World Negro Belief," *American Anthropologist* 39 (1937): 635, 636.

3. Full-length works that have taken up the idea of syncretism in Afro-Latin religions include: George E. Brandon, *Santeria from Africa to the New World: The Dead Sell Memories* (Bloomington, IN, 1993); Roger Bastide, *The African Religions of Brazil: Toward a Sociology of the Interpenetration of Civilizations* (Baltimore, 1978 [1960]); Diana Brown, *Umbanda: Religion and Politics in Urban Brazil* (Ann Arbor, MI 1986); Leslie Desmangles, *The Faces of the Gods: Vodou and Roman Catholicism in Haiti* (Chapel Hill, NC, 1992); Melville J. Herskovits, *Life in a Haitian Valley* (New York, 1937); Claude F. Jacobs and Andrew J. Kaslow, *The Spiritual Churches of New Orleans: Origins, Beliefs, and Rituals of an African-American Religion* (Nashville, TN, 1992); Seth Leacock and Ruth Leacock, *Spirits of the Deep: A Study of an Afro-Brazilian Cult* (Garden City, NY, 1975); Alfred Metraux, *Voodoo in Haiti* (New York, 1972 [1959]); Joseph M. Murphy, *Santeria: An African Religion in America* (Boston, 1988); and Donald Pierson, *Negroes in Brazil: A Study of Race Contact in Bahia* (Carbondale, IL, 1967 [1942]).

4. Andrew Apter, "Herskovits's Heritage: Rethinking Syncretism in the African Diaspora," *Diaspora* 1, no. 3 (1991): 235–60.

5. Ibid., 242.

6. See Apter, "Herskovits's Heritage"; and David H. Brown, *Santeria Enthroned: Art, Ritual, and Innovation in an Afro-Cuban Religion* (Chicago, 2003), 113–21.

7. A full discussion of the uses of "creolization" and the problems associated with it is carried out in Charles Stewart, ed., *Creolization: History Ethnography, Theory* (Walnut Creek, CA, 2007), 18ff. Stewart, as well as several contributors to that volume, think that the term "creolization" has been spread too thin to cover too many cultural processes. He would substitute the term "restructuring" for the phenomenon that interests us.

8. These statements are posted on the official website for Ile Opo Afonja, one of the most prestigious houses of *orisha* veneration at which Mae Stella presides. "Ilé Axé Opô Afonjá," www.geocities.com/axeopoafonja/page11 (accessed 1 June 2003).

9. Charles Stewart and Rosalind Shaw, *Syncretism/Anti-syncretism: The Politics of Religious Synthesis* (London, 1994), 7.

10. Samuel Johnson is content to count Shango as a "mythological" rather than a "historical" king. See *The History of the Yorubas: From the Earliest Times to the Beginning of the British Protectorate* (Lagos, 1921 [1897]), 143–55. Oyo's origins are reviewed by Robert S. Smith, *Yoruba Kingdoms of the Nineteenth Century*, 3rd ed., (Madison, WI, 1988 [1969]), 30–31; and Robin Law, *The Oyo Empire: c1600–c.1836: A West African Imperialism in the Era of the Atlantic Slave Trade* (Oxford, 1977), 30–37. I am indebted to the masterful summary by Miguel Ramos in his "The Empire Beats On: Oyo Batá Drums and Hegemony in Nineteenth-Century Cuba" (MA thesis, Florida International University, 2000).

11. Johnson, *The History of the Yorubas*, 150–52.

12. Ibid., 151.

13. Ulli Beier, *Yoruba Myths* (Cambridge, 1980), 22.

14. E. Bolaji Idowu, *Olodumare: God in Yoruba Belief* (London, 1962).

15. Shango praise texts from Pierre Verger, *Notes sur le Culte des Orisa et Vodun* (Dakar, 1959), 363. Translated by Judith Gleason and published in *Leaf and Bone* (New York, 1980), 165.

16. Ulli Beier, *Yoruba Poetry* (Cambridge, 1970), 31.

17. Figures from Juan Perez de la Riva, *Cuantos africanos fueron Traidos a Cuba?* (La Habana, 1977), 12, cited by Ramos, *The Empire Beats On*, 74. Historian Philip Curtin provides figures for extrapolating the presence of the Yoruba in the slave trade of the mid nineteenth century: Of 13,273 African slaves that were "recaptured" and landed in Sierra Leone by British anti-slaving patrols in 1848, 7,114 of them were Yoruba. See *The Atlantic Slave Trade: A Census* (Madison, WI, 1969), 245. David R. Murray cites a contemporary British estimate of 246,798 African slaves entering Cuba between 1840 and 1867. See his *Odious Commerce: Britain, Spain and the Abolition of the Cuban Slave Trade* (Cambridge, 1980), 111, 112. Other figures are from Manuel Moreno-Fraginals, "Africa in Cuba: A Quantitative Analysis of the African Population in the Island of Cuba," in *Comparative Perspectives on Slavery in New World Plantation Societies*, ed. Vera Rubin and Arthur Tuden (New York, 1977), 190–91, cited by Ramos, *The Empire Beats On*, 73.

18. On African ethnicity in Cuba, see Isabel Castellanos and Jorge Castellanos, "The Geographic, Ethnologic and Linguistic Roots of Cuban Blacks," *Cuban Studies*, 17 (1987): 95–110.

19. See Philip A. Howard, *Changing History: Afro-Cuban Cabildos and Societies of Color in the Nineteenth Century* (Baton Rouge, LA, 1998) and the seminal work by Fernando Ortiz, *Los Cabildos Africanos* (Havana, 1921).

20. Ortiz, *Los Cabildos Africanos*.

21. Howard, *Changing History*, 73–79. See also David H. Brown, "Garden in the Machine: Afro-Cuban Sacred Art and Performance in Urban New Jersey and New York," Ph.D. dissertation, Yale University, 1989, 16–27.

22. Howard, *Changing History*, 75

23. David Brown offers two possible translations: "Shangó who/which is the thunderstone"; and "Shangó who is the red monkey." See "Garden in the Machine," 20 n. 16.

24. *Changing History*, 74.

25. Miguel Ramos offers two other examples of Oyo continuity and Lucumi militancy in the prosecution of Juan Nepomuceno Prieto, director of *cabildo* Lucumi Elló [Oyo], for his role in a slave revolt of 1835 and the famous failed conspiracy of La Escalera in 1844 in which oral traditions uphold that *Cabildo Changó Tedún* played a role. Ramos, *The Empire Beats On*, 78.

26. Ortiz, *Los Cabildos Afrocubanos*, 24.

27. David Brown, personal communication. See *Garden in the Machine*, 382ff.

28. Lydia Cabrera, *El Monte* (Miami, 1970), 24.

29. Ramos, *The Empire Beats On*, 95–97.

30. Ibid., 100. Shango priest Andres E. told me that Shango "owns the religion," and he "brings everybody together; all the powers and mysteries of all the *orishas* are owned by Shango." Personal communication, 11 February 2002.

31. See Ysamur Flores-Peña and Roberta J. Evanchuk, *Santería Garments and Altars: Speaking Without a Voice* (Jackson, MS, 1994).

32. See Robert Farris Thompson, *Black Gods and Kings* (Bloomington, IN, 1976), 12/3–12/6.

33. Ysamur Flores-Peña, "Overflowing with Beauty: The Ochún Altar in Lucumí Aesthetic Tradition" in *Osun Across the Waters: A Yoruba Goddess in Africa and the Americas*, ed. Joseph M. Murphy and Mei-Mei Sanford (Bloomington, IN, 2001), 115.

34. There may be a Yoruba pun at work here as well. Shango is sometimes called "Oba Sokoto" which, depending on the tonal pronunciation, might mean either: King of Sókótó, the Fulani kingdom; or King of Sòkòtò, the short trousers. I was put on to this by Yoruba linguist Adetokumbo Adekanmbi. See R. C. Abraham, *Dictionary of Modern Yoruba* (London, 1958), 592; and Lydia Cabrera, *Anagó: Vocabulario Lucumi* (Miami, 1970), 92.

35. Cover photograph by Reginald L. Jackson for second edition of Murphy, *Santería* (Boston, 1992).

36. William R. Bascom, *Shango in the New World* (Austin, TX, 1972), 15.

37. Robert Farris Thompson, *Face of the Gods: Art and Altars of Africa and the African Americas* (New York, 1993), 21, 240.

38. See *Butler's Lives of the Saints*, ed. Herbert J. Thurston, S. J. and Donald Attwater, 4 vols. (Westminster MD, 1981 [1756–59], 4: 487–88; S. Baring-Gould, *Lives of the Saints* (London, 1877), 25–28; and "St. Barbara," *The Catholic Encyclo-*

pedia, ed. Charles George Herbermann et al., 15 vols. (New York, 1907), 2: 284–85, http://www.newadvent.org.cathen/02284d.htm (accessed 13 June 2011).

39. *Catholic Encyclopedia,* ibid.

40. "The Military Order of Saint Barbara," sill-www.army.mil/pao/pabarbar.htm (accessed 18 January 2002). I'm indebted to Georgetown student Jillian Silva for finding this reference. Francesco Pellizzi of the journal *Res* told me that in late medieval Italian forts the building that housed the gunpowder was called "the santa barbara" and it was a dangerous place. More than occasionally it would explode. The goal of invading cannon was to hit the "santa barbara" and cripple the defenders, if not blow them up. When people saw the images of Santa Barbara with the castle behind her they thought that it was the "santa barbara" building within the fortifications. Personal communication, 16 March 2002.

41. This association was pointed out to me by Georgetown student Connie Razza of the Georgetown University class of 1994.

42. Fredrika Bremer, *The Homes of the New World: Impressions of America,* trans. Mary Howitt (New York, 1986 [1853]), 380.

43. Ibid., 383.

44. *Cuba* (New York, 1910), 150.

45. "Que Viva Chango," *Salsa Bendita* (Havana, 1994), compact disc. My thanks to Alfonso Alanis-Cué for help translating these songs.

46. "Que Tu Quieres Que Te Den," *Salsa Bendita.* Again, thanks to Alfonso Alanis-Cué for translation help.

47. Interview with Andres E., 7 November 2001. Mr. E. said that in requesting a sidesaddle version of the statue he wanted Santa Barbara to "look more like a gentle woman … more of a woman saint."

48. J. Loran Matory argues that the crudity of the metaphor of "mounting" indicates Shango's [and his earthly *alafins'*] assertion of power in the sexual domination of their "wives." He writes: "These parallel verbal associations ["horse," "mount"] suggest the suitability of women and cross-dressing men to a violent and sexually redolent subordination to the royal god." *Sex and the Empire That is No More: Gender and the Politics of Metaphor in Oyo Yoruba Religion* (Minneapolis, MN, 1994), 7, 10, passim.

49. See Aline Helg, *Our Rightful Share: The Afro-Cuban Struggle for Equality, 1886–1912* (Chapel Hill, NC, 1995), 107–16.

50. Ortiz, *Hampa Afrocubana,* 33 (cited by Thompson, *Face of the Gods,* 204).

51. Mary Ann Clark, "Asho Orisha (Clothing of the Orisha): Material Culture as Religious Expression in Santería," (Ph.D. dissertation, Rice University, 1999), 155.

52. Brown, *Garden in the Machine* and Flores-Peña *Santeria Altars and Garments.*

53. See Beier, *Yoruba Mythology;* Harold Courlander, *Tales of Yoruba Gods and Heroes* (New York, 1973); and Randy P. Connor and David Sparks, *Queering Creole Spiritual Traditions: Lesbian, Gay, Bisexual, and Transgender Participation in African Inspired Traditions in the Americas* (New York, 2004).

54. Andres E., personal communication, 11 February 2002.

55. Bascom, *Shango in the New World,* 14.

56. Matory, *Sex and the Empire,* 8.

57. Told to me by Andres E., personal communication, 11 February 2002.

58. Andres E. told me that when women priestesses of Shango attend *batá* ceremonies they will often wear men's clothing beneath their ordinary clothes. If Shango should "mount" them during the ceremony their modesty can be preserved.

59. Interview, 7 November 2001.

60. Melville J. Herskovits, "The Contribution of Afroamerican Studies to Africanist Research," *American Anthropologist* 50 (1948): 4.

61. Andrés I. Pérez y Mena, "Cuban Santería, Haitian Vodun, Puerto Rican Spiritualism: A Multiculturalist Inquiry into Syncretism," *Journal for the Scientific Study of Religion* 37 (1998): 15–27.

62. Clark, "Asho Orisha," 154.

63. "Church of the Lukumí Babalu Aye," http://www.church-of-the-lukumi .org/editorial.html (accessed 1 June 2001).

64. Gary Edwards and John Mason, *Black Gods—Orisa Studies in the New World* (Brooklyn, New York, 1985), v.

65. Judith Gleason, "Oya in the Company of Saints," *Journal of the American Academy of Religion* 68 (2000): 284, 268.

66. Les Blank, *Sworn to the Drum: A Tribute to Francisco Aguabella* (El Cerrito, CA, 1995), film.

67. María Teresa Vélez, *Drumming for the Gods: The Life and Times of Felipe García Villamil, Santero, Palero and Abakuá* (Philadelphia, 2000), 141.

68. Miguel Ramos, "Ashé in Flux: The Transformation of Lukumí Religion in the United States," paper presented at the 47th Annual Conference of the Center for Latin American Studies, University of Florida, Gainesville, 26–28 March 1998, 9–14.

69. Gleason, "Oya," 267.

70. *The Myth of the Negro Past* (Boston, 1990 [1941]), 71–72.

71. "Herskovits's Heritage," 253.

72. Ibid., 249.

73. *Patterns in Comparative Religion,* trans. Rosemary Sheed (New York, 1958).

꧁ 6

INCULTURATION, MISSION, AND DIALOGUE IN VIETNAM: THE *CONFERENCE OF REPRESENTATIVES OF FOUR RELIGIONS*

Anh Q. Tran

INTRODUCTION

Since the seventeenth century, Christianity has been an important part of Vietnamese religious scene[1] in conjunction with the three religions imported from China (Confucianism, Taoism, and Buddhism) and the indigenous cults of Heaven and spirits. Between 1615 and 1870 Catholic Christianity established itself as a significant religion in Vietnam, both in Tonkin and Cochinchina.[2] It took root in the native soil despite being small and often persecuted. An important witness to the encounter of Christianity with the traditional Vietnamese religions during this era is the anonymous *Conference of Representatives of Four Religions* (*Hội Đồng Tứ Giáo Danh Sư*), abbreviated as *Conference of Four Religions* (*Hội Đồng Tứ Giáo*).[3] Written by an unknown author in the demotic Vietnamese scripts (*chữ Nôm*),[4] this work purports to be a report of an actual debate between representatives of Confucianism, Taoism, Buddhism, and Catholic Christianity that took place in 1773 in Tonkin (North Vietnam). The themes and concerns discussed in the debates reflect the task of transplanting a religion to new soil.

This essay presents the *Conference* as a case-study about the challenges of the inculturation of Christianity into Asia, and particularly into Vietnam. Native categories were used and adaptations were made. At the end, one must judge from the evidence presented by the author as to whether Catholic Christianity could be counted as an acceptable expression of Vietnamese religiosity while maintaining its own uniqueness. The *Conference*'s primary purpose was to explain and defend the rationality and legitimacy of Christianity from the charge of being a foreign, false, and harmful religion. In the following sections, I first discuss the background and context of this literary work. Next, I provide a brief analysis of selected issues involved. And finally I draw some implications for understanding the significance of the Catholic inter-religious encounter in pre-modern Vietnam.

THE RELIGIOUS AND LITERARY CONTEXT OF THE *CONFERENCE OF FOUR RELIGIONS*

Traditional Vietnamese Religions

Prior to the arrival of Christianity most Vietnamese practiced some form of what is known as the Triple Religion (*Tam giáo*), a mixture of Confucianism, Buddhism, and Taoism together with the indigenous cult of spirits.[5] After centuries of Chinese domination, many thoughts, customs, and habits were so deeply ingrained into the Vietnamese way of life that to separate what was originally native and what came from its northern neighbor is quite difficult. As a result, Vietnam's traditional religious identity reflects the appropriation of the cultural-religious systems from China. It integrates Buddhist metaphysics, Confucian ethics, and Taoist epistemology into the practice of a Triple Religion without the need to maintain the distinction between them. These teachings offer moral and practical guidance which link personal, family, and social levels of existence.[6]

In the early twentieth century, Léopold Cadière, a French missionary and cultural anthropologist, noted that "the true religion of the Viet people is the cult of the spirits. This religion has no history, because it dates from the origins of the race."[7] This cult of the spirits forms the basis of the Vietnamese religious ethos to which elements of Buddhism, Taoism, and Confucianism were amalgamated. A belief in a personal, benevolent, and just deity called Heaven (*Trời*) who is above all spirits allows the Vietnamese to live according to the will of Heaven, to do good deeds and avoid evil. This belief in Heaven has never been formalized into an organized religion: There are no sacred books, images, temples, formalized rituals or prayers, and no official priests or ministers. All worship to Heaven is done outdoors on an open altar. Although everybody believes in Heaven, only the king—the representative of the people—can perform the annual solemn ritual to heaven (*tê´Nam-Giao*).[8] The common people, however, do not regularly practice the cult of Heaven; instead, they substitute for it the cult of ancestors and the cult of spirits. The ancestors are said to be present even after death residing in the family altar. Ancestor worship is common for Vietnamese of all religious dispositions.[9] At the community level, villagers placate local spirits linked to the village who are charged with protecting it. National heroes receive a royal deification certificate to be honored and worshipped publicly.

Confucianism (*đạo Nho*) was introduced together with other forms of Chinese literature, sciences, and arts in the third century of the common era. Even long after being independent from Chinese rule, the Vietnamese kings and lords decided to appropriate Confucian ideology to obtain royal loyalty, establish law and order, and bring stability to society. Though supported by the state, only the basic ideas of Confucianism reached the masses; the common people held on to customs that were transmitted orally and observed in everyday life. The vast majority of Vietnamese did not understand Confucianism as a cohesive system. Rather, they appropriated fragments of Confucian ethics and supplemented them with local customs and beliefs. Most people continued to seek out help from the local genies as well as Taoist and Buddhist practices for their spiritual needs. Even the erudite were practical; they were less interested in philosophical metaphysics than in rules of conduct and correct ritual. Vietnamese Confucians did not write extensive commentaries on the Confucian classics or engage in debates about Neo-Confucianism like their counterparts in China, Korea, or Japan. They seemed to focus on learning the classics well enough to pass the state civil exam and to spend their energy on poetry. Still, because Confucianism remained a state ideology, it enjoyed the full support of the royal court from the fifteenth century until 1918 when the traditional civil examination was abolished. In the process, Confucian scholars set out to be the spokespeople for Taoism as well as Buddhism, by absorbing those elements that are common to all three.[10]

Taoism (*đạo Lão*) also came to Vietnam during the Chinese occupation. However, Taoist philosophy (Chinese: *daojia*) had limited influence outside of the erudite class. In spite of this, the Taoist spiritual outlook allowed one to be closer to nature and free from the constricted life regulated by Confucian rules of conduct. Because of its resemblance to spirit worship, religious Taoism (Chinese: *daojiao*) was well-received by the common folk. The masses eagerly worshipped Taoist deities and practiced its magical, physical, alchemical, and meditative rituals to achieve longevity and immortality. The animist-Taoist practices blended so seamlessly that even their practitioners could not always tell the difference. In Vietnam, Taoism never gained institutional status; it remains largely a folk religious practice with many superstitious elements.[11]

Vietnamese Buddhism (*đạo Phật*)—predominantly a combination of Pure Land and Zen elements of Mahayana Buddhism—came to Vietnam first from India and then from China some time in the second century. However, it did not take root until the sixth century, when Zen Buddhism became more influential in Vietnamese life. During the early independence era Vietnamese rulers found a cultural force in Buddhism that could counter-balance Confucianism. Many prominent Buddhist monks became national advisors and exerted political influence. Buddhism reached its highest development between the eleventh to fourteenth centuries, becoming one of the three religious-philosophical systems of thought (*Tam giáo*).[12] While the social elite and rulers embraced Buddhist philosophy as part of their education, the masses adopted Buddhism as a religion of salvation. Buddhist doctrines of karma and reincarnation influenced popular piety. The village pagoda became a place of refuge from life-suffering, both communal and personal. Beginning in the fifteenth century, however, Vietnamese Buddhism went into decline and fell out of favor at the royal court. It was only with the revival movement in the twentieth century and Buddhist involvement in Vietnamese politics after World War II that Buddhism came to the center stage again.

Pre-modern Vietnamese were disposed to welcome and accept the possibility of multiple religious sentiments. The native language did not have an equivalent word to the Latin term *religio*; instead, Vietnamese people refer to religion as "way" (*đạo*) or "teaching" (*giáo*). Thus, Confucianism was called, "the Way/Teaching of the Erudite" (*đạo Nho / Nho giáo*); Taoism, "the Way/Teaching of Laozi" (*đạo Lão / Lão giáo*); Buddhism, "the Way/Teaching of the Buddha" (*đạo Phật / Phật giáo*). Since *đạo* means a way of living, it is understandable that the Vietnamese have often adapted newer traditions to their existing belief systems, blending traditions together without seeing them as contradictory.[13] They freely took values from different religious traditions or teachings and incorporated them into their own religious practices and worship. Traditional temples in Vietnam can be places of worship of buddhas and bodhisattvas, of gods and goddesses as well as popular village or national heroes, without becoming exclusive. The deities do not share a common altar. Rather, there are shrines and side chapels on the temple grounds dedicated to different deities and spirits to request different favors.[14] In the minds of the common people, "all religions are good" (*đạo nào cũng tốt*). This understanding, however, should not be taken to mean that there is religious indifference in Vietnamese culture. On the contrary, the Vietnamese religious ethos affirms the goodness of all religions and the need to learn from them all. For example, the Confucian concept of humanness (*nhân*; Chinese: *ren*) and righteousness (*nghĩa*; Chinese: *yi*) is seen as compatible with the Buddhist doctrine of compassion; the Taoist notion of purity and quietude is exchangeable with the Zen idea of emptying the mind. This "harmony" of religions was not free from competition or threats by various political maneuvers at different times in Vietnamese history. A clear distinction among the three religions did not exist among pre-modern Vietnamese. At the time of the encounter with Western missionaries, a Vietnamese person was able to be Confucian in his conduct, but Taoist, Buddhist, or both, in his devotion.

The Arrival of Catholic Christianity

When Jesuit missionaries came to Cochinchina in 1615 and Tonkin in 1626,[15] they found in the Vietnamese religious ethos a natural disposition toward the Christian faith—in the worship of Heaven, a strong belief in fate and the afterlife, and a relational ethics that treated all people as family members, among others. Because many of their converts were from the lower classes with few Confucian literati, the dialogue between Christianity and Confucianism was limited and unsophisticated. The missionaries' main concern was how to adapt the Gospel in a new soil without radically altering its basic message. While some missionaries thought that a total destruction of the old religions and customs was necessary before reconstruction, the Jesuits argued for moderation. For example, knowing how the Vietnamese were deeply devoted to their ancestors and parents, they allowed Vietnamese Catholics to honor the dead according to local custom but with modifications meant to ensure that only God was worshipped. The popularity of Catholic Christianity was due both to the Jesuit strategy of accommodation and the fact that it appealed to the spiritual needs of the peasants who were tired of warfare, poverty, and suffering.[16]

The new religion, however, still found itself at odds with some traditional values. Christianity's insistence on exclusive devotion to a single deity, rejection of polygamy, prohibition of participation in local religious festivals, and its limitations on the rite of ancestor worship were interpreted by its opponents as a rejection of the ancestral way and a promotion of the foreign way. In addition, rumors of Vietnamese Catholics being more loyal to the pope, a foreign monarch,[17] than to their own king and lord aroused suspicion among the ruling class. Much of the clash between Christianity and Vietnamese religions stemmed from court politics and religious jealousy. To understand the Vietnamese rulers' attitude toward Christianity, one might view a royal decree in 1785 by King Nguyễn Nhạc:

> The followers of this religion (Christianity) do not recognize [the authority of] father and king. They do not worship deities and spirits; they gather at night to recite books and prayers. Men and women mingle to-

gether without being [properly] separated, and are not ashamed by such
behaviors. They are lazy and do not work, doing nothing to procure the
goods and inheritance. Finally, they take no shame in being punished.[18]

To consolidate the support of the Confucian elite and avoid a divided
society, Vietnamese rulers banned Christianity and persecuted both
missionaries and believers, at various times between 1625 and 1862.[19]
Although a number of cases of Christian repression were prompted
by considerations of state security and public order, many arose in
part because Vietnamese rulers, both in Tonkin and Cochinchina, saw
Christianity as a threat to established social norms derived from Confucianism. As early as 1663, Vietnamese Christians were criticized for
abandoning the ancestral way. In his edict against Christianity, Lord
Trịnh Tạc, the ruler of Tonkin, claimed:

> Followers of the heterodox way (*tả đạo*) who do not kowtow to the de-
> ceased commit an offense of unrighteousness (*bất nghĩa*, [failure to do the
> duties as expected by society]). They do not worship the ancestors, thus
> they commit an offense against filial devotion (*bất hiếu*, [being ungrate-
> ful to one's ancestors]). The capital offense they commit is to destroy the
> ancestral tablets [i.e., wooden tablets with the name and position of the
> deceased inscribed on it]; this is the utmost disrespectful act (*đại bất kính*)
> that is equivalent to homicide.[20]

The Confucian elites, who were eager to defend the traditional way of
life, saw the destruction of the ancestral tablets in Vietnamese Christian
homes as the ultimate betrayal of Vietnamese culture. Pope Clement
XI's decree against the Chinese Rites—the *Ex Illa Die* (1715)—which
took effect in Vietnam by 1717,[21] succeeded in convincing the Confucian literati and ruler that this "Jesus religion" (*Gia-tô giáo*) was a false
one. This ban on venerating one's ancestors became the main deterrent
to becoming Christian for people of good will.[22]

Thus, in addition to political motives, the bans on Christianity reflected a clash between a Christian culture and a native one. There
appears to be a causal link between orthodox Confucianism and the repression of Christianity. The rise and fall of Confucianism affected how
its adherents viewed other religions. While there was some evidence
of purging Buddhism and Taoism of superstitious elements in the seventeenth and eighteenth centuries, the Confucian elite never viewed
these religions as a threat to its own monopoly. When Christianity, with
its link to foreign Western powers and its defiance of Confucian social
practice, became a competing voice in the culture, it was inevitable that
it would be suppressed by the highest authorities.[23]

A SYNOPSIS OF THE *CONFERENCE OF FOUR RELIGIONS*

Literary Context of the Conference

Against this background, it is reasonable to see why an explanation of Christian beliefs and practices was needed to gain the confidence of the new converts and to refute their detractors. In fact, the aim of a number of Vietnamese apologetic works that appeared in the eighteenth and nineteenth centuries was to persuade the new converts and their critics that Catholics do not commit any faults against the state or their parents and ancestors. On the contrary, Christianity also upheld the traditional virtues—especially those of filial devotion and loyalty—in its teaching and practice, even though its manifestation might seem different to societal expectations. Viewed in this context, the *Conference of Four Religions* sought to justify the presence of Catholic Christianity in the religious milieu of Vietnam.

The *Conference* claims to be a record of a religious debate among the representatives of four religions—the three traditional religions and the "new" religion—that took place in 1773 at the court of the Lord Trịnh Sâm, ruler of Tonkin.[24] In reality, this work is most likely an early nineteenth-century composition.[25] The anonymous author tried to demonstrate the compatibility of the new religion with the traditional Vietnamese way of life. However, at the same time, he firmly rejected what he saw as erroneous beliefs in the traditional religions. While there is no solid evidence that the work depended directly on previous Christian apologetic writings that appeared in China and Vietnam, we must take into account the influence of these works. Here, I would like to cite three examples of such writings: Matteo Ricci's *Tianzhu Shiyi*, Alexandre de Rhodes's *Cathechismus*, and Adriano di St Thecla's *Opusculum de Sectis*.

The Jesuit missionary to China, Matteo Ricci (1552–1610), was a pioneer in Christian-Confucian dialogue. His masterpiece, the *Tianzhu Shiyi* (*True Meaning of the Lord of Heaven*),[26] written in literary Chinese and published in 1603, aimed at expounding Christian doctrines in concepts intelligible to his Chinese audience. This work presents Christianity as compatible with native philosophical suppositions. It appears that the author of the *Conference* was quite influenced by the *True Meaning* both in style and theological concepts. These resemblances, at times verbatim, are evidence of a dependency of the latter work on the former. Many arguments in the *Conference* can be traced to the *True Meaning*.[27] In particular, the *Conference*'s arguments for the existence of God are quoted from almost the same texts in the Chinese classics. Furthermore, the style of argument and refutation of the *True Meaning* was clearly reproduced in the *Conference*, though the latter is much less philosophical.

The second influence on the *Conference* was a 1651 bilingual Latin-Vietnamese catechism composed by the Jesuit missionary Alexandre de Rhodes (1593–1660). The *Cathechismus pro iis, qui volunt suscipere Baptismum in Octo dies divisus* (A Catechism for Those Who Want to Receive Baptism Divided into Eight Days),[28] provided a brief summary of Christian doctrines, from the purpose of life to eschatology. De Rhodes's influence on the *Conference*'s vocabulary and views of the native religions was profound. For example, the use of natural reason, the appeal to Chinese classical sources, the universality of Christianity, the negative attitudes toward Buddhism and Taoism, the teaching on the Three Fathers (*Tam Phụ*: God, king, and father), etc. Apart from these parallels, the *Cathechismus* as a whole does not have any direct literary influence on the *Conference*. This is due to the different purposes of the two works. The *Cathechismus*'s primary purpose was to help missionaries present Christian beliefs and doctrines, whereas the *Conference*'s was to defend the legitimacy of Christianity. De Rhodes's treatment of the traditional Vietnamese religions was brief, negative, and inaccurate and was based on hearsay, even with respect to Confucianism. The author of the *Conference*, on the other hand, allowed each religion to speak for itself, and he used reason, analogy, historical knowledge, and the Chinese classics to refute these religions.

Another apologetic work which appeared shortly before the *Conference* is a 1750 work by an Augustinian missionary named Adriano di Santa Thecla (1667–1775). Written for European missionaries, the *Opusculum de Sectis apud Sinenses et Tunkinenses* (A Small Treatise on the Sects among the Chinese and Tonkinese)[29] was composed in Latin with insertions of many terms in Vietnamese Romanized script (*chữ Quốc-ngữ*) and Romanized Chinese as a survey of religious beliefs and practices in eighteenth-century Tonkin. The *Opusculum* is the first extant systematic work on Vietnamese religion by an educated Western European. Santa Thecla's meticulous description of Vietnamese religious beliefs and practices and his usage of Sino-Vietnamese sources and the Chinese classics allow the reader to understand the background of many discussions in the *Conference*. Generally speaking, while treating a similar topic, Santa Thecla gave a much more detailed and elaborated account than the author of the *Conference* did. There is also an anonymous Vietnamese document entitled *Tam Giáo Chư Vọng* (The Errors of the Three Religions)[30] which covers the same ground as that of the *Opusculum*. This work, a Vietnamese criticism of traditional religious practices, seems to draw from the same sources as the *Opusculum*.[31] It is more likely that the author of the *Conference* had greater access to this Vietnamese text rather than to the Latin *Opusculum*.

In short, the *Conference* is dependent on the literary style, concepts, and sources of its predecessors. Though one cannot establish a direct connection between it and these earlier Christian apologetics, the earlier works illuminate and give details to the later one. They also set the agenda and provide credibility for the anonymous author of the *Conference* who relied on them.

Structure and Content

The actual existence of a conference among the representatives of the four religions is secondary to the message its author wanted to convey to the reader. The *Conference* is framed as a three-day debate, each day with its own theme in dialogical form, which reflects a Christian interest. The topics discussed revolve around three issues that are important for human life, according to Christian anthropology: the origin, meaning, and end of human life. The first debate attempts to answer the question: "What is the origin of humanity and of the cosmos?" The second debate focuses on morality: "What should human beings do in this life?" And the final debate is concerned with the question of the afterlife: "Where does the human person go after death?"

In each of these three debates each religious representative appeals to the religious writings of his own tradition. The dialogues are given in the following order: the Catholic priest, or "the Western Scholar," enters the debates on a particular subject, first with the Confucian scholar, then with a Taoist priest, and lastly with the Buddhist monk. The representatives of the Three Religions present their understandings or views of the subject and the Catholic priest challenges them with reasons and historical examples. After questioning the others' views, the priest presents the Catholic teaching on the same subject. Then his opponents, especially the Confucian scholar, have the opportunity to refute him. At the end of each day, the mandarin gives the final comments on the merit of the arguments and declares the winner, and needless to say, the priest wins every round. Judging from its style and Christian interest, the *Conference* is an imaginative conversation that serves as a catechism for new converts to defend Christian beliefs and practices.

In the conversations, the Confucian scholar acts as the main objector to Christian claims and frequently comes to the rescue of his Taoist and Buddhist partners. He assumes the role of spokesman for the other two traditions when referring to their common beliefs, and is the only one to question the Christian view. In addition to belonging to the educated class, the Confucian scholar's action was also influenced by the political background of seventeenth- and eighteenth-century Vietnam. In a country marked by upheaval due to civil wars, court politics, and rebellion, the masses, being tired of war and political factionalism, sought relief in the spiritual realm of Buddhism and Taoism that Confucian orthodoxy could not provide. Hence, Confucian leaders and intellectuals sought a way to reclaim the authority which was slipping from their grasp.

Always the last speaker, the Christian priest is able to refute the "errors" of his opponents and defend the beliefs and practices of Christianity. He does not shy away from giving a complete presentation of the basic tenets of Christianity such as the nature of God, the soul, the Virgin birth, the enigma of the cross, the universal redemptive work of Christ, and the general resurrection, even if they sound ridiculous to his opponents. While he is the winner at the end of each day, the tone of the conversation is respectful even in the midst of disagreement. The Christian priest, for his part, is willing to validate the teachings of the others when they are reasonable and morally acceptable. Still, the objections from his Confucian interlocutor highlight the tensions in Christian-Confucian relations.

Interpretation of the Conference

To understand and properly evaluate the *Conference,* the reader should bear in mind that the work was written to defend Christian legitimacy against the accusation that "this foreign Portuguese religion (*đạo Hoa Lang* [Christianity])[32] is a false and superstitious teaching, full of lies and irrationality" which seduced "ignorant people."[33] This serious accusation, among other political factors, is the reason behind waves of severe persecution of Christianity by various Vietnamese rulers and Confucian elites from 1625 until the 1880s. In such a hostile environment it was natural for Christians to be defensive and apologetic. I suggest that the *Conference* is not primarily a manual of dialogue aimed at engaging with members of different religious traditions but a type of catechism meant to help Christians solidify their beliefs.

In order to establish the legitimacy of Christianity the author of the *Conference* sought to show the intelligibility of Christian teachings and their compatibility with reason. Since the Confucian gentry class of Vietnam considered themselves to be educated and rational people, any efforts to win their minds and hearts had to demonstrate that Christianity was rational rather than superstitious like the popular Buddhism or

Taoism of the day. The Christian priest in the dialogue takes advantage of the situation by using the concepts and language of his intellectual contemporaries.

Truth has no partiality for the Christian priest. He often cites Confucian classics to refute Confucian claims and defend the Christian position. He exhorts the Confucian scholar to "examine everything according to reason"[34] and chastises him whenever he fails to do so. For him, it is not sufficient to repeat "what was laid down in [their] sacred books."[35] To counter the charge that Christian beliefs are also "human-made legends and myths,"[36] "ridiculous,"[37] "unbelievable,"[38] or "foolish and ridiculous,"[39] he often uses examples drawn from daily life to prove his points. The *Conference* is also unique in the way in which it presents Christian doctrines using examples and analogies from Asian history and historical figures. His preferred method of argument is reasoning based on observation and differentiation. As Ricci did in the *True Meaning*, the Christian priest misses the nuances of Confucian-Taoist metaphysical concepts such as the concepts of *yin* and *yang*,[40] Supreme Ultimate (*taiji*), Way (*dao*), and Principle and Material forces (*li-qi*),[41] as well as the apophatic concepts (e.g., "emptiness," "non-being").[42]

A Major Theme of Concern: the Religious Life

There are many topics one can discuss about the *Conference*. Due to the limited space of this essay I will focus on the views of the Three Religions and Christianity on the theme of religious conduct. This highlights the efforts of Christians to inculturate their new faith into the traditional religious context. For the author of the *Conference*, the heart of the matter is religious practice since there are more discussions on the second day than on the other two days (e.g., 56 verbal exchanges, in comparison to 14 on the first day and 21 on the third day).

Cultic Practice

Traditional Vietnamese cultic life and acts of worship are a mixture of the cult of spirits and other acts of personal or public piety. There are a number of Vietnamese words that describe the act of worship and adoration: *thờ* (worship), *phụng* (serve), *kính* (venerate or respect), *cúng* (offerings), *tế* (sacrificial offerings), *lễ* (ritual), *cầu* (pray or petition), and *khấn* (make a vow or promise). Among these terms, *thờ* deserves more explanation because it is the most debated topic in the *Conference* (40 percent of the conversation).[43] Here *thờ* means an act of devotion that is rendered to beings worthy of respect, which includes worship, veneration, homage, respect, and submission.

While Western theology distinguishes different degrees of worship: between *latria* (worship due to God), *dulia* (veneration of the saints), and *hyperdulia* (veneration of the Blessed Virgin Mary), the Vietnamese language lacks the theological concepts to differentiate between devotion given to a deity or a human. In the Vietnamese context *thờ* is applied to both the living and the deceased, to human beings and deities.[44] External gestures of kneeling or prostrating before the altar or image might remind the missionary of idolatry. Vietnamese custom, however, assigns these gestures a deep reverence and respect toward the subject (not the object) represented by the altar or pictures. One is to serve the dead in the same manner as the living. Thus, if a person is expected to kneel or prostrate before a high official or the emperor, there is nothing wrong with prostrating before one's ancestors. In the same way, *cúng* (offerings) and *giỗ* (memorial feasts) are acts of deep filial piety to remember the well-being of the deceased by offering their favorite food, or praying to them for protection.

Since the official rite of Heaven is exclusively reserved to the "son of Heaven"—namely, the king—the common people turn to other deities and spirits to express their religious sentiments. A strict monotheism did not exist in traditional Vietnam; the worship of and belief in Heaven do not exclude other lesser deities or spirits. As a king is assisted by his ministers, Heaven is assisted by numerous deities and spirits to carry out its will. Thus, we see the common people worship and adore anyone or anything that can support them and grant them good fortune as well as protect them from harm and calamities. This includes demons and deities,[45] spirits of nature,[46] deified heroes and sages,[47] and Taoist gods.[48] Needless to say, this view easily leads to practices that are considered indiscriminate worship or superstition that the author deems unacceptable.

Since there is ambiguity in the language, the author makes a distinction of different degrees of "worship" or "service." For example, the Christian priest states:

> Our way teaches people to worship the "Three Fathers"; however, the three are not worshipped equally. The solemn offering and sacrifice is the highest worship that is reserved to the supreme Father who alone deserves such honor. We the children do not dare to equate the lower father, our parent, to the supreme Father; hence we do not dare to make offerings and sacrifice to our parents [in the same manner as to the Lord of Heaven].[49]

Only the highest Father—God who is the "Most High Unsurpassed Lord of Heaven"—deserves ritual worship and adoration. When applying the notion of "worship" to the king and the parents, the text means to honor and serve these people. The "worship" of the middle Father takes on the meaning of service that is rendered to the kings: Respect him as the highest person of the nation; obey his orders despite their hardship; submit to his will and pay tributes; assist him when he is in need; be grateful and loyal; and never rebel and usurp the throne.[50] Likewise, the "worship" of the lower Father—one's parents—mainly refers to filial duties.

Ancestor Worship

Regarding the controversial topic of ancestor worship, the author of the *Conference* is quite cautious in delineating the proper worship that is due to one's parents. Citing the Fourth Commandment (honoring one's parents) as the top among the commandments that regulate human relations, he lists seven ways that a Vietnamese Christian can honor his or her parents:

> First, respect and fear them; second, obey them; third, take care of them [in their old age]; fourth, bear with them [in their infirmity]; fifth, give them a proper burial; sixth, give alms so to pray to the Lord of Heaven for their souls; and seventh, commemorate their death anniversary by praying and visiting their graves [on that day]. Such are the teachings for children to honor their parents in thought, word, and deed. When parents are still alive, their children must visit them regularly, serve them, and take care of their needs. When they pass away, the children must honor them in spiritual manner, by devotionally praying, giving alms, and doing good works to pray for their souls. That is how we [Christians] honor our parents.[51]

To outsiders, Catholics appear not to honor their parents because they fail to make offerings and sacrifices or keep external signs of mourning according to Vietnamese customs,[52] such as prostrating in front of the deceased, or partaking in the memorial banquet given by their non-Catholic relatives.[53] To respond to these allegations, Catholics insist they are truly filial, but their expressions of filiality do not follow the standard customs. Vietnamese Catholics, then and now, pray for their forebears but do not sacrifice to them. Because they believe that the souls of their parents have already left this world for the next, it is more important to pray for their souls rather than to display what they consider an empty show of respect.[54] Prostrating before a lifeless corpse or offering food that the deceased can no longer eat—because now they are in the spiritual world that requires spiritual sustenance rather than human food—are not filial acts, but a mockery of the dead.[55] If one is to follow the Confucian principle of "treating one's parents in death as in life," it is better that Catholics do penance, perform good works, and pray for the repose of their forebears than to engage in what they consider ineffective ritual acts.[56]

The discussion on ancestor worship highlights a difference in the concepts of the afterlife between Christianity and the traditional Vietnamese religions. The author of the *Conference* acknowledges this fact when he states that:

> Consider two teachings: One teaching [of Christianity] believes that once the souls of parents and ancestors have gone to another realm, they will not come back to eat and drink earthly food; thus their descendants do not have to make offerings and invite them to partake of the food. The other teaching [of the Three Religions] believes that the souls go back and forth between worlds, so that they still need to be fed as if they were still alive, and they have the power to grant fortune and protect their descendants... Now which teaching is true?[57]

The basic anthropological belief of all Vietnamese, regardless of their religious affiliation, is that the human person is composed of body, mind, and soul. At death the body is corrupted, but the soul survives beyond the grave. There are two kinds of soul, the material soul (*phách* or *vía*) which remains on earth, and the spiritual soul (*hồn*) which goes to the next world. Pre-modern Vietnamese believed that life in "the palace of the dead" (*âm phủ*) mirrors life in "the world of the living" (*dương gian*). Hence, those who are dead still need material support to live in the next life. They continue to engage in similar activities as if they still were alive. If they do not get the support they need, the spirit of the dead comes back to disturb the living. That is why offerings were made to appease them. This basic animistic belief was modified by Confucianism, Taoism, and Buddhism to different degrees.

Because of its concern with human affairs, Confucianism did not develop a theory of the afterlife. Neo-Confucianism, with its materialistic view, does not really believe in a continuing existence after death: "when *qi* gathers, there is life; when *qi* disperses, there is death. [Human beings are] no different from animals."[58] Since Confucians emphasize filial piety (*hiếu*), they insist on honoring the dead as if they were still alive. Food offerings are made to parents not so much to appease them as to show respect and keep alive their remembrance. Many Confucians do not believe that the dead actually can come back to this world and eat the offered foods but they consider it a significant moral act that forms a basic attitude of gratitude toward to one's family (and by extension to the country). For example, although being favorably disposed toward Christianity, Lord Nguyễn Phúc-Ánh explained to his advisor, Bishop Pigneau de Béhaine, why he could not agree to convert to Christianity and abandon ancestor worship:

I know that my ancestors are no longer with me. I also know that whatever I do for them (e.g., ritual worship) does not really benefit either them or me. But [I have to perform these rites because] I want to show everyone that I do not forget my ancestors, and I want to demonstrate a good example of filial piety to my subjects. ... In my view, there is no other real obstacle to preventing my whole kingdom converting to Christianity. ... I have prohibited acts of sorcery and divination; I wholly consider the cult of the spirits wrong and ridiculous. But I have determined to keep ancestor worship for the reasons above, because I consider it to be one of the most essential foundations of our moral formation.[59]

Christians' failure to observe these honorable customs was offensive to the ruling elite.

It is useful to remind the reader that the *Conference* was written at a time when the Chinese and Vietnamese rites to honor their ancestors were rejected by Rome as superstitious religious acts. The details of the long and heated Chinese Rites Controversy are beyond the scope of this essay but it can be summarized briefly as follows. When he was working with Chinese converts, Matteo Ricci did not see the custom of honoring the dead as incompatible with the Christian faith. However, other missionaries denounced these customs and traditions on the grounds of superstition, thus prohibiting Chinese Christians from engaging in such activities. In Vietnam, Rhodes and his confreres took a moderate path between the Riccian and the anti-Riccian position, allowing Vietnamese converts to venerate the dead so long as they got rid of the superstitious elements (for example, finding an auspicious time and/or grave for burial, burning of paper money and paper goods).[60] Meanwhile in Europe, the debates between pro-Jesuit and anti-Jesuit factions clouded the issues. After almost sixty years of heated debates between the proponents and opponents of the Chinese rites, Pope Clement XI tried to settle the controversy in 1704, then in 1710 and 1715, forbidding Christians, among other things, from making ritual offerings and sacrifices to ancestors and keeping ancestral tablets on the family altar. The final Papal Bull *Ex quo singulari* (1742) by Pope Benedict XIV ended all discussion, resulting in the regrettable alienation and division of Christians from their countrymen, a division which has taken centuries to heal.[61]

CHRISTIAN SELF-UNDERSTANDING IN THE PRE-MODERN VIETNAMESE RELIGIOUS MILIEU

The *Conference of Four Religions* enjoyed popular success from the time of its publication in the nineteenth century. It survived in texts written in all three scripts: the *Nôm*, the *Quốc-ngữ*, and the Chinese script (*chữ Nho*) and was reprinted in many editions. There are at least nine editions in *Nôm* (1864, 1867, 1869; Phát Diệm: 1867, 1869, 1909; Hong Kong: 1897, 1903, 1905), not counting fourteen *Quốc-ngữ* editions between 1880 and 1959. From a number of extant manuscripts, we can suggest that the *Conference* was first composed in handwritten *Nôm* script years (or decades) before an 1864 printed copy was circulated in North Vietnam. It was then transliterated into the *Quốc-ngữ* script and first printed in South Vietnam in the 1880s. It was finally translated into Chinese in 1887–1888. The *Quốc-ngữ* version was reprinted many times until 1959.[62]

The *Conference* is one of many apologetic works in both the long history of the Christian Church around the world and in its shorter history in Vietnam. Apologetic literature appears whenever a group tries to establish its own identity and legitimacy in an environment that may not be favorable to its survival. The genre of *apologia* allows the reader to understand the motivation and background behind many of the polemical discussions found in the *Conference* as well as in the larger question of the relationship between Christianity and other groups—religious or secular. In writing the *Conference*, the author was trying to build a case for Christianity in Vietnam. His goal was twofold: to dispel the suspicion of foreignness and heterodoxy of Christianity and to promote Christianity as a universal religion that could potentially become acceptable and beneficial for the Vietnamese people.

Christianity as a Challenge to Vietnamese Confucianism

Although it came to Vietnam at least fifteen centuries after Confucianism, Taoism, and Buddhism, Christianity sought to establish itself as the "Fourth Religion" of the Vietnamese people. In both China and Vietnam, Christians found an ideological ally and competitor in Confucianism. Both Ricci and the author of the *Conference* held Confucianism in high regard for its moral teaching and worship of Heaven. Even Alexandre de Rhodes and Adriano di St. Thecla, while critical of the religious practice of the "sect of the literati" (Confucianism), praised Confucian moral values and social relations.

In the *Conference* the author presents Christianity as no more a foreign religion than the Triple Religion. For him the so-called traditional religions were also foreign imports from China and India: "Confucianism originated in the state of Lu [modern Shandong]; Taoism only appeared at the end of the Zhou dynasty in the lands of Hu and Guang [Central China]; and Buddhism arrived from India."[63] They have become "religions of Vietnam" mainly because Vietnamese rulers accepted and promoted them, not necessarily because of their own merits.[64] The author presents Christianity a continuation of the "natural religion" that was practiced by the sages of East Asia who "followed the mandate from Heaven" to govern the people by the "way of Heaven."[65] Christianity is compatible with the Vietnamese religious ethos and it could also become a Vietnamese religion if people are open to it. The "new" religion is as old as the Vietnamese culture itself; its teaching does nothing but continue the path set by the Confucian ethics of Three Duties and Five Relations. By quoting extensively from the references about Heaven in the Confucian classics, the author wants to demonstrate both that Christianity is compatible with the native cult of Heaven, and that the Lord of Heaven is none other than the Supreme Being mentioned in the classics and worshipped by the common people. Because God has engraved that "righteous way" into the human heart,[66] to follow Christianity is to return to the natural state of humanity, which is "the way that has existed from the beginning of creation ... and it should not be considered a new way."[67]

If the teachings of Confucius could be influential outside of China, and even accepted in Vietnam as an honorable religion, then Christianity surely would be able to follow the same path. The author is confident that Christian beliefs and teachings can have universal application beyond the Western world. Quoting the famous Confucian dictum: "Within the four seas, all men are brothers,"[68] he suggests that Christianity, with its belief in one God who is the father of all, and all humanity are brothers and sisters, can potentially be an instrument of healing and peace-building among the war-torn Viet people. He tries to persuade the audience that the Christian mission is not to submit the Viet people to an earthly Western power such as the Portuguese crown, but to follow and worship the true Lord of Heaven and Earth so that everyone is able to "attain happiness in paradise."[69]

The universal claim of Christianity, however, is met with skepticism and resistance by the Confucian scholar. He sees the Christian claim as unreasonable and exclusive. The following passages express such sentiments:

> Such a Lord of Heaven belongs to your land alone and so be it. Do not boast about him in this Eastern land. ... Not only has no one [in this land] ever seen that Lord, but also in the *Five Classics* which our sages have passed down [to us], nothing has ever been written about the name of that Lord of Heaven.[70]

He continued:

> Since the Lord Jesus was born in a certain land, all the meritorious service which he had achieved could only be benefited from by the few people of that land. How could it affect this Eastern land which remains a separate and different world? ... Is not such a claim of yours delirious?[71]

For the Confucian scholar, Christianity is a religion of the West and appropriate for Westerners but it cannot surpass the venerable way of the Confucian (and by extension the Three Religions) which has shaped the culture and life of people in the Eastern word. There is no need for a new religion:

> The way of your Lord of Heaven cannot surpass the sacred way of the Venerable Master Kong (Confucius). Since these eastern countries already commit to what the Venerable Master Kong left behind, it is sufficient teaching for [everyone]. … All families give praises; countries are prosperous; people peaceful. Therefore, who would need to learn about the way of the Lord of Heaven? Is the Confucian way any less praiseworthy?[72]

Here, we see a competing truth claim between the representatives of the two religions. Like medieval Christianity which enjoyed unquestioned support in the whole of Christendom, the Confucians saw their teaching and practice as normative for Vietnam without ever questioning their unique status. Only when confronted with the universal claims from Christian opponents did the Confucians retreat to a defensive position.

Traditional Christian Views of Other Religions

The assessment of non-Christian religions in the *Conference* reflects a largely "exclusivist" view.[73] The attitude of the author toward the traditional religions of Vietnam ranged from dismissive coldness (in cases of Taoism and Buddhism) to reluctant acceptance (Confucianism). The disdain of Taoism and Buddhism is reflected in the author's refusal to engage their representatives in discussing their beliefs. In his assessment, Taoism is a "religion of emptiness,"[74] and Buddhism is a "religion of superstition, emptiness and harmfulness."[75] Needless to say, the author's assessment of Taoism and Buddhism is inaccurate and based on his limited exposure to popular religious practice.

Even Confucianism that was accepted by the majority of the Vietnamese people and especially by their rulers as normative was seen by the author of the *Conference* as inferior to the "religion of the Lord of Heaven." From the author's perspective, Confucian moral exhortation and self-cultivation is praiseworthy and proper; however, he claims that without knowing God and worshipping Him, a moral life alone does not bring eternal reward. Confucianism, for all its goodness, is seen as concerning only the human realm, for it exhorts people "to cultivate themselves, to manage their family, and to govern their country" but does "not teach people about the true Lord [of heaven and earth]… whom they should worship in order to attain eternal life."[76] Thus, it cannot be compared to the teaching of God, which goes beyond the natural realm to be "more significant, more real, and more thorough" than Confucianism.[77]

The exclusivist outlook of the *Conference* reflects a long-standing position of Christianity with regard to the merits of other religions. It parallels the early self-understanding of Christianity within the Jewish community and the larger Greco-Roman world. Because the early Christians felt marginalized by the Jewish community, they developed a theology of replacement, seeing themselves as representing the New Israel and replacing the Old Israel in God's plan. With regard to their environment the emerging Christian community adopted Greek philosophical categories and concepts into Christian theology. However, Christians distanced themselves from the religious and ritual practices of the mystery religions. Furthermore, because they were a small and persecuted minority, Christians had to assert their identity with great zeal and enthusiasm. A concern for survival helped form a defensive attitude among Christians, especially with regard to orthodoxy and heterodoxy. Absolute claims with regard to their faith and morals helped to safeguard Christians from being absorbed by syncretistic movements of the time (such as Gnosticism). Early Christians could not afford dialogue with persecutors and competitors as it would weaken their unity and threaten their own identity. Any compromise of the faith was seen as endangering their survival.[78]

This exclusivist mentality formed by a minority complex did not go away when Christianity became the official religion of the Roman Empire in the fourth century. On the contrary, as Christians embraced the civil structure, language, and culture of their former persecutors they became as intolerant and aggressive towards others. Outside the boundaries of their confessional churches, religious leaders could not perceive any movement of the divine spirit. Soon, the formula *"extra ecclesiam nulla salus"* (outside the Church there is no salvation) was applied not only to schismatics and heretics but also to people outside of Christianity. The conflict with Muslim military forces during the crusades hardened this position.[79]

This superiority complex of the Church and, by extension, of the European monoculture resulted in clashes between Christian missionaries and believers of other traditions in Asia and Africa. Since by the late Middle Ages, Europe had only one dominant religion and culture, missionaries were not theologically and culturally prepared to understand and respect believers of other religions as co-pilgrims on the journey toward God. In addition, unfriendly relations between European Christians, Jews, and Muslims did not foster an acceptance of the followers of other religious traditions as respectable partners in dialogue. Missionaries presented Christianity to the people of East Asia as being superior and more logical than their native religions. Largely out of ignorance and cultural pride, missionaries treated the East Asian religions (especially Buddhism and Taoism) as wholesale superstition.[80]

The Christian exclusivist mentality was reflected in works such as the *Conference*. As members of a minor and persecuted religion in Vietnam, Catholic Christians were taught to be steadfast in their beliefs and distrust their environment which was often hostile to their newly founded faith. Their attitude toward the other religions of Vietnam was not unlike the early Christian attitude toward the Greeks. Vietnamese Christians appropriated the Confucian ethical system and categories of thought while rejecting the Confucian rituals and worships. The approach by the author of the *Conference* to Confucianism is a kind of fulfillment theory in which Christianity complements Confucian ethics or culture by providing the spiritual dimension that it allegedly lacks. The focal point of Christianity has been and still is soteriological, and thus it is natural for Christians to measure other world-views, secular or religious, in terms of its own concerns as was done in the *Conference*.

The Conference and Inculturation

Although "inculturation" has become a major part of contemporary discussion in the past forty years, the concept of inculturation, or the dynamic relationship of faith and culture, is not entirely new.[81] Back in 1659, the *Instruction of the Propaganda Fide* to its vicars and missionaries in the Far East offered the following advice:

> Beware of forcing the people to change their way of life, their customs and traditions, as long as these are not in open contradiction to religion and good morals. Is there anything more foolish than to transplant France, Spain, Italy, or any other European country (that is to say its customs and practices) to China! That is not what you should bring to them, but the faith which neither despises nor rejects the lifestyle of any people or their customs as long as they are not evil in themselves, but rather desires their preservation and promotion.[82]

These words of wisdom did not always translate into practice, but at least we can see an attempt to contextualize the Gospel in the land to which it is preached. In his memoir *Divers Voyages et Missions* (1653), Alexandre de Rhodes told of being scandalized when he saw that Indian converts had to wear Portuguese clothing in Goa, and Chinese Christians had to cut their hair short in European style in Macao. De Rhodes protested these customs, for he thought that being a Christian was about adopting a new faith, not new clothing or hairstyle. In his effort to interact with the local culture, he adopted the Vietnamese tunic and hat and encouraged other missionaries to do the same.[83]

But inculturation is more than adapting to a style of dress or learning a new language. It is about embracing a whole different set of cultural expressions, customs, and beliefs. In broad strokes, there are currently six models of inculturation (or contextual theology), as suggested by Stephan Bevans: (1) translation, (2) anthropological, (3) praxis, (4) synthetic, (5) transcendental, and (6) countercultural.[84] In all six models, Bevans points out that there are interactions of elements of the past (the Gospel message and tradition) with the present (culture and social change). These models differ from one another according to the degrees of emphasis on fidelity to the Gospel message and tradition and on adaptation to the present culture and social change.

The *Conference* is best understood as representing Bevans's "translation model." This model presupposes that all cultures, despite their diversities, possess the same structure, and divine revelation is primarily a communication of truth in propositions that can be discovered by the process of reasoning. This explains the preference of reason by the author of the *Conference*. At the end of the *Conference*, the Christian priest told his dialogue partners that if they were open to listening to reason they would discover the truth: "If the gentleman takes reason as his guide, false teachings will not escape from being discovered by reason."[85]

But the author of the *Conference* did not merely translate Christian doctrines into the Vietnamese language. He wanted to express Christian concepts and terminology in ways that could be understood by his audience. Hence, we see a great deal of borrowing from Confucian terminology and the Chinese classics. He also made some cultural adaptations, especially with regard to one's duties toward the monarch and toward one's parents in the doctrine of the "Three Fathers." Here we see a limited version of Bevans's "synthetic model" which incorporates cultural and sociological elements into the author's expressions of faith.

The author of the *Conference* was limited by his theology of religions and theology of revelation. While he saw a compatible notion of God in the Chinese classics, he could not appreciate the East Asian apophatic approach to God. Abstract words like *Dao* as the Primal Principle did not make sense to him.[86] He appreciated the "natural religion" but he also shared the missionaries' contempt for the traditional Vietnamese religious heritage as paganism and superstition. He did not try to understand the other religions in their proper terms and concepts, especially with regard to their religious practice.

FINAL ASSESSMENT

An apologetic text such as the *Conference*, although limited in its cultural understanding and theology, is an early attempt to indigenize the Christian faith using the categories and style of its times. In quoting from the Confucian classics rather than from Western religious sources, the author attempted to communicate truth in expressions that could be received by his audience. The fact that the author of the *Conference* chose to express his thoughts in *chữ Nôm*, the vernacular language of Vietnam, rather than in *chữ Nho* (Chinese characters) or *chữ Quốc-Ngữ* (at that time it was still associated with foreigners) speaks volumes about his desire to make the Christian faith accessible to the common people. Furthermore, he avoided lengthy philosophical explanations such as those in Matteo Ricci's *True Meaning*. Apart from using the Chinese classics, the author mostly used examples from well-known historical figures and from daily life to explain Christian doctrines. Given that the majority of his audience were Tonkinese peasants, the approach was quite effective.

The addition of Catholic Christianity to the three religions of Vietnam created a new dynamic in religious relations among the religions. It challenged the Confucian domination of society. The chief aims of the Confucian literati were to promote harmony in social relations under their leadership. While Buddhism and Taoism during these centuries were controlled and regulated by Confucian authority, Christianity refused to blend with the Confucian vision of harmony. With its own system of metaphysics, ethics, and religious practice, Christianity was a potential replacement for Confucianism as the religion capable of satisfying the intellectual and religious needs of the people. In the *Conference* the Christian scholar claims his religion is as good as, if not superior to, Confucianism. Since both Confucianism and Christianity claim that they follow the "Mandate of Heaven" (or in Christian terms, God's will), both try to appeal to the basic Vietnamese religious belief in Heaven. Thus, the underlying source of the debate here is an integral Confucian-Christian conflict. This reflects the self-confidence of Christians that their religion could challenge the monopoly of Confucianism.

In today's atmosphere of religious openness, past strategies such as one-sided apologetic, defensive, and exclusivist approaches to religious encounters are no longer adequate. Rather, a spirit of mutual learning, criticism, and enrichment is the way of interreligious dialogue. Nevertheless, in evaluating such an apologetic work as the *Conference of Four Religions*, one must remember the context in which it was composed. Despite its narrow outlook, the *Conference* provides us a valuable window into the self-understanding of Vietnamese Christians who must justify their existence. The work was written for a persecuted group of people who wanted to strengthen their faith and to dispel the fear and suspicion of their adversaries. Through the debates the author of the *Conference* took great pains to show that the Christian worldview and doctrines could be adapted to the audience's existing worldview and ethos, so that a process of indigenization of the Christian faith was possible. Although Catholic Christianity was a latecomer to the religious landscape of pre-modern Vietnam, it should not be seen as a threat to the traditional way of life; rather it could supplement, criticize, and clarify cultural and religious practices in Vietnam.

Notes

1. According to imperial record, a Christian missionary named I-ne-khu (Ignatius) came to North Vietnam in 1533. Prior to the arrival of the Jesuits in 1615, however, there were sporadic missionary activities.

2. During the seventeenth and eighteenth centuries, Vietnam was divided into two separate states which engaged in a civil war: the North, known in the West as Tonkin, was under the control of the Trịnh; the South, Cochinchina (also called Annam) was ruled by the Nguyễn. For a historical study of Tonkin during this period, see Alain Forest, *Les Missionaires Français au Tonkin et au Siam XVIIe-XVIIIe Siècles: Livre II—Histoires du Tonkin* (Paris, 1998); for Cochinchina, see Tana Li, *Nguyễn Cochinchina: Southern Vietnam in the Seventeenth and Eighteenth Centuries* (Ithaca, NY, 1998). For a study of Jesuit missions during this period, see Peter C. Phan, *Mission and Catechesis: Alexandre de Rhodes and Inculturation in Seventeenth Century Vietnam* (Maryknoll, 1998); see also J. Ruiz-de-Medina, "Vietnam," in *Diccionario Historico de la Compañia de Jesus*, ed. Charles O'Neill and Joaquin Dominguez, vol. IV (Roma: Institutum Historicum Societatis Jesu, 2001).

3. I have translated this work into English as a part of my Licentiate of Theology (STL) thesis. See Anh Q. Tran, "*Hội Đồng Tứ Giáo (Conference of Four Religions)*: An Encounter of Christianity with the Three Religions in Eighteenth Century Vietnam," STL thesis, Jesuit School of Theology at Berkeley, 2006, 40–124.

4. Before 1945, there were three systems of writing in Vietnam. Chinese writing was used in official court documents from the first century until its abolition after World War II. In the thirteenth century, *chữ Nôm*, a modified script based on Chinese characters, was invented to accommodate the vernacular language. *Chữ Quốc ngữ*, the Romanized alphabetic script was invented by Jesuit missionaries, and it was adopted by the French colonial government in the early twentieth century for communication and education.

5. For a discussion of the formation of the Triple Religion in Vietnam, see Duong Ngoc Dung, "An Exploration of Vietnamese Confucian Spirituality:

The Idea of the Unity of the Three Teachings," in *Confucian Spirituality,* ed. Tu Weiming and Mary Evelyn Tucker (New York, 2004), 2: 289–319.

6. For a detailed description of Vietnamese traditional religions, see Léopold Cadière, *Croyances et Pratiques Religieuses des Viêtnamiens,* 3 vols. (Hanoi, 1944–57); and Joseph Nguyen Huy Lai, *La Tradition Religieuse, Spirituelle et Sociale Au Vietnam* (Paris, 1981). Also, a brief synopsis of Vietnamese religions can also be found in Phan, *Mission and Catechesis,* 13–28.

7. Cadière, *Croyances et Pratiques* 1: 6.

8. Phan, *Mission and Catechesis,* 92–93, 221–22.

9. Many Vietnamese today maintain an ancestral altar in the home to keep the memory of their ancestors alive, especially on the anniversaries of their death, when incense is burned and offerings are made to them.

10. For a discussion of Vietnamese Confucianism, see Alexander Woodside, "Classical Primordialism and the Historical Agendas of Vietnamese Confucianism," in *Rethinking Confucianism: Past and Present in China, Japan, Korea, and Vietnam,* ed. Benjamin A. Elman, John B. Duncan, and Herman Ooms (Los Angeles, 2002), 116-43; Shawn Frederick McHale, *Print and Power: Confucianism, Communism, and Buddhism in the Making of Modern Vietnam* (Honolulu, 2004), 66–74; and Phan, *Mission and Catechesis,* 20–24.

11. Nguyen Huy Lai, *Tradition Religieuse,* 268–83.

12. For a discussion of the early history of Buddhism in Vietnam up to the fourteenth century, see Cuong T. Nguyen, *Zen in Medieval Vietnam* (Honolulu, 1997), 9–21. Under the Lý and Trần dynasties all educated men had to show competency in the basic thought of the three religions to qualify for the civil examination. This is the philosophical root of *Tam giáo.*

13. The tendency of religious assimilation was so strong that Christianity was seen as the "foreign" way because of its steadfast refusal to conform to native beliefs and customs.

14. For an illustrated description of Vietnamese folk religions, see Ann Helen Unger and Walter Unger, *Pagodas, Gods, and Spirits of Vietnam* (London, 1997).

15. Only the briefest outline of Vietnamese Catholic history is given here. Unfortunately, besides a few general English articles written by Peter C. Phan in encyclopedic dictionaries, such as *A Dictionary of Asian Christianity,* ed. Scott Sunquist (Grand Rapids, 2001), 876-880, or the *New Catholic Encyclopedia,* most historical accounts are written in French or Vietnamese, notably, Adrien Launay's works *Histoire de la Mission de Cochinchine: Documents Historiques* (Tome 1: Paris, 1923; Tome 2: 1924; Tome 3: 1925) and *Histoire de la Mission du Tonkin* (Paris, 1927).

16. Missionary sources reported (perhaps with a bit of exaggeration) that by 1650, over 300,000 people were baptized, with an annual growth of 15,000. Phan, *Mission and Catechesis,* 66.

17. The Vietnamese at that time could not distinguish between the different countries of the West. Since the Portuguese traders were the first ones who came to Vietnam, Catholic Christianity was considered the "religion of the Portuguese" (*đạo Hoa Lang*) and the Roman Pontiff was the "king of Portugal." On this misunderstanding, see Phan, *Mission and Catechesis,* xv.

18. Cited by Adrien Launay, *Histoire de la Mission de Cochinchine*, 3: 119.

19. It is estimated that 300,000 people were killed between the seventeenth and nineteenth centuries. On June 19, 1988, Pope John Paul II canonized 117 of these martyrs, of whom 96 were native Vietnamese.

20. Quoted by Cao Thế Dung in *Việt Nam Công Giáo Sử Tân Biên* (A New History of Vietnamese Catholicism) (Gretna, LA, 2002), 2: 769.

21. Launay, *Histoire de la Mission de Cochinchine*, 1: 601–09.

22. The literature surrounding the Chinese Rites Controversy is enormous. For an introduction and summary of issues involved, see George Minamiki, *The Chinese Rites Controversy from Its Beginning until Modern Times* (Chicago, 1985); D. E. Mungello, ed., *The Chinese Rites Controversy: Its History and Meaning*, Monumenta Serica Monograph Series, 30 (Nettetal, 1994).

23. In Cochinchina, eight decrees prohibiting Christianity were promulgated between 1625 and 1725; in Tonkin, seventeen decrees of prohibition were promulgated between 1629 and 1773, followed by a renewed wave of persecution in 1793.

24. According to the prologue of the *Conference*, the narrator tells us that there was a mandarin named Prince Six, the uncle of the Lord Trịnh Sâm, who took an interest in Christianity. He wanted to learn more about "the Christian way" before he could decide for himself whether he should embrace this new religion: "Thus one day, he summoned a representative from each [of Vietnam's] religious traditions to [a conference at] his palace: a Confucian scholar, a Taoist priest, a Buddhist monk, and the two imprisoned [Catholic] priests. [At this conference] he asked them to debate on religious beliefs, so that he could examine the truth claims of each religion." These Catholic priests were later identified as Dominican fathers Jacinto Castañeda of Valencia, Spain and Vincent Liêm, a native priest from Nam Định province. Both of them were arrested in early October of 1773 during a raid against Christian leaders and executed on 7 November 1773 outside of Hanoi.

25. The dating of this work is problematic. The fact that the first extant printing was in 1864, ninety years after the event, casts doubt on the claim that this work was an eyewitness record. In my thesis, I have proven that this claim is not possible, for the Mandarin Six, the organizer in this conference, had died before such an event could take place. Based on earlier events, it is likely that this work was composed in the early decades of nineteenth century in Tonkin.

26. Translated from Chinese with introduction and notes by Douglas Lancashire and Peter Hu Kuo-chen, SJ (St. Louis, 1985) (hereafter abbreviated as the *True Meaning*).

27. Although this is not an exhaustive list of the similarities between the *True Meaning* and the *Conference*, a brief comparison between the two works reveals the following similarities: 1) the style of dialogue (both were written as dialogues between the Western (Christian) scholar and the representatives of other religions); 2) the use of natural reason (both insist that the true religion must be in accord with common sense or natural reason); 3) the use of canonical writings (both appeal extensively to the Chinese classics to prove their ideas; the author of the *Conference*, however, does not appeal to any Western sources except the Bible); 4) the interpretation of Chinese philosophical concepts (both

misunderstand the Taoist "Non-being" (*wu*), the Buddhist "Nothingness" (*kung*), and the Neo-Confucian "Supreme Ultimate" (*taiji*), "Principle" (*li*), and "Vital Energy" (*qi*)); 5) the name of God (both use the same name for God, "Lord of Heaven" (*Tianzhu*) or "Sovereign-on-High" (*Shangdi*)); 6) the universality of Christianity (both argue that Christianity is neither a new religion nor a Western one, but an ancient and universal religion); 7) the doctrine of Triple fatherhood (both refer to the three degrees of fatherhood—God, king, and one's father—and speak of proper honor and worship that are due to each); 8) and the human soul and reincarnation (both use similar arguments to refute the doctrine of reincarnation).

28. Translated from Latin and Vietnamese by Peter Phan in *Mission and Catechesis*, 211–315 (hereafter abbreviated as the *Cathechismus*).

29. Translated from Latin and annotated by Olga Dror (Ithaca, 2002) (hereafter abbreviated as the *Opusculum*).

30. I recently discovered a *Quốc-ngữ* manuscript titled *Tam Giáo Chư Vọng* (The Errors of the Three Religions) in the archive of the MEP in Paris, catalogue number V-1098. This 205-page unpublished manuscript, dated in 1752, was written in a 10 by 15 centimeter notebook.

31. Di St. Thecla said that he had relied on earlier Vietnamese works *Dị Đoan chi Giáo* (Doctrine of Superstitions) and *Đại Học chi Đạo* (Doctrine of Great Learning), both in *Nôm* script. These works have not yet been located.

32. The misunderstanding of Christianity as a Portuguese religion was so entrenched that Alexandre de Rhodes in his 1651 Catechism vigorously argued against that misconception. He wrote: "Do not say that this law (religion) is the law of the Portuguese. The holy law of the Lord of heaven is a light greater and older than the light of the sun itself ... The holy law (religion) of God, though it has appeared to others kingdom first, should not be seen as belonging to this or that kingdom, but as the holy law of God, the Lord of all things. It is a law nobler and older than any kingdom whatsoever." See also Phan, *Mission and Catechesis*, 233.

33. Tran, translation of *"Hội Đồng Tứ Giáo* (Conference of Four Religions)," 4. Citation number here and in following citations of this work refers to the paragraph number of my translation of the text.

34. Tran, *"Hội Đồng Tứ Giáo,"* 17.

35. Ibid., 23.

36. Ibid., 25.

37. Ibid., 83.

38. Ibid., 93.

39. Ibid., 99.

40. Ibid., 15.

41. Ibid., 13, 17.

42. Ibid., 17, 19.

43. Out of a total of 101 conversations, 41 are devoted to the issue of worship and veneration. See paragraphs 33–43, 51–52, 57–61, 75–82, and 103–19.

44 . For example, the phrase *"thờ cha kính mẹ"* means "honor one's father and respect one's mother"; *"thờ cúng tổ tiên"* means "pay homage or veneration to ancestors."

45. Tran, *"Hội Đồng Tứ Giáo,"* 37–41.
46. Ibid., 41–43.
47. Ibid., 51–52, 78–82.
48. Ibid., 57–61.
49. Ibid., 108.
50. Ibid., 104.
51. Ibid., 106.
52. Ibid., 107, 116.
53. Ibid., 110.
54. Ibid., 117.
55. Ibid., 111.
56. These arguments are similar to De Rhodes' objection in the 1630s. He saw three "gross errors" in the practice of the memorial banquet. First, it presupposes that the deceased parents can freely come and go as they please or when invited, ignoring the barrier separating them from the living. Second, it naively assumes that the dead need food and drink like the living. Third, it wrongly supposes that the deceased have the power to grant requests of protection and fortune to the living. Cf. Phan, *Mission and Catechesis,* 94.
57. Tran, *"Hội Đồng Tứ Giáo,"* 114.
58. Ibid., 120.
59. Launay, *Histoire de la Mission de Cochinchine,* 3: 320.
60. De Rhodes modified the veneration of ancestors with practice acceptable to the Christian faith. See Phan, *Mission and Catechesis,* 93–96.
61. For an analysis of the prohibition of ancestor worship in Tonkin and its relation to the persecution of Christianity, see Cao Thế Dung, *Việt Nam Công Giáo Sử Tân Biên,* 763–808. Note that in Vietnam, it was not until 1965 that Vietnamese Catholics were allowed to pay homage at their ancestral altars and offer memorial banquets for the anniversaries of their parents' deaths.
62. The oldest extant *Nôm* version is an 1864 wood-block printed edition (located at Vietnam's National Library. Catalogue AB 305, 72 pages, size 25 cm by 14 cm). The oldest extant *Quốc-ngữ* version was a third-printing edition, 76 pages long, published in Tân Định (Saigon, South Vietnam) in 1887. My research is based on a 1867 *Nôm* reprint and 1951 *Quốc-ngữ* 13th edition. The *Quốc-ngữ* version is not simply a transliteration of the *Nôm* version; its anonymous editor tried to update the language, adding more explanations and clarifications. The *Quốc-ngữ* version separated the introduction from the dialogues, and divided the discussion sections for ease of reading. The Chinese edition, which claims to be a translation of the literal translation of a *Nôm* text, was printed with a commentary, 94 pages long, and published in 1911.
63. Tran, *"Hội Đồng Tứ Giáo,"* 6
64. Ibid., 7.
65. Ibid., 5.
66. Ibid., 67.
67. Ibid., 72.
68. Confucius, *Analects,* 12: 5.
69. Tran, *"Hội Đồng Tứ Giáo,"* 6.
70. Ibid., 25.

71. Ibid., 87.

72. Ibid., 70.

73. The categories of exclusivism, inclusivism, and pluralism are discussed in contemporary works of theology of religions such as Jacques Dupuis, *Toward a Christian Theology of Religious Pluralism* (Maryknoll, 1997); Paul F. Knitter, *No Other Name? A Critical Survey of Christian Attitudes toward the World Religions* (Maryknoll, 1985).

74. Tran, "*Hội Đồng Tứ Giáo,*" 61

75. Ibid., 66.

76. Ibid., 73.

77. Ibid., 74.

78. Dupuis, *Toward a Christian Theology of Religious Pluralism,* 54–57.

79. Ibid., 84–86. It must be noted that during the Middle Ages, there were some positive attempts to understand and appreciate other religions as seen in the writings of Peter Abelard, Francis of Assisi, Ramon Llull, and Nicholas of Cusa, but these were occasional voices. Cf. Ibid., 102–09.

80. De Rhodes's treatment of Confucianism, Buddhism, and Taoism in his *History of the Kingdom of Tonkin* (1651) showed an unfortunate ignorance and false perception of these religions. His information was second- or third-hand. His goal, however, was to win converts, and he succeeded in converting some monks, who became his effective collaborators. See Phan's assessment in *Mission and Catechesis,* 82–96. We also find a similar attitude in St. Thecla's *Opusculum de Sectis apud Sinenses et Tunkinense.*

81. The popularization of this term is due to the Society of Jesus. One of the earliest usages of the term is attributed to Joseph Masson, SJ of the Gregorian University at Rome. He wrote in 1962: "Today there is a more urgent need for a Catholicism that is *inculturated* in a variety of forms." Quoted in Aylward Shorter, *Toward a Theology of Inculturation* (Maryknoll, 1988), 10.

82. Quoted in the article "Propaganda Fide Congregation" by Joseph Metzler in *A Dictionary of Asian Christianity,* ed. Scott Sunquist (Grand Rapids, 2001), 677. See also "Instructions of 1659," 384-85.

83. De Rhodes' cultural adaptations are summarized by Peter Phan in *Mission and Catechesis,* 75–81.

84. *Models of Contextual Theology,* rev. ed. (Maryknoll, 2002).

85. Tran, "*Hội Đồng Tứ Giáo,*" 148.

86. Ibid., 19.

7

CONCENTRATION OF SPIRITUALITY:
THE TAIPING AND THE ALADURA COMPARED

David Lindenfeld

The comparison of these two geographically and temporally disparate movements—the Taiping Rebellion in China in the mid nineteenth century, and the Aladura churches in West Africa and its diaspora in the twentieth—has a twofold purpose: 1) to draw attention to certain patterns of non-Western adaptations of Christianity that I believe are characteristic of a wide variety of cases; and 2) to suggest some ways of overcoming the distinction between the categories "Western" and "non-Western" themselves, a distinction which, I believe, continues to shape our thinking, if not always at a conscious level.[1] If one surveys the textbooks that are used in college courses in World Religions, for example, one does not find an overtly pro-Western bias; the importance of respecting diversity and a variety of human cultures is duly acknowledged. But vestiges of the old distinction between "advanced" and "primitive" societies nevertheless survive, primarily in the lumping together of non-literate religious practices in a single chapter, regardless of where in the world they originated, and the application of a label such as "indigenous," "primal," "basic," or "tribal."[2] One often finds the term "traditional" applied to many religious practices to distinguish them from those that have been exposed to "world" religions. The implication is that "traditional" societies are static, whereas "world" religions are dynamic—a claim that has been falsified in any number of instances. In trying to come up with new terms to categorize cross-cultural religious interactions, then, we would be well advised to look for ones that point beyond these habits of thought.

Before proceeding to the two cases, a word is in order about the comparative method itself as it is employed in the humanities. The merits of cross-cultural comparative historical studies as a launch pad for theory have been amply demonstrated by Max Weber, who based his sociology of religion on extensive investigations of Confucianism, Hinduism, Buddhism, and Judaism, in addition to the Protestantism which had formed part of his own background. Nevertheless, the methodological, linguistic, and terminological difficulties raised by the comparative approach are formidable and must be considered briefly here. Jürgen Kocka has commented recently on the pitfalls and promises of the comparative approach.[3] Of the pitfalls, he highlights three, all of which are exemplified in this paper: 1) it relies on secondary literature, because the linguistic skills required for cross-cultural comparisons at the level of primary and archival sources exceed the abilities of most historians, including myself (indeed, I initially chose the Chinese and West African cases because there was an abundant secondary literature available); 2) it entails deliberately taking these cases out of their local context and isolating certain features so that they can meaningfully be compared— a procedure which goes against the grain of many historians' training and temperament, which leans towards more contextualization rather than less. This of course renders the comparativist open to criticism by the specialist, but hopefully in ways that can be useful to both; and 3) it suggests that the similarities and differences between any two cases (or more) are likely to emerge most sharply precisely in the absence of causal interactions between them. Thus the point is not to argue for the influence of the Taiping on the Aladura, or of Africa on China with respect to missionary activity—or vice-versa. Kocka has pressed this point further by arguing that the growing interest in world history tends to highlight the connections and influences across cultural lines instead of treating these cultures in isolation—thus taking the wind out of the sails of the comparative enterprise.[4] I do not, however, see why this need be so: Connections can themselves constitute the basis of comparison. Encounters between religions and ideologies with disparate roots are taking place all around us and are the stuff of daily headlines. There is no reason why such types of interactions in the past cannot be themselves isolated and compared. Indeed, there are strong reasons why they should be.

This brings me to the positive dividends of the comparative approach, which Kocka also acknowledges. He warns against over-specialization, particularly in a global age. More specifically, such far-flung, decontextualized comparisons may have great heuristic value. In Kocka's words, "the comparative approach allows one to identify questions and problems that one might miss, neglect, or just not invent otherwise."[5] This is particularly applicable to the study of religious encounters. Comparative study directs our attention to common strategies and processes by which peoples assimilate or otherwise combine the beliefs and practices of a new religion with their own cultural systems—strategies and processes which appear in quite disparate circumstances.

In comparing the Taiping and the Aladura movements, an obvious difference should be stated at the outset. The Taiping ("great peace"), although it began as a religious sect, became directed against the ruling Qing dynasty, fomenting a rebellion (1850–1864) of huge proportions which at its height managed to control a portion of central China roughly equal to the size of France. It had grown from an army of some 300 men in 1850 to about 3 million five years later; the number of deaths from the rebellion as a whole is estimated at about 30 million. It was not the only rebellion against the Qing dynasty in the mid nineteenth century; others occurred in the north and in the Muslim west. All were indicative of a demographic crisis that had overtaken China, compounded with widespread government corruption.[6] The Taiping exemplifies a widely recognized response to crisis situations, namely millenarianism, a belief that the crisis is a prelude to the imminent transformation of society and eradication of evil—surely a feature common to both Eastern and Western religious traditions.[7]

In contrast to the Taiping, the Aladura ("owners of prayer") movement in West Africa was focused less on political and more on religious matters, specifically the power of prayer to heal sickness and overcome evil in the present. The term refers not to a single denomination or church, but to a multiplicity of them which were recognized to have similar outlooks.[8] While it is true that millennial ideas can be found in their sermons, particularly in the early years of the movement, this emphasis declined markedly over time.[9] One can also find expressions of pan-African nationalism in some Aladura churches, but the degree or intensity of this feature pales in comparison to its Taiping counterpart.[10] The contrast nicely illustrates David Aberle's distinction between *transformative* social movements, which seek to change an entire society, and *redemptive* social movements, which work primarily through the lives of individuals.[11]

The Aladura churches originated in the Yoruba lands of southwestern Nigeria and Benin (then Dahomey). The earliest ones arose in response to a specific health crisis, the influenza pandemic of 1918; the movement gained greatly in numbers thanks to a revival that took place in the 1930s, as the region felt the effects of the Great Depression. Like the Taiping, the Aladura was not the only movement of its kind at the time; rather it was part of a vast wave of mass conversions and revivals that swept much of sub-Saharan Africa between 1910 and 1940.[12] The Aladura churches have retained their dynamism down to the present: In the 1940s and 50s they struck roots in Sierra Leone, Liberia, and Ghana, and since the 1960s have established branches in Europe and

North America, where they provide a "home away from home" to West Africans abroad.[13]

We can now turn to the main positive reason for comparing these Chinese and West African phenomena: the centrality of the founder's vision, experienced in an altered state of consciousness, in providing meaning and leadership to the movement. Such leadership is usually associated with the term "charisma," but the comparison offered here is narrower and more precise. Although charismatic authority frequently involves an invocation of supernatural or mystical powers, these are often left vague. Hence the term is applied to an extraordinary range of cases, "as disparate as Jesus, Adolf Hitler, and Leonard Bernstein," as Michael Adas puts it.[14] In the specific type of charismatic authority under consideration here, the visionary experience of the founder, duly recorded and shared, was central.

The Taiping originated with a schoolteacher from Guangdong Province near Canton, Hong Xiuquan, who had studied the Confucian classics for some twenty years in preparation for the official examinations, which he failed four times. In 1837, just after one of these failures, he experienced a period of madness and near-death lasting some forty days, in which he had an extended and vivid dream of being in heaven and facing a heavenly father who ordered him to return to earth to slay the evil demons there. After the battle with the demons, Hong returned to heaven to be welcomed by the father, his wife, an elder brother and sister-in-law. The father and elder brother ordered him, against his own inclination, to return to earth once more to continue fighting evil and to usher in a period of great peace (*Taiping*). Most, though not all, of these dream-images were quite comprehensible in terms of Chinese writings that would have been familiar to Hong. Similar millenarian features could be found in China as far back as the second century A.D. and also existed in other sects which rebelled against the Qing in the nineteenth century. In 1843, however, Hong read a Christian tract which clarified doubtful points in his vision and reinforced its authenticity in his mind: The father was Jehovah, the elder brother was Jesus, and Hong himself was God's second son. Hong was further convinced of this by a partial coincidence of Chinese characters between the transliteration of Je-ho-vah and Hong's own name—a mode of persuasion which been dubbed "glyphomancy" and has been found in other cases of Chinese conversion as well.[15] And as another local study has shown, Hong was by no means idiosyncratic: Several accounts of conversions in the Fuzhou area of Fujian province also took the form of having such visions and incorporating in them a few Christian concepts or Biblical stories within a larger body of Chinese beliefs about the supernatural. This was particularly true in the stage of initial contact between Chinese religion and Christianity.[16]

Hong's early preaching emphasized the Ten Commandments and the importance of right moral action—an emphasis consonant with the Confucian tradition in which he had previously immersed himself. As the Taiping movement turned political—scholars disagree on exactly when—the evil demons become the Qing dynasty. From this point on, the Taiping ideology combined the moral emphasis with the punitive and fearsome aspects of the Old Testament God and the Book of Revelations, which led to a strict military discipline in a highly effective way that reminded Max Weber of Cromwell's model army.[17]

In the West African case, much of the authority of the Aladura leaders was based on their power to heal illnesses through prayer, stemming also from their visionary experiences. At the risk of some simplification, one can point to four different churches: 1) The Cherubim and Seraphim (C&S) traces its beginnings to a prolonged trance by a fifteen-year-old girl in Lagos in 1925, Christiana Abiodun Akinsowon, who had just been confirmed in the Anglican church. Like Hong, she found herself in heaven, addressed by angels, but was told that she would die unless she met someone who could really pray. Her family brought in an older itinerant evangelist, Moses Orimolade Tunolase, the son of a priest in the Yoruba *Ife* cult who had achieved some fame as a visionary, to pray for her, and she recovered. The two began to hold regular prayer meetings, which attracted much public attention and eventually developed into the church. 2) The Christ Apostolic Church (CAC) traced its origins to the influenza epidemic of 1918, which neither Western medicine nor Yoruba medicine could cure. A group met at the home of J. B. Sadare, a goldsmith, who had experienced visions before the epidemic and who believed that prayer alone could heal. Sadare named the group the Precious Stone Society. It continued to meet, affiliating with an American sect, the Faith Tabernacle; during the Depression it experienced a great revival thanks to another powerful visionary, Joseph Babalola, a semiskilled worker of Anglican background. After several other metamorphoses, the movement constituted itself as the Christ Apostolic Church in 1941. 3) The Church of the Lord Aladura (CLA) was founded by Joseph Oshitelu, an Anglican schoolteacher, who had a series of visions between 1925 and 1929, including one of an eye as bright as the sun, but also of witches, which he managed only gradually to overcome. Once having done so, he founded the church in 1930, by holding open air meetings and speaking in tongues. He became known as the "last Elijah." Oshitelu did not pay as much attention to healing at first, but as his church grew in the 1930s he could not afford to ignore the demand for it. 4) The Celestial Church of Christ (CCC) was likewise the child of a single prophetic figure, Joseph Oschoffa, raised a Methodist, who in 1947 assumed the title of "Pastor-Founder."

As did the Taiping, the Aladuras found ample precedent for altered states of consciousness in the Bible, particularly the Old Testament. The 1938 constitution of the Church of the Lord Aladura states, "We believe in dreams and visions because those of ancient days used to speak to God through visions and dreams. People like Abraham, Isaac, Moses, Jacob, Joseph, Solomon, etc. … [a]nd we are directed by the Holy Spirit."[18] The latter reference indicates the affinity with Pentecostalism, at least at the level of belief; the Christ Apostolic Church affiliated with an American Pentecostal church in the 1930s.[19]

Inseparable from vision-based charismatic authority is the problem of its routinization, which both Taiping and Aladura leaders had to face in their lifetimes.[20] In themselves, powerful movements are likely to generate personal rivalries and struggles for power; when such rival claims are supported by rival visions, the effort to maintain stability and continuity is rendered all the more difficult. This was true both of the Taiping and the Aladura churches. In China, Hong's authority was first exercised over a group known as the Society of God Worshippers in a remote area of Guangxi Province in the 1840s; it unleashed among the people a wave of further visions and other shamanistic features which had been part of the folk religion in the area. From this emerged two other powerful leaders, one a peasant, the other a charcoal burner, both without Hong's literary training, and both of whom claimed to be the voices of Jesus and God respectively.[21] The second of these, Yang Xiuqing, became the chief military strategist of the rebellion. From these experiences, Hong probably concluded that the routinization of his charisma could come none to soon. When the rebels took over the city of Nanjing in 1853 and proclaimed it the heavenly capital, Hong hastened to introduce measures modeled on the imperial dynasty with the intent of establishing a new one: a hierarchy of titles and regalia, palaces, concubines, a new calendar, and a new set of civil service exams. This meant that, taken as a whole, the Confucian elements predominated over the Christian ones in the movement.[22] The establishment of this structure did not, however, prevent the rivalry from escalating, as Yang Xiuqing arrogated to himself the additional title of Holy Spirit and began to challenge Hong himself. The result was bloody internecine warfare which began in 1856, when Yang was assassinated. This undermined the physical and moral strength of the rebellion and was a major factor in contributing to its eventual failure.

Hong also realized early on that his personal vision would have to be buttressed by scriptural authority in the religious sphere. During the formative years of the God Worshippers' Society, he was actually in Canton studying the new Chinese translation of the Bible. During the final years, Hong himself withdrew increasingly from public ceremony and view. While most scholars interpret this as a retreat into mental illness, Jonathan Spence argues that Hong was actually working on a Biblical commentary and revision, attempting to bring its stories into line with his moral code and to reconcile the Old Testament genealogy with his original vision and hence to legitimize his lineage and ultimately his dynasty. He came to believe he was the incarnation of King Melchizedek, mentioned fleetingly in Genesis 14 as "priest of the Most High God" at the time of Abraham.[23]

The tendency to factionalism and the subsequent need to buttress vision-based authority with a more stable set of institutional and intellectual structures were also prominent features of the Aladura churches. The most dramatic case was the Cherubim and Seraphim, where a much-publicized split occurred between the middle-aged Orimolade and the 22-year-old Abiodun; this was but the first of six splits in seven years! Clearly age and gender issues were involved—most of the women in the movement sided with Abiodun—but the splintering continued long after Orimolade's death in 1933.[24] Not surprisingly, the other Aladura churches had their share of splits and secessions as well.[25] Remarkably, however, each of these groups managed to weather these storms and arrive at a way of integrating the charismatic and bureaucratic impulses, thus calling into question Weber's contention that the two are incompatible. As Jacob Olupona notes, such a combination is common among independent African churches.[26] In the case of the Christ Apostolic Church, the leaders realized that they needed some guidance apart from their personal visions, and affiliated successively with several foreign organizations—one American, one Canadian, one Welsh—that held to faith healing as a central doctrine.[27] The Church of the Lord Aladura and the Celestial Church of Christ, both more closely tied to a single founder-figure than the other two, were better able to survive the schisms that occurred there as well, because both leaders paid attention to organizational matters early on. Both incorporated a principle which effectively routinized the charismatic impulses: that of splitting the "prophetic" branch of the hierarchy from the administrative one. Prophets were promoted on the basis of their spiritual gifts, of having visions and interpreting those of others, and were not expected to engage in the day-to-day running of the church itself. This structure reflected a widespread African practice, in which mediums such as diviners were clearly separate from elders, headmen, chiefs, etc.[28] And even the Cherubim and Seraphim found a way of channeling certain types of visionary material so as not to endanger the church organization: Visions were reported to the leaders, who decided how they were to be interpreted.[29] Moreover, all the Aladura churches stressed the importance of Bible study to reinforce and stabilize the visionary impulse.

At the same time, however, the churches created rituals as part of the church calendar that were designed to encourage the sharing of visions and dreams on the part of the congregation. The centrality of vision was thus not limited to the founders, but became a part of regular church life. The Cherubim and Seraphim, for example, scheduled a regular Saturday night vigil, lasting from 10 P.M. to 2 or 3 A.M., with singing and clapping invoking the Holy Spirit to descend, leading to people falling into trances and speaking in tongues. In smaller groups, known as praying bands, members actually slept in the church and were awakened to share their dreams and visions in the middle of the night.[30] Thus, in addition to the routinization of charisma, one can also speak of the re-enchantment of routine.

The role of visions and altered states of consciousness as the foundation of religious authority strikes us as something that does indeed transcend the distinction between "traditional" and "world" religions. An ethnographic study of 488 societies in different parts of the world revealed that 90 percent of them reported that such altered states of consciousness were a part of their accepted cultural patterns, although the percentage of societies in the Mediterranean region, which included Europe, North Africa, and the Middle East, was somewhat lower at 82 percent.[31] These findings suggest, however, that vision-based religion in the West, found in innumerable revival movements, has been unduly marginalized and should be better integrated into our cultural and religious history.

In seeking to go beyond syncretism in describing and conceptualizing how the Taipings and Aladuras appropriated Christianity to their own purposes, one might draw on several terms put forth in other papers in this volume, such as vernacular translation or creolization. I would suggest, as a less elegant but more precise term, *selective inculturation*. It is meant to convey that, as far as the cases presented here are concerned, the indigenous society absorbs elements of foreign Christianity into its own cultural matrix, which remains dominant. At the same time, it stresses that this absorption was not wholesale or uncritical. Let me try to justify this with respect to the two cases.

We have already seen that the Taiping leader, Hong Xiuquan, had studied Christianity for only a short time as compared to years of immersion in the Chinese classics. Hence it is not surprising that his incorporation of Christian elements looked a lot more Chinese than Christian. So it appeared, at least, to the British and French in China at the time, who rejected Hong's claims to be a fellow Christian as superstitious nonsense.[32] What I want to emphasize here, however, is the selective character of this inculturation: how much is left out. Some basic doctrinal elements of Western Christianity, such as the idea of original sin and of Christ as the redeemer of sins, are missing in Hong's interpretation. Moreover, it is important to note that Hong deployed the elements of Christianity that he did incorporate to in turn sweep away large portions of his native religion as well. Thus, selectivity operated in two directions, so to speak. The most conspicuous example of this was the campaign against idolatry, based of course on the First Commandment. One of Hong's first acts upon assuming his new calling was to smash the tablets to Confucius in the school where he taught (a gesture to be imitated, incidentally, forty years later by a youthful admirer of Hong who would go on to become one of China's most famous Christians, Sun Yat-Sen).[33] Later the Taipings also destroyed images and temples to local divinities throughout the area they occupied, including Buddhist and Taoist shrines, thus setting themselves in opposition to much of Chinese folk religion.

The Aladura case is somewhat more complicated, but also more illuminating. Unlike the Taipings, the Aladura leaders, and many of their parishioners, had already been exposed to the Christianity of the missionary churches.[34] Thus it is not surprising that the Aladura churches themselves retained many elements of the European-style churches in their rituals and liturgy. Descriptions of their services reveal a mixture of European and African elements that often appear on the surface to be syncretic. There is drumming and dancing, alternating with European-style hymns; Church of the Lord Aladura began with a hymnal consisting entirely of original tunes, but gradually added more hymns drawn from the Anglican and Methodist ones.[35] Indeed, there has been a certain tendency over time for the Aladura churches to become more like the "mainstream" churches rather than more "African."[36]

Nevertheless, these features do not tell the whole story of the interaction that the Aladuras brought about, as J.D.Y. Peel has argued.[37] For one thing, their approach to prayer was derived neither from mission Christianity nor from traditional Yoruba religion, but was something genuinely new. The lethal challenge of the flu epidemic of 1918 demonstrated the incapacity of *both* native healers *and* western medicine to prevent the deaths. Faith healing was a new strategy rather than a continuation of a previous one.[38]

At the same time, these new meanings for Christian ideas and symbols that the Aladuras created remained in accordance with the underlying principles of Yoruba beliefs and practices. In other words, inculturation took place not at the level of individual rituals or objects of worship, but at the level of fundamental assumptions. Thus the emphasis on healing is indicative of the Yoruba conception of spirituality as practical power to alter conditions in this world, rather than salvation in the next. This power is embodied in especially gifted individuals, the healers and prophets. It is noteworthy that the Yoruba word *agbara* means both charisma and power.[39] Likewise, the emphasis on visions and dreams bespeaks an ongoing belief in the multiplicity and proximity of spirits, both good and evil. For example, according the Church of the Lord Aladura's *Book of Rituals*, to be anointed into the special order of Crossbearer means to be "separated for the Lord to be overlord over dark powers, satan, world, witches, wizards, and all spirits of diseases and sickness, to subdue and to cast them out."[40] Similarly, the angels of the Cherubim and Seraphim are seen as spirit-mediators between God and man, and are addressed directly in prayers.[41]

Yet, as with the Taipings, this inculturation was highly selective. Belief in spirits did not mean worshipping them or making sacrifices to them. Once again, Judeo-Christianity was used to sweep away the visible manifestations of the spirit world. The rejection of fetishes, charms, and statues to local deities was a common denominator among the Aladura churches. There was occasionally open strife between Christians and pagans in the early years. Babalola's revival of 1930 featured conspicuous burnings of such objects; Oschoffa summarized his founding vision of the Celestial Church of Christ as follows: "many Christians there [in the mainline churches] who are on their death do not see Christ because they had become idol worshippers before their death. This is the task entrusted to me."[42] This willingness to break with aspects of the past was often a creative act, freeing the churches to come up with new ideas and solutions. All the case studies agree that the Aladura movement is more than simply a reshuffling of previous Yoruba religious elements. Something new is added. To quote H. W. Turner, "Many observers have commented on this central conviction, among the independent groups in Africa—that the 'impersonal and remote (God) had all at once descended from this heaven, and met them as the holy, incorruptible, but also as the loving God.'"[43]

The selective aspect of these cases may also be seen to be symptomatic of a more profound process which is often found in indigenous adaptations of Christianity and which is furthermore characteristic of a broad range of other religious behaviors. I call this process *concentration of spirituality*: the letting-go of religious objects and practices, narrowing them down from relatively many to relatively few, as a means of focusing and thereby heightening the energy of the subject in whatever task the religion calls him or her to do. In the case of the Taiping, that task was military and political efficiency that was needed to overthrow and supplant the Qing; in the case of the Aladura, it was originally physical and mental health, but more than that, the ability to survive and prosper in a new urban environment. In both cases, Christianity was associated with discipline.

Associated with this need to focus and intensify one's energies was another common feature of both movements: asceticism. This took the form of prohibitions against alcohol, addictive substances, gambling, and a distrust of sexuality. During the Taiping rebellion, the leaders enforced strict separation of the sexes in separate camps; even husbands were not allowed to cohabit with their wives. At the same time, women were organized into fighting units with their own officers. The avowed purpose was to concentrate one's strengths for the military task at hand—segregation was promised to end when peace came.[44]

The Aladuras, while not so severe, did insist on separation of men and women in church. The prohibition of tobacco, alcohol, and pork is written into the CCC constitution.[45] A characteristic form of asceticism in the Aladura churches is fasting—not something found in Yoruba tradition. According to Orimolade, "[P]raying and fasting are the only channels through which man can reach God"—a prime example of concentrated spirituality.[46] According to a bishop in the CLA, "Fastings help us to be more clean, in the state of which our guardian angel will be able to come nearer to us. The more we take to hard, harder, and the hardest fasting, the nearer our Angel will come to us, to take our prayer to the Lord with speed."[47] The focus of purification is clearly the church itself as a sacred space, a familiar feature of African religions—as is the exclusion of menstruating women from church.[48] Yet innovation was present in this aspect as well. For example, corpses are not allowed in the church, and funeral rites are at the home and gravesite only. This departs both from the previous Yoruba practice and from that of the mainline Christian churches.[49] The CCC offers a period of spiritual incubation or confinement to individuals who feel threatened by evil spirits. This involves staying inside the church for days, weeks, or even months.[50]

This concentration of spirituality may be contrasted with another form of indigenous response to Christianity that was more characteristic of the mainline Christian churches. Because the latter had remained European in ritual and had not incorporated much of Yoruba practice, the frequent result was a very different form of adaptation, which has been called "dual religious participation," or compartmentalizing one's Christian and native religious behavior. This would mean going both to church and to also the native priest or doctor when the need arose. No doubt the members of the Aladura churches did this to an extent as well, but not to the same degree; their religion served as a new and genuine synthesis of indigenous and Christian elements.[51] Nevertheless, one notices that the dual approach did replicate itself in another form, namely of crossovers between the mainline and the Aladura churches. Some of the latter allow dual membership, and one study has noted a significant number of "clandestine" Aladuras who find it more fashionable to belong to a mainstream church but to visit an Aladura father for individual counseling as well.[52]

Certainly the "quest for purity" is a phenomenon not unique to the Taiping and the Aladura churches; a collection of essays under that title, edited by Walter E. A. van Beek, appeared in 1988 and included case studies of the Taiping, Calvin's Geneva, the New England Puritans, as well as the Wahhabis, the Fulani Jihad, the Iranian revolution, and Communism, among others.[53] Most of these movements shared a political dimension; the editor's introduction stresses the obsession with evil in all the cases under consideration, which invariably led to the failure of the movements to attain their ideals. The Aladura case suggests, however, that this characterization may be too restrictive. Concentrated spirituality and asceticism may involve a quest for purity that focuses on personal and interpersonal dimensions rather than political, the redemptive rather than the transformative. One thinks also of the case with the yogic techniques of Hinduism and Buddhism.

Many will recognize this narrowing of the range of religious beliefs and practices to mobilize one's energies and change one's behavior—and that of the world—as resembling the asceticism which Weber pointed out in *The Protestant Ethic and the Spirit of Capitalism*. For Weber, this asceticism was tied the twin concepts of rationalization and disenchantment, both of which characterized the modern Western world. Rationalization consisted of such features as a consistently worked-out cosmology and a methodical calculation of means and ends to achieve a result (such as salvation). This led to a compartmentalization of the irrational aspects of religion. "The unity of the primitive image of the world," he wrote, "in which everything was concrete magic, has tended to split into rational cognition and mastery of nature, on the one hand, and into 'mystic' experiences, on the other."[54] Peel views the Aladuras' concentration on prayer as a means to healing as an example of such rationalization.[55] In my view, however, Weber's model does not fully capture the phenomena under examination here. The world was energized for the Taipings and the Aladuras, but hardly disenchanted: Emotions and visions were as much a component of the religious experience as was intellect. Although Bible study was important, there was, as we have seen, also a deliberate attempt to preserve the visionary experiences, leading to a more balanced and less compartmentalized combination of the rational and irrational.

A more adequate theoretical interpretation is provided, I believe, by certain ideas of Carl Jung, although not necessarily in ways elucidated by Jung directly. One does not have to subscribe to Jung's notion of a fixed repertoire of archetypes that reside in a human collective unconscious to appreciate his understanding of the power of visions as numinous religious experiences. Like Weber, Jung traced the roots of modern secular Western society to religious changes. He also envisaged a process of disenchantment, which he described in psychological terms as a "withdrawal of projections."[56] By this he meant the growing conviction that deities and spirits are mere superstitions, figments of one's imagination. This could be a very dangerous process, Jung believed, because a person's need to project, i.e., to displace psychic contents onto objects, did not disappear just because these objects were no longer available. The result is that projections become unconscious and thereby more powerful:

> After it became impossible for the demons to inhabit the rocks, woods, mountains, and rivers, they used human beings as much more dangerous dwelling places. ... A man does not notice it when he is governed by a demon; he puts all his skill and cunning at the service of his unconscious master, thereby heightening its power a thousandfold.[57]

Jung mounted a powerful critique of the Enlightenment on this basis, associating its campaign against superstition on the one hand with the fanaticism and destructiveness of the French Revolution on the other. "Our fearsome gods," he wrote, "have only changed their names. They now rhyme with —*ism*."[58] Jung's model, I believe, forces us to relativize the Western version of disenchantment by seeing it as containing the same dynamics of balancing of opposites that we find in the African case.

In any event, the idea of concentration of spirituality, conceived as an ideal-typical model of certain types of religious attitudes and behaviors, seems applicable to a broad range of religions worldwide, certainly transcending the gap between the West and the rest, or between traditional and world religions. It might also help to explain the appeal of Islam and Christianity to Africans in a time of rapid change, since both religions are biased towards concentration of spirituality by virtue of their monotheism and their insistence on the uniqueness of a single messiah/prophet as the prime bearer of God's message. At the same time, I would also tentatively suggest that the dynamic opposite of this concentration, namely the diffusion of spirituality so often associated with the term "animism" is likewise not limited to one brand of religion but is equally trans-cultural and trans-continental, with plenty of manifestations in the so-called "rational" religion of the West. But this is the subject for another essay at another time.

Notes

1. This chapter is a considerably revised version of an article that appeared as "The Taiping and the Aladura: A Comparative Study of Charismatically Based Christian Movements," in *Afrika Zamani. An Annual Journal of African History* (2003–2004) 11 & 12: 119–35, which is used with permission. Some passages are adapted from "Indigenous Encounters with Christian Missionaries in China and West Africa, 1800–1920: A Comparative Study," *Journal of World History* 16 (2005): 327–69.

2. David Lindenfeld, "The Concept of 'World Religions' as Currently Used in Religious Studies Textbooks," *World History Bulletin* 23, no. 1 (2007): 6–7; cf. Rosalind Shaw, "The Invention of 'African Traditional Religion,'" *Religion* 20 (1990): 340–42.

3. Jürgen Kocka, "Comparison and Beyond," *History and Theory* 42 (2003): 39–44.

4. Ibid., 42.

5. Ibid., 40.

6. My account of the Taiping is drawn mainly from Jonathan Spence, *God's Chinese Son* (New York, 1996); Rudolf G. Wagner, *Reenacting the Heavenly Vision: The Role of Religion in the Taiping Rebellion*, China Research Monograph, no. 25 (Berkeley, CA, 1982); Jen Yu-wen, *The Taiping Revolutionary Movement* (New Haven, CT, 1973); and Vincent Y.C. Shih, *The Taiping Ideology* (Seattle, 1967). For a comprehensive picture of Christianity in China, see Daniel H. Bays, ed. *Christianity in China: From the Eighteenth Century to the Present* (Stanford, CA, 1996).

7. See Hillel Schwartz, "Millenarianism. An Overview," *Encyclopedia of Religion*, ed. Mircea Eliade, 16 vols. (New York, 1987), 9: 521–32. For a comparative study of millennial revolts against colonialism, see Michael Adas, *Prophets of Rebellion* (Durham, NC, 1979).

8. The discussion of the Aladura churches is drawn primarily from J.D.Y. Peel, *Aladura: A Religious Movement among the Yoruba* (London, 1968); H. W. Turner, *History of an African Independent Church*, 2 vols. (Oxford, 1967); Akinyele Omoyajowo, *Cherubim and Seraphim: The History of an African Independent Church*

(New York, 1982); and Afeosemimi U. Adogame, *Celestial Church of Christ: The Politics of Cultural Identity in a West African Prophetic-Charismatic Movement* (Frankfurt am Main, 1999).

9. Peel, *Aladura*, 74–75, 99–100, 146, 152.

10. See Turner, *African Independent Church*, 2: 312–14, 321–22, which includes the text of a hymn "Africa Shall Rise" and mentions the fact that some Aladuras believe in a universal sense of mission to spread African Christian religious sensibility to whites as well. The Taipings, on the other hand, believed that their struggle with the Qing was to restore an ancient belief in the Supreme God that had become corrupted over the millennia by the worship of many gods.

11. David F. Aberle, *The Peyote Religion among the Navaho* (New York, 1966), ch. 19.

12. Adrian Hastings, *The Church in Africa 1450–1950* (Oxford, 1994), 531; Graham Duncan and Ogbu U. Kalu, "*Bakuzufu*: Revival Movements and Indigenous Appropriation in African Christianity," in *African Christianity: An African Story*, ed. Ogbu U. Kalu (Trenton, NJ, 2007), 245–69. Some other manifestations of this revival included the prophets William Wade Harris and Garrick Braide in West Africa, Simon Kimbangu in the Congo, and the Zionist movements of southern Africa.

13. On West African expansion, see Turner, *African Independent Church* 1: chs. 6–8; on Europe, see Adogame, "Clearing New Paths into an Old Forest: Aladura Christianity in Europe," in *Orisa Devotion as World Religion*, ed. Jacob K. Olupona and Terry Rey, 247–62, esp. 256–57 (Madison, WI, 2008).

14. *Prophets of Rebellion*, xx–xxi.

15. Spence, *God's Chinese Son*, 32; David K. Jordan, "The Glyphomancy Factor: Observations on Chinese Conversion," in *Conversion to Christianity*, ed. Robert W. Hefner, 285–303 (Berkeley, CA, 1993).

16. Ryan Dunch, *Fuzhou Protestants and the Making of a Modern China, 1857–1927* (New Haven, CT, 2001), 14.

17. Max Weber, *Gesammelte Aufsätze zur Religionssoziologie*, 3 vols. (Tübingen, 1920), 1: 508.

18. Turner, *African Independent Church*, 2: 122. Cf. Peel, *Aladura*, 72–3; Omoyajowo, *Cherubim and Seraphim*, 88; Adogame, "Old Wine in New Wine Bottles: Prophetic Experiences in the Celestial Church of Christ," in *Uniquely African? African Christian Identity from Cultural and Historical Perspectives*, ed. James L. Cox and Gerrie Ter Haar (Trenton, NJ, 2003), 248.

19. Peel, *Aladura* 105.

20. This deviates from Weber's ideal-typical presentation of the concept, in that Weber linked routinization to succession following the death of the charismatic leader. See *From Max Weber: Essays in Sociology*, trans. and ed. H. H. Gerth and C. Wright Mills (New York, 1946), 297.

21. Spence, *God's Chinese Son*, 107–08; Jen Yu-Wen, *Taiping Revolutionary Movement*, 50.

22. Thus Shih's detailed discussion of the sources of Taiping ideology devotes 17 pages to Christianity and 107 pages to the Chinese classics.

23. Spence, *God's Chinese Son*, 254–61, 291–97.

24. Omoyajowo, *Cherubim and Seraphim*, ch. 4, esp. 82; and Peel, 269–76.

25. See Peel, *Aladura,* 111–12; Turner, *African Independent Church,* 1: ch. 5; and Adogame, *Celestial Church of Christ,* 67ff.

26. Cf. Jacob Kehinde Olupona, "The Celestial Church of Christ in Ondo: A Phenomenological Perspective," in *New Religious Movements in Nigeria,* ed. Rosalind I. J. Hackett (Lewiston, NY, 1987), 56. Cf. Weber, *From Max Weber,* 253, 296, 297.

27. Turner, *African Independent Church,* 1: 33; Lamin Sanneh, *West African Christianity: The Religious Impact* (London, 1983), 184–86, 194–97.

28. Turner, *African Independent Church,* 2: 38–39; Adogame, *Celestial Church of Christ,* 75–76, 99.

29. Peel, *Aladura,* 126–27; Omoyajowo, *Cherubim and Seraphim,* 140.

30. Peel, *Aladura,* 164, 169–70, 174.

31. Erika Bourguignon, "A Framework for the Comparative Study of Altered States of Consciousness," introduction to *Religion, Altered States of Consciousness, and Social Change,* ed. Erika Bourguignon (Columbus, OH, 1973), 9–11.

32. Spence, *God's Chinese Son,* 198.

33. Harold Z. Schiffrin. *Sun Yat-sen and the Origins of the Chinese Revolution* (Berkeley, CA, 1968), 15.

34. Peel, *Aladura,* 205; Turner, *African Independent Church,* 2: 9–10.

35. Turner, *African Independent Church,* 2: 111–19, ch. 24; Peel, *Aladura,* 158–65, for descriptions of CAC and C&S services. The CCC is an exception in that it does not admit European hymns (Adogame, *Celestial Church of Christ,* 134).

36. Turner, *African Independent Church,* 1: 100; Omoyajowo, "The Aladura Churches in Nigeria Since Independence," in *Christianity in Independent Africa,* ed. Edward Fasholé-Luke et al. (Bloomington, IN, 1978), 101.

37. "Syncretism and Religious Change," *Comparative Studies in History and Society,* 10 (1968): 121–41.

38. Turner *African Independent Church,* 2: ch. 13.

39. Peel, *Aladura,* 135–41; Adogame, *Celestial Church of Christ,* 53.

40. Turner, *African Independent Church,* 2: 10–11.

41. Omoyajowo, *Cherubim and Seraphim,* 117, 132.

42. CCC Constitution, quoted in Adogame, *Celestial Church of Christ,* 17. Cf. Peel, *Aladura,* 95; Omoyajowo, *Cherubim and Seraphim,* 16, 94; Turner, *African Indepndent Church,* 2: 85; and Peel, *Aladura,* 232–33.

43. *African Independent Church,* 2: 337. The internal quote is from Ephraim Andersson, *Messianic Movements in the Lower Congo* (Uppsala, 1958), 180.

44. Spence, *God's Chinese Son,* 120–22, 184–85; Jen Yu-Wen, *Taiping Revolutionary Movement,* 120–21.

45. Adogame, *Celestial Church of Christ,* 131.

46. Omoyajowo, *Cherubim and Seraphim,* 16. There are examples of other indigenous Christian movements in which prohibition of alcohol consumption played a central role. See Paul Stuart Landau, *The Realm of the Word. Language, Gender, and Christianity in a Southern African Kingdom* (Portsmouth, NH, 1995), on the Ngwato kingdom in southern Africa; and Bengt G. Karlsson, "Entering into the Christian Dharma: Contemporary "Tribal" Conversions in India," in *Christians, Cultural Interactions, and India's Religious Traditions,* ed. Judith M.

Brown and Robert Eric Frykenberg (Grand Rapids, MI, 2002), 146–47, 150 on the Rhabas of west Bengal.

47. Quoted in Turner, *African Independent Church*, 2: 81.

48. Turner, *African Independent Church*, 2: 43; Olupona, "Celestial Church of Christ," 61. Andrew F. Walls, *The Missionary Movement in Christian History* (Maryknoll, NY, 1996), 118.

49. Adogame, *Celestial Church of Christ*, 171; Turner, 2: 254–55; Omoyajowo, *Cherubim and Seraphim*, 148.

50. Adogame, "Old Wine in New Bottles," 251.

51. The point is made by Turner, *African Independent Church*, 1: 12; Omoya-jowo, *Cherubim and Seraphim*, 182; Omoyajowo, "Aladura Churches," 109. The phrase "dual religious participation" comes from anthropologist William K. Powers and his study of Christianity among the Sioux in *Beyond the Vision: Essays on American Indian Culture* (Norman, OK, 1987), ch. 5.

52. Gabriel I. S. Amadi, "Continuities and Adaptations in the Aladura Movement: The Example of Prophet Wobo and His Clientele in South-Eastern Nigeria," in *New Religious Movements in Nigeria*, ed. Hackett, 89.

53. Walter E.A. van Beek, ed. *The Quest for Purity. Dynamics of Puritan Movements* (Berlin, 1988). The editors stress the negative side—the continuous campaign against sin and evil which ultimately renders these movements self-defeating. The Aladura, I think, provide a counter-example of a "puritanical" church with a positive attitude.

54. Weber, *Religionssoziologie*, 1: 254; trans. In *From Max Weber*, 282.

55. Ibid., 251–53; trans. in *From Max Weber*, 280–81. On Peel's interpretation, see *Aladura*, 64–65, 120–21, 294–95.

56. C. G. Jung, *Psychology and Religion* (1937), in *The Collected Works of C. G. Jung*, ed. Herbert Read et al., 20 vols. (Princeton, NJ, 1953–1979), 11: 82–83.

57. Jung, *Marginalia on Contemporary Events* (1945), ibid., 18: 594.

58. Jung, *Two Essays in Analytical Psychology*, ibid., 7: 203.

🪷 8

ACCULTURATION AND GENDERED CONVERSION: AFRO-AMERICAN CATHOLIC WOMEN IN NEW ORLEANS, 1726–1884

Sylvia Frey

Ordinarily when we think of Christian missionaries we mean missionaries from North America or Europe who go to a non-Christian place somewhere on the globe. When we think of enslaved Christians in the United States South, we think of one or another of the evangelical Protestant denominations, which attracted the great majority of enslaved peoples.[1] I want to invert that perspective by putting my focus on the process by which a predominantly white "foreign" church represented by a vanguard of French nuns evangelized a black diasporic community. I have chosen New Orleans as the site of my study. A unique location, it was European, Caribbean, American, black and white, enslaved and free. Organized in a complex racial order composed of whites, free people of color and enslaved, New Orleans was the exception to the rule of black Protestant America and it offers a distinctive model of female missionary activity.

The designation of the United States as a mission field by the *Propaganda Fide*—the Vatican congregation responsible for overseas missions—created a mission tradition in North America that pre-dated an American Catholic organization for foreign missions by a full century.[2] Although priests and monks of various orders began proselytizing Africans in the fifteenth century and became heavily engaged in the imposition of orthodoxy on indigenous populations in the Spanish Atlantic world, neither Protestantism nor Catholicism had developed missionary programs in North America aimed at enslaved people. Until the creation of the Catholic Board for Mission Work Among the Colored People, incorporated in 1907, the Catholic Church more or less yielded the mission field to evangelical Protestants, with the consequence that the vast majority of all peoples of African descent in North America belonged to one or another evangelical Protestant denominations—except in New Orleans, the epicenter of North American Catholicism and the focal point of African-American Catholicism.

No single model of acculturation can encompass the range of cultural interactions between African descendants and white missionaries. In New Orleans, acculturation was an urban, extended multi-generational, multi-dimensional process involving the chief components of Catholic worship, baptism, and the Eucharist. The trajectory of change encompasses four distinct stages beginning with baptism. Carried out initially by white missionaries, it involved a creative and dynamic relationship with African descendants who quickly claimed the ritual as their own. As the mission period progressed, formal religious training was initiated by white female missionaries. Under their highly scripted tutelage, the most ardent among the young black female converts took up the apostolate of teaching and, contrary to conventional wisdom about structural assimilation, gathered their own society of faith within the church. As the illusion of the universal church faded over time, black female leaders reclaimed their spiritual independence by creating their own separate institutions of learning. Ultimately the gulf between how they understood and experienced Catholicism created divisions within the black religious community and inadvertently contributed to racial separation.

BAPTISM

In response to the mandate by the French Crown to use religion as a vehicle for national consolidation, the Company of the Indies made contracts with three male religious orders, the Jesuits, Capuchins, and the Carmelites, to assume responsibility for the spiritual lives of all inhabitants of French territories in North America. The territory was divided into three jurisdictions, each of which was assigned to one of the three religious houses. Louisiana was the exclusive mission field of the Capuchins.[3] As part of their pastoral responsibilities Capuchins baptized several thousands enslaved adults and infants between 1730 and 1803. Through a close analysis of sacramental records between 1800 and 1813 Emily Clark and Virginia Gould show that almost 7,000 enslaved people were baptized in St. Louis Cathedral, often in group baptisms during the Easter holy days. Although it varied, roughly 40 percent of baptisands were adult Africans, the great majority of them from Kongo and the Senegambia regions from which most of Louisiana's enslaved population was taken. Over 50 percent of all black baptisands were women.[4] The number of African Catholics waxed and waned depending on a number of factors, among them the rate of natural increase, the opening and after 1808 the closing of the international slave trade, and the influx of American slaves following the Louisiana Purchase and of refugees from St. Domingue during the Haitian Revolution.

But is baptism a reliable index of faith? The most obvious question is, of course, the extent to which Catholicism was merely a cover concealing the enduring presence of African spiritual traditions, such as conjure, root working, and voodoo. Because voodoo rituals took place in secrecy, we know little about the early history of African spiritual traditions in Louisiana. Enslaved people in Louisiana were taken predominantly from the Senegambia region and Kongo in West Central Africa and carried with them various cultural practices and religious traditions such as the Kongolese practice of *minkisi,* and Fon-Ewe-Yoruba voodoo.[5] These cultural traditions were probably reinvigorated by the arrival in 1809–10 of over 3,000 enslaved Haitians, the majority of whom had Kongo roots and practiced a Haitian version of *vodou,* which incorporated Catholic elements.[6]

Rather than disprove the sincerity of Afro-Louisiana Catholicism, Louisiana voodoo appears to have been a transatlantic extension of Kongolese popular religion. Conditioned by several generations of contact with Capuchin missionaries, Kongolese people had a "genuine and sustained interest in Catholicism" in pre-colonial Africa, which they brought with them to Haiti.[7] That combined with the virtual absence of African religious specialists during the hiatus of the African slave trade from 1743 through the 1760s, probably accounts for the popularity of Catholicism among adult Africans from the Senegambia and Kongo. For many people of African descent in New Orleans, Catholicism was adopted because the rituals, prayers, songs, and images were already at least vaguely familiar, because in the absence of traditional ritual practitioners, Catholicism was spiritually effective, and because they saw no incompatibility between it and their own spiritual heritage.[8]

There was to be sure an element of coercion imposed by the 1724 *Code Noir* requiring masters to have slaves instructed and baptized in the Catholic faith. There was also a lack of choice. French and Spanish colonial laws banned both Protestants and Jews until the last Spanish governor, Estevan Miró, overhauled immigration policy. Consequently not a single Protestant church was established in Louisiana before 1804, when Bishop Joseph Willis, the first black Baptist preacher arrived from Mississippi. The first Baptist church was not formed until 1812 in Bayou Chicot, a deeply rural area nearly 200 miles west of New Orleans. The first black Baptists in New Orleans were members of a biracial church formed in 1817. When William Winans, the first Methodist itinerant preacher, arrived in New Orleans in 1813, he found that "aside from two or three obscure white people and some twenty persons of colour, there were none ... who had evinced any partiality for Methodism, and very few with Protestant predilections." After a "succession of discouragements," Winans went on to preach, but it was not until 1825 that the Methodists had a continuous presence in the city.[9] In that year there were only 147 black Methodists in the Louisiana District. Ten years later the Louisiana District contained only 189 black and 695 white members while the New Orleans District, which included surrounding rural parishes, reported 933 black and 1,198 white members.[10]

While it can be argued that adult black Catholics assented to the faith through public ritualized demonstrations such as baptism, baptismal records alone do not constitute incontrovertible evidence of religious self-determination. Linguistic differences would have made it very difficult for newly arrived Africans to comprehend complex church doctrines such as the Trinity. The practice of infant baptism, a later development in Louisiana, also raises questions about the genuineness of "conversion." "Cradle Catholics" clearly are incapable of individual choice but are rather absorbed into the faith of their parents, who by choosing to baptize their children do demonstrate a commitment.

The family history of Henriette Delille is a core text. Shortly after she arrived in Louisiana as an enslaved person, an African woman, Marie Ann, also called Nanette, was baptized sometime after 1731 in St. Louis Parish Church (later Cathedral). Nanette was probably evangelized by her mistress, Marie Payen Dubreuil, a devout Catholic and a member of the Children of Mary. Marie Dubreuil was the wife of Claude Joseph Dubreuil, Sr., a prosperous planter, Royal Engineer, contractor of the King of France, and the father of Nanette's children. Nanette had her three children baptized and they in turn had their children baptized. Nanette's great-grand-daughter, Marie Joseph Diaz, a quadroon woman, was baptized on 8 June 1787. The three children she bore with Jean Baptiste Lille Sarpy—Cecile, Marianne, and Henriette—were also baptized. The family belonged to the large and prominent free mixed race community of New Orleans. According to oral tradition, the young Henriette was sent to study at an elite boarding school operated by the Sisters of the Sacred Heart at a convent outside the city. By the time she was fourteen years old, Henriette was a lay catechist, teaching the rudiments of the faith to members of her own caste in the French Faubourg Marigny, where her family lived, and to enslaved people on outlying plantations.[11]

The choices of baptismal godparents made by enslaved people also suggests the internalization of Catholic values and the penetration of Catholicism more generally among the black community. Godparenting, a practice unique to Catholic countries, argues strongly for individual and collective choices and for a changing consciousness.[12] Clark and Gould's analysis of baptismal records reveals that Creole[13] and African parents increasingly assumed ritual responsibility for baptizing their children in the Catholic faith and standing as godparents to one another's children: In 1733, people of African descent were godparents in only 2 percent of all baptisms; by 1750, they represented 21 percent; in 1765, 68 percent; 1775, 89 percent.[14] Catechisms in use in New Orleans stressed the responsibility of godparents *"pour qu'ils puissent promettre au nom de l'enfant ce que l'enfant lui-meme promettrait s'il avait l'usage de la raison"* [so that they can promise in the name of the child that which the child itself would promise if it had the use of reason]. Those who stood as god-parents accepted a commitment *"d'instruire l'enfant dans les devoirs de la Religion, au défaut de ses parents"* [to instruct the child in the duties of religion in default of its parents].[15]

A liturgical expression of community, in New Orleans godparent- ing was mediated through black female leadership. In contrast to white Catholic practices, the same African female sponsors stood repeatedly. Between 1845 and 1860 there were seventy-eight baptisms recorded in St. Augustine Church in Faubourg Tremé. Forty-six were slaves, the ma- jority adults. Henriette Delille, who as a young woman knelt before the altar in St. Augustine and committed herself to an apostolate mission, is named as a sponsor of twenty-eight; Josephine Charles, her companion and co-founder of the black sisterhood, sponsored forty three; Juliette Gaudin, the third founder of the black religious community, sponsored four. Delille and other devout women carried out the same ministry in other parishes, especially nearby St. Mary's, or Bishop's chapel as it was also known.[16]

For Catholics as for most Protestants, baptism represented the induc- tion of the individual into religious life and theoretically at least bridged racial and class divides through acceptance into the community of faith. The first of seven sacraments, it differed from Protestant baptism in sev- eral essential points. A religion of the heart, evangelical Protestantism emphasized the importance of effecting an emotional transformation in the congregation as a necessary prelude to the conversion experience, a pre-requisite for baptism. Intensely emotional, the conversion pro- cess frequently began with an exhortation and was followed by a long period of agonized soul-searching and involved personal confessions before the sinner finally achieved conviction. Baptism, the ritual climax of the conversion experience, consisted of sprinkling or full immersion depending on the denomination, and occurred in a mass ceremony in a river or stream. Because young children did not possess the capacity to experience religious conversion, baptism was reserved for adults. It was the only public event in which a parental role was recognized, and then only informally when preachers spoke briefly to the mother before performing the ritual.[17]

ACCULTURATION

Catholicism favored a more traditional, ordered alternative through catecheses. For a variety of reasons, including a chronic shortage of missionaries, lack of support from the Company, and indifference on the part of the Capuchins themselves, the vital work of catechistical training in Louisiana was largely left to Catholic nuns from France.

More than any other doctrinal controversy, different interpretations of how sinful humans can achieve reconciliation with God divided the various denominations of Christians during the tumultuous years of the Protestant Reformation and Catholic Counter-Reformation. Catholics and Protestants agreed that humans are incapable of gaining salvation by their own efforts. But whereas Protestant reformers insisted that the gift of salvation could only be bestowed by God, Catholicism interpreted the demands of salvation to include baptism, the Eucharist, and good works. In carving out a place for human initiative the Catholic Church had forged a weapon in the battle against Protestantism and unwittingly placed it in the hands of female religious activists. By insisting on the necessity of performing good works they would need to obtain salvation (and that were, in any case, extensions of sanctioned women's work), religious women took advantage of the spirit of the Counter-Reformation in some cases to escape the cloister altogether, and in other cases to redefine its meaning and purpose. Like it or not, the Old Regime was absolutely dependent on female religious. It not only tolerated their activities in France but sent them on apostolic missions in the North American wilderness.[18]

While French female religious orders were not explicitly missionaries in an institutional sense, their fervent sense of apostolic mission laid the foundation stones for the rise of Catholicism in New Orleans and of Afro-Catholicism in particular. Once the faith was implanted, white female religious orders in New Orleans turned to Africans to convert Africans, a model deployed by Capuchin missionaries in West Central Africa, by Moravian missionaries in the Dutch Caribbean, and by evangelical Protestant denominations during the First and Second Great Awakenings. Although some of the enslaved population of New Orleans had probably already been introduced to Catholicism by the Capuchins in West Central Africa or to Islam in the Senegambia, the arrival of Ursuline nuns in New Orleans in 1726 signaled the beginning of the creation of an indigenous African-Catholic population. The commitment of French Catholic nuns to the inclusion of Africans in Catholicism coincided with the imperial design put into play in Louisiana by the *Code Noir* of 1724.

In contrast to the household origins of evangelical Protestantism, the Catholic school was the institutional foundation for acculturation. For many black parents and children the school was the first contact with Catholicism. In 1727, the Ursulines established an Indian mission in Louisiana and the first academy for women's education in what is now the United States.[19] Far from a state of contemplative isolation, the small community of Ursulines in New Orleans was bound by strong and intimate ties to the local social and economic complex virtually from the beginning. Their little compound, located on the outskirts of the turbulent frontier town, welcomed a steady stream of Indian and African girls to the boarding and free day schools they operated. The female confraternity they organized accommodated a broad spectrum of women, and through it democratized significantly the female religious population of New Orleans. The range and intensity of their work in the education of women and girls, in founding hospitals and orphanages, provided stable foundations for the chaotic frontier community and created much of the institutional framework and the infrastructure of social services that supported colonial life.[20] In fact, the active and proselytizing Catholicism practiced by Ursuline nuns produced a shift from the educational responsibility of women in the home to the educative responsibility of the school.

The multi-racial school for girls established by the Ursulines in New Orleans was an essential step in the process of acculturation. Young females, recruited at a point when they were consolidating their identities, passed through a conditioning process designed to teach them the rules and requirements and to internalize the new culture. What little we know about what was taught and how comes from the *Règlemens*, or rules of the order found in the Ursuline library in New Orleans. Volume one sets out clearly the purpose of the Ursuline mission: "*Les Religieuses Ursulines étans principalement établies, pour s'employer à l' instruction and conduite des jeunes filles*" [the Ursulines Religious are established to employ themselves in the instruction and behavior of young girls]. In contrast to the first missionaries in New Spain, who baptized thousands of native Americans without any pre-baptismal instruction, the Ursuline regimen depended upon daily instruction in reading, writing, and numeracy. Mornings and afternoons "pensionnaires," or boarders, attended reading classes, one in Latin, one in French, which forecasted the important role that language would play in the development of acculturation. Students learned by repetition: the *"maitresse"* read five or six lines; the students, following along in a text, then repeated word for word. As part of their training, students also learned the fundamentals of female piety, which were modeled largely on French notions of gendered piety. Teachers were required to warn their students about inappropriate forms of recreation such as *"comédies, danses, cartes, et autres semblables, et ne les laissent chanter des chansons mauvaises"* [comedies, dances, cards and other similar things, and not to allow them to sing bad songs].[21]

The catechism was the centerpiece of religious instruction and preparation for first communion, which consumed seven weeks and was the final act of acceptance of the major tenets of Catholicism. Chapters four and five of the *Règlemens* outline in elaborate detail the fundamentals of religious instruction. In contrast to the question and answer format most commonly used in religious indoctrination, the Ursulines discouraged learning the basic tenets of the faith by rote, in order to ensure *"qu'elles ne retiennent pas seulement par memoire, mais comprennet bien"* [that they do not retain only by memory, but understand well]. Students learned the doctrine by communally reciting the Creed and the acts of faith, hope, charity, and contrition, but the *Règlemens* stressed the importance that they be taught not only why the sacraments were instituted but their form and purpose.[22] Although not part of the formal curriculum religious instruction also encompassed liturgical music and art, such as the stations-of-the-cross prominently displayed in St. Louis Cathedral, and through participation in elaborate processions, such as Palm Sunday, and other dramatic displays of Catholic liturgy.

Collectively the young women who were educated at religious schools stood at the center of the kinship network that defined the emerging black Catholic community. Godparental relationships formed from a coalescence of networks of female influence extended outward to embrace kinship and neighborhood connections. St. Louis Cathedral, the nucleus around which parish life coalesced, centered missionary efforts in a continuous core for black Catholic life. The absence of formal racial separation within the church marked out in symbolic and social fashion the notion of the universal Catholic Church. During his travels around the United States in the early nineteenth century, Benjamin Henry Latrobe visited New Orleans and attended Sunday Mass in St. Louis Cathedral. Perhaps because Latrobe was more familiar with the differentiated space which had already begun to distinguish biracial Protestant churches in the rest of the country, he was struck by the physical and spiritual unity of collective public worship in New Orleans and in particular the presence "of all the beautiful girls in the place, and of two or three hundred quadroons, negroes and mulattoes, and perhaps of 100 white males to hear high mass ..." On another occasion Latrobe attended Good Friday services, and reported that at least three-quarters of the congregants were black or colored, and of those "a very large number were women."[23]

Baptismal records confirm Latrobe's impression of a feminized and Africanized church. In 1820, when Latrobe attended worship, whites made up only 39 percent of the baptisands; free persons of color 23 percent, and slaves, 38 percent. Of 1,402 baptisms in St. Louis Cathedral and nearby St. Mary's in 1830, 460 were whites [33 percent]; 286 were free persons of color [20 percent]; and 656 slaves [47 percent].[24] Until the era of Jim Crow in the 1890s, whites of both sexes, who never made up more than 35 percent of the Catholic population of early New Orleans, worshipped with a roughly two-thirds majority African Catholic community. Whites only began to equal black Catholics with the influx of Americans following the Louisiana Purchase in 1803, and only after the entry of Irish Catholics and Germans beginning in the 1820s and 1830s did white Catholics equal and eventually exceed those who were black.[25]

SEPARATION

Although white religious orders such as the Ursulines provided spiritual preparation and training for young black women interested in taking religious vows, they did not admit them to the novitiate, in part because church authorities acquiesced in social conventions of racial discrimination, and in part because state segregation laws prohibited it.[26] Black women who wanted to devote their lives to the teaching ministry were forced to form their own orders. Two of the pioneering sisterhoods were the Oblate Sisters of Providence, the oldest black female religious order in the world, founded in Baltimore in 1829, and the Sisters of the Holy Family, founded in New Orleans in 1842. The Catholic Directory's announcement of the founding of the Oblate order betrays the central ambiguity between Catholic universalism and race and gender. In describing the target and the content of the order's work the Directory noted that "these girls will either become mothers of families or household servants. In the first case ... the solid virtues, the religious and moral principles, which they acquired, when in this school, will be carefully transferred as a legacy to the children ... As to those whose future is as servants, they will be instructed with domestic concerns, &

the care of young children." In order to instill "religious principles," and "habits of modesty, honesty and integrity," the school's curriculum included in addition to religion, English, French, cyphering and writing, sewing in all its branches, embroidery, washing and ironing.[27]

Despite differences in the socio-cultural contexts in which the black sisterhoods emerged, both shared certain common characteristics. Most conspicuous is the fact that lineage and color correlate with female leadership. The founding members of both groups were émigrés, bound together by racial heritage, French language and culture, and the Catholic faith. The founders of both religious houses were part of the nineteenth century diasporic stream that brought persons of African descent first to the Caribbean and later to the United States. Of the first four Oblate Sisters, one was a Haitian émigré and two were émigrés from Santo Domingo. The principal foundress of the Sisters of the Holy Family, Henriette Delille, was born in New Orleans but her co-foundress, Josephine Gaudin, was born in Cuba of refugee parents from St. Domingue.

Nineteenth-century African-American sisterhoods followed a general pattern of developing community life. Both sisterhoods evolved from previously existing associations formed by lay black women teachers in cities that were havens for émigrés from Haiti, to vowed women living in community, to approved congregations. Both followed the Catholic tradition of women evangelizing women through catechetical instruction. Marie Elizabeth Lange, Madeleine Marie Balas, Rosine Boegue, and Almaide Therese Duchermin established a home-based school in the Fells' Point area of Baltimore to serve the black Francophone community clustered there. In New Orleans the most important activity of the female ministry was acting as sponsors and witnesses for enslaved people and people of color. Both female orders not only survived the heightened tensions of the antebellum period but expanded their teaching missions to create a nexus of religious societies and educational institutions to serve black America.[28]

The Sisters of the Holy Family serve as an example of proselytizing Catholicism practiced by black women. As transitional figures they formed evangelical links between the white sisterhoods who brought the first young women into the community of faith and the vast parochial school system that was the principal vehicle for the transformation of the demographic face of Catholicism. Delille herself defined the mission of the society of devout women: "*[D]ans le but 1e de soigner les malades, 2e de secourir les pauvres; 3e d'instruire [sic] les Ignorantes*" [for the purpose of 1. caring for the sick, 2. aiding the poor, 3. instructing the ignorant].[29] Their work was cut out for them. In 1852 a French priest wrote to the prefect of the *Propaganda Fide:* "The slaves of Catholics are baptized, a goodly number among them are taught their prayers, but the immense majority do not approach the sacraments."[30] The small group of holy women led by Henriette Delille would carry out their mission to care for "the sick, the infirm and the poor" and to "teach the principal mysteries of religion and the most important points of Christian morality" to the free black and enslaved populations in complex interaction with the demographic, social and cultural changes that were transforming the region.[31] From 1803 until 1840, people of African descent made up a majority of Louisiana's total population. New Orleans' population of over 100,000 remained divided into a three-tiered social system, a demographic distillation of the elaborate system of racial classification introduced by Spain during the colonial period and unparalleled in any other city in North America.

But New Orleans was on the threshold of a major demographic transformation as the flood of Americans following the Purchase of 1803 and the influx of German and Irish immigrants produced a new white majority by 1840. The intense competition engendered by the spread of cotton production and the development of the port of New Orleans intensified racial animosities, which found expression in new legal restrictions on the entry of free people of color from other states or foreign countries. Although free people of color maintained an extraordinary presence in the city, more intense professional competition from immigrants robbed them of jobs as porters, small merchants, or dockworkers—jobs that would be completely lost to Irish and German laborer families by 1850. One other feature of the new demographic profile was of particular importance to the mission of the holy women: the gender and age structure. In 1840 in all age groups among both enslaved and free people of color, women outnumbered men. Free black women between the ages of 25 and 55 made up 61 percent of the total population of color in New Orleans while enslaved women accounted for 58 percent.[32] It was to this constituency that Delille and her disciples aimed their mission and it was from this constituency that they built their spiritual community.

The black sisterhood's strategies for carrying out their apostolic mission were shaped by several different factors, prominent among which was the problem of navigating between racial cultures and class within race. Because they had no legal right to exist as a religious community for the first ten years of their existence, the founding women functioned as an "association," a term deployed to draw a racial distinction between the white "Madames" of the Sacred Heart or the "Dames" Hospitaliers and their black sisters. The first official recognition of their existence was not until 1846, when the Directory for the Archdiocese of New Orleans mentioned "an association of colored persons, for the nursing of the sick and the destitute."[33]

Because they were not canonically recognized, black religious women were not allowed to wear a habit, an important historical emblem to differentiate Catholic from Protestant women, or one order from another, and as an indicator of social status.[34] Rather than offend the racial sensibilities of the white community, the black religious women wore a simple blue percale dress, which differentiated them from lay women but made no claim to the special status of female virtue signified by the formal habit.[35] After the community received formal religious rule in 1852, they exchanged their blue percale dresses for a simple black dress. The first formal habit was adopted in 1873, nearly half a century after they launched their ministry. But white religious women were not immune to the virulent racism that permeated post-Civil War society. According to Sister Mary Deggs, whose historical narrative is one of the few literary sources for the founding years of her order, "after 45 or 50 years that we had worked to have a religious habit," the black sisters were "persecuted" by the French Sisters of St. Joseph of Medaille, who "tried all that they could to make us take off our habits...." Deggs's protest that "[n]o one would think we were anything if we were not dressed in the holy habit," suggests a sophisticated appreciation of the fact that nuns were both teachers and symbols, set apart by the wearing of a habit that made their word more powerful in an increasingly race-conscious environment and within a patriarchal structure that subordinated women.[36]

A deeply embedded communal ethnic identity also informed their antebellum mission. Although the old, complex racial categories based on blood lineage were weakening as a result of immigration, the Creole status of the founding generation influenced the way its members perceived themselves and others and the way they defined their mission. They were, almost without exception, from elite black Creole families, the "very first families of the city," as Sister Mary Deggs words described them.[37] Most of them claimed French, Spanish, or German paternity, but their decision about how to identify themselves was influenced by how and where they were reared. What little knowledge we have of the early years of their apostolate suggests that the founders of the religious community were deeply marked by the fundamental influence of French ideas and religion. Like most of their Creole sisters, the charter generation received their formal religious education from white French female orders, principally the Ursulines [1727], Sisters of the Sacred Heart [1821], or the Sisters of Mount Carmel. Some were educated in Europe in keeping with the local tradition of sending children to the father's native country.[38] As "an enclave within the Gallic community," they grew up in relative isolation from most white and black New Orleanians.[39] Until the 1840s, New Orleans' free black population was spatially segregated in the back-of-town neighborhood or Faubourg Tremé, said to be the oldest existing black neighborhood in the nation, while the enslaved population was spatially integrated with the white population.[40]

Torn between European culture and race, they continued to claim their "Frenchness," in part as a way to differentiate themselves from the enslaved population, in part to distinguish themselves from "outsiders." The French language was a critical component of their French cultural identity. The constitution and rules of the order of 1876 and 1877 were written in French, as were modifications adopted as late as 1894.[41] In contrast to the Oblates, all of whom learned English to accommodate black Anglophone Catholics, founding Mother Juliette Gaudin "could speak but a very few words of English together with many of the children who could not speak a word of French." French linguistic identity and Francophone Catholicism inhibited their ability to expand their mission beyond the French-speaking faubourgs where they grew up and launched their apostolic mission. Forty years after Delille and Gaudin dedicated themselves to live in community Marie Magdaline Alpaugh, mother superior from 1882–1888, still spoke "only the French language well." Later "she became more anxious to speak English," after recognizing that "had she known how to speak English about twenty years sooner, she would have saved many good and fervent souls who was no doubt lost for want of instruction in the true faith."[42]

Traditional identities of class and color were also essential components of their community identity and shaped their mission in fundamental ways. Holy Family and Oblate sources differ significantly in their respective emphases on physical appearance and family history. Sister Mary Deggs made frequent allusions to skin and hair color, noting, for example the "German complexion" and "honey colored hair" of Mother Marie Magdaline, and the "fair and rare" skin of Mother Josephine Charles.[43] Despite a common faith and a shared linguistic and ethnic identity, Holy Family sisters viewed the Oblates of Providence, who had a brief stay in New Orleans between 1866 and 1872, as "strangers," a social category commonly used in reference to people from other states. When the Oblates "accused our sisters of having influenced the people against them and also said we wanted their places," Sister Mary Deggs's defensive response revealed both ethnic and class bias: "Our people have more confidence in us, who are their own people, than in the Oblates, who were strangers." Although Oblate membership before 1850 drew from Baltimore's black middle class, Oblate family backgrounds were more modest than the New Orleans' sisterhood as Deggs's arch observation that Holy Family sisters hailed from "fine and select families" implied.[44]

Whether the charter generation adhered to or accommodated local racial and class conventions out of necessity is unclear but class divisions within race appear to have informed their ministry in the antebellum years. As a community, the Oblates did not discriminate against candidates on the basis of color or operate racially segregated schools. Their antebellum membership included free-born and enslaved, Francophone and Anglophone women.[45] The rule of the first motherhouse of the Sisters of the Holy Family stated that "we accept only those of free and well-known families." An "Indian, red-skinned," and Chloe Preval, a freed slave, were both refused admission to the community. During Reconstruction, as racial hostilities intensified, class distinctions gradually relaxed. Mother Josephine Charles [1867–1882], who "did not respect human conventions" admitted the first two sisters, who, the color-conscious Deggs noted, "were as dark as the head of a jet-pine." One of them was the widow Preval, who was received as Sister Mary Joachim in 1870. It was not until 1872, when Preval took vows, that the class barriers were finally breached.[46]

Delille and her disciples began their apostolate exclusively to black New Orleanians in the old French-speaking part of the city. The charter generation had begun their ministry as sponsors for baptisms and as witnesses for the marriages of enslaved people and free people of color. As non-vowed "associates," they evangelized from their family households for the first five or six years. After incorporating as the Society of the Holy Family in 1847, they moved from one temporary house to another before finally settling provisionally in 1851 on Bayou Road, now Governor Nicholls Street, near Rampart Street in the French Quarter. This first motherhouse of the community was the center for their ministry, the first years of which were marked by poverty so extreme that they often had nothing to eat but "cold hominy that had been left from some rich family's table." They supported themselves by begging, doing laundry, making vestments and altar cloths for local clergy, and sewing trousseaux for "thousands of the richest and best families of this state."[47] During the 1850s there were approximately 65,000 Catholics in New Orleans. Perhaps 12,000 to 15,000, or about 50 percent of the total black population, were at least nominal Catholics.[48] Although their original mission was to evangelize women and young girls, ultimately the varied relationships between black and white, between enslaved and free people of color, between "French" and American, Catholic and Protestant complicated the missionary work of the black sisterhood. As they struggled to establish a distinct community and identity, they unwittingly contributed to a racially divided Catholic community by perpetuating the institutional separations triggered by the Ursulines' surrender of the biracial St. Claude School to the Sisters of Mount Carmel.

Fragmentary sources on the early years of the black sisterhood suggest that their evangelizing efforts reflected their neighborhood and mirrored class and residential patterns. They began with a home for the elderly, the first institution of its kind in the United States, and in 1852 opened a small boarding school for girls that taught basic literacy. In certain essentials these early day schools functioned like later parochial schools. Their mission was to preserve and protect the faith and cultural values of the community and gain an entrance to the home through the school. Mary Deggs explained how it worked in practice: "[A]ll the little ones would wait for Mother Marie Magdalene and ask her if she would tell them all about God and His mother so that they might tell their papas and mamas on the days that they were at home and so that they might ask their friends not to go to bed at night before they had made their night prayers."[49]

According to the Catholic Directory, in the early years the principal evangelical work of the Sisters of the Holy Family was to prepare "Catholic colored girls and women" for baptism and communion.[50] Legal restrictions on education meant that the vast majority of the enslaved population was illiterate so the sisters probably relied on oral instruction to avoid running afoul of the law. There are no extant documents describing the methods used for instruction, but at their convent in Grand Coteau, where Delille is believed to have received her religious training, the Religious of the Sacred Heart relied on singing to inculcate basic Catholic tenets to the 100 to 200 enslaved people who met together for that purpose on Sunday afternoons: "What attracts them is the singing of hymns. In fact, they do not say to me I am going to instruction but I go to learn singing. We have discovered a twofold advantage in having them learn their religion and to replace the profane songs, which resound through the shops and over the fields, with the praise of their Creator and holy Mother."[51]

The basic text that was probably used was the *Catéchism Imprimé par l'Ordre de Monseigneur Blanc,* which was set up in question and answer format and contained various exercises for children but no special prayers or exercises for Afro-Catholics. During the daytime the nuns held classes for poor girls and adults from St. Mary's Parish and during evening hours conducted Latin and music classes for working girls and prepared "sixty to seventy year old mothers and grandmothers, with their violet colored dresses and blue veils on their heads and white shawls and gloves on their hands" for their first communion. Their teaching methods probably consisted of ritual repetition, beginning with the Trinitarian doctrine, "du mystère de la tres-sainte Trinité," the mystery of the incarnation, the Eucharist, which "*contient réellement et en verité de Corps, l'âme et la Divinité de Notre Seigneur Jesus-Christ*" [contains really and in truth the body, the soul and the divinity of our Lord Jesus Christ].[52] Many of the older women "had never known how to make the sign of the cross," much less "tell how many persons there were in the Blessed Trinity. If one would ask them who was the first person, one would say, 'St. Joseph' and the other would say, 'the son.'" Mother Josephine "was obliged to take their hands, one by one, and teach them both by words and song to make the sign of the cross and also to pronounce the names of the three persons of the Holy Trinity."[53]

"Just at the time the Civil war broke out our dear little work began to sprout its timid buds," Deggs recalled.[54] The Civil War and Union occupation [1862–1877] "demolished the whole country and put a stop to the unbounded charity of our noble-hearted Catholic families." In the bitter aftermath of the war, Sister Mary Deggs looked back with nostalgia at the relatively peaceful pre-war years: "It is only since the Civil War that this state has become so very prejudiced and the people of this city have so many hard feelings against the colored class. We have always been like one and the same family, going to the same church, sitting in the same pews, and many of them sleeping in the same bed. If we had any entertainment, the whites would come by."[55] Although Deggs exaggerated the racial harmony of the pre-war years, she correctly anticipated the massive transformation in race relations that would cleave the universal church into black and white.

SEGREGATION

Despite the hardships of those years, the Reconstruction era stands as a brief interlude when some political divides, mostly involving race, were temporarily narrowed, and others, mostly involving faith, were widened. The state constitutions of 1868 and 1870 made all males eligible to vote, and in 1869 Louisiana became the only Southern state to create an integrated public school system. In 1870 the state repealed the ban on interracial marriage, while the Civil Rights Act of 1875 banned segregation in public places. Despite the hardships and the devastation wrought by the war, under the protective umbrella of Reconstruction the Sisters of the Holy Family built organizations for health care and relief work that laid the foundations for the social infrastructure of modern Catholic life. In 1867 they opened St. Mary's Academy on Chartres Street, New Orleans' first high school for free girls of color and the oldest school in continuing existence for black children in the United States; in 1874 they took over operation of St. Augustine School for Colored Children; and in 1877 established the Old Women's Asylum on St. Bernard Avenue and took charge of the Louisiana Asylum for Colored Girls. After frequent moves from house to house, in 1881 they finally established the motherhouse at 717 Orleans Avenue in the old Orleans Ballroom. In addition to the motherhouse, the sisters established five other houses in New Orleans, and expanded their mission to rural communities in Opelousas, [1876], Baton Rouge [1881], and Donaldsonville [1886].[56]

Almost all of the educational facilities and social institutions they built to serve the black community were clustered downriver from Canal Street in the French-speaking First and Third municipalities where almost all free black creoles lived. St. Mary's Church adjacent to the old Ursuline Convent on Chartres Street and the nearby St. Augustine Church were flourishing centers around which the institutional life of an emerging Afro-Catholic community clustered. Through their creation of networks throughout the black neighborhoods, the Sisters of the Holy Family had unwittingly perhaps facilitated the emergence of the black parish as a separatist institution in its relation to St. Louis Cathedral, the historic center of integrated worship for over a century and a living symbol of the universal Catholic Church. The umbilical link between black Catholics and the Sisters of the Holy Family was manifest in the marked tendency of black Catholics to flock to St. Mary's for Sunday Mass, even during Holy Week, a trend that did not escape the notice of Cathedral priests, who "complained about the church being empty."[57] In an effort to restore the ecumenical character of the church through integrated worship the Dutch-born Archbishop Francis Janssens ordered all Catholics to attend services in their own parish, which for most black Catholics meant a return to St. Louis or to St. Augustine. Sister Mary Deggs's account of the new boundaries of participation they found in the Cathedral describes a dramatically different Catholic universe than the one witnessed by Benjamin Henry Latrobe some sixty years earlier.[58]

"When we were there on any grand day for a ceremony in the church, all the other religious communities were allowed to pass in front of us," Deggs wrote. "They said that they were older communities than ours and took all the front seats. That threw our sisters so far back that we could scarcely see anything." In a scene reminiscent of the eviction of Richard Allen and Absalom Jones from the communion rail at St. Georges in Philadelphia, the Sisters of the Holy Family found themselves summarily removed from the pews of honor traditionally assigned according to the founding date of religious orders: "We went to the expense of putting up a small gate to our pew to prevent anyone from going in before us. But that was all in vain, for others would break the gates saying that they were the oldest in the church and had the right to pass in front of us." Archbishop Janssen responded to their protest by restoring the sisters' "proper place" based on seniority and allowed "our children" to conduct the singing. "This, however, caused us and the children a great many insults from the other side."[59]

For 150 years the Catholic Church had been the central institution of faith and a vital hub of social and cultural life in the city for black and white New Orleanians. But the collapse of the Reconstruction experiment in 1877, the return of Louisiana to Democratic rule, the rapid re-segregation of public schools, the disfranchisement of black men, the enactment of Jim Crow laws, and the economic depression of 1894 ushered in a decade of incorrigible and violent conflict between whites and blacks that changed the religious landscape of the city. The racial divides are reflected in the racial composition of St. Augustine Parish. At its founding in 1841 the parish was almost evenly divided between whites and blacks. As racial tensions intensified the racial composition of the parish changed from 53 percent white and 47 percent black in 1880, to 54 percent white and 46 percent black in 1890, to 75 percent white and 25 percent black in 1900.[60]

The statistics also reflect a dramatic exodus of black Catholics from the church. The Dutch-born Archbishop Francis Janssens estimated that 20,000 black Catholics left the church in the forty years following the Civil War. Janssens's assumption that it was "the poor darkey that is led astray from the church to the Baptist and Methodist shouting houses" is probably true.[61] The church's own internal investigation showed that black Catholics were also alienated by discrimination within the church, by the neglect of black parishioners by white priests, by the refusal of the church to ordain black priests, and by the absence of schools to educate their children. Many black Catholics felt only a tenuous loyalty to Catholicism and were ready to explore new religious options once freedom made it possible.

Baptist and Methodist itinerates had been trying to gain a foothold in Louisiana for almost a century but they did not become permanently established until the late 1830s. Because they had no settled churches, itinerant preachers held worship services in gin houses, warehouses, shops, private homes, outdoors, and on plantations. By 1827 there were enough black Baptists to separate from the biracial church on St. Charles Avenue and to organize as an all-black church on Girod Street, in the old Faubourg St. Marie, or former American quarter of the old city. Later they would move to Third Street as the First African Baptist Church. By 1867, there were 5,000 black members, and by 1910, black Baptist associations in Louisiana counted over 50,000 members.[62] Black Methodism also made a permanent establishment in New Orleans with the organization of Wesley Chapel in 1838. Wesley started in a warehouse stable on Gravier Street between Carondelet and Baronne. By 1845 Wesley's biracial membership was over 500, and the church moved to South Liberty as an all-black congregation.

As a minority faith, black evangelical Protestant churches tailored their evangelicalism to accommodate the racial attitudes of the white community. In keeping with the law, a white overseer was always present during services and, although pastored by white men "promising Negro preachers were used" by evangelical churches, and their "spirit-filled sermons" often "out-preached some of the white preachers." Wesley Chapel posted ads for runaways or announcements of slave auctions on the church door. But the church also functioned as a "City Market," where people could gather to look for work as domestics, steamboat hands, midwives, or farm laborers.[63] Moreover, certain evangelical rituals assumed great importance in the choice of an alternative spiritual order. Hundreds were drawn to revivals that lasted for days, sometimes weeks, and to worship that permitted the full range of expression. The evangelical emphasis on emotional conviction was more attractive to many than Catholic catechesis, however perfunctory it might have been. Total water immersion practiced by Baptists had a greater attraction for some than the more restrained Catholic sprinkling.

As their congregations blossomed, both Baptists and Methodists began laying the institutional foundations that would challenge Catholic hegemony. Significantly, they established their institutions upriver from Canal Street where Americans and the recent immigrant population tended to cluster, thus pressing forward the pattern of forming religious life around ethnic groups, particularly those defined by language. "Out of the loins of Mother-Wesley," a host of institutions to serve the freed black community emerged: In 1866, the Freedman's Aid Society was chartered; in 1867, the Sunday school was turned into a regular day school; in 1869, the Tomson Biblical Institute was established; in 1870, the Winans Chapel Home Missionary Society was chartered with 200 members, and Faith Kindergarten was established by the Women's Home Missionary Society; in 1873 came Union Normal School and in 1889, the Peck School of Domestic Science and Art.[64]

The competition from evangelical Protestantism forced the Catholic hierarchy to consider what the black community needed and wanted from the church.[65] Rather than a consensus, what the Archbishop found was a deep social divide within the black community, separating the shrinking Creole population from the emancipated population, the educated from the less educated, the Catholic from evangelical Protestant. Convinced that the withdrawal of black Catholics was "because we cannot give them in the church the same accommodations as the whites; that is mix them together, as they desire; for then we drive the whites away… ," Archbishop Janssens concluded that the only solution was to establish a separate church.[66] In 1895, Janssens negotiated an agreement with the French Assumption Fathers which contained four articles: the Assumption fathers were granted *"plein et entière jurisdiction sur les gens de couleur de l' archediocese de la Nouvelle-Orléans"* [full and complete jurisdiction over the people of color of the archdiocese of New Orleans]; other articles effectively established racial separation by creating a distinct congregation for black Catholics while prohibiting whites from renting pews in the church. Significantly Article 4 reserved a special role for the Sisters of the Holy family *"qui ont evangelisé les populations de couleur …"*[67]

Janssens's promotion of a separate church as a gesture toward equality exposed the dilemma of the post-bellum church, caught as it were within a spiritual universe divided not only by race but by class within race. Janssens's intention in creating a separate church was to keep black people within the Catholic fold. The Jim Crow laws that secular authorities were enacting were designed to keep them out of public places. Ironically the two formed a mutually reinforcing choreography that inevitably cleaved the church, along with society, into black and white. The issue of a separate church brought the nascent divisions within the black community to the surface. The mental maps that people in different sub-cultures have formed are infinitely complex. The divisions, however, seem to reflect divisions of relationships to white hegemony as well as old divisions of class and color within the black community.

One part of the African-Catholic community favored a church *"specialement destinée a notre population."* Demands for a separate church under the auspices of St. Abraham, *"patron de l'illustre Presidente des États Unis,"* followed the Emancipation Proclamation and came from an association of colored people who called themselves "Congrégation Unioniste de Bienfaisance de la Ville de la Nouvelle-Orléans."[68] But the notion of a separate church struck powerfully at the heart of the mostly mixed-race Catholic community. "I am in a pickle just now," Janssens conceded. "Some of our colored people are up in arms against me and the proposed colored church."[69] Although Janssen's proposal did not oblige black Catholics to attend the black church, for Creole elites a black church struck at the very heart of their understanding of justice and equality. Signing themselves "practical Catholics," 134 men and women protested the "injustice" of plans to establish a church exclusively for colored people. As "faithful subjects of the church "we do most emphatically protest against this class legislation for no other reason than to humble, and humiliate one class of God's children without elevating the other."[70] The issue was especially important for the Comité des Citoyens, which had suffered a stinging defeat in *Plessy v. Ferguson*. In an audience with the Archbishop committee members denounced plans to renovate the old St. Joseph Church on Common Street for the exclusive use of black Catholics: "To us a Jim Crow or Negro Church is as distasteful, we might say as impious to use a mild term, as a Jim Crow or Negro car."[71]

The fragmentation of the black Catholic community was a kind of tipping point for the Sisters of the Holy Family. While they had an enviable record of growth and accomplishment, the sisterhood had to have cultural salience in the new environment. The schools, orphanages, and institutions for the sick and elderly they had founded in black neighborhoods laid the foundation for stable parishes and commanded the loyalty of French-speaking African Catholics. Yet if they were recognized as a sympathetic presence they were also associated with the differentiation of classes among blacks. The policy of admitting only free girls of color to St. Mary's Academy presupposed a logic of social separation that was completely at odds with the aspirations of the emancipated population for education as a pathway to mobility.

Having weathered the storms of racism to found their mission and win for themselves formal recognition as vowed religious women, the Sisters of the Holy Family once again re-shaped their ministry in fundamental ways. First, they distanced themselves from the more radical elements in the black community represented by the Comité de Citoyens. According to Sister Deggs, "there are some who had never dreamed of such things but are now the hardest cases of all. If anyone says to them a word about any colored person, they get insulted and say that they did not know anything about color, but about respect and virtues which make a man a person in the sight of Almighty God and also in the eyes of society." It was, Deggs complained, "the presumptuous ones who caused the great prejudice in this country. They wanted everyone to remain in their rank as they had done before." Deggs' annoyance was aimed at Homer Plessy, a member of the St. Augustine Parish Church, and of the Comité de Citoyens for trying "to impose themselves on persons of a more superior rank and did not keep in their places until they were invited to a more superior place. And what is the result?" Deggs demanded. "They are driven from their presence and are not allowed to even ride in the steam car with them." The sisters, who presumably knew their place, "were still well received by all classes," and "were admitted to the Captain's table when they passed on the steamboats."[72]

As French influence in the city began to decline both politically and demographically, the Sisters struggled to transcend their Francophone cultural origins by assimilating African American cultural identity. The election of Mary Ellen Jones, the sixth mother superior [1891–1909], who took the name Sister Mary Austin, signaled the shift. Sister Mary Austin was born upriver in rural Donaldson in 1861 and entered the postulancy when she was only sixteen. When she was not quite thirty-three, she was elected "the only *American* superior who has ever governed our dear little community since its foundation."[73] How far the order had adapted is suggested by the fact that in 1896, Austin presented Sister Mary Joachim, the daughter of slaves, the silver crown of twenty-five years service in the community. By 1890, the community had grown to thirty professed sisters, most of whom were young and from increasingly diverse backgrounds, as women from other southern states and countries were admitted to the novitiate. Linguistic influences remained strong, but by the end of the century, English was the "legal" language of the state, and it was perhaps for that reason that Deggs wrote her history of the order in English even though French was her native language. Under Sister Mary Austin's leadership, school instruction became bilingual and by the turn of the century English was the primary language of instruction.[74]

Under the leadership of the reform-minded Mary Austin, the sisterhood extended its mission to new constituencies and expanded into "American" areas of the city. They opened a kindergarten for poor children of working mothers; and they opened their schools to older girls who "can only come two or three times a week to learn well some branch of learning that does not require as much application as books do in general classes," and to Protestant girls whose parents had "great admiration" for "our measures of raising girls." Although their primary mission was female education, in 1891 they opened a day and boarding school for boys and a year later opened St. John Berchmans Girls' Home, the Carrollton German School; moved the St. Bernard Street home for the elderly to a new facility on Bayou Road; moved the Louisiana Asylum for Colored Girls to St. Bernard's School; and opened St. Maurice's School for boys and girls.[75] Archbishop Janssens's tribute to the Sisters of the Holy Family reflects how broadly Church authorities recognized their successful evangelizing efforts: The Sisters of the Holy Family were "gaining in membership, and increasing their work. They make admirable religious."[76]

Despite their success, the schools they established scarcely met the needs of the newly freed population and in a way replicated the prejudices built into society. The Sisters of the Holy Family had begun to downplay ethnicity and class in the convent and in the school, but when they expanded their educational mission to include the daughters of former slaves, they discovered that color and class lines within the black Catholic community were almost as intractable as race. Black creoles "of a better class" objected to "those with whom their children were playing ... and said that they did not want their children to mix with those whose mothers had been slaves. That gave our sisters much pain. But what could we do.... If we could have lived without their tuition, it would have been more agreeable to us. Unfortunately we were too poor...."[77] A year later, an epidemic of yellow fever and cholera forced the closing of the boarding school and the day school and the suspension of catechism classes. When the school reopened, classes were segregated by caste, with free-born children in one room, and children of former enslaved families in another.

To the emancipated population education was a central part of the very meaning of freedom. A decade before Archbishop Janssens launched his experiment with separate churches, L.A. Chasse, chancellor of the Archdiocese of New Orleans, had tried to explain this to Archbishop Janssens: "experience has taught that the colored people prefer to come to mass and to the sacraments with their white brethren as it is done now in all the churches where the French language is spoken. What we need most is the establishment of free colored schools to counterbalance the evil effects of the free public schools."[78] Reverend Chasse was referring to the seventy-six integrated public schools, all of which were under-funded and poorly equipped. In addition to the public schools there were more than one hundred private schools, over half of them Catholic, but they served only a small part of the black population. In 1891 Catholic schools enrolled 10,124 white children and only 1,505 black children.[79]

Faced with a burgeoning immigrant population and a sharp decline in the number of black Catholics the church hierarchy finally bowed to circumstances. In 1884, the Third Plenary Council of Baltimore issued a binding degree requiring each Catholic parish to build a parochial school within two years to combat "the deadly blight of indifferentism and the corruption of morals "associated with secular education.[80] A milestone in the history of education in the United States, the decree produced few immediate results due to a lack of financial support and personnel. Eventually it led to the establishment of the vast parochial school system and changed the demographic face of Catholicism. It would take another quarter century before the church launched an organized mission movement similar to the highly successful Protestant organizations that were changing the religious landscape of the South. In the meantime, female religious orders like the Sisters of the Holy Family would continue to serve as the unheralded backbone of Catholic evangelism.

Although the Sisters of the Holy Family played a pioneering role in the advancement of Catholic missionary work, to a large extent they remain invisible in the history of Christian missions. They are in a sense transitional figures in a transitional time and place in the continuum of Catholic evangelism. They took as their model the active and proselytizing Catholicism pioneered by the Ursulines and from it developed a formidable religious tradition and a corporate identity as pious women. In a period of history when laws restricted black access to education and before the white church hierarchy targeted blacks for conversion, they had made a beginning by establishing schools, which were intrinsically bound to the family, the neighborhood, and the church and helped transform them into a new hybrid, the parochial school system—a major milestone in the history of American Catholicism.[81] Their genius in building organizations and institutions for health care and relief work laid the foundations for the social infrastructure of New Orleans black community life when government provided no services. Convinced that God had destined the Sisters of the Holy Family to "evangelize his people all over the world,"[82] they spread their apostolic ministry across the country from California to the District of Columbia, and around the Atlantic from Central America to West Africa. Perhaps the most enduring testimony to the success of their evangelizing efforts is the fact that well before the organized mission movement was launched in the early twentieth century, the largest and most stable black population in the United States was in New Orleans.

Notes

1. Sylvia R. Frey and Betty Wood, *Come Shouting to Zion: African American Protestantism in the American South and British Caribbean to 1830* (Chapel Hill, NC, 1998).

2. Comparatively little work has been done on Catholic evangelization in North America. For recent studies see Angelyn Dries, *The Missionary Movement in Catholic America* (Maryknoll, NY, 2002); Dana L. Robert, *American Women*

in Mission A Social History of Their Thought and Practice (Macon, GA, 1996), 318–22.

3. For details of the contracts see Roger Baudier, *The Catholic Church in Louisiana* (New Orleans: Privately published, 1939), 64–65, 66, 74, 76–77, 152–53. For the early history of the Ursulines mission to African Americans see Emily J. Clark, *"Masterless Mistresses" The New Orleans Ursulines and the Development of a New World Society, 1727–1834* [Published for the Omohundro Institute of Early American History and Culture by the University of North Carolina Press, 2007], 81, 166–67, 168.

4. Emily Clark and Virginia Meacham Gould, "The Feminine Face of Afro-Catholicism in New Orleans, 1727–1852," *William & Mary Quarterly*, 3, no. 59 (2002): 409–48; the data on Africans are drawn from the unpublished database derived from sacramental records by Jean Pierre LeGlaunec and from LeGlaunec's unpublished paper, "The Louisiana Purchase or the 'Dark Years' of the Catholic Church." I am grateful to Professor LeGlaunec for sharing his data with me.

5. Michael A. Gomez, *Exchanging Our Country Marks: The Transformation of African Identities in the Colonial and Antebellum South* (Chapel Hill, NC, 1998), 137, 153.

6. Hein Vanhee, "Central African Popular Christianity and the Making of Haitian Vodou Religion," in *Central Africans and Cultural Transformations in the African Diaspora*, ed. Linda M. Heywood (Cambridge, 2002), 258–59.

7. Terry Rey, "Kongolese Catholic Influences on Haitian Popular Catholicism," in *Central African*, ed. Heywood, 279.

8. Yvonne P. Chireau, *Black Magic: Religion and the African-American Conjuring Tradition* (Berkeley, CA, 2003), 12; Gomez, *Exchanging Our Country Marks*, 153.

9. William Hicks, "History of Louisiana Negro Baptists"; Ray Holder, "Methodist Beginnings in New Orleans, 1813–1814," in *Religion in Louisiana*, ed. Charles E. Nolan, 19 vols., Louisiana Purchase Bicentennial Series in Louisiana History (Lafayette, LA, 2004), XIX: 227–236, 237–250 (quote is from Holder, 238).

10. *Minutes of the Annual Conferences of the Methodist Episcopal Church for the Years 1829–1839*, 2 vols. (New York, 1840), 1: 457; 2: 399.

11. Sister Mary Bernard Deggs, *No Cross, No Crown: Black Nuns in Nineteenth Century New Orleans*. ed. Virginia Meacham Gould and Charles E. Nolan (Bloomington, IN, 2001), xxvi–xxvii, 202 n. 9, 205 n. 23; and Clark and Gould, "The Feminine Face," 408–48.

12. Jane Landers, *Black Society in Spanish Florida* (Urbana, IL, 1999), 121.

13. The term "creole" is controversial and has different meanings, which vary over time and according to ethnicity, race, and class. I use it here as a shorthand reference to free, French-speaking persons of African and European descent who were born in Louisiana. The term came into use in the late eighteenth and early nineteenth centuries. See Richard Campanella, *Time and Place in New Orleans: Past Geographies in the Present Day* (Gretna, LA, 2002), 115–16.

14. Clark and Gould, "The Feminine Face," 408–48, esp. 412, 413, 424–25. Much less is known about Catholic missionary activity in the French Antilles.

See Sue Peabody, "'A Dangerous Zeal': Catholic Missions to Slaves in the French Antilles, 1635–1800," *French Historical Review* 25 (2002): 53–90.

15. Catéchisme de la Doctrine Chrétienne, ordonné par le Troisième Concile Plenier de Baltimore et Traduit en Français par l'Ordre de Monseigneur l'Archevêque de la Nouvelle-Orléans (1885), in Catechisms Accession No. 72-026, Archdiocese of New Orleans (hereafter AANO).

16. Cyprian Davis, O.S.B., *Henriette Delille Servant of Slaves Witness to the Poor* (New Orleans, 2004), 49, 50.

17. Frey and Wood, *Come Shouting to Zion*, 142–43; Cynthia Lynn Lyerly, *Methodism and the Southern Mind, 1770–1810* (New York, 1998), 68.

18. Ruth Liebowitz, "Virgins in the Service of Christ: The Dispute Over an Active Apostolate for Women During the Counter-Reformation," in *Women of Spirit: Female Leadership in the Jewish and Christian Traditions*, ed. Rosemary Ruether and Eleanor McLaughlin (New York, 1979), 140; Susan E. Dinan, "Spheres of Female Religious Expression in Early Modern France," in *Women and Religion in Old and New Worlds*, ed. Susan E. Dinan and Debra Meyers (New York, 2001).

19. Emily J. Clark, "*Masterless Mistresses: The New Orleans Ursulines and the Development of A New World Society, 1727–1834* (Chapel Hill, NC, 2007); McNamara, *Sisters in Arms*, 481.

20. Clark, "Masterless Mistresses," 202–05; see also Emily J. Clark, "'By All the Conduct of Their Lives': A Laywomen's Confraternity in New Orleans, 1730–1744," *William and Mary Quarterly*, 3, no. 54 (1997): 790–91.

21. *Règlemens des Religieuses Ursulines de la Congrégation de Paris* (Paris: 1775): 30–31, 36. I am grateful to Emily Clark for generously sharing this document with me.

22. *Règlemens*, 45, 47.

23. Benjamin Henry Latrobe, *Journals of Benjamin Henry Latrobe, 1799–1820: From Philadelphia to New Orleans*, ed. Edward C. Carter II et al. (New Haven, CT, 1980), 175; *Impressions Respecting New Orleans: Diary and Sketches, 1818–1820*, ed. Samuel Wilson, Jr. (New York, 1951), 122.

24. I am grateful to Charles Nolan for calling this data to my attention. See *Sacramental Records of the Roman Catholic Church of the Archdiocese of New Orleans*, ed. Charles E. Nolan, 19 vols. (New Orleans, 2004), 19: xix.

25. I am drawing here on LeGlaunec's unpublished database developed from the New Orleans sacramental records.

26. Diane Batts Morrow, *Persons of Color and Religious at the Same Time: The Oblate Sisters of Providence, 1828–1860* (Chapel Hill, NC, 2002), 118.

27. Convents & Academies: 1833, *Catholic Directories* [1833–1904] 02-16-04, 124-25, AANO.

28. For the Oblate Sisters of Providence, see Morrow, *Persons of Color*, especially 14, 17–19, 33; Morrow, "Embracing the Religious Profession. The Antebellum Mission of the Oblate Sisters of Providence," in *Diasporic Africa: A Reader*, ed. Michael Gomez (New York, 2006), 105–06. For the Sisters of the Holy Family, see Gould and Nolan, eds. *Henriette Delille*, and Deggs, *No Cross, No Crown*, 4, 7, 10, 12, 14–16, 17, 19; see also Cyprian Davis, O.S.B., *The History of Black Catholics in the United States* (New York, 1993), 98–115.

29. Quoted in Davis, *Henriette Delille*, 36.

30. Ibid, 26–27.

31. Quoted in Deggs, *No Cross, No Crown*, xxxiii.

32. For the growth of the free black population in the period before 1803, see Kimberly S. Hanger, *Bounded Lives, Bounded Places Free Black Society in Colonial New Orleans, 1769–1803* (Durham, NC, 1997); the most comprehensive demographic study of antebellum period is Marjorie Bourdelais, "La Nouvelle Orléans: Une Ville Francophone, 1803–1860," unpublished diss., 2 vols. (Écoles des hautes études en science social, 2007), 2: 288 (table 5.1), 292 (table 5.2), 302–03, 313, 425 (table 5.4 and 5.5), 314 (table 5.6). Although the population of free people of color continued to decline as a proportion of the total population, it continued to increase numerically, reaching 20,000 in 1840, then falling back to 10,000 in the last two decades of the antebellum period. See Paul F. La Chance, "The Formation of a Three-Caste Society: Evidence from Wills in Antebellum New Orleans," in *New Orleans and Urban Louisiana,* ed. Samuel C. Shepherd, Jr., Louisiana Purchase Bicentennial Series, vol. XIV: 588–89.

33. Charitable Institutions, 1846, *Catholic Directories,* AANO.

34. Rebecca Sullivan, "Breaking Habits: Gender, Class and the Sacred in the Dress of Women Religious," in *Consuming Fashion: Adorning the Transnational Body,* ed. Anne Brydon and S. A. Niessen (New York, 1998), 116, 123.

35. Sister Audrey Marie Detiege, *Henriette Delille, Free Woman of Color* (New Orleans, 1976), 42.

36. According to Deggs it was not until 1881 that they were allowed to wear a regular habit. Deggs, *No Cross, No Crown,* 14, 25, 206 n. 37; quote is on 41.

37. Ibid., 42.

38. Ibid., 8, 10, 13, 29, 41–42, 94, 133, 195.

39. La Chance, "Formation of a Three-caste System," 588.

40. Campanella, *Geographies of New Orleans,* 4, 9.

41. Davis, *History of Black Catholics,* 287 n. 50.

42. Deggs, *No Cross, No Crown,* 18, 61, 106. Although Francophones still represented a majority of the population until the Civil War, by 1840 Anglophones made up roughly 35 percent of the population, and their numbers rose sharply after 1850. Morrow, *Persons of Color,* 77.

43. Morrow, *Persons of Color,* 30; Deggs, *No Cross, No Crown,* 6, 7, 29, 114.

44. Morrow, *Persons of Color,* 61–73. The Oblates opened a school for orphan girls in New Orleans in 1868 or 1869 but they returned to their motherhouse in Baltimore in 1875, see Deggs, *No Cross, No Crown,* 38, 163–64, 211 n. 36.

45. Morrow, *Persons of Color,* 20, 30, 162, 192.

46. Deggs, *No Cross, No Crown,* 197; Sister Mary Francis Borgia Hart, SSF, "Violets in the King's Garden. A History of the Holy Family of New Orleans "[typescript, n.p., 1976] Amistad Research Center, Tulane University, hereafter ARC.

47. Deggs, *No Cross, No Crown,* 27, 41, 83, 108–09, 124.

48. Robert C. Reinders, "The Churches and the Negroes in New Orleans, 1850–1860," *Phylon* V, no. 22 (1961): 241.

49. Deggs, *No Cross, No Crown,* 106.

50. Religious Communities in the Diocese of New Orleans, 1869, 69, 94–95, *Catholic Directories,* AANO.

51. Quoted in Davis, *Henriette Delille*, 63.

52. *Catechisme Imprimé par l'Ordre de Monseigneur Antoine Blanc Archevêque de la Nouvelle-Orléans* (New Orleans, 1845). In Catechisms Accession No. 72–119: 24, 25, 36, 88, AANO.

53. Deggs, *No Cross, No Crown*, xxxv, 9, 46–47.

54. Ibid., 98.

55. Ibid., 84, 91–92.

56. Ibid., 26.

57. Ibid., 112.

58. Ibid., 66, 112.

59. Ibid., 91, 214 n. 44.

60. I am grateful to Charles Nolan for calling my attention to this data *Sacramental Records*, ed. Nolan et al., vol. 19, n.p.

61. Janssens to Drexel, 29 April 1894, quoted in Annemarie Kasteel, *Francis Janssens, 1843–1897 A Dutch-American Prelate* (Lafayette, LA, 1992), 303.

62. Rev. Nelson Sanders, brought to the city by slave traders in 1833, gathered a small following on Gentilly Road and despite persecution began organizing in different parts of the city. There were no day schools or Sunday schools, but newly emancipated ministers, most of whom were illiterate, began preaching. See Hicks, "History of Louisiana Negro Baptists," in *Religion in Louisiana*, ed. Nolan, 231–36.

63. *113 Years. Wesley Methodist Church, 1838–1951, History,* Pamphlet compiled by W. Scott Chinn. Microfilm, Wesley Methodist Records, 1864–1951, Amistad Research Center, New Orleans, LA.

64. Ibid. 18, 19, 23.

65. Janssen to Drexel, 29 April 1894, quoted in Kasteel, *Francis Janssens,* 303.

66. Archbishop Janssens to Katherine Drexel, quoted in Kasteel, *Francis Janssens,* 297.

67. Regulations for Assumption Fathers, 16 July 1895 [copy among letter file No. 45, 1895], 156; Mission Chez le people de couleur en Louisiane, 27 August 1895, between pages 156–57, Diary of Francis Janssens Archbishop of New Orleans [1888–1897], AANO.

68. Les Sociétés de Bienfaisance, November 1863, in Negro Church, Protest against building, 1888–1894, (Colored Missions), AANO.

69. Janssens to Drexel, 29 April 1894, quoted in Kasteel, *Francis Janssens,* 303.

70. To Archbishop Janssen, 3 January 1894, in Negro Church, Protest against building, 1888–1894 (Colored Missions), AANO.

71. Jim Crow Catholic Church, 14 February 1895, *The Daily Crusader,* copy in AANO.

72. Deggs, *No Cross, No Crown,* 91–92.

73. Ibid., quote 38 (emphasis added); see also 29, 181, 185, 186.

74. Deggs, *No Cross, No Crown,* x, 137, 181, 183, 217 n. 12; 1890: Religious Communities and Convents, *Catholic Directories,* 94.

75. Deggs, *No Cross, No Crown,* 180, 184.

76. Archbishop Janssens's Report, in *Mission Work Among the Negroes and the Indians*, 1898, 18, AANO.

77. Deggs, *No Cross, No Crown*, 5, 12, 29, 197.

78. L. A. Chasse to the Secretary of the Commission for the Catholic Missions among the Colored People and the Indians, 19 June 1888, quoted in Dolores Labbé, *Jim Crow Comes to Church: The Establishment of Segregated Catholic Parishes in South Louisiana* (Lafayette, LA, 1971), 19.

79. 1891, Province of New Orleans: Recapitulation, *Catholic Directories* [1833–1904], 238, AANO.

80. Acts and Decrees of the Third Plenary Council of Baltimore, in *Creative Fidelity: American Catholic Intellectual Traditions*, ed. R. Scott Appleby, Patricia Byrne, and William L. Portier (Maryknoll, NY, 2004), 83–89.

81. The first time that the word parochial was used in 1888 was in reference to a "colored" girls school operated by the Sisters of the Holy Family, see Book of Parish Statistics, 1888–1918, AANO.

82. Deggs, *No Cross, No Crown*, 171.

♨ 9

COLONIAL CONSTRUCTS AND CROSS-CULTURAL INTERACTION: COMPARING MISSIONARY/INDIGENOUS ENCOUNTERS IN NORTHWESTERN AMERICA AND EASTERN AUSTRALIA

Anne Keary

NARRATIVES OF FIRST ENCOUNTER

In 1835, Samuel Parker and Marcus Whitman, both Presbyterian missionaries with the American Board of Commissioners for Foreign Missions (A.B.C.F.M.), embarked on an expedition across the continent to the American Northwest in order to locate sites for missions to the Nimiipuu (Nez Perce) and Salish (Flathead) peoples on the Columbia Plateau.[1] Although they knew little of the people they hoped to convert and nothing of their languages, they felt confident of evangelical success. Accompanied by traders from the American Fur Company, they arrived at the Green River "Rendezvous" in the Rocky Mountains in August. It was there that they encountered Nimiipuu and Salish people for the first time.

In his published account, *Journal of an Exploring Tour Beyond the Rocky Mountains,* Parker reported that he and Whitman called a meeting with a group of men he identified as "chiefs" of the assembled "Indians" and asked them if "they wished to have teachers come among them and instruct them in the knowledge of God, his worship, and the way to be saved...." In response, Parker wrote: "The oldest chief of the Flatheads arose and said, 'he was old, and did not expect to know much more; he was deaf, and could not hear, but his heart was made glad, very glad, to see what he had never seen before, a man near to God.'" According to Parker, another Flathead chief, "Insala," followed, declaring that his "heart," too, was "made so glad to see a man near to God." And finally "Tai-quin-su-watish," a Nez Perce chief, declared that "he had heard from white men a little about God, which had only gone into his ears; he wished to know enough to have it go down into his heart, to influ-

ence his life, and teach his people." The meeting, as Parker presented
it, promised the imminent conversion of the "Indians" to Christianity.
With a Nimiipuu guide, Parker then traveled on into the country of the
Nez Perce "nation," while Whitman returned home to ask for missionary reinforcements.[2]

Across the Pacific, in eastern Australia, another Protestant missionary, Lancelot Threlkeld, wrote a very different story of first encounter. After serving several years as a missionary in Tahiti, Threlkeld had
been asked by the London Missionary Society (L.M.S.) to establish a
new mission to the "Aborigines" near the colonial town of Newcastle,
100 miles north of Sydney. Shortly after he arrived with his family in
late 1824, Threlkeld reported overhearing the "Aborigines" singing one
night in "different parts of the settlement." Their tune, he wrote, was
"rather dismal," but he noted with surprise, "some have attempted
with no bad effect to imitate the sacred music of the church...."[3] Then,
several weeks later, he reported that the "natives" had invited him to
a dance "on account of our arrival among them." In his journal he described the dance, observing that it was

> performed in exact time to the beating of two pieces of stick one upon
> the other by an old man who sings during the performance.... The whole
> unite in the tune which begins high and sinks gradually raising again, the
> compass is perhaps two octaves. The women join in the dance and song
> but all are naked not in consequence of the dance but because they are
> allways [sic] so.[4]

Not long after this he made his first attempt to discuss religious matters. As he put it, he:

> [h]ad some conversation with 4 or 5 Natives who could speak a little
> broken English, questioned them concerning who made the Sun, moon,
> stars &c. One of them replied that long while ago one Black fellow threw
> the vermin from his head into the fire and they jumped up (for become)
> these things. When they were informed God made them, Me don't see
> was the reply for I do not know.

Although alarmed by their "ignorance," Threlkeld was happy to report
that they wanted to learn about the "object of [his] mission" and asked
where he should reside in "the interiour [sic]."[5]

INTRODUCTION

There are obvious differences between these two reports of first encounter. In Parker's account, indigenous people are depicted as more

or less known quantities and as promising candidates for conversion: Parker confidently names and places the headmen as "chiefs" of the "Nez Perce" and "Flathead" "nations"; his chiefs speak, apparently in English, in stylized primitive but noble language; they already appear to know who "God" is and desire to learn more. In Threlkeld's writings, by contrast, Aboriginal people are portrayed as altogether unfamiliar and their potential for evangelization is far less certain: Threlkeld does not refer to them using specific tribal names; he places them in a rather vaguely defined "interiour"; he depicts their modes of communicating as strange; and he makes it clear that they have no idea who "God" is, although they were apparently willing to tell him a story about one of their own creator beings.

It would be easy to read these differences as simply the product of different experiences of encounter. However, as this essay will attempt to demonstrate, these differences, in and of themselves, provide a means of analyzing the complex colonial and cross-cultural histories of missionary/indigenous relations in each place. Read carefully, the two reports offer a first glimpse at the ways in which concepts of identity, space, communicative practice, and religious life informed patterns of cross-cultural interaction at each mission site. Situated in historical context and examined comparatively, such a re-reading can also show how these concepts were, at the same time, shaped or inflected by different histories of colonialism.

On the most general level there were significant similarities between the Plateau region of northwestern America and inland east coast Australia as colonial sites for missionary activity. In the nineteenth century both were the territories of indigenous hunter-gatherer peoples that had been claimed by European powers interested in acquiring lands for agricultural settlement. The L.M.S. and A.B.C.F.M. missionaries entered both territories as members of colonizing societies. And in both cases these missionaries sought to convert indigenous peoples who had deep spiritual attachments to their lands during the very period that those lands were being invaded or threatened with invasion. But there were also significant differences. In the American Northwest, under the Convention of 1818, Britain and the United States had agreed to joint occupancy of the region they called "Oregon Territory." In this territory, Euro-Americans (British, French-Canadians, and white Americans) classed indigenous peoples generally as "Indians" while also recognizing indigenous groups as distinct tribal entities with relations to particular lands;[6] indigenous and Euro-American peoples had established exchange relations with each other through the fur trade; and despite epidemic outbreaks, indigenous people were the majority in the region when the A.B.C.F.M.

missionaries arrived in the 1830s. Although the Hudson's Bay Company (HBC) had established trading posts from the coast to the Plateau, the full-scale invasion of "Oregon Territory" by American settlers in the 1840s had not yet begun.[7] In Australia, by contrast, the British colonized the country in 1788 on the principle of *terra nullius*, that is, a land without landowners or a sovereign power.[8] The British did not recognize Aboriginal peoples as distinct tribal entities with rights to lands; nor, for various reasons, did they establish significant commercial relations with them. Operated first as a penal settlement, the colony began attracting free settlers in the early nineteenth century. When Threlkeld arrived in late 1824, the colonial invasion of Aboriginal lands was escalating, and violence, dispossession, and disease were rapidly reducing indigenous populations along the eastern seaboard.[9]

The differences between these histories of colonialism, I will argue, had significant consequences for the development of the terms of cross-cultural interaction at each mission site. In the American Northwest, I pay particular attention to how American conceptions of the "Indian," and, at the same time, their practice of recognizing indigenous peoples as distinct tribal entities—and, crucially, indigenous interest in being "recognized"—shaped the development of missionary/indigenous relations. In Australia, on the other hand, I look at how missionaries and indigenous people came to understand each other and work out terms for interacting in the absence of the constructs that came with recognition and in the face of an increasingly virulent colonial racism. In both cases I consider how colonial constructs and practices—and missionary and indigenous positions within particular colonial formations—affected each party's understandings of the identities of their interlocutors, the space of their interactions, the nature of the other's communicative practices, and the character of the other's religious life.

As a study of colonialism and missions, this essay is not primarily or solely concerned with the question of the various ways in which missions advanced or challenged colonial agendas[10] (although it does not ignore this issue); rather it remains focused on how the constructs that emerged from different colonial histories affected and informed everyday missionary/indigenous interactions. My interest is in the connections between the macro-politics of colonial structures and ideologies and the micro-politics of localized cross-cultural encounters—in other words, the ways in which colonial categories were variously accessed, instantiated, altered or rejected through linguistic and cultural exchange.[11] I adopt a comparative approach in order to better discern particular patterns and processes in each case. As Mark Daunton and Rick Halpern argue, comparative history, "by acquainting one with what goes on elsewhere," can "inspire a critical awareness of what is taken for granted in one's own country."[12] I use comparison then, not as a way of generating abstract sociological models about religious change, but as a means of highlighting and calling into question terms or concepts that might otherwise go unremarked if each case was considered in isolation. Lastly, it should be added that as a contribution to *Beyond Conversion and Syncretism*, this essay is not directly concerned with either conversion or syncretism. Indeed, in the cases examined here, there were few converts in any sense of the term, and while there were syncretic developments in both regions, many of the indigenous engagements with missionary Christianity that I consider fall outside these categories. Rather, in focusing on how missionary and indigenous conceptions of identity, space, communicative practice, and spiritual life articulated with colonial structures, this essay is offered as an attempt to think more precisely about missionary/indigenous interactions in colonial environments.

I begin, then, with an analysis of the opening scenes of first encounter. Situating each in its colonial and cultural context, I examine them as key moments in the constitution of the terms of cross-cultural interaction. Then, focusing on the A.B.C.F.M. mission to the Nimiipuu and the L.M.S. mission to the Aboriginal people who came to be known as the Awabakal, I discuss the ways in which these terms continued to shape interaction, paying particular attention to the indigenous reception of Christianity in the face of colonization.

FIRST ENCOUNTERS: SAMUEL PARKER AND THE NIMIIPUU AND SALISH HEADMEN

Let us begin with Parker's report of his encounter with the Nimiipuu and Salish headmen at Green River. Although highly dramatized, it can be re-read to illuminate the colonial and cross-cultural dynamics of the meeting. In order to understand this interaction in all its dimensions, Parker's report must be analyzed in the context of American colonial practices of recognizing and representing indigenous people, and then re-examined using indigenous language materials and other historical and anthropological sources.

The Missionary Perspective

The first point to be made is that Parker suppresses any mention of the process of translation in his narrative of the Green River encounter.

Rather, as noted, his account proceeds as if he already knew who the headmen were, could understand what they said, and could, in turn, speak to them. However, without any knowledge of the headmen's languages, Parker and Whitman must have used an interpreter. In this instance, it was most likely a French-Canadian voyageur by the name of "Compo," to whom Parker refers as "my interpreter" in his account of his subsequent travels through Nez Perce country.[13] (It is also evident, as we shall see from the slightly different versions of the headmen's speeches that appear in Whitman's unpublished reports of the encounter, that a translator was present.) Parker's omission is significant. As David Murray has pointed out, in order to maintain an image of assured cultural dominance, colonial writers frequently repressed any "knowledge of the process of translation … in favor of a reassuring image of mutual intelligibility which [did] not register as significant who … had to 'translate'."[14] In this way, any difficulties with communication could be cast as a failure of the colonized, not the colonizer. In Parker's case, the mediating work of the interpreter enabled him to avoid directly engaging with indigenous conceptions of identity, space, or religion while his suppression of the work of translation allowed him to promote and preserve the authority of his own distinctly colonial representations of the headmen and their words.

Parker's reliance on colonial constructs is evident, first of all, in the names he used to identify the headmen: "Nez Perce" and "Flathead."[15] Both were Euro-American inventions; these names were not originally used by Plateau people to refer to themselves. It was Euro-American traders, interested in identifying indigenous groups with whom they might exchange goods for furs, who created "Nez Perce" and "Flathead." These names (anglicized as "Pierced noses" in the case of Nez Perce) were then adopted by the explorers Lewis and Clark under instruction from Thomas Jefferson to name the "nations" they encountered and the "extent and limits of their possessions."[16] In renaming the peoples of the Plateau and redefining them as nations, Euro-Americans were, in effect, simplifying and rationalizing what was a complex multilingual, village-based political geography for the purposes of trade, and ultimately, treaty negotiations for land. Indeed, it is not insignificant that this renaming of peoples occurred at the same time as traders and explorers went about renaming, and thereby imaginatively possessing, the country even before they took formal possession.[17] When Parker identified the headmen as chiefs of the Nez Perce and Flathead nations, then, he was adopting a Euro-American colonial viewpoint; he was assuming a knowledge of their political and territorial organization that served Euro-American purposes and obscuring the ways in which Plateau peoples identified and related to their lands themselves.

The other term Parker used to identify the headmen, "Indian," was, of course, even more explicitly colonial.[18] While "Nez Perce" and "Flathead" implied that Plateau peoples were organized as nations, "Indian" classed them as members of an undifferentiated collective and carried with it a host of colonial implications. "Indian," even more explicitly, effaced Plateau peoples' relations to specific territories by grouping them with unrelated indigenous peoples in the east; it also cast them in the same historical role: as "uncivilized" peoples who would eventually have to make way for white settlers. Although it was Parker's hope that these "Indians" would avoid war and make land available by giving up hunting and gathering and becoming settled Christian farmers, he had no doubt that their lands were, or would soon be, American territory. Indeed, in a later chapter in his narrative he envisioned the region as a fertile country for future American farmers and manufacturers, thanked his god for creating passes for future railways, and imaginatively erased the presence of the Nimiipuu and Salish altogether.[19] Parker's use of "Indian," in short, enabled him to assimilate the headmen into an American narrative of colonial expansion and deny the very existence of alternate indigenous geographies and histories in the Plateau.

Having defined the space of encounter and the identities of the Nimiipuu and Salish headmen in American terms, Parker was then able to turn to well-established images of "Indians" to interpret their words and actions. His representation of the headmen declaring that their "hearts" were made glad to see a "man near to God" drew on one of the most common stereotypes of the period: the Indian chief as noble orator. In many ways, this was not surprising. In popular literature, cultural nationalists had long promoted the Indian orator as an example of American simplicity and dignity in opposition to the artifice and hypocrisy of the Old World. Their Indian orators typically spoke in short declarative sentences and used a standardized "Indian" vocabulary: They "showed their heart," "opened their ears," and acknowledged the authority of the "Great Father" and the power of "the Great Spirit." Notably, they used the same (English) expressions regardless of their supposed tribal affiliation.[20] But for evangelical advocates like Parker, the Indian orator was a particularly useful figure. First, the notion that Indians always spoke from the "heart" was a powerful way of representing potential Indian converts. In evangelical thinking, the heart, as the locus of the true feeling self, was the site of conversion, requiring not simply an intellectual statement of belief, but a fundamental change of heart. The Indian who spoke from or about his heart was signaling his readiness to undergo the change of heart necessary for the salvation of his soul.[21] Second, evangelicals often used the image of the Indian orator speaking about God or the "Great Spirit" to imply that Indian people already possessed a God-given instinct for the Christian truth.[22] Indeed, early nineteenth-century mission advocates often suggested that Indian religions were indigenous versions of a Christian cosmology in which a "Great Spirit" acted as both supreme creator and judge.[23] Parker himself later declared that all "Oregon Indians" believed "in one Great Spirit, who has created the earth and in an afterlife in which people were either rewarded or punished for their deeds."[24] From this perspective, evangelization was then simply a matter of awakening the Indians' instinct for the truth and fulfilling God's plan for America. It is not surprising, then, that Parker drew on these images in his representation of the headmen's speeches, especially, as we shall see, it was in fact not unlikely that the Nimiipuu and Salish headmen spoke of their hearts and expressed an interest in learning more about Christianity. It should nevertheless be noted that in his reports of the event, Whitman used the terms "inward parts" or "vital parts" where Parker wrote "heart"—a difference that points both to the difficulties of translation and the extent to which Parker chose to represent the headmen's words in accordance with popular American understandings of "Indian" speech.[25] In doing so, Parker cast the headmen as Indian orators in an evangelical drama of conversion and salvation, a move that precluded any recognition that the men would have been speaking in accordance with their own cultural codes and might have had their own reasons for seeking a knowledge of the white man's god.

Finally, what are we to make of Parker's account of his and Whitman's own address to the headmen? As Parker tells it, they asked if the "chiefs" wished to have "teachers come among them, and instruct them in the knowledge of God, his worship, and the way to be saved." This statement—both simple and grand—suggests that the missionaries may have been using language they believed "Indians" would understand. In this, there is an element of the cultural phenomenon that Philip Deloria has termed "playing Indian," that is, the adoption of supposedly "Indian" ways by Euro-Americans seeking, temporarily, to imaginatively indigenize themselves. But while Deloria has argued that Euro-Americans who played "Indian" in eighteenth- and nineteenth-century social protests or in the ceremonies of fraternal organizations were engaging in a "mythic historic construction of American identity" that served the interests of the emergent nation, historical records show that Euro-Americans also "played Indian" in their interactions with actual Indians.[26] And, in the encounter at Green River, Parker and Whitman adapted "playing Indian" for a new evangelical purpose. Elements of their play are also suggested in Parker's apparent acceptance of the role he believed the headmen assigned him: "a man near to God." In "playing Indian," the missionaries could imagine themselves to be speaking about God in "Indian" terms to "Indian" people, although, again, these terms were American constructs.

The Indigenous Perspective

The indigenous side of the Green River encounter is not, of course, easy to reconstruct. However, using other sources, it is possible to re-trieve something of the ways in which the Nimiipuu and Salish head-men might have approached their exchange with the missionaries. As we shall see, their conceptions of identity, territory, communicative practice, and spiritual life must have differed markedly from those of Parker. Nevertheless, an important point to be made here is that, to some extent, Parker was able to maintain his ideas about the headmen, first because of an indigenous interest in being "recognized" by Euro-Americans, and second because there were a number of *apparent* points of convergence between missionary ideas and indigenous practices.

A knowledge of the differences and similarities between each party's understandings of identity and geography provides a starting point for understanding the dynamics of the Green River encounter. First, as noted, the headmen would not have called themselves "chiefs" of the "Nez Perce" and "Flathead" "nations" in their interactions with each other. For Plateau people, the village, led by a headman and usually named after a nearby river, stream, or feature of the landscape, was the primary source of identity and political organization—not the nation led by a chief. For Nimiipuu and Salish people, the European idea of a nation as a linguistic, political, and territorial unity was quite foreign. On the Plateau, trade networks and kinship ties meant that villages were often multi-lingual; political organization beyond the village was lim-ited to inter-village (band) meetings and, only occasionally, inter-band councils to discuss trade or war.[27][28] Further, Plateau peoples' identities were closely tied to their lands. Through stories passed on through gen-erations, and varying from village to village, Plateau peoples learned of the sites made by the creator trickster figure, Coyote, and other power-ful mythic beings. Lands, mythically endowed and alive with sacred power, were created for specific groups. Stories, and the place names they established, taught Plateau peoples who they were; where to hunt, fish, and gather; where to access spirit beings; and how to live properly in relation to the human and non-human world.[29]

However, even as they held to their own conceptions of identity and geography, it is highly likely that by the 1830s the Nimiipuu and Salish headmen had become familiar with the new tribal names used by Euro-Americans. Traders of the Northwest Company and later the Hudson's Bay Company had established a number of fur trade posts or forts in the region which they named after the Indian "nations" of the region. These included Fort Nez Perce in 1818 and Flathead House in 1823.[30] For Plateau people interested in acquiring European goods and guns, answering to such names as "Nez Perce" or "Flathead" in their exchanges with Euro-Americans at these posts made sense. And, in the competitive societies of the Plateau, this was particularly the case for headmen interested in increasing their status through profitable relations with the traders.[31] Certainly the traders themselves used the names frequently. One trader, Alexander Ross, claimed that his colleagues used "Nez Perces" "indiscriminately."[32] Whether or not indigenous peoples understood that such names implied the existence of nations, by the 1830s "Nez Perce" and "Flathead" had become part of a new, if still evolving, set of identities on the Plateau. If Parker and Whitman used "Nez Perce" and "Flathead" at Green River, the headmen would have recognized the names.

It is possible, too, that the other term of identity used by Parker— "Indian"—was also known to the headmen. Certainly they would have been familiar with the rough equivalent, *siwash*. *Siwash* was a term from the Chinook jargon, the fur trade lingua franca spoken throughout the Pacific northwest by both Euro-Americans and Plateau peoples. The word was derived from the French *sauvage* and was used, like "Indian," to refer to all indigenous peoples.[33] Adopted by Plateau people, the word points to their awareness of the Euro-Americans' inability or unwillingness to distinguish between different groups. It also suggests the emergence on the Plateau of a new, if not deeply held, collective identity in relation to Euro-Americans. In this sense, *siwash* was not only a new identity, but a new form of identification: Unlike traditional Plateau identities, *siwash* did not define people in relation to particular places, but rather as a generalized collective in relation to others. The headmen at Green River, then, would have been aware that Parker and Whitman, like the traders, were ignorant of Plateau forms of identity and inclined to identify them generally with terms like "*siwash*" or even as "Indians."

How would the headmen have identified the missionaries? Just as the Chinook jargon taught Plateau people how Euro-Americans identified them, it also provided them with terms for identifying Euro-Americans. These included: *Boston* to refer to Americans; *Kintshosh* (King George) to refer to the British; *Pasaiuks* to refer to French-Canadians; and *Soyapo* to refer to Americans or white people generally.[34] Most likely, *soyapo* was derived from the jargon word for hat, *seapo* (chapeau), to indicate "hat wearers," and was first used among Nimiipuu peoples before spreading to Salishan-speaking groups.[35] Parker himself later recorded the word as "suéapo" in a short vocabulary of Nimiipuu words that he appended to his *Journal*.[36] In all probability, then, the Nimiipuu and Salish headmen at Green River would have identified the missionaries as *soyapo*. Significantly, *soyapo*, like *siwash*, classed peoples as members of a undifferentiated collective, defined in relation to others rather than in relation to place. In identifying the missionaries as *soyapo*, the headmen would have been identifying them as white men who shared the same languages, customs, and general appearance as the traders, and as people who were outsiders in Plateau country and of unknown origin.

The identities Nez Perce, Flathead, *soyapo*, and possibly *siwash* or "Indian" established the starting points, then, for cross-cultural interaction at Green River. To varying degrees, these terms of identity were shared, but missionary and indigenous understanding of these names, and the ways in which the names served to locate people in imagined social fields, differed considerably. Understanding this, what are we to make of headmen's addresses to the *soyapo* religious men? They did not, of course, speak as the primitive Indian orators of Parker's imagination, but they would have spoken as leaders thoroughly skilled and long practiced in the proper use of words. Typically they would have spoken in accordance with particular conventions of delivery and in response to verbal expressions of support, but in addressing the missionaries it seems likely that they would have modified and shortened their statements, knowing that the *soyapo* missionaries and their interpreter were ignorant of proper etiquette.[37] Still, it is probable that the headmen did seek to impress the missionaries with their ability as speakers—and they likely noted the missionaries' interest in their speech-making. Each party understood that the headmen's addresses involved the display of authority. To a limited extent, then, there was some convergence between indigenous practice and missionary conceptions of "Indian oratory." It should be noted, though, that while Parker chose to downplay the work of the interpreter, the headmen may well have viewed him as a buttress to their authority. On the Plateau, interpreters were common in inter-band transactions. Further, headmen frequently employed criers, men who repeated a headman's words in a louder voice to his audience. Criers served to deflect resentment if necessary, amplify the headman's message, and uphold a headman's dignity.[38] The headmen at Green River, then, may well have viewed the interpreter—even the trader, Compo—as a kind of crier and, as such, a figure who enhanced their authority as principal men.

This brings us to the question of what the headmen might have actually said. Although Parker obviously relied on American conventions
for representing their speeches, his account need not be completely dismissed. In the first place, it is in fact quite likely that the Nimiipuu and
Salish leaders did express an interest in learning more about the *soyapos'*
god. Historical records show that Plateau people had been seeking access to this god for some time. In 1824, when the HBC governor, George
Simpson, directed his chief traders to offer Christian instruction, Plateau people had responded with interest. Indeed, two headmen sent
their sons to a Church Missionary Society school in the HBC's Red River
settlement to the north in order to learn more. When one of these sons,
Spokan Garry, returned, he began preaching about the new religion and
encouraging Plateau communities to hold Sunday ceremonies in which
people gathered to listen to exhortations and participated in devotional
dances. These ceremonies appear to have involved the incorporation of
new Christian elements into Plateau religious practice; they also show
links to an indigenous prophetic tradition that emphasized the need
for renewed commitment to spiritual life in times of crisis. Inspired by
these developments, a delegation of Nimiipuu and Salish men traveled
to St. Louis in 1831 to request more Christian teachers. It is, then, highly
likely that when the headmen encountered the missionaries at Green
River they were pleased to see them and expressed interest in receiving
further instruction about the white man's god.[39]

But Parker's account must be more fully re-examined in indigenous
terms. The god that the headmen sought was not the god of Protestant
Christianity nor the "Great Spirit" that Americans imagined to be the
object of "Indian" belief. Further, Plateau leaders would not have conceived of a relationship to this god in the evangelical terms of conversion and salvation. Rather, as other scholars have argued, the headmen
would have been seeking access to the *soyapos'* god in accordance with
their own cultural principles. For Plateau people, human relations to
the spirit world were understood primarily in terms of sacred power.
Individuals received personal powers as gifts from guardian spirits or
wéyekin and, most commonly, they obtained these powers as children
through lone vision quests in spiritually powerful locations. However,
it was also possible for people to seek more spiritual power from other
wéyekin in times of need. Confronted, then, with the material wealth
of the traders, and, even more importantly, their evident immunity to
the epidemic diseases that were affecting Plateau communities, it made
sense for people to seek access to the source of the soyapo's apparent
power. When the headmen told Parker and Whitman that they wanted
"a man near to God" to come among them, they were most likely ask-

ing for teachers who could show them how to acquire the white man's apparent spiritual strength and wealth.[40]

Exactly how the headmen conceived of the *soyapos'* god is more difficult to determine. Historical and linguistic records suggest that they may well have viewed him as an altogether new kind of being. Certainly they would have understood that this god was not like their own *wéyekin* who usually took the form of an animal, insect, plant, or natural feature of the Plateau world. They would have also been aware that he was quite unlike Coyote, their mythic creator and trickster figure.[41] And whereas both *wéyekin* and Coyote were related to particular sites in the Plateau landscape, the soyapo's god was not. Plateau people appear to have understood that it resided in an indeterminate place "above": "God" in the Chinook jargon was "*sakali-taie*," meaning "the Chief above or on high";[42] in Nimiipuu people came to refer to this god as "*ʔaqámkiniko*," or "the person above, higher one."[43] Perhaps, then, the Nimipuutimt and Salish headmen were seeking not only access to the new god's powers, but also more knowledge of a spiritual being that was clearly altogether different from their own.

One further point to be made is that on the Plateau it was headmen, rather than traditional religious leaders, who appear to have been most interested in accessing the power of the soyapo's god.[44] It was headmen who first learned of the new god through their interactions with traders, and it was headmen, not shamans, who directed the Sunday ceremonies. Most likely, in acting as advocates for the new god, headmen sought to increase their status and authority. It is probably safe to assume, then, that when the Nimiipuu and Salish headmen invited Parker and Whitman to come among them, they hoped thereby to enhance their authority through relationships with the *soyapo* religious men.

It is in this context, lastly, that we should consider the possibility that the headmen spoke of their "hearts" in their declarations to the missionaries. For Plateau people, speaking from the heart was not an expression of "primitive" purity, as the Americans would have had it, but a powerful cultural concept of their own. They understood the heart to be the locus of emotion *and* intellect, not, like American evangelicals, that of emotion in opposition to the intellect. The Nimiipuu word *timíne* was (and is) used to talk about both matters of feeling—as in "*timíne?ew'níse*" (I give her my heart)—and matters of thought—as in "*timíne haníya*" (he made up his mind); or, significantly, "*timínéćiqce*" (I am thinking: I am saying in heart).[45] If the headmen spoke of their hearts to the missionaries, then, they would have been speaking not as noble savages but as men trying to convey the seriousness of their request.

Reconstructed in the context of these different histories, it is evident that the A.B.C.F.M. missionaries and the Nimiipuu and Salish headmen brought quite different, but not completely disparate, understandings of space, identity, and purpose to their encounter at Green River. These understandings, in turn, articulated very differently with the cultural constructs of American colonialism. Although Parker's narrative is, to be sure, a literary reconstruction of the Green River meeting, it clearly shows that he aligned the A.B.C.F.M. missionary project with Euro-American colonial expansion and strongly suggests that he borrowed its constructs to make sense of his interaction with the headmen. In identifying the Nimiipuu and Salish leaders as chiefs of the Nez Perce and Flathead "nations" and classifying them as "Indians," he defined the space of interaction in Euro-American colonial terms. He was then able to rely on American stereotypes of Indians to represent their speeches and their interest in the Christian god. At the same time, he downplayed the importance of the process of translation and, with that, any recognition of, or possibility of insight into, indigenous difference. The headmen operated with very different understandings of their identities and their relationships to their lands. They had their own conventions for communicating, little understood by the missionaries, and while they sought access to the Euro-American god, they did so in the interests of acquiring power, not salvation. At the same time, though, these headmen were familiar with the forms of identity that the Euro-Americans used and with the terminology of Christianity. In a sense, they were able to work with American colonial constructs without accepting all their colonial implications. In this space of interaction, then, there were enough apparent points of convergence to make the interaction work; but there were also enough points of divergence to make the relationship come undone.

FIRST ENCOUNTERS: LANCELOT THRELKELD AND THE AWABAKAL

The Missionary Perspective

Let us now turn to Lancelot Threlkeld's reports of his first encounters with Aboriginal people in eastern Australia. His account illuminates the very different interplay between colonial constructs and cultural forms that shaped the dynamics of cross-cultural interaction at his mission site.

For a start, it is notable that, unlike Parker, Threlkeld did not identify the indigenous people he met as members of tribes or nations: he referred to them using only the general terms "natives" or "Aborigines." This was not an omission. In doing so, Threlkeld was following British colonial practice in Australia. Having colonized the country on the principle of *terra nullius*, the British had little interest in naming and recognizing Aboriginal peoples as nations or tribes and thereby recognizing their claims to particular territories.[46] An important consequence of this was that Threlkeld did not, like Parker, assume that establishing his mission involved taking up residence in the territory of an indigenous nation. Rather, in his report of first encounter, he uses the vague term "interiour [sic]" to describe his future mission site. While Parker operated with the seemingly contradictory view that the A.B.C.F.M. missions would be established in the territory of the "Nez Perce" and "Flathead" "nations" and that this was also (or soon-to-be) American territory, Threlkeld's use of "interiour" suggests both a settler's view that the land was simply available for the taking and a sense that the land was still unknown, as yet undefined.

The terms Threlkeld did use—"native" and "Aborigine"—were both more general and somewhat less charged than the Euro-American term "Indian." "Native" and "Aborigine" classed the indigenous peoples of Australia in the same group as the indigenous peoples of Africa, Asia, or the Pacific and, as such, they were even broader generalizations than "Indian." But while both "native" and "Aborigine" in contemporary European usage often implied a host of colonial ideas about non-European peoples' lack of "civilization," they did not have quite the same ideological weight attached to them as "Indian" did for the American missionaries. Whereas "Indians" had become symbolically central in American nationalist discourse, whether cast as noble orators to be admired, or as bloodthirsty savages against which the republic needed to defend itself, the "Aborigines" occupied no such position in British discourses about the Australian colony. And whereas many American evangelicals viewed the conversion of the "Indians" as the fulfillment of God's plan for America, the conversion of Aboriginal people carried no such import in Australian settler narratives. In fact, in the early nineteenth century even sympathetic evangelicals viewed the "Aborigines" as the most abject of native or Aboriginal peoples and the most resistant to "civilization" or Christianization, while the settler majority opposed missions altogether in the self-justifying belief that Aboriginal people were doomed to extinction.[47]

In this regard it is important to note that Threlkeld favored using the term "Aborigine" rather than the more distinctly racial term "Black." "Aborigine," at the very least, implied a prior and original relationship to the land, and was the preferred term among evangelicals and humanitarians in colonial Australia.[48] "Black," by contrast, had gained currency among colonists as the pastoralist frontier expanded and settlers came into violent conflict with indigenous peoples. Use of the term "Black," unlike Aborigine, conveniently effaced any indigenous relation to the land and was all too frequently accompanied by assertions that Aboriginal people were less than human. In the late 1820s one British traveler, echoing prevailing colonial views, described the "Blacks" as the "link between man and the monkey tribe."[49] When Threlkeld arrived, he was dismayed to find that many settlers "supposed that they were a species of Baboon, and had no regular language...."[50] As a missionary committed to the conversion and salvation of Aboriginal people, Threlkeld vigorously rejected such views. And, for the most part, he held to the identification "Aborigine" with that term's implied associations of humanity and rights.

Threlkeld's relationship to the dominant colonial society and its conceptions of indigenous people was, then, very different from that of Parker's. While Parker (and the other A.B.C.F.M. missionaries) actively promoted colonial expansion into the American Northwest and the Christianization of the "Indians" as part of God's plan for America, Threlkeld, though generally favoring colonization, was appalled by the violence of settler society toward Aboriginal people and had to defend his missionary endeavor against both local evangelical pessimism and settler hostility. And while Parker could draw upon well-established colonial stereotypes of "Indians" as primitive orators and pure-hearted noble savages, Threlkeld, having rejected the racist views of the settler majority, found few usable colonial constructs with which to make sense of the indigenous people he hoped to convert.

It is in this context, then, that we should understand Threlkeld's accounts of the Aboriginal people he encountered in Newcastle. It was, I would like to suggest, the very absence of preconceived ideas about indigenous speech that led him to pay attention to their particular forms of communicating. In his account of Aboriginal singing he noted that their songs began "high and end about an octave below the pitch." In reporting their dance performance he observed details with an ethnographer's eye: the old man beating two sticks and singing, the whole uniting "in the tune which begins high and sinks gradually raising again...." And in his description of his first conversation on religious matters, he noted that the Aboriginal men spoke to him "in broken English," that they were, in other words, speaking in a language that was not their own. In doing so, Threlkeld did not, like Parker, efface the work of translation; rather he made it apparent. Lacking usable stereotypes, he assumed no knowledge of Aboriginal forms of communication. In the very process of noting details, he made it clear that he did *not* fully understand their words and actions—and that they did not fully understand his. He was clearly perplexed by their singing of church music, aware that they were doing something meaningful to them alone. And while his description of the Aboriginal dance performance could be read as a proof of their "savagery"—particularly in its pointed reference to the nakedness of the women—his observation of specifics nevertheless suggests both an effort to comprehend their actions and an awareness of cultural difference.

This awareness is also evident in Threlkeld's reports of Aboriginal religious beliefs and responses to Christianity. Although he generally viewed Aboriginal people as heathen, he did not, like Parker, presume to understand their conceptions of the sacred; and he certainly did not assume that they already knew of a "Great Spirit." In his account of the Aborigines singing church music, he is, if anything, all too aware that they had translated the music into another cultural register. And in his report of his conversation about creation, while there is, to be sure, a strong implication that the men were speaking from heathen ignorance—"One of them replied that long while ago one Black fellow threw the vermin from his head into the fire and they jumped up (for become) these things"—there is also, for all that, still some recognition of an alternative indigenous framework, a recognition that is strikingly absent from Parker's narrative.

The Indigenous Perspective

Again, as with Parker's narrative, it is difficult to retrieve the indigenous side of this encounter, but Threlkeld's writings and other sources provide some clues. Read carefully, the evidence suggests that these indigenous people, unlike the Plateau headmen, did not, for the most part, work with the concepts and identities used by the colonists. Rather, they rejected the racist constructs of the settler majority, as Threlkeld did, but from their own cultural perspective. Their actions, in imitating the colonizer's songs, performing a dance, and telling the missionary a part of one of their own sacred stories, can be considered assertions of their own conceptions of identity, space, and the sacred in the face of colonization. Through these actions, it would appear that they were reaching out to Threlkeld and trying to accommodate him in terms of their own cultural codes.

For a start, the indigenous people at Newcastle would not have considered themselves "Aborigines" or "Blacks," as the colonists used these terms. Like Plateau peoples, they were divided into different groups, in this case family clans or bands who were closely tied to particular lands. Bands were also connected to each other through sacred and familial ties. Throughout southeastern Australia cycles of songs, each telling of the creative journeys and acts of ancestral beings, communicated a knowledge of each band's territory, its sacred sites, and each site's relations to other sites. As band members passed on these songs to other bands, the journeys of the ancestral beings and the connections they created were affirmed and animated. Further, because each individual, through conception, birth, and burial was related to different sites and their particular spirits, marriages between members of different bands created social and spiritual connections across space.[51] Like indigenous peoples of the Plateau, then, the indigenous peoples around Newcastle were not a homogenous mass but distinct groups whose identities were closely tied to their lands in their own culturally unique ways.

Unfortunately, the precise name or names these people used to identify themselves are no longer known. Scholars, since the late nineteenth century, have labeled the indigenous people of this region the Awabakal, and that name will hence be used in this essay, but Threlkeld himself never recorded it.[52] Although he did record other place names (as we shall see), the only name for the group that he noted was "*Mulubinbakal*," meaning "belonging to *Mulubinba*," the name of the site on which the British had established Newcastle. However, it is not clear that this was their primary identification.[53] In this case, the lack of certainty attests to the lack of colonial interest in recognizing and identifying Aboriginal people as distinct groups in the early nineteenth century.[54]

This is not to imply, however, that colonization had no effect on the ways in which the Awabakal people identified themselves. Threlkeld's own account of an Awabakal man explaining a creation story — "long while ago one Black fellow threw the vermin from his head into the fire and they jumped up (for become) these things" — shows that by the 1820s the Awabakal had begun using the term "blackfellow." "Blackfellow," like *siwash*, was a jargon word, and it was similarly used to identify all indigenous peoples. In the Australian case, the jargon was a lingua franca primarily used by convicts, settlers, and Aboriginal peoples to facilitate the exchange of European goods for indigenous labor or sexual relations with Aboriginal women.[55] Most likely, "blackfellow" came into use during the same period that "black" gained currency, but it did not carry quite the same racist connotations. Records indicate that Aboriginal people used "blackfellow" without any sense that it might imply racial inferiority, and that they considered it as a counterpart to "whitefellow," another jargon word.[56] The combination of the two, and the addition of "fellow" to both, hints at the possibility that Aboriginal people, at least, sought less hostile and hierarchical relations (albeit only between men) than those which otherwise prevailed.[57] At the same time, indigenous use of "blackfellow," like *siwash*, indicated both a concession to British ignorance of indigenous differences and the emergence of a new collective identity. When the Awabakal man used "blackfellow" while recounting a creation story to Threlkeld, he was no doubt referring to an ancestral being; "blackfellow" provided a usable term to convey to the whitefellow missionary the fact that this Being was indigenous and human in form, but it also inevitably limited what he could communicate.

Exactly how the Awabakal viewed the "whitefellow" colonists in their country is difficult to determine, but the history of their relations with the British provides some clues. When the British first established the penal colony of Newcastle in 1804 (a year before the Nimiipuu encountered Lewis and Clark's expedition) the Awabakal initiated and maintained limited but generally peaceful relations, occasionally trading food for goods and acting as guides through the surrounding country. There is also some evidence to suggest that they formed a friendly relationship with the town's chaplain, the Rev. Middleton, although he did not attempt to convert them.[58] However in 1821, three years before Threlkeld arrived, Newcastle became a port for free settlers, and a wave of colonists invaded the lands of the Awabakal's neighbors (the Wonaruah and Geawegal peoples), and soldiers crushed indigenous resistance.[59] This invasion was accompanied by a general surge in violence as soldiers and the convict laborers assigned to work on settlers' pastoral runs attacked Aboriginal men and assaulted Aboriginal women.[60] The Awabakal were subject to these attacks and to the racist hostility that licensed them. However, their own lands to the south of Newcastle, around the lagoon that the British named Lake Macquarie, remained relatively untouched. Indeed, Threlkeld would be the first colonist to establish a settlement there in 1825. They were therefore able to continue fishing, hunting, and gathering and, importantly, to preserve their spiritual connections to sacred sites through the performance of ceremonies and the passing on of songs.[61] By the time of their encounter with Threlkeld, then, the Awabakal had acquired some knowledge of the British. While no doubt horrified by the hostility exhibited by many of the incoming settlers, they had experienced positive relations with some individuals: They understood that there were differences. Still largely in control of their own lands, they remained interested in establishing relations with the British on their own terms rather than in the terms of the emerging, more racist colonial order. It is in this context that we need to understand their actions following Threlkeld's arrival.

First, in imitating and singing British church music, it would appear that the Awabakal were attempting to acquire and/or display a knowledge of the newcomers and draw them into their own networks of cultural exchange. Although Threlkeld was puzzled by what he overheard, he later learned that all indigenous groups in the region had their "itinerant professors" who went from "tribe to tribe" teaching new songs.[62] Through this activity they acquired new knowledge and maintained relations with each other. In singing church music, then, the Awabakal were acting in accordance with their own custom of learning and passing on new songs. Their actions suggest that they were seeking ways of relating to the British on indigenous, not colonial, terms.

The Awabakal's dance performance for Threlkeld can similarly be viewed as an attempt to establish a relationship on their own terms. The dance, as Threlkeld understood it, was "on account of [his] arrival among them." As such, it was an act that cast his arrival in Newcastle as an arrival in Awabakal, not British, country. It can also be understood as an Awabakal assertion that they were hosts, not subject peoples, of the British. It is, however, notable that the Awabakal evidently knew that the British, unlike other Aboriginal groups, would not attempt to learn their songs and dance movements. Their actions in inviting Threlkeld to watch and then thanking him and wishing him "goodnight" show that they had adapted to a colonial propensity to view their dances as spectacles to be watched rather than performances to be imitated and passed on. Nevertheless, even if they were aware of the ways in which the British approached their performances, it would appear that the Awabakal were intent on asserting their identity as the people of the country and the validity of their own modes of establishing relationships with others.

And lastly, it is clear from Threlkeld's report of the creation story conversation that the Awabakal were interested in exchanging religious knowledge: evidently they wanted to tell the missionary something about their own traditions and, according to Threlkeld, they were pleased to learn that he was going to teach them more about Christianity. Again, it would appear, they were seeking to establish a relationship with the missionary on their own terms. Unlike Plateau people, the Awabakal did not have a tradition of acquiring powers from new spirits, but they did have a tradition of exchanging stories about spirit beings. Further, in Aboriginal cultures throughout the southeast the acquisition of sacred knowledge was a means of heightening one's authority, particularly for initiated men.[63] Perhaps when the Awabakal met with Threlkeld, then, they recognized him as a man possessed of religious knowledge and interpreted the missionary's desire to tell them about his sacred stories as an expression of interest in exchange. Clearly, they wanted him to understand that they had their own stories and traditions.

To sum up: unlike the A.B.C.F.M. missionaries and the people of the Plateau, Threlkeld and the Awabakal, in the absence of the structures of recognition and in the face of colonial racism, had few useful colonial constructs with which to work. Rather, both opposed the most racist views of the colonial majority, albeit to varying degrees and from different perspectives. At the same time, although there were few useful points of convergence, the Awabakal were clearly interested in reaching out and exchanging knowledge with the missionary, while Threlkeld, though not interested in exchange on Awabakal terms, was open to learning more about the people he had come to convert.

THE COLONIAL AND CROSS-CULTURAL DYNAMICS OF MISSIONARY/INDIGENOUS RELATIONS

In different ways, the terms of cross-cultural interaction established at first encounter continued to inform the evolution of missionary/indigenous relations at each site. In the latter half of this chapter, I discuss some of the ways in which each party's conceptions of space, identity, communicative practice, and the sacred were variously reproduced or reconstituted in these two different colonial environments. What follows is not in any way a complete account of each mission's history; rather, I remain focused on the terms of cross-cultural interaction as these articulated with the structures of colonialism in each region.

The American Northwest

The A.B.C.F.M. established four missions on the Plateau: one, led by Marcus Whitman, among the Cayuse and Walla Walla; another among the Salish; and two among the Nimiipuu. I will focus on the Nimiipuu missions. The first was established by Henry Harmon Spalding and his wife, Eliza, in 1836; the second was established by Asa and Sarah Smith in 1840, after they had spent two years with the Spaldings.

One of the first points to be made is that despite the many years the Spaldings and Smiths lived among the Nimiipuu, they acquired surprising little knowledge of indigenous geography or forms of identity. Aside from the place names of their mission sites—the Spaldings established his mission at the riverine site of Lapwai, the Smiths moved to the village of Kamiah in 1840—their writings contain remarkably few references to other indigenous villages or sites.[64] Rather, they continued to refer to the "Nez Perce nation" and continued to rely on a Euro-American geography of names for the region's rivers, mountains, and lakes. They also continued to use the colonial generalizations "Indian" and even "Red Man."[65] One of the few facts about indigenous identity that they did learn was that the people called their language "Nimipuutímt" and those who spoke it "Nimipu."[66] (Possibly, the missionaries themselves promoted this as a form of identity instead of village names.) The Nimiipuu, for their part, may have been content for the missionaries, as for the traders, to rely on the general terms "Nez Perce" or "Nimipu," as a usable identity. They did not, so far as one can ascertain from historical records, press the missionaries to understand the more complex ways in which they identified or related to their lands. As a result, the dense network of village and place names, along with all their spiritual and ecological associations, remained outside the missionaries' frame of reference. In a sense, Spalding and Smith never fully realized they were in a foreign country.

Points of convergence between indigenous speech practices and missionary conceptions of Indian oratory also continued to shape missionary/indigenous interaction at the Nimiipuu mission. This was particularly the case in the relationship between Spalding and the headmen at Lapwai. When headmen interested in establishing an alliance with the *soyapo* religious man spoke on his behalf at village meetings, Spalding praised their efforts. His reports also show that a cross-cultural language of the "heart" continued to be central, functioning as both a bridge to communication and a barrier to each party's full understanding of the other's intentions. In a letter to his missionary colleague Hiram Bingham in Hawaii, Spalding proudly reported that one unnamed "chief" had declared, on behalf of his people: "We wish you to ... tell us how to worship; for ... we have one and all thrown away our bad hearts."[67] On another occasion he wrote to the secretary of the A.B.C.F.M. board, David Greene, that a headman whom he had named "Joseph" as a mark of his allegiance to the mission, had spoken "most affectingly" to a gathering of Nimiipuu, "urging all present to give their hearts to Jesus without delay."[68] Spalding, of course, interpreted such statements as expressions of their readiness for conversion conceived of as an emotional surrendering of the self to Christ. The Nimiipuu, on the other hand, while evidently interested in the *soyapos'* god, would more likely have understood giving their hearts to Jesus as a matter of focusing their thoughts and feelings on him as a way of accessing his powers.

In addition, Spalding was evidently attracted to the practice of "playing Indian" and the Nimiipuu, for their own reasons, accommodated him. In dramatic language, similar to that used by Parker, Spalding told the Nimiipuu upon his arrival that he had "not come to trade with them but do them good, to live and die with them, to teach them about God...."[69] Then, when the Nimiipuu made arrangements for Spalding to address them, he accepted their terms. In a letter to Greene, he explained the approach he had worked out with the headmen:

> We have represented in paintings, several events recorded in the Scriptures.... These I explain first to my crier. I then go over the subject to the people the crier correcting my language and carrying out my history.... They return to their tents, and sometimes spend the whole night in perfecting what they but partly understood on the Sabbath. If one is to leave camp for some distant part of the country, my crier and the paintings are sent forth and the whole night spent in going over with the subjects, to prepare himself to instruct others. Several are already preaching in different parts of the nation.[70]

From Spalding's perspective, this arrangement enabled him to perform the role of preacher/orator and, in doing so, believe he was communicating Christianity in "Indian" fashion. It is worth noting, however, that unlike Parker, he acknowledged the role of his crier/interpreter. Quite possibly his interest in "playing Indian" actually led Spalding to acquire some understanding not only of the Nimiipuu language but of their speech practices. Under the direction of the A.B.C.F.M. secretary, Spalding, with the other missionaries, had begun learning the language soon after he arrived with the goal of being able to preach in the vernacular and, importantly, translate the Bible.[71] For instruction he relied primarily on the headman Hallalhotsoot, also known as "Lawyer" among the fur traders because of his skill as a speaker. Spalding's colleague, Asa Smith, described him as a "a man of mind" who "will speak with the eloquence of an orator."[72] From observing Hallalhotsoot and other Nimiipuu speakers, Spalding no doubt noted their use of criers. It is quite possible that he came to understand, then, that the employment of a crier/interpreter could buttress his authority as a speaker.

For the Nimiipuu, on the other hand, the arrangement positioned Spalding as a figure of authority, but it also contained him and allowed the transfer of real power to the headmen who enhanced their authority and elaborated a new role for themselves as tellers of Biblical stories. This was a new development for the headmen and a new development, too, in the Nimiipuu engagement with Christianity. As Asa Smith later observed, the headmen "manifest a great fondness for hearing something new & telling of it & by so doing they gather many about them & increase their influence & sustain their dignity among the people."[73] They were especially fond, he noted, of the "historical parts [of the Bible] which they remember extremely well ..."[74] Although the evidence

Illustration 9.1. | *This portrait of Hallalhotsoot, one of the few Nimiipuu to express a sustained interest in Christianity in the early mission era, was drawn by Gustav Sohon at the 1855 Walla Walla treaty council meeting. Source: Washington State Historical Society, NO. 1918.114.9.53. Used with permission.*

is fragmentary, it would appear that the headmen around Kamiah and Lapwai abandoned the practice of leading devotional dancing on Sundays after the missionaries condemned it, and sought another way of sustaining their authority as advocates of the *soyapos'* god.[75] In taking up the telling of Bible stories, they may have been influenced by Spalding's Protestant emphasis on preaching the Word of God and his admiration for their public speaking, but they were also, no doubt, acting in accordance with their own cultural principles. In Plateau cultures, stories were the source of mythic, moral, and life-sustaining knowledge and those who told them were highly regarded. Indeed, stories could be owned and given as gifts.[76] In this cultural context, Spalding's telling of Biblical stories may have been regarded as an offering of gifts to the Nimiipuu headmen who then took ownership of the stories and used them to enhance their own authority. Further, it seems likely that they looked to these stories to make sense of the *soyapo's* religious traditions. As one contemporary Plateau story-teller has said: "Stories are what we have to explore with."[77] The retelling of Biblical stories would have enabled the headmen to explore the nature of the *soyapo* god and human relationships to him, and work out ways of integrating that knowledge into their own cultural and spiritual world.

One of the few records that offer some insights into the Nimiipuu interpretation of Biblical stories is an unnamed headman's speech that was translated by Spalding with the assistance, most likely, of Hallalhotsoot, and published by Spalding's colleague, Hiram Bingham, in the *Hawaiian Spectator* in 1838. Indeed, in many respects the speech illuminates the points of convergence and divergence between missionary and indigenous understandings of the communication of Christianity. While Spalding presented the speech as evidence of his evangelical success in bringing the Word to the Nez Perce, much of the speech points to a specifically Nimiipuu process of interpreting and communicating Christianity. The speech reads, in part, as follows:

> ... my heart told me to come and see you.
> What I now see and hear is new to my eyes and ears.
> ...
> I see these good books [the paintings],
> I have heard you explain them:
> I have heard you sing and worship.
> It is not a small thank you I return for all these things;
> It is one of mountain size.
> I have eaten all your heart.
> I never before heard the name of Jesus Christ:
> This news is a bright morning sun,
> Rising over a near mountain.

...
We have sometimes heard a little said,
...
About one God at some of the forts.
We always took great care to make it fast about our persons,
But in riding a short distance we invariably lost it:
...
But now it is very different with me.
The pack I have corded up since yesterday is immense:
The strap cuts deep into my forehead;
The load presses heavy on my shoulders:
Even now I am obliged to raise my hands to the straps,
To give support to my neck, which already begins to bend.
But I will carry it all home, and occupy many days
In pouring out its contents before my people.
I will soon drive away the darkness,
Which has hung over my country from before the days of my fathers.
There will soon be day light.
...
My heart is glad to hear of this good Being.[78]

Clearly, much of the oration reproduces standard Euro-American "Indian" vocabulary, attesting to the missionaries' ongoing fascination with the genre. Indeed, Bingham asked his readers to imagine "this aged chieftain [pouring] forth his ardent feelings in a torrent of true aboriginal eloquence, exhibiting fine sentiments, in striking and appropriate figures ..."[79] Nevertheless, there are elements that point to a Nimiipuu frame of reference.

For a start, the speech makes it clear that it was the headman, not the missionary, who delivered Christian knowledge to the people: The missionary is thanked and then displaced. It is the headman who carries home the pack of knowledge and pours "out its contents before [his] people." Moreover, it is notable that the speaker discusses the reception of Christianity not only in terms of the people, but also in terms of the land. The news of Christ is as a "bright morning sun rising over a near mountain"; it will "drive away the darkness which has hung over [his] country." The speaker makes it clear that it is *his* country and seems to suggest that for the new spiritual power to be accessible to the people, it had be made effective in the land.

In addition, the speech contains references to Nimiipuu history and mythology. On one level, the story of the headman carrying and losing a small pack from the fort and then carrying and giving a larger pack of knowledge to the people recalls the practice of headmen obtaining goods from trading posts and dispensing them in their villages. As such it reflects the connection many Nimiipuu appear to have initially made between the material wealth and spiritual power of the *soyapo*. On another level, the story is reminiscent of a Nimiipuu myth story about the creator/trickster Coyote in which Coyote follows his daughter to the land of the dead only to be ordered to return to the land of the living, carrying a heavy pack across five mountains without looking back. Just as the pack "presses heavy" upon the headman's shoulders in the speech, Coyote's pack becomes heavier and heavier in the story, until finally he drops it and looks back just before crossing the fifth mountain. The consequence of Coyote's failure to fulfill his task is that the dead, including his daughter, have to remain in the land of darkness. Death, thereby, became a permanent condition.[80] By contrast, in the speech the chief's heavy pack of Christian knowledge enables him to drive away darkness. These parallels and points of connection suggest that the Nimiipuu headmen may have turned to Coyote stories to interpret Spalding's biblical ones.[81]

Another indication of the headmen's interpretive use of Coyote stories is the remarkable expression "I have eaten all your heart." Clearly not derived from American evangelical literature about the sincerity of Indian hearts, this phrase evokes stories of Coyote obtaining power over others by taking possession of their hearts. For instance, in a story in which Coyote is consumed by "Monster" along with mythic "people," Coyote frees himself and the people by cutting out the fat around Monster's heart and feeding it to the people, and then cutting out the heart itself.[82] In another story, Coyote destroys some "Humming Birds" who leave their hearts on a mountainside while they go off to battle by dashing up the mountain and "plucking" their hearts.[83] The phrase, "I have eaten all your heart," then, suggests not the change of heart desired by the missionaries, but an interest in obtaining power over, or from, the missionaries.

Significantly, despite such indications that the Nimiipuu were interpreting Bible stories in the light of their own traditional stories, Spalding and the other A.B.C.F.M. missionaries seemed to have remained remarkably ignorant of Nimiipuu mythology and cultural life in general. Spalding made no records of indigenous traditions and on only two occasions did Whitman make notes on indigenous beliefs. Once he reported to Greene: "Their legend is that the present race of beasts birds reptiles & fish were once a race of men who inhabited the globe before the present race."[84] In another letter he related that a "prominent Nez Perces" had told him that "they did formerly worship the Prairie Wolf who is the subject of many traditions + to whome [sic] they ascribe many wonderful changes in nature + even the formation of the world."[85] But Whitman did not see fit to record any of these traditions. And even when Spalding and Smith began learning the Nimiipuu language, their translations suggest that they remained focused on finding equivalents for a limited number of English words without considering the possibility that the language might offer useful insights into Nimiipuu ways of thinking. Spalding produced a series of primers aimed at teaching the Nimiipuu about Euro-American morality and agriculture and the uses of European tools, clothes, and foods.[86] Smith made a more concerted effort to grasp the rules of the language, but his unpublished grammar indicates little interest in Nimiipuu spiritual vocabulary—with the exception, notably, of a translation for the word "heart" —*timíne*.[87] Indeed, he came to the view that there was "an entire destitution of terms to apply to religious subjects."[88] In the apparent absence of equivalents he substituted modified English words such as *"Godnim"* and *"Holy Ghostki,"* rather than considering any Nimiipuu words.[89]

The Nimiipuu, for their part, seem to have been either uninterested or unwilling to tell Spalding or Smith their stories or teach them about their ways of living in the world. While they might have invited members of other indigenous groups to gatherings in which traditional stories were told, they issued no such invitations to the missionaries. No doubt they soon came to realize that Spalding and Smith were hostile to their spiritual and cultural practices. The headmen must also have realized that the missionaries' admiration for their skills as speakers was restricted to those occasions in which they spoke in support of the Christian god. In this situation, it seems that the headmen decided to learn what they could of the *soyapos'* religious traditions, exploiting Spalding's admiration for their speaking skills and drawing on an apparent convergence between their own story-telling traditions and the evangelists' telling of Biblical stories; but they did not and could not engage the missionaries in any sustained exchange of religious and cultural knowledge.

By 1839 relations between the missionaries and the headmen were beginning to break down. Asa Smith started to question the Nimiipuu's apparent interest in Christianity and called for a new method of instruction. The hearts of the Nimiipuu, Smith argued, were not the pure hearts of noble savages but the selfish "natural" hearts of fallen men.[90] Nor, in his opinion, did the Nimiipuu already believe in God or a Great Spirit. Contrary to Spalding's reports, he wrote that "it is very evident that their hearts are very opposed to God & we find them extremely selfish." Instead of telling Bible stories, Smith advocated a policy of communicating only the "plain" truths of Protestant Christianity. As he put it, the Nimiipuu needed "to have their hearts searched by a plain presentation of gospel truth."[91] The headmen responded to this new approach with hostility. As Smith himself noted, "As long as they listened to the interesting historical parts of the bible, they were pleased, but the great truth that all are under condemnation & exposed to the penalty of the law ... is very offensive to them...."[92] Indeed, two headmen confronted Smith at his mission station, ordering him "not to talk to the people again."[93] Smith's policy prevented the headmen from elaborating their role as story-tellers and undermined the convergences upon which Spalding and the headmen had built their cross-cultural relationship.[94]

By the mid-1840s, the breakdown of cross-cultural relations at the Nimiipuu missions was everywhere apparent. Spalding claimed a total of twenty-one converts in all—mainly headmen and their families who had decided to ally themselves with the missionary.[95] Hallalhotsoot, the missionaries' language teacher, did not become a formal member of the church at this time, although, according to Smith, he had "more knowledge of the truths of the gospel than any one of the natives with whom I have conversed," was recognized by most as Christian, and regularly participated in church services.[96] Most Nimiipuu, however, were turning away from the *soyapo* religious leaders. The missionaries had not increased their access to material wealth; their god had not given them immunity to diseases that were again bringing illness and death to the Plateau; and Marcus Whitman's trek to the east and return with a large party of settlers in 1842 increased Nimiipuu fears that *soyapo* were coming to take their land. In the face of these threats, and in defiance of the missionaries, shamans reasserted themselves and began encouraging the people to look to the spirits of their own country as sources of spiritual strength and renew their participation in traditional rituals.[97]

In response, Spalding and Smith abandoned any notions that the Nimiipuu might be "noble savages" and turned to another, older American stereotype of "Indians" as devil-worshippers. Derived from the Puritan past, the image of the Indian devil-worshipper conflated a colonial and spiritual enemy and offered the missionaries a powerful explanation for indigenous resistance to Christianity. The performance of traditional ceremonies became proof, as Spalding put it, that the Nimiipuu were "very much under the power of the devil."[98] The missionaries collectively dismissed indigenous spiritual practice as "sorcery" and its chief practitioners as "conjurers." David Greene, Secretary of the Board, encouraged this view, reminding the missionaries that the "Indians" were "benighted, passionate, deluded, superstitious beings, infatuated and led astray by the devil ..."[99] The ease with which the A.B.C.F.M. missionaries adopted this explanation is striking. It attests to the hold of colonial stereotypes on their thinking, a hold that was both cause and consequence of their failure to engage with the Nimiipuu and comprehend their spiritual and cultural life. It also points to the deep ideological links between their evangelical project and American colonial expansion.

A final point to be made here is that as part of this shift the missionaries also abandoned the image of the noble Indian orator. Instead, they began characterizing indigenous speech as the speech of demons or the incomprehensible talk of savages. When Nimiipuu headmen asked Smith to leave, for instance, he wrote that their talk "was warm" and that they "seemed more like demons from the bottomless pit than human beings."[100] And when resistance to the missionaries mounted, Spalding complained to Greene that the whole valley now rang "with [Indian] gambling songs & hideous yells, rendering it almost impossible to sleep & dangerous to go out of doors."[101] Spalding also reported being "violently threatened" when he preached and that one evening "after the camp had retired to rest," a headman made a speech against him. He wrote: "This is a common practice among the people. If any one has anything of importance to communicate to the people, he waits till night, when all are at rest, then steps out and delivers his speech seemingly to the winds, not a person in sight, but all in hearing."[102] In this account Spalding notes, for the first time, some specifics of Nimiipuu speech practices that could in no way be interpreted in terms of the construct of the Indian orator. It would seem that without that construct, Spalding was finally able to recognize that the Nimiipuu had their own communicative practices and, indeed, their own communicative spaces that he could not enter and did not understand. It was a rare recognition that he was, in fact, an outsider in their country.

The Closing of the A.B.C.F.M. Mission and Its Aftermath

All A.B.C.F.M. missions in the Plateau were finally closed in 1847 after the killing of the Whitmans by some Cayuse at Waiilatpu, who were acting in response to another outbreak of disease and an influx of *soyapo* settlers.[103] Nevertheless, despite the collapse of the mission, and the invasion of Oregon Territory by Euro-American settlers, some of the colonial constructs that shaped missionary relations with Plateau people continued to inform indigenous interactions with Euro-Americans. In the 1855 Walla Walla treaty council convened by U.S. government officials to demand land cessions from northwestern tribes, both Plateau headmen and American officials returned to the forms that had governed earlier interactions. Records of the treaty proceedings also offer further insight into Plateau peoples' continuing reinterpretation of the *soyapos'* god or Great Spirit. It would appear that even if many

Nimiipuu and other Plateau people rejected mission Christianity, they did not reject the existence of the spiritual being about whom the missionaries and other Euro-Americans had spoken; rather they reinterpreted his nature within the framework of an indigenous spirituality.

The council began with Governor Isaac Stevens "playing Indian," and telling the assembled headmen through a crier:

> My children, the sky is clear, the ground is dry, my heart is glad to day. Our hearts are glad.... I came from the great waters beyond the mountains, across the mountains, and you have all been friends to me.[104]

He requested that the headmen "open their hearts" to him and outlined his plan to place all the tribes on reservations. The headmen made speeches in response. Possibly they hoped to appeal to Euro-American admiration for "Indian" oratory. They spoke of their hearts. They appealed to the concept of the nation. As one headman put it: "Our hearts are Nes Perses [sic] hearts and we know them." And, most strikingly, they repeatedly appealed to the idea of a creator god or Great Spirit who had made their lands for them. As one Yakima headman declared: "God ... named our lands for us to take care of." Looking Glass, a Nimiipuu headman, put it slightly differently: "The Great Spirit spoke to his children the law with tracks on the ground strait ..." and thereby marked that ground for his children.[105] And then a Cayuse headman, "Young Chief," told the Americans:

> The Earth says, God has placed me here. The earth says that God tells me to take care of the Indians on this earth.... The earth and water and grass says God has given our names and we are told those names. Neither the Indians nor the whites have a right to change those names.[106]

In these speeches, God or the Great Spirit appears not as a judge or supreme deity above, but as a creative force in and of the land. If the headmen whose speech Spalding recorded in 1837 had described the reception of the new god in terms of the land and its peoples, the headmen who spoke at the treaty council in 1855 had come to view this god as the creative power alive in the landscape. The Great Spirit made tracks on the earth; the earth, the water, and the grass speak back to him. Their statements point to the possibility, suggested by contemporary indigenous theologians, that Plateau headmen had come to apply the name God to the creative power that they understood to exist in all things in the world.[107] This God could be represented as the same as the Christian God when the headmen argued with American officials that both they and the *soyapo* should be subject to his "law" of creation. Yet he was also a figure who had been reinterpreted in terms of Plateau conceptions of the sacred, and as such, he was distinct from, but equal to, the *soyapos'* Christian god.

In the end, the headmen's arguments fell short as a means of defending their lands. In appealing to U.S. officials by using the constructs of nationhood, oratory, and the Great Spirit—constructs used and developed in their relations with the missionaries—Plateau people were ultimately unable to compel them to comprehend, let alone respect, their relationship with their lands. American officials asked them to look not to the God of creation but to the Protestant God of industry and purpose. In urging them to consider relocation, Governor Stevens told them, "I do not think God will be angry if you do your best for yourself and your children. Ask yourself ... Will not God be angry with me if I neglect this opportunity to do them good?"[108] After much debate, Plateau peoples, constituted as nations, accepted treaties ceding portions of their ancestral territories and began the move onto reservations.

The reservation period marked the beginning of a new chapter in the religious history of the Nimiipuu. After the treaty of 1855, and following the incursions of increasing numbers of white miners and settlers, the U.S. government pressed the Nimiipuu to cede a much greater area of their land in the treaty of 1863. This treaty was accepted by Hallalhotsoot and his followers and rejected by Chief Joseph. The result was the division of the Nimiipuu between reservation and off-reservation groups, a division that soon came to be expressed in religious affiliation. Of those who moved onto the reservation, the majority converted to Christianity. This movement began with a revival led by a Yakima Methodist minister, and continued following the return of American missionaries in 1871 (including, for a period, Spalding himself) and, most importantly, the emergence of Native churches led by ordained Nimiipuu ministers. Typically, as Deward Walker has noted, people converted not as individuals but as members of villages or bands. For many, Christianity may have been viewed as offering some protection against further land loss; it was certainly central to the formation of a new Nimiipuu identity within their now colonized country.[109]

For those who rejected reservation life and later fought with Chief Joseph against the U.S. Army in the war of 1877, a nativist movement led by a number of prophets, including Smohalla, offered hopes of a different future. Although there was some variation, the movement centered on people's spiritual connections with a sky-dwelling creator God and a Mother Earth, the rejection of white ways, the return of the dead, and the reestablishment of an Indian world. Followers were urged to sing the songs of the visionaries, perform dances, and practice a strict set of rituals. As such, the movement displayed both continuities with the indigenous past and the incorporation and reinterpretation of elements from Euro-American Christianity.[110] Certainly, as Peter Nabokov has argued, their faith in an "Earth Mother and a sky-dwelling Creator" was a faith in beings "who could hold their own against a non-Indian Almighty God."[111] As a faith that evolved in dialogic opposition to a colonizing American Christianity, it became central to the constitution of a new anti-colonial Nimiipuu identity.

Eastern Australia

In eastern Australia, the dynamics of cross-cultural relations at Threlkeld's mission developed very differently. In the face of mounting racial hostility and in absence of established colonial structures for recognizing or interacting with indigenous peoples, Threlkeld and the Awabakal engaged in a more sustained (albeit unequal) cross-cultural dialogue than ever took place at the A.B.C.F.M missions.

In late 1825, almost a year after their first encounter, Threlkeld established his mission station on the shores of the salt-water lagoon known to the British as "Lake Macquarie" but at a site the Awabakal called "Bah-tah-bah."[112] From an Awabakal perspective he was, in this respect much like other colonists, but as the missionary became increasingly involved in their lives and concerned about settler hostility, it no doubt became apparent that he was a colonist of a different kind. Motivated by his evangelical belief in the fundamental, and therefore redeemable, humanity of Aboriginal people, Threlkeld became the Awabakal's defender, denouncing both the violence of the colonists and the racist prejudices that licensed their attacks.[113] It was perhaps for this reason that, as part of their own effort to resist colonial racism, the Awabakal continued trying to teach the missionary about their world and establish a relationship with him on their own terms, while Threlkeld, holding fewer preconceived ideas about the people he had come to convert, continued to be more inclined to pay attention and more willing to enter into cross-cultural conversation.

One of the first consequences of this very different interplay between colonial structures and the terms of cross-cultural interaction is that in response to Awabakal efforts to instruct him, and in the absence of any conception of indigenous nationhood, Threlkeld, unlike the A.B.C.F.M. missionaries, did come to some understanding of indigenous geography and identity. Threlkeld's principal teacher in this matter was his language "tutor," Biraban, a young man who had acquired a knowledge of English after being captured as a boy.[114] It is clear from Threlkeld's personal writings and from his published grammar that Biraban and other Awabakal wanted him to understand how they related to their country. Threlkeld's report that they were "connected [to other tribes] in a kind of circle extending to the Hawkesbury and Port Stephens" and that their own land was bounded by "the entrance to Lake Maquarie, N by Newcastle & Hunter's River, W by the five Islands on the head of Lake Macquarie 10 miles west of our station," clearly shows that they undertook to explain to him the boundaries of their land and their relations to others.[115] Further, Biraban and other Awabakal evidently told him numerous place names: Threlkeld recorded over 40 in his grammar and made notes on the animals, plants, or minerals to be found at each.[116] And, significantly, Threlkeld clearly tried to comprehend how they conceived of their relationship to place. In his grammar, for example, he recorded the phrase, "*Mulubinbah kah-laan bountoah,*" translating it both as "She belongs to Newcastle" (Mulubinba being the indigenous name for the site), and, in the indigenous idiom, as "Newcastle being has she," a translation that conveys a conception of relation to place not as a matter or residence but as a form of active identification.[117] And finally, Biraban taught the missionary, and Threlkeld recorded, several stories associated with sacred sites. These included the story of *Kur-rur-kur-rán*, the place of petrified wood which was formed when a large rock "fell from this heavens and killed a number of blacks ... they being collected together in that spot by command of an immense Guana;" the story of *Mul-lung-bu-la*, the name of two upright rocks created when "two women ... were transformed into rocks, in consequence of their being beaten to death by a Blackman;" and the story of *Yi-rán-ná-lai* where Biraban had once compelled Threlkeld to be quiet for fear that he would anger the Being who lived there.[118]

The ways in which the Awabakal and Threlkeld understood these sacred stories was, of course, quite different. For Biraban and other Awabakal these stories were parts of their "Law journeys," stories about the journeys of ancestral beings that the scholar Heather Goodall has described as "powerful dramas of ethical and emotional struggles, as well as physical conflicts, between the great protagonists of the creation stories."[119] Although much was clearly lost or distorted in translation, these stories would have conveyed important information about the rules of Awabakal life, relations between people and places, and proper modes of behaving at sacred sites.[120] As I have argued elsewhere, the act of telling the missionary these stories can be read, then, as a powerful assertion of the persistence of an Awabakal sacred geography in the face of colonization.[121] Indeed, without being able to rely on or appropriate any concept of indigenous nationhood, as Plateau people did, it was the only way the Awabakal could assert their relationship

Illustration 9.2. | *This portrait of Biraban was drawn by Alfred Thomas Agate, an artist for the U.S. Exploring Expedition during its visit to Australia in 1839. It was later included in L. E. Threlkeld's book* A Key to the Structure of the Aboriginal Language *(1850) (Public domain).*

to territory. The telling of these stories was also, for the Awabakal, a way of reframing their relationship with the missionary as a relationship in their space, a space in which they controlled the terms of their interaction. For Threlkeld, on the other hand, these stories were both evidence of Awabakal heathenism—he dismissively characterized their beings as "imaginary"[122]—and, at the same time, information that was nevertheless worthy of being recorded. Indeed, it should be noted that Threlkeld was one of the first Europeans to record indigenous "Law" or, as they are more commonly known, "Dreaming" stories. In contrast to the A.B.C.F.M. missionaries who relied on the colonial conceptions of indigenous nationhood, Threlkeld, through Biraban and others, acquired a knowledge, albeit limited, of an indigenous geography that was altogether distinct from the colonial geography of the country.

A similar dynamic can be observed in Threlkeld and the Awabakal's cross-cultural conversation about the nature of sacred beings. When Biraban took it upon himself to instruct the missionary about the beings who governed Awabakal life, Threlkeld evidently listened. Although the missionary did, to be sure, hold to the evangelical—and colonial—view that the "heathen" Aborigines lived in a state of "darkness, error, superstition, and misery," this did not prevent him from paying attention to the particular nature of their "superstitions."[123] Indeed, unlike the A.B.C.F.M. missionaries, Threlkeld held to an Enlightenment view of non-Christian religions as the fabrications of ignorance rather than as the inventions of the devil and, in the absence of preconceived notions about indigenous religion as either a belief in a "Great Spirit" or as devil-worship, he was more inclined to approach Awabakal spiritual practice with detached curiosity. He therefore took care to record Awabakal descriptions of their sacred "Beings," making notes for instance on Biraban's account of *Koun*, the sacred law-giver of initiated men, who appeared as a man, flew like a bird, visited men in their dreams, and threatened to carry them away. He also described Koun's frightening wife, the variously named *Tip-pa-kal-lé-un*, *Mail-kun*, or *Bim-póin*, who carried off "the natives in a large bag beneath the earth" and speared children dead. And, when Biraban invited Threlkeld to a preliminary ceremony held prior to the sacred and restricted ceremony of male initiation, he accepted, taking the opportunity to record some of the rituals associated with the event.[124]

Threlkeld's willingness to learn about Awabakal spirits and ceremonial practices did not, of course, indicate a willingness to accept them: Their sacred order was precisely that which he sought to displace. But his efforts to turn the Awabakal away from "heathenism" and communicate the "truths" of Christianity were complicated by his approach to translation. While the A.B.C.F.M. missionaries, out of hostility to Plateau beliefs and practices, rejected Nimiipuu vocabulary and substituted their own or, alternately, focused on a few terms (e.g., heart) in accordance with their preconceived ideas of indigenous religiosity, Threlkeld seems to have been more inclined to use Awabakal vocabulary and was also more aware of the cross-cultural shifts of interpretation that such an approach entailed. Whereas Smith, for example, used "Holy Ghostki," Threlkeld borrowed *"yirriyirri"* to convey "holy" and *"marai"* to convey "spirit," making *"marai yirriyirri"* even though he evidently realized that these words conveyed quite specific Awabakal meanings. As he learned from Biraban, *"yirriyirri"* did not express a general conception of holiness but referred, rather, to the exclusive sacredness of initiated men's spiritual domain; and *marai* was not the same as the English "spirit" but referred to the "spirit, soul of a living being" as opposed to *mamuya* which was the "spirit of a dead person."[125] (Threlkeld did, however, use the Hebrew word Eloi, or Jehovah, to name his god after determining that the Awabakal had no equivalent term in their language to name a supreme being—Koun, one of their most highly regarded beings, being decidedly not god-like.[126]) Similarly, Threlkeld's efforts to find a term to convey the crucial Christian concept of belief drew him into an exploration of the very different world of Awabakal epistemology. From his discussions with Biraban, the missionary came to understand that the Awabakal did not distinguish knowledge from belief but differentiated ways of knowing according to the bodily sense involved and, in some cases, whether the object known was a person or a thing. Threlkeld recorded that "to know a person by sight is *gi-mil-liko*," but "to know a thing by sight, '*na-killiko;*'" "to know by touch was *nu-mulliko,*" while *"ngurrulliko"* was "to know, to perceive by the ear, to understand," or "to hear, to obey."[127] Of these, Threlkeld selected *ngurrulliko* to translate as both "to know" and "to believe," on the basis, perhaps, that belief followed not from seeing but from hearing God's Word. And lastly, it would appear that when it came to finding terms to convey the more personal aspects of a relationship with a Christian god, Threlkeld ventured with Biraban into a discussion of Awabakal emotional vocabulary. In the absence of any emphasis on indigenous hearts—a term that is strikingly absent in Threlkeld's writings—the missionary recorded such remarkable expressions as: *"yi-mul-liliko*—to make light, as fur is caused to lie lightly before the blacks twist it into a cord, ... to encourage, to cheer up," and *"bur-kul-li-ko*—to be light as a bird, to fly, to be convalescent."[128] Translating the Christian message into these terms, rather than relying on substituted words or preconceived notions such as "Great Spirit" or "heart" must necessarily have entailed recognizing, to some degree, that translation was an unstable and unpredictable exercise. Threlkeld's writings, unlike those of the A.B.C.F.M. missionaries, show an awareness that the process of translating Christianity involved grappling with the complexities of cultural difference.[129]

This awareness of cultural difference also characterizes Threlkeld's approach to the work of communicating Christianity. Unlike the A.B.C.F.M. missionaries, he did not attempt to "play Aborigine": no such construct existed in Australian settler colonial culture. Nor did the Awabakal, as the Nimiipuu had done, seek to position the missionary as a speaker in accordance with their own communicative customs; there simply was no usable point of convergence between the missionary's interest in preaching and Awabakal forms of communication. Threlkeld was clearly not an indigenous composer of songs, nor was he an indigenous messenger or *puntimai*.[130] It is significant, though, that Threlkeld did make note of their communicative practices and even expressed the hope, at one point, that "the same custom which promulgates the new Song will convey throughout Australia, 'The glad tidings of a Saviour Christ the Lord'."[131] However, for his own purposes, Threlkeld followed the practice of simply reading and preaching from translated Scripture. This suited his image of himself as a man of the Word but he remained mindful that it was a foreign practice to the Awabakal. Threlkeld recorded the words the Awabakal invented to describe both his particular kind of "book-speak" and his strange practice of writing. Their word for book, *wiyalikane*, was derived, he noted, from "*wiyelli*," to speak; and from the word, "*upali*, to perform," he observed that the Awabakal developed "*upaiye*" (writer), "*upalikane*" (pen), and "*upaliyeil*" (desk.)[132] Threlkeld also noted: "*upilli ngél kolai ta birung*," or "a wooden table, or acting place of wood,"[133] a peculiar phrase that suggests that the Awabakal regarded the missionary's desk not as a passive object, but as a site of communicative action.

For all of Threlkeld's apparent awareness of Awabakal cultural difference, indigenous responses to his evangelizing efforts were predominantly negative. In part, this rejection may have been a consequence of the stark differences between Christian and Awabakal conceptions of human relations to the sacred. The missionary's representation of his Jehovah as a judging deity above who required worship, obedience, and love and offered salvation to all who believed, may well have had little appeal to the Awabakal whose connections to the sacred were tied to their country and determined by their individual relationships to particular Ancestral Beings. Further, unlike the Nimiipuu, the Awabakal had no tradition of acquiring new powers from other spirit beings.[134] But the Awabakal's experience of colonization was probably an even more important factor in their decision to reject the missionary's message. In contrast to the Nimiipuu, the Awabakal had no history of mutually profitable relations with Europeans. Rather, through the late 1820s and through the 1830s, they suffered a series of devastating losses at the hands of the British: They lost more land to settlers; imported livestock drove away their game and destroyed their gathering grounds; diseases wreaked their toll on the population; and as they were compelled into relations of dependence on the colonizers, assaults on Awabakal women increased.[135] In this context, it is not surprising that the majority of the Awabakal rejected the missionary's god. Threlkeld's insistence that it was his god who had created all things was met with doubt. At one meeting he reported that a woman interrogated him, asking "if Jehovah created the Moon as well as the Sun?"[136] On another occasion, a boy told him "he thought it was all gammon [lies] that master had told him about the Creation, for who was there who saw God create man!"[137] Given the colonial implications of Threlkeld's assertion that it was his god, not their ancestral beings, who had created their country and its peoples, such responses are not surprising. Others argued that one of their own beings was more powerful than the Christian god. One man told Threlkeld, "The Blacks had a much more powerful Being than the Whites had, who ... would if he were executed, put out the eyes of all the Whites, and smite them with total blindness!"[138] Such an assertion suggests the attribution of new powers to an indigenous Being that mirrored the great powers that the colonizers attributed to their own deity. It also most surely reflected a desire to return upon the colonists the devastation they had inflicted upon Aboriginal people.

However, if most Awabakal turned against the missionary's god, this was not the only response. Although Threlkeld never considered any Awabakal as candidates for conversion some appear to have developed their own understanding of the missionary's deity. One of the most interesting interpretations of the Christian being came from Biraban, Threlkeld's language teacher. In 1836, Biraban told the missionary that he had had a remarkable dream. As related by Threlkeld, in the dream, Biraban and his "party" of men were in the "Heavens" when "Jehovah," he "about whom the whites speak," appeared wearing "clothing of fire, red like a flame." Jehovah then went past the men, without speaking to them, "flying like fire with a great shining." After this, Biraban told his men, "[L]et us go down, lest he take us away." They descended to a mountain and awoke when they reached the ground. Biraban told the missionary, "We often dream of this mountain, many blacks fancy themselves on the top when asleep."[139]

This dream narrative is significant on a number of counts. For the Awabakal, dreams were the realm of encounters with the supernatural. It was in dreams that Awabakal spiritual leaders, *karakul*, traveled into the sky and obtained their special powers from Koun. Dreams also enabled cultural innovation: ancestral beings revealed new songs to spiritual leaders in dreams.[140] For Biraban, then, to dream of an encounter with a supernatural being, including, and perhaps especially, a being "about whom the whites speak," was to demonstrate spiritual leadership and introduce new sacred knowledge in a recognized and legitimate manner. It is notable, in this regard that Threlkeld's own records show that Biraban had begun acting as a messenger, telling other bands about the missionary's sacred being.[141] His authority to speak, however, was grounded not in the missionary's book, but in his dream, in an indigenous form of experiencing the sacred. It is also clear that Biraban's Jehovah was very different from the missionary's god. In the dream, Jehovah appears not as the Christian god of judgment and salvation; rather he bears a strong resemblance to Koun, the powerful law-giver of initiated men. Like Koun, Biraban's Jehovah is a male being who visits Awabakal men in their sleep, flies in the sky, is associated with fire (Koun carried a firestick), and threatens to carry men away. Notably, Biraban's reference to the mountain also firmly situated the encounter within an Awabakal sacred geography. There is much to indicate, then, that Biraban remade the Christian deity as an indigenous sacred being, incorporated him into an Awabakal cosmological and geographical order, and portrayed him as a special *yirriyirri* figure for Awabakal men while claiming for himself the role of Jehovah's interpreter. In doing so, it would appear that he was asserting a relationship with the god of the colonizing culture, but on his own terms and in the context of the Awabakals' relationship to their country.[142]

End of the Mission and Aftermath

Threlkeld's mission to the Awabakal was closed in December 1841 after the colonial government withdrew its support. Disease and dispossession had devastated the Awabakal: In 1840, Threlkeld counted only sixteen in his annual return.[143] Biraban himself became a victim of alcoholism and died a few years afterwards. Unlike the Nimiipuu, the Awabakal were never given the opportunity to defend their lands and lives through treaty negotiations and Biraban was never in a position to use his relationship with "Jehovah" to argue for his people's rights to their country.[144]

Threlkeld, however, continued to write about the Awabakal, producing a series of *Reminiscences* and a study of their language, *Key to the Structure of the Aboriginal Language,* in 1850. Both texts reveal a striking portrait of the complexity of Awabakal cultural life, a portrait dramatically at odds with the prevailing colonial view of Aboriginal people as lacking culture altogether. These texts show that in the face of racism and in the absence of usable colonial stereotypes, Biraban and other Awabakal were able to push Threlkeld to an awareness, albeit limited, of the existence of their conceptions of space, identity, speech, and the sacred life. Yet, without the structures of formal recognition, neither they nor Threlkeld were able to use this awareness to empower Aboriginal people in Australian settler society.

CONCLUSION

The histories of the A.B.C.F.M. mission to the Nimiipuu and the L.M.S. mission to the Awabakal can of course be studied as unique cases. However, as I have tried to show here, by situating these histories alongside each other, and examining them comparatively, one can gain a better understanding of each. The differences revealed by comparative study illuminate the ways in which colonial concepts and structures informed cross-cultural interaction at each mission site. In Northwestern America, the A.B.C.F.M. missionaries aligned their evangelical project with American expansionism and made full use of colonial constructions of indigenous identity, space, speech, and the sacred. The Nimiipuu, for their part, were able to use colonial conceptions of indigenous identity and, where possible, exploit apparent convergences between their cultural practices and missionary conceptions for their own purposes. These constructions facilitated interaction but, at the same time, masked significant cross-cultural differences and profoundly limited missionary understanding of the peoples they sought to convert. In eastern Australia, by contrast, missionary and indigenous relations to the larger colonizing society produced a very different cross-cultural dynamic. Here, the British refusal to recognize Aboriginal people as political entities, and the emergence of a powerful and persistent racism, meant that there were no usable colonial constructs of indigenous identity, space, speech, or conceptions of the sacred for either Threlkeld or the Awabakal. However, the absence of such constructs—and the absence too of any useful points of convergence between European and indigenous cultural categories or practices—ironically created a situation in which Threlkeld and the Awabakal were able to engage in a more open cross-cultural dialogue than was ever the case in northwestern America. In both cross-cultural encounters the terms of colonialism mattered, by which I mean not only the particular colonial policies or developments that structured relations between Europeans and indigenous peoples, but the colonial vocabularies through which, or against which, missionaries and indigenous peoples imagined and spoke to each other.

From another direction, this comparative study also points to some interesting parallels between Awabakal and Nimiipuu responses to evangelization in the context of their experiences of colonization. In a broad sense, both the Awabakal and the Nimiipuu were peoples with highly developed oral cultures whose spiritual lives were based on deep relationships with their lands and their lands' non-human creatures. Further, both Nimiipuu and Awabakal peoples were accustomed to the exchange of sacred stories or songs with peoples from other places, with the understanding that other stories belonged to other places. In their encounters with missionaries, both peoples were interested in stories about the Christian god; in the case of the Nimiipuu this interest was linked to their desire to access the *soyapo* god's powers; in the case of the Awabakal it appears to have been an interest in acquiring knowledge and establishing a connection with the colonizers on indigenous terms. Indigenous leaders, both Nimiipuu headmen and Biraban, also used the telling of Christian stories to enhance their authority as sources of the new knowledge. And lastly, in both cases, it appears that indigenous leaders reinterpreted the Christian god, and their people's relationship to him, in terms of their spiritual relationship to their own lands. The Nimiipuu headmen redefined the Christian god as the Creator, a manifestation of creative spiritual power in the land; Biraban, on the other hand, recast this god, Jehovah, as an indigenous being in an Awabakal sacred landscape. For peoples whose spiritual lives were so closely tied to their lands, such reinterpretations of the Christian deity made sense, but they also worked differently in the face of colonization. For Plateau people, the creator god, albeit redefined in indigenous terms, could still be spoken of as being one and the same as the Christian god and could therefore be called upon in appeals to Euro-Americans to respect Plateau peoples' relations to their lands. The Plateau concept of god worked as an apparently shared construct in cross-cultural interaction, but it masked deep differences. Biraban's reinterpretation of Jehovah, on the other hand, may have been his way of attempting to make a connection with the colonizers' culture on his own terms, but his Jehovah was distinctly different from the Christian god. The reinterpreted Jehovah of the Awabakal could never have served as a common construct with which to mount a defence of Awabakal claims to their land, but nor, in colonial Australia, were the Awabakal ever given an opportunity to present such a defense.

Notes

1. In this chapter, I use Nimiipuu and Salish to identify these groups, as these are the names currently used by these peoples to refer to themselves. Nimiipuu and Salish are now the names of both languages and peoples. As will

be discussed, these names would not have been the primary sources of identity for these peoples in the nineteenth century. J. Diane Pearson makes the point that "'Nez Perce' is an assigned name that was used by non-Natives, treaty-makers and federal authorities." *The Nez Perces in the Indian Territory: Numiipuu Survival* (Norman, OK, 2008), 6. However, it should also be noted, as the title of her work makes clear, that Nez Perce has become the official identification of the tribe and is important to the U.S recognition of tribal sovereignty.

2. Samuel Parker, *Journal of an Exploring Tour Beyond the Rocky Mountains* (New York, 1838), 81–82, 100.

3. Lancelot Threlkeld, Public Journal, 13 March 1825, in *Australian Reminiscences and Papers of L. E. Threlkeld, Missionary to the Aborigines, 1824–1859*, 2 vols., ed. Niel Gunson (Canberra, A.C.T., 1974), I: 86.

4. Ibid., 88.

5. Ibid.

6. In the early years Euro-American recognition was informal, limited to naming indigenous groups and mapping their territories. Official political recognition of indigenous groups as peoples with claims to particular lands came with the formalization of treaty relations, beginning in 1855.

7. For a general account of the early history of "Oregon Territory," see Carlos A. Schwantes, *The Pacific Northwest: An Interpretive History* (Lincoln, NB, 1996), Part I; Richard Somerset Mackie, *Trading Beyond the Mountains: The British Fur Trade on the Pacific, 1793–1843* (Vancouver, 1997).

8. On the doctrine of *terra nullius* and its consequences for Aboriginal peoples, see Alan Frost, "New South Wales as *Terra Nullius*: the British Denial of Aboriginal Land Rights," *Historical Studies* 19, no. 77 (1981): 513–23; Henry Reynolds, *The Law of the Land* (Ringwood, Australia, 1988), 7–9, 12–18, 51–54.

9. For an account of the colonization of eastern Australia during this period, see T. M. Perry, *Australia's First Frontier: The Spread of Settlement in New South Wales, 1788–1829* (Melbourne, 1963); see also Barry Morris, *Domesticating Resistance: The Dhan-Ghadi Aborigines and the Australian State* (Oxford, 1989). On the colonization of the region where Threlkeld established his mission, see Keith Clouten, *Reid's Mistake: The Story of Lake Macquarie from Its Discovery until 1890* (Lake Macquarie Shire Council, 1967).

10. The relationship between missionary activity and empire has been discussed from a variety of scholarly perspectives. For studies that focus on the imperial connections between missions and colonial expansion, see: Brian Stanley, *The Bible and the Flag: Protestant Missions and British Imperialism in the Nineteenth and Twentieth Centuries* (Leicester, UK, 1990); Andrew Porter, *Religion Versus Empire?: British Protestant Missionaries and Overseas Expansion, 1700–1914* (Manchester, UK, 2004); and, on the American side, William R. Hutchison, *Errand to the World: American Protestant Thought and Foreign Missions* (Chicago, 1987). For studies that consider the complex relationship between missions and cultural colonialism, see Jean and John Comaroff, *Of Revelation and Revolution*, 2 vols. (Chicago, 1991 and 1997); Elizabeth Elbourne, *Blood Ground: Colonialism, Missions, and the Contest for Christianity in the Cape Colony and Britain, 1799–1853* (Montreal, 2002); Vicente Rafael, *Contracting Colonialism: Translation and Spanish Conversion in Tagalog Society under Early Spanish Rule* (Durham, NC, 1993);

Susan Neylan, *The Heavens Are Changing: Nineteenth-Century Protestant Missions and Tsimshian Christianity* (Montreal, 2002); Nicholas Thomas, "Colonial Conversions: Differences, Hierarchy, and History in Early Twentieth-Century Evangelical Propaganda," *Comparative Studies in Society and History* 34, no. 2 (April 1992): 366–89; David J. Silverman, *Faith and Boundaries: Colonists, Christianity, and Community among the Wampanoag Indians of Martha's Vineyard, 1600–1871* (New York, 2005). See also the informative essays in Norman Etherington, ed., *Missions and Empire* (Oxford, 2005).

11. My interest in the politics of cross-cultural communication has been influenced by the works of linguistic anthropologists and socio-linguists, in particular: Erving Goffman, *Frame Analysis: An Essay on the Organization of Experience* (New York, 1974) and *Forms of Talk* (Philadelphia, 1981); William Hanks, *Language and Communicative Practices* (Boulder, CO, 1995); Dell Hymes, "Towards Ethnographics of Communication: the Analysis of Communicative Events," in *Language and Social Context*, ed. P. P. Gigioli, 21–44 (Harmondsworth, 1972); and *Ethnography, Linguistics, Narrative Inequality: Toward an Understanding of Voice* (London, 1996); and Alessandro Duranti, *From Grammar to Politics: Linguistic Anthropology in a Western Samoan Village* (Berkeley, CA, 1994).

Scholars who examine the work of translation at mission sites tend to focus on the construction of missionary linguistic texts, or on the indigenous translation of Christianity, rather than on the dynamics of cross-cultural communication in particular. Nevertheless, a number of such studies offer important insights into the nature of linguistic and cultural exchange between missionaries and indigenous people. See Johannes Fabian, *Language and Colonial Power: The Appropriation of Swahili in the Former Belgian Congo, 1880–1938* (Cambridge, 1986), ch. 1; Louise Burkhart, *The Slippery Earth: Nahua–Christian Moral Dialogue in Sixteenth Century Mexico* (Tucson, AZ, 1989); Rafael, *Contracting Colonialism;* Paul Stuart Landau, *The Realm of the Word: Language, Gender, and Christianity in a Southern African Kingdom* (Portsmouth, NH, 1995); John Lonsdale, "Kikuyu Christianities: A History of Intimate Diversity," in *Christianity and the African Imagination: Essays in Honour of Adrian Hastings,* ed. David Maxwell and Ingrid Lawrie (Leiden, 2002), 157–98; Isabel Hofmeyr, "Jonah and the Swallowing Monster: Orality and Literacy on a Berlin Mission Station in the Transvaal," *Journal of Southern African Studies* 17 (1991): 633–53, and *The Portable Bunyan: A Transnational History of The Pilgrim's Progress* (Princeton, NJ, 2004); Derek Peterson, "Translating the Word: Dialogism and Debate in Two Gikuyu Dictionaries," *Journal of Religious History* 23, no. 1, (1999): 31–50; Laura J. Murray, "Joining Signs with Words: Missionaries, Metaphors, and the Massachusett Language," *The New England Quarterly* 74 (2001): 62–93; Helen Bethea Gardner, "'New Heaven and New Earth': Translation and Conversion on Aneityum," *The Journal of Pacific History* 41 (2006): 293–311; and Rachel Gilmour, *Grammars of Colonialism: Representing Languages in Colonial South Africa* (New York, 2006.)

12. "British Identities, Indigenous Peoples and Empire," introduction to *Empire and Others: British Encounters with Indigenous Peoples, 1600–1850* (Philadelphia, 1999), 8. For a thoughtful discussion of comparative history, see Ann Laura Stoler, "Tense and Tender Ties: The Politics of Comparison in North American History and (Post) Colonial Studies," *The Journal of American His-*

tory 88 (2001): 829–65. On the advantages of adopting a comparative approach to the study of missions and Christianization in particular, see Peggy Brock, ed., Introduction to *Indigenous Peoples and Religious Change* (Leiden, 2005), 6. Other studies that use comparison to illuminate the history of missionary/indigenous relations include: Peggy Brock, "Mission Encounters in the Colonial World: British Columbia and South-West Australia," *Journal of Religious History* 24 (2000): 67–96, and "Two Indigenous Evangelists: Moses Tjalkabota and Arthur Wellington Clah," *Journal of Religious History* 27 (2003): 348–66; Thor Wagstrom, "Broken Tongues and Foreign Hearts: The Religious Frontier in Early Nineteenth-Century South Africa and New Zealand," in *Indigenous Peoples*, ed. Brock, 51–78; Gilmour, *Grammars of Colonialism*; Etherington, ed., *Missions and Empire*.

13. See Parker, *Journal of an Exploring Tour*, 83.

14. David Murray, *Forked Tongues: Speech, Writing and Representation in North American Indian Texts* (Bloomington, IN, 1991), 6.

15. It is worth noting that Whitman wrote the name as *"Napiersas"* in his report of the encounter, an indication that the spelling and pronunciation of the name among Euro-Americans was still in flux in the 1830s. See Marcus Whitman, "Journal and Report by Dr. Marcus Whitman of his Tour of Exploration with Rev. Samuel Parker in 1835 Beyond the Rocky Mountains," ed. F. C. Young, *Oregon Historical Quarterly* 28 (1927): 248.

16. "Jefferson's Instructions to Lewis," in Meriwether Lewis and William Clark, *The Original Journals of the Lewis and Clark Expedition*, ed. Reuben G. Thwaites, 8 vols. (New York, 1959), 7: 248.

The precise origin of the terms Nez Perce and Flathead is unknown. When Clark met with the Nimiipuu he observed: "Their diolect [sic] appears verry different from the flat heads ...," adding, "They call themselves *Cho pun-nish* or *Pierced noses.*" Clark, *Original Journals*, 3: 78. It is possible that "Chopunnish" was a variant on Sahaptin, the name now used for the language family to which Nez Perce or Nimiipuutímt belongs. Nez Perce soon became the more commonly used name. As the fur trader Ross Cox wrote, "The natives of this district are called the Pierced-nose Indians; but as French is the language in general use among traders in this country, owing to most part of their working men being Canadians, we commonly called them *Les Nez Perces.*" *The Columbia River: or Scenes and Adventures During a Residence of Six Years on the Western Side of the Rocky Mountains among Various Tribes of Indians Hitherto Unknown, Together with "A Journey across the American Continent,"* ed. Edgar I. Stewart and Jane R. Stewart (Norman, OK, 1957), 87. However, very few of the Nimiipuu practiced nose-piercing, and the custom, if practiced at all, seems to have died out by the 1830s. One possibility, suggested by Haruo Aoki, is that "Chopunnish" derived from *"tsoopnit,"* the act of punching a hole with a pointed object, and by extension, *tsoopnitpeloo* meaning "piercing people." See Haruo Aoki, "What does 'Chopunnish' Mean?" *Idaho Yesterdays* 10 (Winter, 1966–67): 10–11.

The term Flathead is also somewhat of a misnomer. Few of the Salish speaking people who came to be called Flathead actually practiced head flattening as did the Chinook or the coastal Salish. The fact that Lewis and Clark used the term suggests that they may have heard the name before meeting Salish speakers and it is possible that the sign-language term for the Salish used by the Hidatsa-Mandans suggested head-flattening. Alvin Josephy suggests that the Plains tribes told French and British traders that the country west of the mountains was inhabited by people who flattened their heads and that this was the origin of the term. See Alvin Josephy, *The Nez Perce Indians and the Opening of the Northwest* (Boston, 1997), 647; and John Fahey, *The Flathead Indians* (Norman, OK, 1974), 5.

17. As Ned Blackhawk has argued, the processes of naming and mapping were a means of inscribing colonial power: "By producing the knowledge from which conquest could flow, those who extended American claims in the region became agent for the most violent forms of imperialism." *Violence Over the Land: Indians and Empires in the Early American West* (Cambridge, MA, 2006), 148.

18. For a discussion of the origin and colonial uses of the generalization "Indian," see Robert F. Berkhofer, *The White Man's Indian: Images of the American Indian from Columbus to the Present* (New York, [1978] 1979).

19. Parker, *Journal of an Exploring Tour*, 220–222.

20. Though the evolution of this vocabulary is yet to be studied, its emergence is apparent from a reading of any popular collection of Indian speeches. See, for example, *I Have Spoken: American History Through the Voices of the Indians,* ed. Virginia Irving Amstrong (Chicago, 1971). On the history and uses of "Indian oratory," see David Murray, *Forked Tongues,* 39–48; and William M. Clements, *Oratory in Native North America* (Tucson, AZ, 2002). See also Elise Marienstras, "The Common Man's Indian: The Image of the Indian as a Promoter of National Identity in the Early National Era," in *Native Americans and the Early Republic,* eds. Frederick Hoxie, Ronald Hoffman, and Peter J. Albert (Charlottesville, VA, 1996), 261–96.

21. Indians speaking from the heart became common figures in American evangelical literature. In December 1827, for instance, the Reverend John Allan presented a typical speech from a Choctaw chief to readers of the *Missionary Herald:* "Take away from us our bad hearts and give us new hearts. Our bad hearts hurt us.... we hear your word ..." (December 1827), 381.

22. Documentary evidence suggests that the expression "Great Spirit" originated in seventeenth-century cross-cultural conversations between French Jesuits and Native people in the northeast, first in Jesuit translations of indigenous references to the European god, and then as a term used to refer to powerful creator spirits in their own traditions. In 1611, Samuel de Champlain noted that the Huron people, the "Attigouantan," called one of their spirits, "Oqui" or, he wrote, "as we should say, a great spirit." *The Works of Samuel de Champlain,* trans. H. H. Langton, 6 vols. (Toronto, 1932), 4: 320. The original French reads: "*ils l'appellent Oqui, comme si nous disions un grand esprit....*" In 1638, Father François Joseph le Mercier related that a Huron headman was complaining about the Jesuits' constant talk of "their Oki, — that is, the great Spirit they worship." "Relation de ce qui s'est passé an la Nouvelle France, en l'année 1638," in *The Jesuit Relations and Allied Documents: Travels and Explorations of the Jesuit Missionaries in New France, 1610–1791,* ed. Reuben Gold Thwaites, 73 vols. (Cleveland, 1898), XV: 51. Thirty years later, an Algonquin convert told another Jesuit, Father Aloez, that he became a Christian because all his life "he had

acknowledged a great Spirit who included himself in Heaven and Earth; that he had always invoked him in his sacrifices." Le Mercier, "Relation," LII: 99. It was subsequently adopted by the Iroquois, in the eighteenth century, who used the phrase in diplomatic negotiations with European powers, and it was also used by the prophets Neolin and Tenskwatawa in their pan-Indian spiritual resistance movements of the late eighteenth and early nineteenth centuries.

23· The following evangelical account of Choctaw beliefs from 1822 is typical. According to the writer, the Choctaws believed that there is a "Great Spirit, who made the earth, and placed them on it, and who preserves them in their hunting journeys, and gives them their 'luck in life'; ... that all who die, go to the Spirit country; but that some suppose it is divided into two nations; the one abounding in fine woods, and deer, and buffaloes; the other destitute of both — ... that when the spirit of bad men leaves the body, ... it takes the way to the bad country ... — that many expect a day when the world will be burnt and made over again ... when the spirits will return." *Missionary Herald* (May 1822), 153. Such a conception of "Indian" religion also has links with a longer-standing American idea that the Indians came from the Lost Ten Tribes of Israel and that their religion should therefore contain vestiges of the true faith. See Bernard Sheehan, *Savagism and Civility: Indians and Englishmen in Colonial Virginia* (Cambridge, 1980), 50–55.

24. Parker, *Journal of an Exploring Tour*, 239–40.

25. Whitman, "Journal and Report," 248; Whitman to Greene, 7 November 1835, in *Marcus Whitman, Crusader, Part One*, eds. Archer Butler Hulbert and Dorothy Printup Hulbert, vols. 3–6 of *Overland to the Pacific* (Stewart Commission of Colorado College and the Denver Public Library, 1936), 6: 169.

26. Philip J. Deloria, *Playing Indian* (New Haven, CT, 1998), 92.

27. For a description of the indigenous Plateau as a linguistic and cultural region, see Deward E. Walker Jr.. Introduction to *Handbook of North American Indians. Plateau*, ed. Deward E. Walker and W. C. Sturtevant, 17 vols. (Washington, DC, 1998), 12: 1; and Elizabeth Vibert, *Trader's Tales: Narratives of Cultural Encounter in the Columbia Plateau, 1807–1846* (Norman, OK, 1997), 23–28.

28. On village names and village autonomy see Eugene Hunn, *Nch'i-Wána: "The Big River:" Mid-Columbia Indians and Their Land* (Seattle, 1990), 58; and Alvin Josephy, *Nez Perce Country*, (Lincoln, NB, 2007), 6–9. For an account of relations among village, band, and tribe, see Verne Ray, *Cultural Relations in the Plateau of Northwestern America* (Los Angeles, 1939), 4–17. On kin and trade networks, see Josephy, *The Nez Perce Indians*, 16–20; Fahey, *The Flathead Indians*, 12–20; and Theodore Stern, *Chiefs and Chief Traders: Indian Relations at Fort Nez Percés, 1818–1855* (Corvallis, OR, 1993). On the (limited) development of more centralized forms of governance following the acquisition of the horse, see Verne Ray, "Native Villages and Groupings of the Columbia Basin," *Pacific Northwest Quarterly*, 27, no. 2 (April, 1936), 113–14; and Christopher Miller, *Prophetic Worlds: Indians and Whites on the Columbia Plateau* (New Brunswick, NJ, 1985), 38–39. Miller probably overstates the extent to which villages lost their political autonomy.

29. On Plateau peoples' spiritual connections to their country, see Rodney Frey, ed., *Stories that Make the World: Oral Literatures of the Indians Peoples of the*

Inland Northwest as Told by Lawrence Aripa, Tom Yellowtail, and Other Elders (Norman, OK, 1995); Jarold Ramsey, ed., *Coyote Was Going There: Indian Literature of the Oregon Country* (Seattle, 1980); Deward E. Walker and Daniel N. Matthews, *Nez Perce Coyote Tales: The Myth Cycle* (Norman, OK, 1998); and Peter Nabokov, *Where Lightning Strikes: The Lives of American Indian Sacred Places* (New York, 2006), ch. 9.

30. On the history of relations between traders and the Numipu at Fort Nez Perces, see Stern, *Chiefs and Chief Traders*.

31. Competitiveness seems to have characterized many Plateau societies. Certainly competition for status was common among the Nimiipuu. Deward Walker writes that Nimiipuu life was characterized by "a general rivalry for limited rewards in the forms of prestige, ecoomic wealth, and religious power." "Nez Perce," in Walker and Sturtevant, eds., *Handbook of North American Indians. Plateau*, 12: 426–27.

32. Alexander Ross, *Fur Hunters of the Far West*, ed. Milo Milton Quaife (Chicago, [1855] 1924), 175.

33. On the origin and development of the Chinook trade jargon, see Chester Fee, "Oregon's Historical Esperanto—the Chinook Jargon," *Oregon Historical Quarterly* 41 (1941): 176–85; S. G. Thomason, "Chinook Jargon in A Real and Historical Context," *Language* 59 (1983): 820–70; and J. V. Powell, "Chinook Jargon Vocabulary and the Lexicographers," *International Journal of American Linguistics* 56 (1990): 134–51.

34. The philologist Horatio Hale recorded all these terms, with the exception of *soyapo*, in the first scholarly account of the trade jargon. See *Ethnology and Philology*, United States Exploring Expedition, 1838–42, (Philadelphia, 1846), 6: 640.

35. Samuel Black, the chief trader at the Nez Perce Fort from 1825 to 1830, documented "*Shouiwapo*" as meaning "Americans." "Vocabulary" in "Report by Chief Trader Samuel Black to the Governor and Committee of the Hudson's Bay Company, 1829" (HBC Archives, B146/e/2). Subsequently, *Shouiwapo*, or *soyapo* came to be used more generally by Sahaptian and Salishan language speakers to refer to "white people." See Powell, "Chinook Jargon Vocabulary and the Lexicographers," 136. The linguist Haruo Aoki suggests that the term signified "hat wearers," see his *Nez Perce Dictionary* (Berkeley, 1994), 658. Another possibility, suggested by Alvin Josephy, is that soyapo was a Salish word for "long-knives," the term used by eastern tribes to designate the Americans. He suggests that the Nimiipuu acquired this term when a woman from one of their villages was taken captive, sold east, and later returned. See Josephy, *Nez Perce Indians*, 34.

36. Parker, *Journal of an Expedition*, 388.

37. On Plateau speech practices, see Frey, *Stories that Make the World*, 20–23.

38. On the role of the crier in Plateau cultures, see Hunn, *Nch'i-Wána*, 84; and Josephy, *Nez Perce Country*, 9.

39. On the HBC's decision to offer Christian instruction, see Theodore Stern, *Chiefs and Change in the Oregon Country: Indian Relations at Fort Nez Perces, 1818–1855* (Corvallis, OR, 1996), II: ch. 1. On the development of the "devotional dance" and indigenous prophetic traditions, see Deward E. Walker, *Conflict and*

Schism in Nez Perce Acculturation: A Study of Religion and Politics (Pullman, WA, 1968), ch. 3; Christopher Miller, *Prophetic Worlds*, ch. 3; and Larry Cebula, *Plateau Indians and the Quest for Spiritual Power* (Lincoln, NB, 2003), ch. 4. On the St. Louis delegation, see Josephy, *Nez Perce Indians*, 77–95. It was reports of the delegation that had, in fact, inspired Parker and Whitman's own expedition. Stories of the delegation also prompted the Methodist Missionary Society to establish a mission on the Plateau in 1834. Albert Furtwangler provides a interpretative account of the delegation and the evangelical response to it in *Bringing the Indians to the Book* (Seattle, 2005), ch. 1.

40. On the central role of *wéyekin* in Plateau cultures, see Walker, *Conflict and Schism*, 18–24; Josephy, *Nez Perce Country*, 23–24; and Nabokov, *Where Lightning Strikes*, 155. On Plateau people's interest in acquiring the spiritual powers of the white man's god, see Walker, *Conflict and Schism*, 32–35; and Walker, "New Light on the Prophet Dance Controversy," *Ethnohistory* 16 (1969): 245–55.

41. According to Deward Walker, tutelary spirits have been recorded not only for animals and insects but the "sun, moon, stars, clouds, trees, mountains and rivers." See "Nez Perce," in *Handbook of North American Indians*, 12: 427.

42. Hale, *Ethnography and Philology*, 647.

43. Aoki, *Nez Perce Dictionary*, 975.

44. Walker makes this point in *Conflict and Schism*, 38.

45. Aoki, *Nez Perce Dictionary*, 74, 747.

46. In the early period of contact, a few British officers made some effort to ascertain the names of different bands around Sydney. However, by the second decade of the nineteenth century, the British had adopted the policy of naming Aboriginal groups after the nearest colonial town or landmark.

47. In the judgment of the leading colonial clergyman, Samuel Marsden, the Aborigines were "the most degraded of the human race and never seem to wish to alter their habits and manner of life." Keith Wiley, *When they Sky Fell Down: The Destruction of the Tribes of the Sydney Region 1788–1850s* (Sydney, 1979), 188–89. The Attorney General at the time, Saxe Bannister, warned Threlkeld that "there were many who would banish [him] from the Colony and prevent every attempt of a Missionary nature among the Blacks if they could." Bannister to Threlkeld, 10 August 1826, in *Reminiscences and Papers*, II: 213.

48. The humanitarian preference for the term "Aborigine" is reflected, of course, in the name of the Aborigines Protection Society founded in 1837 to protect the rights of indigenous people as the British conceived of them at the time.

49. Peter Cunningham, *Two Years in New South Wales: A Series of Letters, Comprising Sketches of the Actual State of Society in That Colony; of Its Peculiar Advantages to Emigrants; of Its Topography, Natural History, &c, &c.*, 2 vols. (London, 1827), II: 45–46. On racism in colonial Australia, see Henry Reynolds, *Dispossession: Black Australians and White Invaders* (St. Leonards, 1996), ch. 4.

50. L. E. Threlkeld, "Memoranda," 14 December 1825, in Gunson, ed. *Reminiscences and Papers*, I: 91.

51. On southeastern Aboriginal peoples' relations to their lands, see Heather Goodall, *Invasion to Embassy: Land in Aboriginal Politics in New South Wales, 1770–1972* (St. Leonards, 1996), Ch.1. On the spiritual connections between peoples

and places, see Tony Swain, *A Place for Strangers: Towards a History of Australian Aboriginal Being* (Cambridge, 1993), 33–34.

52. The name "Awabakal" appears to have been given to the Aboriginal people who lived in the region of Newcastle and Lake Macquarie by John Fraser when he edited and republished Threlkeld's writings under the title *The Australian Language as Spoken by the Awabakal, the People of Lake Macquarie, Being an Account of Their Language, Traditions, and Customs* (Sydney, 1892). Fraser may have created this name on the assumption that "Awaba" was the indigenous name for Lake Macquarie and that Aboriginal people in the east used "kal" to denote belonging to a place. But Threlkeld himself recorded "Nik-kin-ba" or "a place of coals" as a name for the lake region. See L. E. Threlkeld *An Australian Grammar Comprehending the Principles and Natural Rules of the Language, as Spoken by the Aborigines in the Vicinity of Hunter's River, Lake Macquarie &c. New South Wales* (Sydney, 1834), 83; and Threlkeld, "Reminiscences," *Reminiscences and Papers*, I: 64.

53. On Mulubinba as an Awabakal name and site, see Threlkeld, *An Australian Grammar*, 15–16. For a discussion of the different bands that likely made up the people now known as the Awabakal, see Kellie Austin et al., *Land of Awabakal* (Hamilton, NSW, 1995), 4–5; and Gunson, "Introduction," Threlkeld, *Reminiscences and Papers*, I: 72.

54. When the American philologist Horatio Hale visited New South Wales in 1839 he was struck by the fact that Threlkeld could not give him any "general word by which to designate all those who speak their tongue." Hale, *Ethnography and Philology*, 482.

55. On the New South Wales jargon, see Jakelin Troy, *Australian Aboriginal Contact with the English Language in New South Wales 1788 to 1845* (Canberra, 1990).

56. As one Aboriginal man reportedly declared (in an interesting reversal of colonial hierarchies): "white fellow works, not black fellow; black fellow gentleman." Hale, *Ethnography and Philology*, 109.

57. As Roger Oldfield reported in 1828, "The Aboriginal inhabitants … are colloquially termed—*black fellows;* an appellation which they accept in good part; and in return entitle us—*white fellows*." "Account of the Aborigines of N.S.W.," in *Reminiscences and Papers*, II: 351.

58. For an account of early relations between the Awabakal and the British, see David Andrew Roberts, "Aborigines, Commandants, and Convicts: the Newcastle Penal Settlement," http://www.newcastle.edu.au/centre/awaba/awaba/group/amrhd/awaba/history/convicts.html, 23 January 2003 (accessed 15 June 2011). On Middleton's relationship with the Awabakal, see Threlkeld's Public Journal, 15 January 1825, *Reminiscences and Papers*, I: 85.

59. On the invasion of the Hunter River Valley, see T. M. Perry, *Australia's First Frontier*, 66; and Henry Dangar, *Index and Directory to Map of the Country Bordering upon the River Hunter; the Lands of the Australian-Agricultural Company; with the Ground-plan and Allotments of King's Town, New South Wales, etc.* (London, 1828), 126–27. For reports of the military operation in the Hunter River Valley, see Governor Ralph Darling, *Dispatches*, September 1826, Mitchell Library of Australia, A 1197 Reel CY 522.

60. On the colonization of Awabakal country in particular, see Clouten, *Reid's Mistake*, 52.

61. On the continued performance of Awabakal rituals in this early period, see Threlkeld, "London Missionary Society Report, December 1825," *Reminiscences and Papers*, II: 189–93.

62. Threlkeld, "London Missionary," *Reminiscences*, I: 57.

63. On the link between knowledge and status in many Aboriginal societies, see W.E.H. Stanner, *White Man Got No Dreaming: Essays 1938–1973* (Canberra, 1979), 39.

64. Spalding does mention four indigenous place names, without further explanation, in the journal of his travels through the region in July 1839. See Spalding's Diary in *The Diaries and Letters of Henry H. Spalding and Asa Bowen Smith Relating to the Nez Perce Mission, 1838–1842*, ed. Clifford Drury (Glendale, CA, 1958), 257–67.

65. Ibid.

66. Asa Smith titled his first book in the language, *Numipuain Shapahitamanash Timash* (Lapwai, 1840). This can be translated as Nez Perce Reading Book.

67. Spalding, Diary, 9 October 1837, *Diaries and Letters*, 238.

68. Ibid., 248.

69. Spalding to Greene, 8 July 1836, A.B.C.F.M. letters, vol. 71, Oregon Historical Society Mss 1200.

70. Spalding to Greene, 16 February 1837, reprinted in *Missionary Herald* (December 1837), 499.

71. Greene to Whitman, 4 March 1836, reprinted in Hulbert and Hulbert, eds., *Marcus Whitman, Crusader, Part One*, 196. Preaching in the vernacular, rather than instructing potential converts in English, became established A.B.C.F.M policy in the 1840s. See Paul William Harris, *Nothing but Christ: Rufus Anderson and the Ideology of Protestant Foreign Missions* (New York, 1999), 134.

72. Asa Smith to his parents, 11 March 1839, in *The Mountains We Have Crossed: Diaries and Letters of the Oregon Mission, 1838*, ed. Clifford Drury (Lincoln, NB, 1999), 169. For an account of Lawyer's life, see Clifford M. Drury, *Chief Lawyer of the Nez Perce Indians, 1796–1876* (Glendale, CA, 1979).

73. Smith to Greene, 27 August 1839, *Diaries and Letters*, 107.

74. Smith to Greene, 25 February 1840, *Diaries and Letters*, 146–47.

75. Parker condemned the practice of Sabbath dancing and successfully urged the Nimiipuu to abandon the practice during his stay among them. Parker, *Journal of an Exploring Tour*, 253.

76. Frey, *Stories that Make the World*, 153.

77. Ibid., 172.

78. *Hawaiian Spectator* (July 1838), 382–83.

79. Ibid., 382.

80. "Coyote, the Interloper," in Archie Phinney, *Nez Percé Texts* (New York, 1934), 268–82.

81. Headmen may have taken up the very practice of telling Bible stories as a similar to the practice of telling Coyote stories, known in Nimiipuutímt as the practice of *titwati*. Aoki, *Nez Perce Dictionary*, 763.

82. See "Coyote and Monster," in Phinney, *Nez Percé Texts*, 18–29. On the relationship between Coyote and monsters, see Deward E. Walker, *Blood of the Monster: The Nez Perce Coyote Cycle* (Worland, WY, 1994), 185–88.

83. "Coyote and Humming Bird," Phinney, *Nez Percé Texts*, 54–62.

84. Whitman to Greene, 7 April 1843, Hulbert and Hulbert, eds., *Marcus Whitman Crusader, Part Two*, 298.

85. Whitman to Greene, 12 March 1838, in ibid., 296.

86. Spalding's primers include: *Nez Perces First Book: Designed for Children and New Beginners* (Clear Water, [Or. Ter.] 1839); *Talapusapaian Wanipt Timas* (Lapwai, 1842); and *Shapahitamanash Suyapu Timtki* (Lapwai, 1845).

87. See Asa Bowen Smith, "Peculiarities of the Nez Perce Language," A.B.C.F.M. Papers, vol. 138, Reel 783.

88. Smith to Greene, 6 February 1840, Drury, *Diaries and Letters*, 140.

89. These are the terms Smith uses in his primer, *Numipuain Shapahitamanash Timash*.

90. As he put it, "to suppose that … any thing but selfish motives," could account for Native interest in Christianity, "is to suppose that good can come out of the natural heart." Smith to Greene, 27 August 1839, Drury, *Diaries and Letters*, 107.

91. Smith to Greene, September 1838, ibid., 88.

92. Smith to Greene, 27 August 1839, ibid.,108.

93. Asa Smith, 1840, copied by Gray and included in Gray to Greene, 4 October 1840, Oregon Historical Society Mss 1207 (typescript).

94. Similar conflicts erupted between Whitman and the Cayuse. When Whitman adopted the same policy of "plain talking," Narcissa reported that the Cayuse "try to persuade him not to talk such bad talk to them, as they say, but talk good talk, or tell some story, or history, so that they may have some Scripture names to learn." Narcissa Whitman to her father, 10 October 1840, in Narcissa Whitman, *The Letters of Narcissa Whitman* (Fairfield, WA, 1986), 102.

95. For an account of the converts, see Drury, ed., *Diaries and Letters*, 327. Smith was very critical of Spalding's decision to admit many of these individuals into the church.

96. Smith to Greene, 25 February 1840, ibid., 147; Lawyer was eventually baptized in 1871. See Drury, *Chief Lawyer*, 75.

97. On the outbreak of illnesses, fears of a *soyapo* invasion, and the resurgence of the shamans, see Josephy, *Nez Perce Indians*, 229–41.

98. Spalding Diary, October 1841, in Drury, ed., *Diaries and Letters*, 324.

99. Greene to Whitman, 16 April 1846, A.B.C.F.M. 1:3:2 Letters to Missionaries to Indians (Houghton Library), vol. 8.

100. Smith to his brother, 10 June 1840, Drury, ed. *Letters and Diaries*, 195.

101. Spalding to Greene, 24 January 1846, Washington State University Archives, Cage 143, Box 2, Folder 30.

102. Spalding to Greene, 3 February 1847, Washington State University Archives, Cage 143, Box 2, Folder 30.

103. The men probably suspected that Whitman's activities as a medical doctor had caused the deaths of several Cayuse following the disease outbreak. In doing so, they were likely following the customary Plateau practice of killing

shamans believed to be using their powers for evil. In this case, however, the murder of Whitman's wife, Narcissa, and several other Euro-American workers who had recently become associated with the mission, indicates that tensions arising from the breakdown of cross-cultural relations and Cayuse fears of the Euro-American influx had provoked a more bloody and widespread assault. See Cameron Addis, "The Whitman Massacre: Religion and Manifest Destiny on the Columbia Plateau, 1809–1858," *Journal of the Early Republic* 25 (2005): 221–38.

104. Darrell Scott, ed., *A True Copy of the Record of the Official Proceedings of the Council in the Walla Walla Valley held jointly by Isaac I. Stevens Gov. & Supt. W.T. and Joel Palmer, Supt. Ind. Affairs O.T. on the part of the United States with the Tribes of Indians named in the Treaties made at that Council June 9th and 11th 1855,* (Fairfield, WA, 1985), 38.

105. Ibid., 55, 31, 80, 99.

106. Ibid., 77.

107. Clara Sue Kidwell, Homer Noley, and George E. "Tink" Tinker, *A Native American Theology* (Maryknoll, NY, 2001), 57.

108. Scott, ed. *Proceedings at the Council in the Walla Walla Valley,* 87.

109. Deward E. Walker, *Conflict and Schism,* 52–73. On the development of an indigenous Christian ministry, see Bonnie Sue Lewis, *Creating Christian Indians: Native Clergy in the Presbyterian Church* (Norman, OK, 2003).

110. On the evolution of this movement, see Deward E. Walker, *Conflict and Schism,* 48–52; Clifford E. Trafzer and Margery Ann Beach, "Smohalla, the Washani, and Religion as a Factor in Northwestern Indian History," *American Indian Quarterly* 9 (1985): 309–24.

111. Nabokov, *Where Lightning Strikes,* 168.

112. Threlkeld noted that "[t]he Aborigines call the place Biddobar." He later spelled it "Bah-tah-bah." See Threlkeld, *Reminiscences and Papers,* I: 90, II: 215.

113. As he wrote to the L.M.S. Directors, "If I do not speak then my conscience says I become accessary [sic] to their death—God will give me wisdom and prudence...." Threlkeld to G. Burder and W. A. Hankey, 4 September 1826, *Reminiscences and Papers,* II: 213. On Threlkeld's efforts to defend Aboriginal people, see Henry Reynolds, *This Whispering in Our Hearts* (St. Leonards, NSW, 1998), 60–69. From a different perspective, the literary critic Anna Johnston has analyzed the ambivalences in Threlkeld's relationship to colonial society. See *Missionary Writing and Empire, 1800–1860* (Cambridge, 2003), chs. 8, 9.

114. Biraban was taken by the British and assigned as a servant to a Captain John M. Gill at the military barracks in Sydney sometime in the second decade of the nineteenth century. Gill renamed him M'Gill as a mark of his claim to the boy. When Gill returned to England he attached Biraban to a Captain Francis Allman who took him first to Port Macquarie in 1821, and then to Newcastle in 1824. During these years Biraban worked as an interpreter, guide, and "bush constable" tracking runaway convicts. On Biraban's early career, see Niel Gunson, Introduction to *Reminiscences and Papers,* I: 6.

115. Threlkeld to Saxe Bannister, 27 September 1825; Threlkeld to Alexander M'Leay, 19 February 1828, ibid. II: 186, 241.

116. Threlkeld, *Australian Grammar*, 82–85.

117. Ibid., 14.

118. Ibid., 83–85. Of *Yi-rán-ná-lai*, he later related that when he called out while walking beneath some rocks there, Biraban "instantly beckoned me to be silent" and told him the "tradition of the place." *Reminiscences and Papers*, I: 65.

119. Goodall, *Invasion to Embassy*, 3.

120. On stories of ancestral beings as sources of knowledge about the foundation of Aboriginal social institutions, see Stanner, *White Man Got No Dreaming*, 28–30.

121. Anne Keary, "Christianity, Colonialism, and Cross-Cultural Translation: Lancelot Threlkeld, Biraban, and the Awabakal," *Aboriginal History* 33 (2009): 117–55.

122. Threlkeld *Australian Grammar*, 80.

123. Threlkeld, "London Missionary Society Report, December 1825," in *Reminiscences and Papers*, II: 189.

124. Threlkeld, *Australian Grammar*, 80–81; Threlkeld, "London Missionary Society Report, December 1825," in *Reminiscences and Papers*, II: 192–93.

125. In his own notes on the word's definition, Threlkeld first defined *yir-riryirri* as "Sacred, reverend, holy, not to be regarded but with awe," but then added that *yirriyirri* also described "the place marked out for mystic rites . . . not to be profaned by common use, hence holy …" — in other words, a men's initiation site, and he observed that a sacred messenger could be described as "*yirriyirri-lang*, one who acts sacredly, one who is holy." Threlkeld, *A Key to the Structure of the Aboriginal Language; Being an analysis of the particles used as affixes, to form the various modifications of the verbs; shewing the essential powers, abstract roots, and other peculiarities of the language spoken by the Aborigines in the vicinity of Hunter River, Lake Macquarie, New South Wales; together with a comparison of Polynesian and Other Dialects etc* (Sydney, 1850), 49, 59. A dialogue fragment in Threlkeld's 1834 grammar makes this gendered meaning explicit: "Why do not women go with the men? Because it is a sacred concern … *Yanoa yirriyirr ka ke.*" See Threlkeld, *Australian Grammar*, 129. On the meaning of *marai*, see Threlkeld, "Lexicon to the Gospel According to Saint Luke" (1859), reprinted in Fraser, ed. *An Australian Language*, 222–23 (see n. 46). In a note attached to some translated scriptural selections he elaborated: "Marai" is "the spirit … in opposition to corporeal substance … and *mamuya* is a 'ghost'." Threlkeld, *Key*, 59.

126. Threlkeld, *Key*, 51.

127. Ibid., 54, 61.

128. Threlkeld *Australian Grammar*, 96, 104.

129. Hilary Carey has also discussed Threlkeld's translation work. Her analyses, however, pay surprisingly little attention to Threlkeld and Biraban's translation of religious terminology. See Hilary M. Carey, "Lancelot Threlkeld and Missionary Linguistics in Australia to 1850," in *Missionary Linguistics*, selected papers from the First International Conference on Missionary Linguistics, Oslo, 13–16 March 2003, ed. Otto Zwartjes and Even Hovdhaugen (Amsterdam, 2004) 253–76; and "Death, God and Linguistics: Conversations with Missionaries on the Australian Frontier, 1824–1845," *Australian Historical Studies* 40 (2009): 161–77.

130. Threlkeld, *Australian Grammar*, 91.

131. Threlkeld, "5th Report 1835," in *Reminiscences and Papers*, I: 123.

132. The philologist, Horatio Hale, included these words in a vocabulary of invented words that he obtained from Threlkeld. See Hale, *Ethnography and Philology*, 500 (see n. 28).

133. Threlkeld, *Australian Grammar*, 121.

134. Also, the Awabakal's relationships with the spiritual beings of their land were arguably more fixed, established by the facts of conception and birth, rather than acquired through vision quests, as was the case for the Nimiipuu.

135. Threlkeld later estimated that at his first mission site, "upwards of sixty Blacks lie mouldering in the dust, of whom many were destroyed by ... the epidemic of the time." He also wrote of sexual assaults on Aboriginal women in his report of 1837, noting that the "usual consequences" were "disease and death." "Annual Report of Mission to the Aborigines New South Wales, 1837," in *Reminiscences and Papers*, I: 137. Colonization exacerbated the effects of disease by reducing game and access to gathering grounds. By 1841, ten land grants totaling several thousand acres had been issued by the New South Wales government for lands around Lake Macquarie. See Clouten, *Reid's Mistake*, 52–67 (see n. 10).

136. Threlkeld, Memoranda, June 1837, *Reminiscences and Papers*, I: 134.

137. Threlkeld "The 6th Annual Report of the Mission to the Aborigines, Lake Macquarie for MDCCCXXXVI," in ibid., 134.

138. "5th Report, 1835," in ibid, 121–22.

139. Threlkeld, "The 6th Annual Report of the Mission to the Aborigines, Lake Macquarie for 1836," in *Reminiscences and Papers*, I: 134.

140. On dreams and the making of medicine men or karakul, see A. P. Elkin, *Aboriginal Men of High Degree*, 2nd ed. (St. Lucia, Queensland, 1977), 80, 86–88. On the function of dreams in Aboriginal spiritual life, see A. W. Howitt, *The Native Tribes of South-East Australia* (London, 1904), 434–42. On dream travel as a cultural phenomenon, see Roger Ivar Lohmann, "Introduction," *Dream Travelers: Sleep Experiences and Culture in the Western Pacific* (New York, 2003), 1–18.

141. Threlkeld was often surprised at the reach of Biraban's efforts: "[T]he Christian knowledge which has been communicated to M'gill and other Aborigines, has been the subject of discussion amongst the remnant of the tribes forty miles distant." "8th Annual Report, 1838," *Reminiscences and Papers*, I: 144. M'Gill was the colonial name applied to Biraban.

142. I discuss this dream narrative and the variety of Awabakal responses to Christianity in greater depth in Keary, "Christianity, Colonialism, and Cross-Cultural Translation," 143–46. Penny van Torn has also discussed this dream, arguing that Biraban envisioned Jehovah as the south-eastern sky-god Baiami, but this interpretation ignores the evidence of Biraban's translation work, his description of Koun, and the fact that he is never recorded as mentioning Baiami. See Penny van Toorn, *Writing Never Arrives Naked: Early Aboriginal Cultures of Writing in Australia* (Canberra, 2006), 47–52.

143. "Return of the Aboriginal Natives, taken at Lake Macquarie on 1st May 1840," Colonial Secretary's In-Letters, 4560, Archives of New South Wales.

144. On Biraban's final years, see Gunson's account in *Reminiscences and Papers*, II: 317. On the last years of the mission, see Gunson, Introduction to ibid., I: 28–29; and Clouten, *Reid's Mistake*, 93–97.

✿ SELECT BIBLIOGRAPHY

Adams, Abigail E. "Making One Our Word: Protestant Qéqchi'Mayas in Highland Guatemala." In *Holy Saints and Fiery Preachers: The Anthropology of Protestantism in Mexico and Central America,* ed. James W. Dow and Alan R. Sandstrom, 205–33. Westport, CT: Praeger, 2001.

Adas, Michael. *Prophets of Rebellion: Millenarian Protest Movements against the European Colonial Order.* Chapel Hill, NC: University of North Carolina Press, 1979.

Adelman, Jeremy, and Stephen Aron. "From Borderlands to Borders: Empires, Nation-States, and the Peoples in Between in North American History." *American Historical Review* 104 (1999): 814–41.

Adogame, Afeosemimi U. *Celestial Church of Christ. The Politics of Cultural Identity in a West African Prophetic-Charismatic Movement.* Frankfurt am Main: P. Lang, 1999.

Apter, Andrew. "Herskovits's Heritage: Rethinking Syncretism in the African Diaspora." *Diaspora* 1 (1991): 235–60.

Asad, Talal. *Genealogies of Religion: Disciplines and Reasons of Power in Christianity and Islam.* Baltimore: Johns Hopkins University Press, 1993.

Axtell, James. *The Invasion Within: The Contest of Cultures in Colonial North America.* New York: Oxford University Press, 1985.

Banerjee-Dube, Ishita, and Saurabh Dube, eds. *Ancient to Modern: Religion, Power, and Community in India.* New Delhi: Oxford University Press, 2008.

Barnstone, Willis. *The Poetics of Translation: History, Theory, Practice.* New Haven, CT: Yale University Press, 1993.

Bascom, William R. *Shango in the New World.* Austin, TX: African and Afro-American Research Institute, University of Texas, 1972.

Bastide, Roger. *The African Religions of Brazil: Toward a Sociology of the Interpenetration of Civilizations.* Baltimore: Johns Hopkins University Press, 1978. Original French edition, 1960.

Bays, Daniel H., ed. *Christianity in China: From the Eighteenth Century to the Present.* Stanford, CA: Stanford University Press, 1996.

Berkhofer, Robert F. *The White Man's Indian: Images of the American Indian from Columbus to the Present.* New York Knopf, 1978.

Bevans, Stephan B. *Models of Contextual Theology,* rev. ed. Maryknoll, NY: Orbis Books, 2002.

Brandon, George E. *Santeria from Africa to the New World: The Dead Sell Memories.* Bloomington, IN: Indiana University Press, 1993.

Brock, Peggy. "Mission Encounters in the Colonial World: British Columbia and South-West Australia." *Journal of Religious History* 24 (2000): 67–96.

Brock, Peggy, ed. *Indigenous Peoples and Religious Change.* Leiden: Brill, 2005.

Brown, David H. *Santería Enthroned: Art, Ritual, and Innovation in an Afro-Cuban Religion.* Chicago: University of Chicago Press, 2003.

Cadière, Léopold. *Croyances et Pratiques Religieuses des Viêtnamiens,* 3 vols. Reprint, Paris: École Française d'Extreme-Orient, 1992.

Cannell, Fenella, ed. *The Anthropology of Christianity.* Durham, NC: Duke University Press, 2006.

Carlsen, Robert S. *The War for the Heart and Soul of a Highland Maya Town.* Austin, TX: University of Texas Press, 1997.

Cebula, Larry. *Plateau Indians and the Quest for Spiritual Power.* Lincoln, NB: University of Nebraska Press, 2003.

Chakrabarty, Dipesh. *Provincializing Europe: Historical Thought and Postcolonial Difference.* Princeton, NJ: Princeton University Press, 2000.

Chireau, Yvonne P. *Black Magic: Religion and the African-American Conjuring Tradition.* Berkeley, CA: University of California Press, 2003.

Clark, Emily J. *"Masterless Mistresses": The New Orleans Ursulines and the Development of a New World Society, 1727–1834.* Chapel Hill: University of North Carolina Press, 2007.

Clark, Emily J., and Virginia Meacham Gould. "The Feminine Face of Afro-Catholicism in New Orleans, 1727–1852." *William & Mary Quarterly* 3, no. 59 (2002): 409–48.

Coates, Ken S. *A Global History of Indigenous Peoples: Struggle and Survival.* New York: Palgrave Macmillan, 2004.

Comaroff, Jean, and John Comaroff. *Of Revelation and Revolution,* 2 vols. Chicago: University of Chicago Press, 1991, 1997.

Cooper, Frederick, and Ann Stoler, eds. *Tensions of Empire: Bourgeois Cultures in a Colonial World.* Berkeley: University of California Press, 1997.

Davis Cyprian, O.S.B. *The History of Black Catholics in the United States.* New York: Crossroad, 1990.

De Craemer, Willy, Jan Vansina, and Renee C. Fox. "Religious Movements in Central Africa: A Theoretical Study." *Comparative Studies in Society and History* 18, no. 4 (1976): 458–75.

Deggs, Sister Mary Bernard. *No Cross, No Crown: Black Nuns in Nineteenth-Century New Orleans,* eds. Virginia Meacham Gould and Charles E. Nolan. Bloomington, IN: Indiana University Press, 2001.

Delâge, Denys. *Bitter Feast: Amerindians and Europeans in the American Northeast, 1660–1664.* Vancouver: UBC Press, 1993 (orig. published as *Le pays renversé,* 1985).

Deloria, Philip J. *Playing Indian.* New Haven, CT: Yale University Press, 1998.

Desmangles, Leslie. *The Faces of the Gods: Vodou and Roman Catholicism in Haiti.* Chapel Hill, NC: University of North Carolina Press, 1992.

Dinan, Susan E., and Debra Meyers, eds. *Women and Religion in Old and New Worlds.* New York: Routledge, 2001.

Dries, Angelyn. *The Missionary Movement in Catholic America.* Maryknoll, NY: Orbis Books, 2002.

Dube, Saurabh. "Paternalism and Freedom: The Evangelical Encounter in Colonial Chhattisgarh, Central India." *Modern Asian Studies* 29 (1995): 171–201.

———. *Untouchable Pasts: Religion, Identity, and Authority among a Central Indian Community, 1780–1950.* Albany, NY: State University of New York Press, 1998.

———. *Stitches on Time: Colonial Textures and Postcolonial Tangles.* Durham, NC: Duke University Press, 2004.

Dube, Saurabh, ed. *Enchantments of Modernity: Empire, Nation, Globalization.* New Delhi: Routledge, 2008.

Dunch, Ryan. *Fuzhou Protestants and the Making of a Modern China, 1857–1927.* New Haven, CT: Yale University Press, 2001.

Duong, Ngoc Dung. "An Exploration of Vietnamese Confucian Spirituality: The Idea of the Unity of the Three Teachings," in *Confucian Spirituality,* ed. Tu Weiming and Mary Evelyn Tucker, 2: 289–319. New York: Crossroad, 2004.

Dupuis, Jacques. *Toward a Christian Theology of Religious Pluralism.* Maryknoll: Orbis Books, 1997.

Early, John D. *The Maya and Catholicism: An Encounter of Worldviews.* Gainesville, FL: University of Florida Press, 2006.

Eaton, Richard M. "Comparative History as World History: Religious Conversion in Modern India." *Journal of World History* 8 (1997): 243–71.

Elbourne, Elizabeth. *Blood Ground: Colonialism, Missions and the Contest for Christianity in Britain and the Eastern Cape, 1799–1853.* Montreal: McGill-Queens University Press, 2002.

Elphick, Richard, and Hermann Giliomee, eds. *The Shaping of South African Society, 1652–1840,* rev. ed. Middletown, CT: Wesleyan University Press, 1989.

Elphick, Richard, and Rodney Davenport, eds. *Christianity in South Africa: A Political, Social and Cultural History.* Berkeley, CA: University of California Press, 1997.

Etherington, Norman, ed. *Missions and Empire.* Oxford: Oxford University Press, 2005.

Falla, Ricardo. *Quiché Rebelde: Religious Conversion, Politics, Ethnic Identity in Guatemala,* trans. Phillip Berryman. Austin, TX: University of Texas Press, 2001.

Fasholé-Luke, Edward, et al., eds. *Christianity in Independent Africa.* Bloomington, IN: Indiana University Press, 1978.

Fischer, Edward F. *Cultural Logics and Global Economics: Maya Identity in Thought and Pratice.* Austin, TX: University of Texas Press, 2001.

Fisher, Humphrey J. "Conversion Reconsidered: Some Historical Aspects of Religious Conversion." *Africa, Journal of the International African Institute* 43 (1973): 27–40.

———. "The Juggernaut's Apologia: Conversion to Islam in Black Africa." *Africa, Journal of the International African Institute* 55 (1985): 153–73.

Forest, Alain. *Les Missionaires Français au Tonkin et au Siam XVIIᵉ-XVIIIᵉ Siècles: Livre II—Histoires du Tonkin.* Paris: L'Harmattan, 1998.

Frey, Sylvia R., and Betty Wood. *Come Shouting to Zion: African American Protestantism in the American South and British Caribbean to 1830.* Chapel Hill, NC: University of North Carolina Press, 1998.

Frykenberg, Robert Eric. "On the Study of Conversion Movements: A Review Article and a Theoretical Note." *Indian Economic and Social History Review* 17 (1980): 121–38.

Garrard-Burnett, Virginia. *Protestantism in Guatemala: Living in the New Jerusalem.* Austin, TX: University of Texas Press, 1998.

Geertz, Clifford. "Thick Description: Toward an Interpretive Theory of Culture." In *The Interpretation of Cultures.* New York: Basic Books, 1973, ch. 1.

Gleason, Judith. "Oya in the Company of Saints." *Journal of the American Academy of Religion* 68 (2000): 265–92.

Gomez, Michael A. *Exchanging Our Country Marks: The Transformation of African Identities in the Colonial and Antebellum South.* Chapel Hill, NC: University of North Carolina Press, 1998.

Goodall, Heather. *Invasion to Embassy: Land in Aboriginal Politics in New South Wales, 1770–1972.* St. Leonards: Allen & Unwin, 1996.

Gort, Jerald, et al., eds. *Dialogue and Syncretism. An Interdisciplinary Approach.* Grand Rapids, MI: W.B. Eerdmans, 1989.

Graymont, Barbara. *The Iroquois and the American Revolution.* Syracuse, NY: Syracuse University Press, 1972.

Greenfield, Sidney M., and André Droogers, eds. *Reinventing Religions: Syncretism and Transformation in Africa and the Americas.* Lanham MD: Rowman and Littlefield, 2001.

Hanger, Kimberly S. *Bounded Lives, Bounded Places: Free Black Society in Colonial New Orleans, 1769–1803.* Durham NC: Duke University Press, 1997.

Harkin, Michael E., ed. *Reassessing Revitalization Movements: Perspectives from North America and the Pacific Islands.* Lincoln, NB: University of Nebraska Press, 2004.

Hastings, Adrian. *The Church in Africa 1450–1950.* Oxford: Clarendon Press, 1994.

Hefner, Robert, ed. *Conversion to Christianity: Historical and Anthropological Perspectives on a Great Transformation.* Berkeley, CA: University of California Press, 1993.

Herskovits, Melville J. "African Gods and Catholic Saints in New World Negro Belief." *American Anthropologist* 39 (1937): 635–43.

———. "Problem, Method, and Theory in Afroamerican Studies." In *The New World Negro: Selected Papers in Afroamerican Studies,* ed. Frances S. Herskovits, 43–61. Bloomington, IN: Indiana University Press, 1966.

Heywood, Linda M., ed. *Central Africans and Cultural Transformations in the African Diaspora.* Cambridge: Cambridge University Press, 2002.

Hilton, Anne. *The Kingdom of Kongo.* Oxford Clarendon Press, 1985.

Hinderaker, Eric. "The 'Four Indian Kings' and the Imaginative Construction of the First British Empire." *The William and Mary Quarterly* 3, no. 53 (1996): 487–526.

Horton, Robin. "African Conversion." *Africa, Journal of the International African Institute* 41 (1971): 85–108.

———. "On the Rationality of Conversion." *Africa, Journal of the International African Institute* 45 (1975): 219–35, 373-99.

Horton, Robin, and J.D.Y. Peel. "Conversion and Confusion: A Rejoinder on Christianity in Eastern Nigeria." *Canadian Journal of African Studies / Revue Canadienne des Études Africaines* 10 (1976): 481–98.

Johnston, Anna. *Missionary Writing and Empire, 1800–1860.* Cambridge Cambridge University Press, 2003.

Josephy, Alvin. *Nez Perce Country.* Lincoln, NB: University of Nebraska Press, 2007.

Kalu, Ogbu, ed. *African Christianity: An African Story.* Trenton, NJ: Africa World Press, 2007.

Kelsay, Isabel. *Joseph Brant, 1743–1807: Man of Two Worlds.* Syracuse, NY.: Syracuse University Press, 1984.

Knitter, Paul F. *No Other Name? A Critical Survey of Christian Attitudes toward the World Religions.* Maryknoll, NY: Orbis Books,1985.

Kocka, Jürgen. "Comparison and Beyond." *History and Theory* 42 (2003): 39–44.

Landau, Paul Stuart. *The Realm of the Word: Language, Gender, and Christianity in a Southern African Kingdom.* Portsmouth, NH: Heinemann, 1995.

Launay, Adrien. *Histoire de la Mission du Tonkin.* Paris: Librarie Orientale et Américaine, 1927.

Lewis, Bonnie Sue. *Creating Christian Indians: Native Clergy in the Presbyterian Church.* Norman, OK: Universitiy of Oklahoma Press, 2003.

Lindenfeld, David. "Indigenous Encounters with Christian Missionaries in China and West Africa, 1800–1920: A Comparative Study." *Journal of World History* 16 (2005): 327–69.

Makdisi, Ussama. *Artillery of Heaven: American Missionaries and the Failed Conversion of the Middle East.* Ithaca, NY: Cornell University Press, 2008.

McHale, Shawn Frederick. *Print and Power: Confucianism, Communism, and Buddhism in the Making of Modern Vietnam.* Honolulu: University of Hawaii Press, 2004.

Mignolo, Walter. *The Darker Side of the Renaissance: Literacy, Territoriality, and Colonization.* Ann Arbor, MI: University of Michigan Press, 1995.

Miller, Christopher. *Prophetic Worlds: Indians and Whites on the Columbia Plateau.* New Brunswick, NJ, Rutgers University Press, 1985.

Minamiki, George. *The Chinese Rites Controversy from Its Beginning until Modern Times.* Chicago: Loyola University Press, 1985.

Morrow, Diane Batts. *Persons of Color and Religious at the Same Time: The Oblate Sisters of Providence, 1828–1860.* Chapel Hill: University of North Carolina Press, 2002.

Mungello, D.E., ed. *The Chinese Rites Controversy: Its History and Meaning.* Monumenta Serica Monograph Series, No. 30. Nettetal: Steyler Verlag, 1994.

Murphy, Joseph M. *Santeria: An African Religion in America.* Boston: Beacon Press, 1988.

———. "Yéyé Cachita: Ochún in a Cuban Mirror." In *Osun Across the Waters: A Yoruba Goddess in Africa and the Americas,* ed. Joseph M. Murphy and Mei-Mei Sanford, 87–101. Bloomington, IN: Indiana University Press, 2001.

Murray, David. *Forked Tongues: Speech, Writing and Representation in North American Indian Texts.* Bloomington, IN: Indiana University Press, 1991.

Nabokov, Peter. *Where Lightning Strikes: The Lives of American Indian Sacred Places.* New York: Viking, 2006.

Newton-King, Susan. *Masters and Servants on the Cape Eastern Frontier, 1760–1803.* Cambridge: Cambridge University Press, 1999.

Neylan, Susan. *The Heavens are Changing: Nineteenth-Century Protestant Missions and Tsimshian Christianity.* Montreal: McGill-Queens University Press, 2002.

Nguyen, Cuong T. *Zen in Medieval Vietnam.* Honolulu: University of Hawaii Press, 1997.

Nguyen Huy Lai, Joseph. *La Tradition Religieuse, Spirituelle et Sociale Au Vietnam.* Paris: Beauchesne, 1981.

Oddie, Geoffrey, ed. *Religious Conversion Movements in South Asia: Continuity and Change.* Richmond, UK: Curzon Press, 1997.

Omoyajowo, Akinyele. *Cherubim and Seraphim. The History of an African Independent Church*. New York: NOK Publishers International, 1982.

Peabody, Sue. "'A Dangerous Zeal': Catholic Missions to Slaves in the French Antilles, 1635–1800." *French Historical Review* 25 (2002): 53–90.

Peel, J.D.Y. *Aladura: A Religious Movement among the Yoruba*. London: Oxford University Press, 1968.

———. "Syncretism and Religious Change." *Comparative Studies in History and Society* 10, no. 2 (1968): 121–41.

Penn, Nigel. *Forgotten Frontier: Colonist and Khoisan on the Cape's Northern Frontier in the 18ᵗʰ Century*. Athens, OH: Ohio University Press, 2006.

Pérez y Mena, Andrés I. "Cuban Santería, Haitian Vodun, Puerto Rican Spiritualism: A Multiculturalist Inquiry into Syncretism." *Journal for the Scientific Study of Religion* 37 (1998): 15–27.

Phan, Peter C. *Mission and Catechesis: Alexandre de Rhodes and Inculturation in Seventeenth Century Vietnam*. Maryknoll, NY: Orbis Books, 1998.

———. *In Our Own Tongues. Perspectives from Asia on Mission and Inculturation*. Maryknoll, NY: Orbis Books, 2003.

Porter, Andrew. *Religion versus Empire? British Protestant Missionaries and Overseas Expansion, 1700–1914*. Manchester, UK: Manchester University Press, 2004.

Powers, William K. "Dual Religious Participation. Strategies of Conversion among the Lakota." In *Beyond the Vision. Essays on American Indian Culture* ed. William K. Powers.. Norman, OK: University of Oklahoma Press, 1987.

Rafael, Vicente. *Contracting Colonialism: Translation and Christian Conversion in Tagalog Society under Early Spanish Rule*. Ithaca, NY: Cornell University Press, 1988.

Ranger, Terence O. "African Conversion." *African Religious Research* 1 (1973): 41–53.

Ranger, Terence O., and Isaria N. Kimambo, eds. *The Historical Study of African Religion: With Special Reference to East and Central Africa*. London Heinemann, 1972.

Richardson, Miles. *Being-in-Christ and Putting Death in its Place: An Anthropologist's Account of Christian Performance in Spanish America and the American South*. Baton Rouge, LA: Louisiana State University Press, 2003.

Richter, Daniel. *The Ordeal of the Longhouse: The Peoples of the Iroquois League in the Era of European Colonization*. Chapel Hill, NC: University of North Carolina Press, 1992.

———. "'Some of them … would always have a minister with them': Mohawk Protestantism, 1683–1719." *American Indian Quarterly* 16 (1992): 471–85.

———. *Facing East from Indian Country: A Native History of Early America*. Cambridge, MA: Harvard University Press, 2001.

Robbins, Joel. *Becoming Sinners: Christianity and Moral Torment in a Papua New Guinea Society*. Berkeley, CA: University of California Press, 2004.

Robert, Dana L. *American Women in Mission: A Social History of Their Thought and Practice*. Macon, GA: Mercer University Press, 1996.

———. *Christian Mission: How Christianity Became a World Religion*. Chichester, UK: Wiley-Blackwell, 2008.

Samson, C. Mathews. *Re-enchanting the World: Maya Protestantism in the Guatemalan Highlands.* Tuscaloosa, AL: University of Alabama Press, 2007.

———. "From War to Reconciliation: Guatemalan Evangelicals and the Transition to Democracy, 1982–2001." In *Evangelical Christianity and Democracy in Latin America,* ed. Paul Freston, 63–96. New York Oxford University Press, 2008.

Sanneh, Lamin. *West African Christianity: The Religious Impact.* London: Hurst, 1983.

———. *Translating the Message: The Missionary Impact on Culture.* Maryknoll, NY: Orbis Books, 1989.

Schreuder, Deryck, and Geoffrey Oddie. "What is Conversion? History, Christianity and Religious Change in Colonial Africa and South Asia." *Journal of Religious History* 15 (1989): 496–518.

Scotchmer, David G. "Symbols of Salvation: A Local Mayan Protestant Theology." *Missiology* 17 (1989): 293–310.

Shell, Robert. *Children of Bondage: A Social History of the Slave Society at the Cape of Good Hope, 1652–1838.* Hanover, NH: University Press of New England, 1994.

Shih, Vincent Y. C. *The Taiping Ideology.* Seattle: University of Washington Press, 1967.

Shorter, Aylward. *Toward a Theology of Inculturation.* Maryknoll, NY: Orbis Books, 1988.

Spence, Jonathan. *God's Chinese Son.* New York: W.W. Norton, 1996.

Steigenga, Timothy J., and Edward L. Cleary, eds. *Conversion of a Continent: Contemporary Religious Change in Latin America.* New Brunswick, NJ: Rutgers University Press, 2007.

Steiner, George. *After Babel: Aspects of Language and Translation.* London: Oxford University Press, 1975.

Stewart, Charles, ed. *Creolization: History, Ethnography, Theory.* Walnut Creek, CA: Left Coast Press, 2007.

Stewart, Charles, and Rosalind Shaw, eds. *Syncretism/Anti-syncretism: The Politics of Religious Synthesis.* London: Routledge, 1994.

Stoler, Ann. "Rethinking Colonial Categories: European Communities and the Boundaries of Rule." *Comparative Studies in Society and History* 31 (1989): 134–61.

———. "Tense and Tender Ties, The Politics of Comparison in North American History and (Post) Colonial Studies." *The Journal of American History* 88 (2001): 829–65.

Strathern, Alan. *Kingship and Conversion in Sixteenth-Century Sri Lanka: Portuguese Imperialism in a Buddhist Land.* Cambridge: Cambridge University Press, 2007.

———. "Transcendentalist Intransigence: Why Rulers Rejected Monotheism in Early Modern Southeast Asia and Beyond." *Comparative Studies in Society and History* 49 (2007): 358–83.

Swain, Tony. *A Place for Strangers: Towards a History of Australian Aboriginal Being.* Cambridge Cambridge University Press, 1993.

Tambiah, Stanley J. *Magic, Science, Religion, and the Scope of Rationality*. Cambridge: Cambridge University Press, 1990.

Taylor, Alan. *The Divided Ground: Indians, Settlers, and the Northern Borderland of the American Revolution*. New York: Knopf, 2006.

Tedlock, Barbara. *Time and the Highland Maya*, rev. ed. Albuquerque, NM: University of New Mexico Press, 1982.

Thomas, Nicholas. "Colonial Conversions: Difference, Hierarchy and History in Early Twentieth Century Evangelical Propaganda." *Comparative Studies in Society and History* 34 (1992): 366–89.

Thompson, Robert Farris. *Face of the Gods: Art and Altars of Africa and the African Americas*. New York: Museum for African Art, 1993.

Turner, H. W. *History of an African Independent Church*, 2 vols. Oxford: Clarendon Press, 1967.

Unger, Ann Helen and Walter Unger. *Pagodas, Gods, and Spirits of Vietnam*. London: Thames and Hudson, 1997.

van Beek, Walter E. A., ed. *The Quest for Purity: Dynamics of Puritan Movements*. Berlin: Mouton de Gruyter, 1988.

van der Veer, Peter. *Imperial Encounters: Religion and Modernity in India and Britain*. Princeton, NJ: Princeton University Press, 2001.

Vásquez, Manuel, and Marie Marquardt. *Globalizing the Sacred*. New Brunswick, NJ: Rutgers University Press, 2003.

Wagner, Rudolf G. *Reenacting the Heavenly Vision: The Role of Religion in the Taiping Rebellion*. Berkeley, CA: Institute of East Asian Studies, University of California, 1982.

Walker Jr., Deward E. *Conflict and Schism in Nez Perce Acculturation: A Study of Religion and Politics*. Pullman, WA: Washington State University Press, 1968.

Wallace, Anthony F. C. "Revitalization Movements: Some Theoretical Considerations." *American Anthropologist* 58, no. 2 (1956): 264–81.

———. *The Death and Rebirth of the Seneca*. New York, Knopf, 1970.

Walls, Andrew F. *The Missionary Movement in Christian History: Studies in the Transmission of Faith*. Maryknoll: Orbis Books, 1994.

White, Richard. *The Middle Ground: Indians, Empires and Republics in the Great Lakes Region, 1650–1815*. Cambridge: Cambridge University Press, 1991.

Wilson, Richard. *Maya Resurgence in Guatemala: Q'eqchi' Experiences*. Norman, OK: University of Oklahoma Press, 1995.

Woodside, Alexander. "Classical Primordialism and the Historical Agendas of Vietnamese Confucianism." In *Rethinking Confucianism: Past and Present in China, Japan, Korea, and Vietnam*, ed. Benjamin A. Elman, et al., 116–43. Los Angeles: UCLA Asian Pacific Monograph Series, 2002.

Young, Richard Fox, and S. Jebanesan. *The Bible Trembled: The Hindu-Christian Controversies of Nineteenth-Century Ceylon*. Vienna: Sammlung de Nobili, 1995.

Young, Richard Fox, and G.P.V. Somaratna. *Vain Debates: The Buddhist-Christian Controversies of Nineteenth-Century Ceylon*. Vienna Institut für Indologie der Universität Wien, 1996.

Yu-wen, Jen. *The Taiping Revolutionary Movement*. New Haven, CT: Yale University Press, 1973.

🏵 CONTRIBUTORS

Saurabh Dube is Professor of History in the Center of Asian and African Studies at El Colegio de México in Mexico City. His authored books include *Untouchable Pasts* (State University of New York Press, 1998, reprint Sage, 2001); *Stitches on Time* (Duke University Press, 2004; Oxford University Press, 2004); *After Conversion* (Yoda Press, 2010); as well as a quartet in historical anthropology in the Spanish language published by El Colegio de México. Among his dozen edited and co-edited volumes are *Postcolonial Passages* (Oxford University Press, 2004); *Historical Anthropology* (Oxford University Press, 2007); and *Enchantments of Modernity* (Routledge, 2009).

Elizabeth Elbourne is Associate Professor in the Department of History, McGill University. Her work includes *Blood Ground: Colonialism, Missions and the Contest for Christianity in Britain and the Eastern Cape, 1799–1853* (McGill-Queens University Press, 2002). She is currently co-editor of the *Journal of British Studies*. Her current research explores struggles over the status of indigenous peoples in the white settler colonies of the late eighteenth- and early nineteenth-century British empire.

Sylvia R. Frey is Professor of History Emerita at Tulane University. She is the author of *Water from the Rock: Black Resistance in a Revolutionary Age* (Princeton University Press, 1991), *The British Soldier in America: A Social History of Military Life in the Revolutionary Period* (University of Texas Press, 1981); and co-author of *Come Shouting to Zion: African American Protestant Christianity in the American South & the British Caribbean* (University of North Carolina Press, 1997). Her edited works include *New World, New Roles: A Documentary History of Women in Pre-Industrial America* (Greenwood Press, 1986), and *From Slavery to Emancipation in the Atlantic World* (Frank Cass, 1999).

Anne Keary is an Australian scholar who received her Ph.D. from the University of California, Berkeley in 2002. She has taught Native American and Pacific history at the University of Utah. Currently, she is living with her family in Toronto, Canada, where she is completing a book manuscript titled "Comparing Cross-Cultural Histories: Christianity, Colonialism, and Translation in Eastern Australia and Northwestern America."

David Lindenfeld is Professor of History at Louisiana State University. Trained as a Europeanist, he has published *The Transformation of Positivism: Alexius Meinong and European Thought* (University of California Press, 1980), and *The Practical Imagination: The German Sciences of State in the Nineteenth Century* (University of Chicago Press, 1997); and co-edited with Suzanne Marchand *Germany at the Fin de Siècle. Culture, Politics, and Ideas* (Louisiana State University Press, 2004). He has taught world history since 1998 and has been researching a comparative study of indigenous encounters with missionary Christianity since 2002.

Joseph M. Murphy is the Paul and Chandler Tagliabue Professor of Interfaith Studies and Dialogue in the Theology Department at Georgetown University. He teaches courses in foundational theology, comparative religions, and the religions of the African Diaspora. He is the author of *Santería: An African Religion in America* (Beacon Press, 1988) and *Working the Spirit: Ceremonies of the African Diaspora* (Beacon Press, 1994). With Mei-Mei Sanford he has edited the volume *Osun across the Waters: A Yoruba Goddess in Africa and the Americas* (Indiana University Press, 2001).

Miles Richardson is Professor Emeritus in the Department of Geography and Anthropology at Louisiana State University. As a cultural anthropologist he did field work in Latin America and the American South for more than 40 years. His most recent book is *Being-in-Christ and Putting Death in its Place: An Anthropologist's Account of Christian Performance in Spanish America and the American South* (Louisiana State University Press, 2003). Since his retirement he has been retooling himself as a biological anthropologist and is currently working on a book tentatively titled "Hominid Evolution: The Trajectory of You and Me," co-authored with Julia Hanebrink. His syncretic tastes include Bach, Vivaldi and, redneck that he is, Hank Williams.

C. Mathews (Matt) Samson is Visiting Assistant Professor of Anthropology at Davidson College in Davidson, North Carolina. His research interests include religious change, ethnic identity, and human rights in Mesoamerica, humanistic anthropology, and human-environment relations in Mexico, Central America, and the borderlands of the U.S. Southwest and South, of which he is a native. He is the author of *Reenchanting the World: Maya Protestantism in Guatemalan Highlands* (University of Alabama Press, 2007).

Anh Q. Tran, S.J. received his Ph.D. in Theological and Religious Studies from Georgetown University in 2011. His research interest is religious pluralism and Christian missions in Asia. His dissertation examines traditional religious practices in premodern Vietnam. He will join the faculty of the Jesuit School of Theology of Santa Clara University as an Assistant Professor of Historical and Systematic Theology.

Richard Fox Young holds the Timby Chair in History of Religions at Princeton Theological Seminary. An Indologist by training, he works in mission studies, world Christianity, and contiguous areas. *Resistant Hinduism* (1981), *The Bible Trembled* (1995), and *Vain Debates* (1996) (all in Sammlung de Nobili, Vienna) are several of his most widely-cited monographs on the encounter of Hindus and Buddhists with Christian missions in nineteenth-century South Asia.

🪷 INDEX